INFLUENCE AND INTERTEXTUALITY
IN LITERARY HISTORY

D1494581

Influence
and Intertextuality
in Literary History

Edited by

JAY CLAYTON
&
ERIC ROTHSTEIN

The University of Wisconsin Press

Undergraduate Lending Library

The University of Wisconsin Press
114 North Murray Street
Madison, Wisconsin 53715

3 Henrietta Street
London WC2E 8LU, England

Copyright © 1991
The Board of Regents of the University of Wisconsin System
All rights reserved

5 4 3 2 1

Printed in the United States of America

Library of Congress Cataloging-in-Publication Data
Influence and intertextuality in literary history / edited by Jay
  Clayton and Eric Rothstein.
    360 pp.   cm.
    Includes bibliographical references and index.
    ISBN 0-299-13030-4   ISBN 0-299-13034-7
    1. English literature—History and criticism—Theory, etc.
    2. American literature—History and criticism—Theory, etc.
    3. Influence (Literary, artistic, etc.) 4. Intertextuality.
    I. Clayton, Jay, 1951–   . II. Rothstein, Eric.
    PR21.15   1991
    820.9 dc20   91-11892
                    CIP

WITHDRAWN

Undergraduate Lending Library

Contents

Contributors

William L. Andrews, the General Editor of Wisconsin Studies in American Autobiography, has written and edited six books on Afro-American literature and culture, including *The Literary Career of Charles Chesnutt* and *To Tell a Free Story: The First Century of Afro-American Autobiography, 1760*–1865.

Jay Clayton works on contemporary literature and cultural theory, as evidenced in articles, and on the history of literary forms, as in his book *Romantic Vision and the Novel.* He has also published several short stories.

A. N. Doane has published editions of *Genesis A* and *Genesis B,* and articles on Old English literature; in addition, he writes on composition theory.

Betsy Draine is the author of *Substance under Pressure: Artistic Coherence and Evolving Form in the Novels of Doris Lessing,* and is Associate Editor of *Contemporary Literature.*

Susan Stanford Friedman, author of *Psyche Reborn: The Emergence of H.D.,* has written extensively on feminist issues and psychoanalysis as they relate to traditions of modern literature.

Lynn Keller specializes in modern and contemporary poetry, as in her book *Re-making It New: Contemporary American Poetry and the Modernist Tradition.*

Cyrena N. Pondrom wrote *The Road from Paris,* about Franco-Anglophone literary traditions in the earlier twentieth century, and has concentrated on the role of female authors in modern literary movements.

Tilottama Rajan's two books deal with early-nineteenth-century thought and hermeneutics: *Dark Interpreter: The Discourse of Romanticism* and *The Supplement of Reading: Figures of Understanding in Romantic Theory and Practice.*

Eric Rothstein has written three books on Restoration drama, one on the history of British poetry from 1660 to 1780, and one on the later eighteenth-century novel, as well as having served as editor for *Literary Monographs.*

Thomas Schaub has published *Pynchon: The Voice of Ambiguity, American Fiction in the Cold War,* and other work on the modern American novel.

Jeffrey Steele's books include *Unfolding the Mind: The Unconscious in American Romanticism and Literary Theory* and *The Representation of the Self in the American Renaissance.*

Andrew D. Weiner has written *Sir Philip Sidney and the Poetics of Protestantism,* and articles on Erasmus, More, Sidney, Spenser, Bruno, Milton, and Shakespeare.

Preface

This book issues from a relationship—both intertextual and influential—among members of the English Department of the University of Wisconsin. All the contributors worked together in a collegial association called the Draft Group, which has met monthly since 1986. Though the essays differ about many issues, their common themes developed out of our regular discussions, and the Group's support, insights, rigorous criticism, and spirited debates contributed to each of the essays collected here. We cannot easily sort out what ideas began where or with whom, but in this environment we learned to understand not only influence, with its enabling sense of personal effect, but also the intertextual, as we each found in others different versions, different transpositions, different images of our own "original" ideas, like Doppler effects, recognizably the same and yet not the same. Cooperative research, so common in many disciplines, remains rare in the humanities. The growth of literary theory and interdisciplinary studies, however, has made us as humanists readier to engage in the kind of intellectual exchange from which this shared product emerged, and from which others, we hope, will emerge in the years to come.

The volume poses questions about influence and intertextuality within the context of the renewed interest in historical approaches to literature. The Wisconsin English department has long had a commitment to the historical study of literature. But more recent engagement with literary theory has led many of us to think critically about the method, status, and goal of historical investigations. Our collective road toward assembling these essays, each written specifically for this volume, has made for an exhilarating journey; we wish the same to our readers. We also wish to thank the Department of English and Joseph Wiesenfarth, the Chair at the time the Draft Group began, for their support of the Group specifically, and more generally, for creating and maintaining an atmosphere in which collegial enterprises can flourish.

INFLUENCE AND INTERTEXTUALITY
IN LITERARY HISTORY

CHAPTER 1

Figures in the Corpus:
Theories of Influence and Intertextuality

JAY CLAYTON AND ERIC ROTHSTEIN

Over the last two decades, the concepts of influence and intertextuality have been sites of generational conflict: to many people, influence has smacked of elitism, the old boy networks of Major Authors and their sleek entourages; others have suspected that the intertextual web flowed from the knitting needles of Mme. Defarge. More routinely, the new and voguish "intertexuality" has served as a generational marker for younger critics who end up doing very much what their elders do with influence and its partners, like "context," "allusion," and "tradition." As terms of art, influence and intertextuality do not have the precision of "iconology" or "iambic pentameter." Strictly, influence should refer to relations built on dyads of transmission from one unity (author, work, tradition) to another. More broadly, however, influence studies often stray into portraits of intellectual background, context, and the other partners of influence that we have just mentioned. The shape of intertextuality in turn depends on the shape of influence. One may see intertextuality either as the enlargement of a familiar idea or as an entirely new concept to replace the outmoded notion of influence. In the former case, intertextuality might be taken as a general term, working out from the broad definition of influence to encompass unconscious, socially prompted types of text formation (for example, by archetypes or popular culture); modes of conception (such as ideas "in the air"); styles (such as genres); and other prior constraints and opportunities for the writer. In the latter case, intertextuality might be used to oust and replace the kinds of issues that influence addresses, and in particular its central concern with the author and more or less conscious authorial intentions and skills. Theoretical treatments of intertextuality have all leaned heavily toward the model of substitution, though many practicing critics, perhaps especially Americans, have used the term "intertextuality" in a context of enlargement.

We do not intend to utter battle cries for either side or even to insist that there must *be* sides, but rather to address the theories that explicitly set agendas for influence and intertextual studies, agendas not always followed in practice. Since both terms have too many operative definitions for us to fix on one for each, we will start with the generalization that influence has to do with agency, whereas intertextuality has to do with a much more impersonal field of crossing texts. We therefore begin with author-centered theories, then discuss the decline of the author as a necessary focus of literary attention, and end with theories in which the author is "dead" as in Barthes or, as in Foucault, merely "the principle of thrift in the prolif-eration of meaning," replaceable by something else (Foucault, "Author" 159).

"Theory," we recognize, is our own principle of thrift in the face of so much practice that might be labeled influence-based or intertextual but that does not use either term or uses them casually or loosely. Our limiting ourselves to theories should not be taken to deny that practicing critics have developed distinctive, sometimes thoughtful attitudes toward both in-tertextuality and influence outside the context of full-dress theories. We also agree that "theory" may not be quite the right word for our genealogy of influence, in that over the years the fact of influence was so universally assumed that most discussion centered upon validation claims: what a belief in influence might entail rarely came up while scholars looked at a question logically subsequent to it, whether Professor X could justly say that Plotinus, Milton, or Godwin influenced Shelley. Our discussion, finally, reflects the wholly pleasant irony that the study of influence, because so tied to particular cases, has largely proceeded anonymously, while that of the far more egalitarian intertextuality has had great impetus from a series of masterful, highly personal critics, such as (in alphabetical order) Bakhtin, Barthes, Derrida, Foucault, Kristeva, Lacan, and Riffaterre.

I

Influence seems like an ancient given, in contrast with the recent term in-tertextuality, which dates from Julia Kristeva's *Séméiotikè: recherches pour une sémanalyse* (1969). A genealogy of the word "influence" as it is used in literary studies, however, would not have to trace its lineage much further than the mid-eighteenth century. "In English," Harold Bloom comments, "it is not one of Dryden's critical terms, and is never used in our sense by Pope. . . . For Coleridge, two generations later, the word has substan-tially our meaning in the context of literature" (*Anxiety* 27).

Concern with influence arose in conjunction with the mid-eighteenth-century interest in originality and genius, and the concept still bears the marks of that origin. For the authors of *Conjectures on Original Composition* (1759) and *An Essay on Original Genius* (1767), Edward Young and William Duff, originality was a key to a work of literature and the only true sign of an author's genius. In such a climate, it was only natural for critics, bent on evaluation, to look for influences that lessen an author's claim to genius and for poets, bent on immortality, to guard against such influences by searching for the new in both style and subject matter. Shakespeare and Spenser were commonly praised as "natural geniuses," who, like the first primitive poets, imitated nature rather than art. Their art then shed influence in the sense that the word has in Nathan Bailey's *Universal Etymological English Dictionary* (1721): "a flowing into, a sending forth Power or Virtue; the Power of a Superior over an Inferior." This formula of natural hierarchy and priority played a prominent role in the first literary history of English poetry, that by Thomas Warton (1774). From the very beginning, influence was an author-centered and evaluative concept, and an important tool for literary historians.

Tracing influences was an essential element in the rise of nineteenth-century historicism, developed as it was under the aegis of idealistic theories that stressed agency. As Ferdinand Brunetière (1849–1906), one of the founders of the comparativist method, wrote about the charting of literary change: "In considering all the influences which operate in the history of literature, the influence of works on works is the main one" (quoted in Wellek 44). As the principal method employed by comparativists in the nineteenth-century tradition, influence study at its best was capable of contributing to such magisterial achievements as Ernst Robert Curtius' *European Literature and the Latin Middle Ages* (1948). At its worst, discovering parallels between the literature of two nations was put to the service of a crude cultural imperialism; a work, a movement, or an entire national literature was exalted to the degree that it was able to exert a hegemony over the literature of other countries, so that twentieth-century scholars such as René Wellek or Claudio Guillén saw its improper use as a major stumbling block to the field of comparative literature as late as the 1950s.[1] During the first half of this century, the method also dominated the historical study of English literature (or philology), so much so that F. W. Bateson, in his long debate with F. R. Leavis over the respective merits of literary history and literary criticism, defined the difference between these two activities in terms of the former's reliance on establishing relations of influence.[2]

As we have remarked, the chief theoretical question about influence was in fact one of method. Scholars worried throughout the twentieth century how to discriminate genuine influences from commonplace images, techniques, or ideas that could be found in almost any writer of a given period, how to "distinguish between resemblances that inhere in the common subject-matter of two poems and resemblances that may really be due to direct imitation" (Dodge 215–6).[3] Until the late 1960s, at about the time that intertextuality was entering into currency, there is very little interesting reflection on other theoretical problems implicit in influence. A partial exception is Ihab Hassan's "The Problem of Influence in Literary History" (1955), which takes issue with what Hassan saw as the naive expressionism — treating the feelings, ideas, and values of an author as if directly manifested in the literary work — which buttressed much influence criticism. Hassan was not interested in exiling the author from the work, as were some of his New Critical contemporaries, but rather in complicating the notion of literary expression by enlarging artistic expressionism, so as to take into account the biographical, sociological, and philosophical perspectives that can help the critic uncover the play of the unconscious involved in every instance of influence.[4]

A larger body of sophisticated theoretical work on influence did appear if one extends the term influence to include the notions of context, of allusion, and of tradition, none of which is influence in a narrow sense but all of which are needed if the narrow sense is to be useful even for the purposes of charting originality. An expanded sense of influence allows one to shift one's attention from the transmission of motifs between authors to the transmutation of historically given material. This shift does not do away with author-centered criticism so much as broaden it to take into account the multifarious relations that can exist among authors. The art historian Michael Baxandall has eloquently stated the case for the greater analytic capability one gains by turning the theory of influence on its head and talking about the agency of the author being influenced:

 "Influence" is a curse of art criticism primarily because of its wrong-headed grammatical prejudice about who is the agent and who the patient: it seems to reverse the active/passive relation which the historical actor experiences and the inferential beholder will wish to take into account. If one says that X influenced Y it does seem that one is saying that X did something to Y rather than that Y did something to X. But in the consideration of good pictures and painters the second is always the more lively reality. . . . If we think of Y rather than X as the agent, the vocabulary is much richer and more attractively diversified: draw on, resort to, avail oneself of, appropriate from, have recourse to, adapt, misunderstand, refer to, pick up, take on, engage with, react to, quote, differentiate oneself from, assimilate oneself to, assimilate, align oneself with, copy, address, paraphrase, absorb, make a variation on, revive, continue, remodel, ape, emulate, travesty, parody, extract from, distort, attend to, resist, simplify, reconstitute, elaborate on, develop, face up to, master, subvert, perpetuate, reduce, promote, respond to, transform, tackle. . . . — everyone will be able to think of others. Most of these relations just cannot be stated the other way round — in terms of X acting on Y rather than Y acting on X. To think in terms of influence blunts thought by impoverishing the means of differentiation. (58–59)

Baxandall, of course, is not the first to make this point, and in work such as D. W. Robertson's on Chaucer and Earl Wasserman's on Pope, the point is not only illustrated but also given theoretical framing.

We should add that Baxandall's more liberal version of influence also enriches the means of understanding intention and agency, which is one of the things influence study claimed to do in the first place. An author, after all, becomes a "precursor" only when someone else uses his or her work, so that at best the line of intentionality runs from the later to the earlier author, or else does not run at all, since one usually does not intend to be influenced by another. T. S. Eliot did not choose to be influenced by San Juan de la Cruz in the same way that he chose to employ San Juan's ideas and words. For the later author, influence is more like an act of perception, in which one's observation causes an action. For the earlier author, influence again is rarely an intentional action: one can respond to the question "why did Horace influence Ben Jonson?" in terms of Horace's intentions toward his own work but not in terms of his intentions toward Jonson. (There are exceptions; cf. the question "why did Pound influence Eliot?") Part of the honorific force of influence is that its action occurs merely as a by-product, an exercise of strength without really trying, but this very fact makes it a weak and oblique way of supporting a "liberal humanist" conception of individual agency. The narrow sense of influence, however, does support efforts to draw up a lineage of the great authors (if one wants to do that) more effectively than the broader sense, because the broader sense might well focus on an allusion to something déclassé, like a London street cry or an Australian ballad. In this way, the broader sense of influence is more democratic, a short step, if one wants to take that step, to the still more egalitarian procedures of intertextuality.

To broaden influence so as to encourage a stress on the receiving author as agent, in turn, psychologizes lineage: a later author may regard an ancestor less as a benefactor than as a despot. This is the scenario for the two most important postwar theories of influence, those of Walter Jackson Bate and Harold Bloom. In their interest in how works are generated, both men broke with the New Criticism that dominated literary studies during the fifties. Although the New Critics never wholly excluded literary history from the critical enterprise, their view of the poem as a self-contained artifact tended to diminish the utility for them of biography, history, or other information deemed "extrinsic" to literature.

For Bate, the biographer of Johnson, Coleridge, and Keats, this information was vital. Questions of influence went hand-in-hand both with
biography and with a reflective approach to literary history. Bate's *The
Burden of the Past and the English Poet* (1970), however, is less about the
problem of influence than about a period when influence first becomes
a problem. He centers his study on the mid-to-later eighteenth century as
the pivotal era when increasing concern with originality brought with it
the self-consciousness, fatigue, and depression he thinks characterize the
modern age. Bate dramatizes in personal, psychological terms the theme
of diminished achievement, of weakness in the shadow of departed giants,
of the past as burden. "We could, in fact, argue that the remorseless deep-
ening of self-consciousness, before the rich and intimidating legacy of the
past, has become the greatest single problem that modern art (art, that
is to say, since the later seventeenth century) has had to face, and that it
will become increasingly so in the future" (4). Unlike idealizing critics
such as Curtius, who saw literary tradition as "the medium by which the
European mind preserves its identity through the millenniums" (395), Bate
echoes the pessimism he perceives in the eighteenth century; he fears that
"the arts could, over the long range, be considered as by definition suicidal: that, given the massive achievement in the past, they may have no
further way to proceed except toward progressive refinement, nuance, in-
direction, and finally, through the continued pressure for difference, into
the various forms of anti-art" (10). One need not accept his generalizations about the eighteenth or the twentieth century to appreciate that he
has tapped a significant strain in the discourse of influence.

The most interesting way of evading the burden of the past that Bate
discusses is the habit of gazing beyond one's immediate predecessors to
find in a still-earlier period a source of authority "remote enough to be
more manageable in the quest for your own identity" (22). Here and elsewhere Bate anticipates many of the principal stands that Harold Bloom
was to elaborate in *The Anxiety of Influence* three years later, such as a
refusal to idealize tradition, an insistence that strong poets feel the burden
of the past more sharply than minor writers, a belief that the relationship
of influence may be more important to poets than any extraliterary factors, and a reliance on parental imagery to characterize that relation.

We will not rehearse the details of Bloom's wonderfully Byzantine theory,
with its six revisionary ratios, later correlated with six Freudian mechanisms of defense, six rhetorical tropes, six forms of poetic imagery, three
Kabbalistic stages, and three dialectical movements—it has been discussed
in many forums, from news magazines to scholarly book reviews, from
handbooks on contemporary criticism to challenging works of literary
theory.[5] Instead, we want to turn to the aspects of his work that are ger-

mane to the relation between influence and intertextuality, since Bloom
has sometimes been characterized as a theorist of the latter, despite the
"influence" in his title. Indeed, Bloom sounds very much like a theorist
of intertextuality when he writes: "The meaning of a poem can only be
another poem"; "Criticism is the art of knowing the hidden roads that go
from poem to poem"; and "Influence, as I conceive it, means that there
are *no* texts, but only relationships *between* texts" (*Anxiety* 94, 96; *Map* 3).
If one considers intertextuality as enlarging upon influence, then this characterization makes enough sense to show the smooth transition between
them. But Bloom's unyielding insistence on the centrality of the author
in criticism distances him from those theories of intertextuality that view
it as a substitute for the older procedures of influence study. We sustain
a terrible "humanistic loss," Bloom writes, if we yield "to those like Derrida and Foucault who imply . . . that language by itself writes the poems
and thinks"; "influence remains subject-centered, a person-to-person relationship, not to be reduced to the problematic of language" (*Map* 60, 77).

Three aspects of Bloom's theory significantly conflict with the theory of
intertextuality or reflect, with a difference, issues that intertextuality brings
to the fore. The first we have already mentioned, his insistence on the subject. Influence is a personal agon, a struggle of one individual with a
strong precursor, modeled on the son's conflict with the father in the
Oedipus complex. Bloom urges the priority of the will in the poetic act
against both his fathers, the New Critics, who denied the relevance of the
poet's intention to the finished poem, and his sibling rivals, the poststructuralists, who deny the very existence of that intention as anything more
than a kink in the signifying chains. His conception of the poetic will is
expressionist, as Hassan argues that any theory of influence must be, but
it does not rely on biography or other historical evidence to establish its
claims. Bloom relegates such details as whether or not a poet actually read
a specific work by the strong precursor to that "wearisome industry of
source-hunting" (*Anxiety* 31). This dismissal of "extrinsic" critical procedures brings us to our second point, that Bloom's theory is resolutely
nonreferential. He repeatedly asserts his interest in the poet qua poet,
which he takes to mean that the overt subject matter of poems is irrelevant. If the meaning of a poem is only another poem, then poetry is never
about anything but the act of writing poetry. The events to which a poem
refers, whether personal, historical, mythic, or divine, are merely the backdrop against which the central drama of poetic influence is acted out. This
tenet of the nonreferential character of the literary text reappears in most
theories of intertextuality, although with a different emphasis. Third, Bloom
unashamedly employs influence to construct a severely limited canon, in
which strong poets compete only with other similarly strong figures. The

only influences that matter are those that come from the departed great; echoes of minor poets, allusions to one's contemporary competitors, or borrowings from nonliterary sources cannot figure in an account of the poet qua poet — or if they do, then they are an index of that poet's weakness. Not surprisingly, the political implications of this restrictive vision of the canon have provoked much criticism.

Bloom's theory, like the notion of influence from the eighteenth century onward, has remained committed to an author-centered criticism, concerned with issues of originality and genius, an evaluative rhetoric, and an emphasis on literary history. With some alteration, these traditional emphases have suited the needs of feminist and minority critics who wish to enlarge the canon, to praise the achievement of wrongly neglected writers, and to construct an alternative history that supplements the long annals of white, male triumphs. Annette Kolodny, for one, objects to Bloom for portraying influence as an oedipal struggle between *fathers* and *sons,* but her objections pertain equally to any literary history that has excluded women from the tradition, whether tradition is conceived of as continuity or as strife. "Bloom's paradigm of poetic history, when applied to women, proves useful only in a negative sense: for by omitting the possibility of poet-mothers from his psychodynamic of literary influence . . . Bloom effectively masks the fact of an *other* tradition entirely — that in which women taught one another how to read and write about and out of their own unique (and sometimes isolated) contexts" (59–60). The idea of another tradition, in which women influence women, has been central to the development of a large body of American feminist research, beginning with Moers's *Literary Women* (1976) and Showalter's *A Literature of Their Own* (1977). Influence has also been important to works such as Gilbert and Gubar's *The Madwoman in the Attic* (1979), which sees women as struggling against not only a male literary tradition but also the constraints on female authorship imposed by patriarchal society. Alternative models of influence help Adrienne Rich, in "When We Dead Awaken," and Alice Walker, in *In Search of Our Mothers' Gardens,* make a case for the importance of nonliterary creativity by women to the development of contemporary feminist writing. Finally, influence figures in Barbara Smith's call for a black feminist criticism, and she lists the identifying of a "verifiable historical tradition" (174) as that criticism's first task. Many political or oppositional criticisms are ready to put influence study to work for them, and the renewed sanction for such study, after the New Criticism, has proved remarkably empowering for revisionists as well as defenders of the old order.

For many kinds of political criticism, a broad version of influence probably works better than does intertextuality. Some issues that most intrigue contemporary minority and feminist critics (as well as their mainstream predecessors) can far more conveniently by framed in terms of allusion than of intertextuality: for example, how women writers in the 1860s subverted a hegemonic patriarchal idiom. To treat this matter as intertextual, at least in the radical version of the theory that sees intertextuality as a substitute for older preoccupations, would mean alleging that an anonymous cultural text produces or even authorizes everything the women writers do; that the subversion of patriarchal authority is part of the always already known; that novelty is a mere bourgeois illusion. Such a treatment of these authors would produce a coarse analysis, since no apparatus exists for explaining, for example, the production of any specific piece of writing from the meshing of a Boston sociolect of 1864 with an intertextual nexus denoted by the name of a Massachusetts woman.

For the majority of interested readers, we suspect, the method would also produce an unsatisfying story about the women as writers, in that it would attenuate their currently positive image as freedom fighters by casting them as role-players in a social dynamic that permitted, perhaps even caused, their rebellion, a rebellion that would turn out to be another, not necessarily bourgeois, illusion. Those whose ability to act has for centuries been confined and depleted by the social structure have not been eager to surrender that hard-won ability in the name of new theories, mostly produced by white, well-educated males. Many recent feminists have worked to recover the notion of the agent — Nancy K. Miller's *Subject to Change* is a recent example — and to broaden the notion of influence, at times coupling it with an intertextuality that augments rather than substitutes for influence theories, so as to explore the connections among women writers (one thinks, for instance, of essays by Susan Stanford Friedman and by Elaine Marks). These Anglo-American feminist critics and black critics have felt that to postulate an intending agent as the epicenter of an eclectic, allusive motion is to raise the issues of opportunities and constraints with which the women or minority writers worked but without returning to the expressionist assumptions of a narrower influence theory.

II

Despite the partial revival of influence in the seventies, Kristeva's neologism, "intertextuality," won partisans fast. It did not do so because of its own coherence: the face of "intertextuality," as a new master term, is less a simple, single, and precise image, a bronze head by Rodin, than something shattered, a portrait bust by an avid exponent of analytic cubism too poor to afford a good chisel. Theories, of course, try to regularize it,

and we shall survey them in the third part of this introduction. Here, however, we shall concentrate on some reasons why, after a long reign, influence began to fall into decline.

The reasons that led critics to prefer the new term ranged from a perception of influence's weakness, to a suspicion that it carried unwanted implications, to a belief in its outright tendentiousness as a concept. Influence,
for example, seemed ill suited to accomodate the discoveries of psychoanalysis, the benefits of simply reading two texts against each other without
regard to historical priority, and the desire of many to play down literary
canons, new and old alike. The narrow form of influence, which intrigued
many nineteenth-century critics, may simply have begun to seem outworn,
a victim of the ongoing rationalization of society that Weber describes.
The traditional concept of influence, that is, seems to stand somewhere
in the middle of the Weberian process by which Western societies moved
from the rule of tradition to that of flexible, rationalized calculations of
purpose. It values individual creativity but continues to rely on the powerful *traditum,* that which is handed down, though — in this individualizing
stage — commonly the legacy of a person ("the influence of Milton") rather
than anonymous practice ("the influence of the picaresque"). It smacks
of the system of earned rule that supplanted lineage, the capitalism of
bold, oblivious robber barons. The practice of allusion comes much closer
to modern Western ideals of action, and its problematic is more intriguing
to critics as to artists nowadays.

More destructive to the reign of influence has been a falling off, among
many critics, of interest in its central figure, the author as agent. In this
decentering of the author, we can identify at least four movements, sometimes companionable with each other. None of these has elbowed out its
competitors but each has created a good bit of elbow room for itself. The
four are: (1) behind an idea of influence lie dubious normative judgments
about originality; (2) the biographical issues crucial to influence are at
best merely ancillary to texts; (3) a stress on the author's being influenced
or influencing tends to make that author authoritative, thus to brush aside
the activity of readers, let alone their freedom of interpretation and response; and (4) a concern about influence promotes an outworn humanism. Each of these four — first a notion of evaluation, then of expression,
next of legitimation, and finally of ideology — names a dynamic that operates to exclude influence or push it to the periphery of concerns. In each
dynamic, some other means of textual gloss also absorbs one or more
roles that influence had previously played. We must emphasize, however,
that we do not put forward these arguments against influence in order to
indict the term but rather to explain why a certain critical practice has
been waning.

1. Normative judgments. To see historical change working through influence has been to envision tradition not as smooth but as disjunctive, progress by the fiats of charismatic figures and works. In our discussion of Bate we alluded to the high value that comes to be placed on originality as a means of altering the status quo and, correspondingly, the lower value that is assigned to the unoriginal, the influenced. In a long account of influence as a normative criterion — the more influential an artist, the better she or he is — Göran Hermerén points to the normative implications of the economic metaphors with which influence is expressed, *owing* and *indebtedness,* normative implications especially strong, we suppose, among the upright who hate dulling the edge of husbandry (130–31, 143, 133). Over the last fifty years, the normative force of influence studies has waned markedly. The ideal of a single, communal, consensual artistic tradition, in which progress takes place, has waned. The deliberate and elaborate borrowings of much canonical twentieth-century art, and the extravagant iconoclasm of much modern avant-gardism that at once adopts the name of "Art" and flaunts its undermining, cooled critics' fervor for exalting the original as a supreme value. Unless one refuses to have a theory of art that accommodates, say, Man Ray's metronome as sculpture, one ends up shifting the locus of originality from the language of art to a meta-language, a statement about Art. Doing that calls attention to the inter-text, the "surround" in terms of which — and only in terms of which — the metronome can be understood *as* art.

Artistic and critical ideals over the past twenty-five years, of course, have further enfeebled the evaluative force of influence.[6] As the old standard of "self-reliance" has turned into the mixture of accelerated commerce and semi-enlightened self-interest that marks the modern economy, "owing" and "indebtedness" have lost their moral sting; Americans think they still frown on debt but they thrive on the "leverage" they get from their mortgages, their credit cards, and the business practices that support their pension funds. More generally, the multiplication of cultural goods and the complexity of their entrance into play make hierarchies of value hard to establish and hardly worth the effort. Since part of the charm of influence studies was their use in assigning praise and blame, sapping these hierarchies also enfeebled the fascination with whether Coleridge was a mere sneaking epigone of Schlegel's or, per contra, made his silk purses from Schlegel's sow's ears. At the same time, the methods of close reading, widely practiced from the mid-thirties on, made this sort of evaluative tack seem beside the analytic point or, one might say, vulgar. What became important was not an author's source but the textual shaping of materials at hand, not debt but the leverage that the appropriation of resources might offer.

Influence has turned out to be unnecessary even to lionize or demote an author historically, an activity still going very strong. One can easily replace it with a more broadly conceived relationship to what used to be called "tradition," as in "tradition and the individual talent," but now is more likely to be assigned to a convention (speech-act, genre), an ideology, an episteme, or a horizon of expectations.[7] The lionized author moves and shakes his or her past, defies the reigning ideology or the audience's horizon of expectations, strongly misreads, or playfully subverts. If in influence earlier people act upon later ones, here systems rather than people "act upon," for the great precursors in Eliot's tradition and Bloom's paternal canon exist as such only as selves who dominate and exemplify a system, a corporate understanding.[8] Again one comes back to a Weberian model, since the late stages of "rationalization" include the interlocking dynamic of both charisma and bureaucracy, innovation fighting routine and then being absorbed by it. This dynamic is dramatized in the literary scenario by the agon of individual and society, whether in the conservative phase of Eliot's pietas or the leftish one of brave new literary history. In either case, effectively, an old-fashioned heroic romance now appears renewed, touting previously excluded authors, or the same old authors for novel reasons, or some (recently) canonical critical theorist who saves the oppressed and slays literary dragons, who are always someone else's literary lions. With the displacement of the historical value structure that influence had generated, the study of influence loses one of its founding purposes.

2. The irrelevance of biography. The charismatic effect of influential authors and works paradoxically led to taking the work both as part of a biography, an expressive act, and as an autonomous quasi-organism speaking with a life of its own. This doubleness, with a life of *its* own, has helped diminish the influence of influence which it was partly spawned to support. Influence depends on the lives of authors, and in our accounts of these lives, incident should illustrate character and character determine incident. During the last half-century or more, however, critics have split being from doing—character from incident—as the autonomy of the text has gained adherents. Consequently, expressive theories of art have had a hard time, and even their attenuated form, by which great art emerged from a great or at least capacious soul, has paled: "Considering 'the poet in his poem,'" Patricia Meyer Spacks writes in an introduction to a collection titled *The Author in His Work,* critics "concentrate on what the poet does rather than who he is. When they touch on the latter issue, they often betray uneasiness. . . . The author presents himself in his work by a series of artifices; the author in his work *is* in fact an artifice" (xii–xiii). If biography does appear, then, critics treat the work as an intricate euphemism rather than language of "a man speaking to men," as Wordsworth put it in 1802 (and as M. H. Abrams approvingly reput it as late as 1979 [566]).

For either the earlier or the later author, such influence as counts is likely to be a nonliterary, nonintellectual influence from infancy (let the Oedipus complex be its token), which in later life emerges in recognizably sublimated form or unrecognizably, when it remains concealed behind acts of rhetoric or ideological funneling. With this occluding of personality, influence simply stops being of much interest for the understanding of a work just as, under (1) above, it stops being of much interest for the evaluation of a writer's achievement. At most, knowing something about the author adds coherence to already framed hypotheses about a text that, like the early Protestants' Bible, provides the matter to be interpreted and the code by which the interpretation takes place.

Once more, some of the heuristic and historical functions of influence, removed to the level of system, can be displaced into a practice of intertextuality. Arthur Danto ingeniously postulates a necktie painted smoothly, uniformly blue by the aged Picasso as a rejection of 1950s flaunting of paint and brushstroke. In some sense this tie is a deliberate archaism. A second necktie, exactly like the first, is painted by a child with paint from the same manufacturer; a sly opportunist forges a third "Picasso" tie; and someone discovers a fourth tie, again indiscernible from the others, painted (perhaps to go with a blue velvet jacket) by Cézanne. The Picasso, Danto argues, is an artwork from the man who had already sculpted "a chimpanzee out of a toy, a bull out of a bicycle seat," while the Cézanne is not, for "there would have been no room in the artworld of [his] time for a painted necktie" ("Artworks" 329; the points are elaborated in *Transfiguration* 40–41). The child's tie is not an artwork, even if it is mistaken for Picasso's and hung in an art museum. Though the forger's tie *is* potentially an artwork, it makes no statement, unlike Picasso's, even if Picasso by error authenticates the forger's tie as his own. The four physically identical ties, Danto contends, are four different kinds of object as art.

The form of Danto's argument, whether or not one accepts its particulars, suggests how intertext can take over and define elements that in the past were often assigned to biography, such as allusion, originality, and expression (the differentia among the four blue neckties). In this example, each tie is historically defined, and since all the ties look identical, each is defined only by historical difference, thus refuting any claim that one can talk about the priority or autonomy of the text. These differences, though, are intertextual: one can talk about reference, expression, and originality as one does in regard to the Picasso necktie only because it has been classified as an artwork and vice versa; the other ties' relation to these properties results from and causes their taxonomic status, by which they are

created as facts in a biography. Danto's argument begins with influence —
De Kooning's, say, on Picasso, and Picasso's (as sculptor) on Picasso (as
tie painter) — but ends by making it simply a mode of intertextuality.

3. The authority of the author. In de-authoring texts and stressing the
primacy of interpretation, criticism of the last fifty years has sporadically
shifted attention to the reader, encouraging the procedures of intertextuality. This shift sometimes occurs even where it seems not to. We would
argue, for example, that the more influential of the two well-known New
Critical essays by Wimsatt and Beardsley, "The Intentional Fallacy" (1946),
discounts the author's intention in the phenomenological sense of "awareness" as well as the narrower sense, which Wimsatt and Beardsley had in
mind, of intended meaning; it attacks more than it sets out to attack. By
contrast, "The Affective Fallacy" (1949), the essay about the reader, begins
with a broader agenda — exposing "a confusion between the poem and its
results" (21) — than it ends up with, by skipping cognitive results and limiting
itself to emotional results alone. By the structure of Wimsatt and Beardsley's
arguments, the reader is thus given extra leeway, the author less, and this
undetected surplus is effectively transferred to the reader's cognitive authority as a textual analyst.

Still more plainly, in most versions of "reader response," influence is
at once asserted and nullified, for the reader's intertextual web traps whatever is public of the writer's influence. Unless the writer and reader are
the same, a given book or idiom that has served to influence the writer
can only appear to the reader as intertext, a section of a pattern in terms
of which he or she makes sense of what is now read. Similarly, reader-
response criticism takes over and converts for its own use a category important to influence, temporal priority. Priority returns in a new form, the
past experience that affects a reader or, more consistently in logic, a reading. We shall suggest below that explicit theories of intertextuality tend
to have strong reader-response components; we would argue the reciprocal
here, that a strong reader-response theory tends toward some form of
intertextuality.

4. Ideology. Perhaps the reason that has most directly led various theorists to try to substitute intertextuality for influence is, in a literal as well
as a loose sense, political. Centering on the author as intentional agent
looks outworn or ominous to many who believe that interest in the author
emerges from a "humanist" scheme of values widely charged with distorting cultural inquiry and political understanding. By distinguishing between
those "major" works of art that radiate effects (sources, influences) and
those mere social products that are "minor" works, influence also seems
to endorse a liberal culture that worships successful individual effort. A
more radical agenda urges intertextualists' suspicion of authorial canons

and canonized authors and insists upon the treatment of all works, not just "minor" ones, as social products. Partisans of these agendas may have widely different political ends, from creative and playful anarchy to a utopian vision of ordered social justice. Two separable but often not separate impulses, moreover, are at work here. One is an eagerness to expropriate, to make the haves share their wealth and acclaim with some have-nots. Critics may be spurred here by iconoclasm and *ressentiment* about the Establishment as well. The other impulse is to get rid of the whole system of literary hierarchies and authorial property, to consider every text to be in the public domain once it is uttered in our common language.

For the advocates of substitution on political grounds, then, the principles of influence (a literary history about agents) and intertextuality (a literary history of meshing systems) preside more as rival subjugators in various kinds of commentary than as co-workers in a continuous, flexible scheme. Thus influence assigns intertextuality, under the slave names "context" and "allusion," to an accessory role in a scenario that features imperious, charismatic Major Works. For its part, once intertextuality has reassigned to the provinces influence's concern with an author's intentions and his or her consciousness of them, it organizes what is left, textual comparison, into a formalist idiom where "society," "culture," and "history" share legibility with the verbal sequences that have traditionally been called "texts" or "works." Likewise, while influence prefers what the anthropologists call "emic" explanations, those in keeping with patterns of thought that would make sense to the men and women being written about, the critics who practice intertextuality often prefer "etic" explanations, those geared for the analyst and not for the ideologically blinded analysand.

III

By the mid-to-late 1960s, the stage had long been set for a theory of intertextuality. On this side of the Atlantic, the most astonishing and influential work of postwar theory, Northrop Frye's *Anatomy of Criticism* (1957), assumed what would come to be known as intertextual principles. It presents, in part, a "conception of literature as . . . containing life and reality in a system of verbal relationships" (122). It subsumes the work of "major" authors with that of "minor" figures in a multiply positional typology based on relation and difference. Like the contemporary French prophet of structuralism and therefore of French intertextuality, Claude Lévi-Strauss, Frye put forth an ideal of scientific objectivity and sweep. These principles immediately captured the imagination of upcoming North American academics. Brought up with New Critical textualism, a new generation learned from Frye how to expand a spatial, formal criticism beyond the individual poem. If close readings of the 1950s showed tensions and multiplicity reconciled within the single text, so in Frye's system the order of literature itself reconciled conflicts within an eclectic canon. What critics took from him was an improvement in techniques they were already using; what a still later group of critics were to be offered through the similar assumptions of intertextuality, however, was a call to scrap the old techniques in favor of something new. The lexicography of the term "intertextuality" took on its force through its French introducers, but the underlying complex of ideas—some of them venerable and many of them rooted in ongoing academic practice—remained so varied as to make the term unstable in meaning. Susan Friedman, in her essay for this volume, remarks on the vain attempts of the term's begetters to restrict it as they would wish.

Kristeva's own development of the term "intertextuality" was itself a complex intertextual event, one that involved both inclusion and selectivity. She initially used it in her dialogue with the texts of Mikhail Bakhtin. One of the first to introduce Bakhtin in France, she employed his ideas as a lever to displace semiotics, shifting it toward a more openly ideological criticism. Her dialogue with Bakhtin, however, was mediated by the texts of Derrida and Lacan, so that her account of Bakhtin as well as of semiotics was destabilized.

For Kristeva, Bakhtin represents the possibility of opening linguistics to society. "Bakhtin situates the text within history and society, which are seen as texts read by the writer, and into which he inserts himself by rewriting them" (*Desire* 65). Bakhtin authorizes this attention to history by shifting linguistic analysis from the grammatical, atemporal plane to that of the individual utterance, which is always caught up in a context of other utterances. A sign can never be analyzed in isolation, for its meaning is always informed by the many often conflicting ways it has been used by other speakers. Thus one focuses not on the usual linguistic unit, the sign, but on the relation of one sign to other signs. "Every word," Bakhtin writes, "is directed toward an *answer* and cannot escape the profound influence of the answering word that it anticipates" (280). Every word, in short, is "dialogic," and must be analyzed as part of a dialogue. Bakhtin calls his project "translinguistics," for he has expanded the unit of analysis across the boundaries of ordinary linguistics.

Following Bakhtin, Kristeva attempts to transform semiotics into something she also calls "translinguistics" (*Desire* 37), a method of analysis that allows her to confront the literary work on the formal and the social levels simultaneously. At the same time, however, she transforms Bakhtin's concepts by causing them to be read in conjunction with ideas about textuality that were emerging in France in the mid-sixties. For instance, she slips "text" into a paraphrase of Bakhtin: "each word (text) is an intersection of words (texts) where at least one other word (text) can be read" (*Desire* 66). Though the parentheses imply that Kristeva is only supplying a synonym, or at most, a neutral expansion of Bakhtin's concept, this textualization of Bakhtin changes his ideas — changes them just enough to allow the new concept of intertextuality to emerge. Thus she characterizes Bakhtin's "conception of the 'literary word' as an *intersection of textual surfaces* rather than a *point* (a fixed meaning), as a dialogue among several writings" (*Desire* 65, italics in original). One cannot help but see Derrida's critique of voice behind this slight shift toward a dialogue of "writings" not "utterances," particularly since Kristeva cites *Of Grammatology* on the first page of her essay. A Derridean view of "writing" supplies a dimension that was not present in Bakhtin originally, the dimension of indeterminacy, of *différance,* of dissemination. Although Bakhtin's notions of "heteroglossia" or "hybridization" might seem near equivalents to the poststructuralist concepts, Bakhtin's emphasis on the historical uniqueness of the context of every utterance distances his terms from the endlessly expanding context of intertextuality. In Kristeva's usage, the intersection of textual surfaces in a literary word can never be circumscribed, is open to endless dissemination.

A crucial step in this transformation had occurred in Derrida's reading of Saussure in *Of Grammatology* (1967). There he subordinates the difference between signifier and signified, a foundational concept of semiotics, to the difference between one signifier and another. Consequently, Derrida must be regarded as a crucial intertext of most theories of intertextuality. His frequently quoted formula, "there is nothing outside of the text" (158), provides ample space within the object of study for a multitude of intertexts. Under the name of "grafts," he pursues an active intertextual practice, in which intertextuality becomes the critic's method of probing, fissuring, disorienting, and dangerously supplementing the text at hand so as to exhibit its implications and implicatedness.[9]

In much the same way, Lacan functions as a largely unacknowledged intertext for Kristeva's reading of Bakhtin. She notes that Bakhtin's claim that the language of epic is univocal cannot withstand a psychoanalytic approach to language. It is psychoanalysis, as well as the semiotics she cites (the theory of Benveniste), that reveals dialogism to be inherent in every word, as the "trace of a dialogue with oneself (with another), as a writer's distance from himself" (*Desire* 74). This psychoanalysis is Lacan's, and his ideas, we suspect, also lie behind Kristeva's choice of the term "ambivalence" to describe certain forms of dialogism: "Confronted with this dialogism, the notion of a 'person-subject of writing' becomes blurred, yielding to that of 'ambivalence of writing'" (*Desire* 68). To conceive of

alogical nature of an utterance in terms of the "ambivalence of writ-
...g rather than in terms of the speaker's situation within language involves a textualization, under the aegis of psychoanalysis, similar to the
textualization of voice that occurred within the Derridean framework.

From this intertextual modification of Bakhtin,[10] then, emerge Kristeva's
several definitions of intertextuality: "in the space of a given text, several
utterances, taken from other texts, intersect and neutralize one another";
"any text is constructed as a mosaic of quotations; any text is the absorption and transformation of another"; "Bakhtin considers writing as a
reading of the anterior literary corpus and the text as an absorption of
and a reply to another text"; "The writer's interlocutor, then, is the writer
himself, but as reader of another text. The one who writes is the same
as the one who reads. Since his interlocutor is a text, he himself is no more
than a text rereading itself as it rewrites itself. The dialogical structure,
therefore, appears only in the light of the text elaborating itself as ambivalent in relation to another text" (*Desire* 36, 66, 69, 86–87).

For the practicing critic, Kristeva's conception of intertextuality opens
several lacunae not in Bakhtin. The first involves a vagueness about the
relation of the social to the literary text. Kristeva does not discuss what
happens to a fragment of the social text when it is "absorbed" and "transformed" by literature, nor does she account for how specific social texts are
chosen for "absorption." John Frow organizes a convincing critique of
Kristeva's work around this point. He argues that her account is dynamic but
not genuinely historical, for it fails to consider the way prevailing social
norms are either reinforced or modified by quotation within literature: "the
social text is transformed into the terms and conventions of literary discourse. To ignore this mediation of the literary system, to relate a text to . . .
a cultural text which is completely or predominantly nonliterary, is to ignore
the complexity of the enunciative shift involved in the elaboration of one
generic structure by another" (128). A second problem, an inability to construct a convincing literary history, follows from the first. Kristeva claims,
for example, that "a break occurred at the end of the nineteenth century"
(*Desire* 71) that clearly marks off the dialogism of Joyce, Proust, and Kafka
from the dialogical novels of the past, including Bakhtin's principal examples, Rabelais and Dostoyevsky. But her conception of intertextuality
generates no means of distinguishing the modern novel from earlier poly-
phonic novels, and she merely has recourse to standard honorifics about
literary modernism. Moreover, her Lacanian demonstration that all words
are dialogical would argue against basing a literary history on progressive
degrees of dialogism. Hence Kristeva follows only one part of Bakhtin's
system by turning to an ahistorical "typology of discourses" rather than
continuing her speculations about historical developments.

Among theorists of intertextuality, Kristeva seems at first unique in not emphasizing the role of the reader. Her subsequent rejection of the term in favor of "transposition" indicates her continued interest in the positionalities of writing rather than the responses of reading. "The term *intertextuality* denotes this transposition of one (or several) sign system(s) into another; but since this term has often been understood in the banal sense of 'study of sources,' we prefer the term *transposition* because it specifies that the passage from one signifying system to another demands a new articulation . . . of enunciative and denotative positionality" (*Revolution* 59–60). The only reader in Kristeva is the writer reading another text, a figure that becomes "no more than a text rereading itself as it rewrites itself." Post-Kristevan writers in her line do supply a reader, but rarely an empirical figure in the manner of American reader-response critics such as Norman Holland, David Bleich, or Stanley Fish, or of German Rezeption aestheticians such as Hans Robert Jauss, whom we shall discuss shortly. This reader, the figure of a well-versed decoder of signs, "transposes" into poststructuralist terms the earlier phenomenological or existentialist reader, encountering a text with all of its depths and deceptions, current in francophone theory after World War II.

Later theories of intertextuality have kept and further textualized Kristeva's strong basis in semiotics: the science of signs developed by Saussure and still intact in Barthes's *Elements of Semiology* (1964) is treated less as a *science* with objective aims and verifiable results, and more as a mode of *interpretation.* Theories proceeded from this point in three directions: (1) the deconstructive path of aporia and the reader's puzzlement or play; (2) a semiotic path that argues for increased certainty for the reader; and (3) the social or political path taken by cultural materialism or new historicist criticism. Barthes will serve to exemplify the first; Michael Riffaterre and Jonathan Culler, aspects of the second; Rezeption and Foucauldian critics, aspects of the third.

In essays published in the late sixties and in *S/Z* (1970), Barthes advances a theory of intertextuality that depends entirely on the reader as the organizing center of interpretation:

A text is made of multiple writings, drawn from many cultures and entering into mutual relations of dialogue, parody, contestation, but there is one place where this multiplicity is focused and that place is the reader, not, as was hitherto said, the author. The reader is the space on which all the quotations that make up a writing are inscribed without any of them being lost; a text's unity lies not in its origin but in its destination. Yet this destination cannot any longer be personal: the reader is without history, biography, psychology; he is simply that *someone* who holds together in a single field all the traces by which the written text is constituted. ("Death" 148)

This notion of the reader introduces several concepts that distance inter-textuality from most theories of influence. The study of influence, we argued, is an author-centered project that generally relies on the disci-plines that Barthes excludes from his conception of the reader—history, biography, and psychology. The expressivist assumptions latent in influ-ence theories equally locate a work's unity in the controlling vision of its author. Finally, the evaluative dimension of most influence criticism is missing from a practice that sees relations among texts in terms of dia-logue, parody, and contestation.

Barthes's vision of intertextuality also highlights the frequent anonym-ity of the "sources" of intertextual quotations. This idea was implicit in Kristeva's discussion of the "absorption" of social texts, because the social may be thought of as the network of anonymous ideas, commonplaces, folk wisdom, and clichés that make up the background of one's life. As we noted, traditional influence studies primarily hunted for allusions to celebrated works of the past, so distinguishing a genuine influence from a commonplace was the chief concern of most theoretical writing on in-fluence, at least in the narrow sense, prior to the 1960s. Barthes, however, makes the commonplace central: "the citations which go to make up a text are anonymous, untraceable, and yet *already read*" ("Work" 160). The "already read" in Barthes encompasses more than the idea that we all possess conventional knowledge whose sources we cannot recall. It extends toward a notion of the subject as constituted by the texts of its culture, the subject *as* the already read. Barthes puts it clearly in *S/Z*: "This 'I' which approaches the text is already itself a plurality of other texts, of codes which are infinite or, more precisely, lost" (10).

The power of Barthes's notion of intertextuality can best be seen in his discussion of realism in *S/Z*. Balzacian realism is effective, for Barthes, not because it refers us to a world outside of literature but because of its continuous reference to anonymous textual codes that are always already read. The "'realistic' artist never places 'reality' at the origin of his dis-course, but only and always, as far back as can be traced, an already writ-ten real, a prospective code, along which we discern, as far as the eye can see, only a succession of copies" (*S/Z* 167). A beautiful woman, Barthes notes, can be described only in terms of a citation of other women in paint-ing, literature, and mythology: "thus, beauty is referred to an infinity of codes: *lovely as Venus*? But Venus lovely as what?" (*S/Z* 34). The circular-ity of reference itself insures the effect of the real. "Once the infinite cir-cularity of codes is posited, the body itself cannot escape it. . . . Thus, even within realism, the codes never stop" (*S/Z* 55).

Valuable as Barthes's account of intertextuality is for understanding the literary, it does not provide the critic with a particularly effective tool for analyzing literary texts. The infinite circularity of codes makes every text, potentially, the intertext for every other text: "by degrees, a text can come into contact with any other system: the inter-text is subject to no law but the infinitude of its reprises" (*S/Z* 211). If the codes never stop, then where does one draw the line between relevant and irrelevant references? How can Barthes's reader "without history, biography, psychology" have interests that would supply such a line? This theory makes for a criticism more stimulating than informative, providing of course that the critic has a stimulating mind. In fact, Barthes's reading practice in *S/Z* is less radical than his theory. Culler (*Structuralist* 203) points out the restrictiveness and insufficiency of the codes with which Barthes unweaves Balzac's narrative, and his interpretive results do not take one further than a highly skilled, subtle formalist might go. We do not want to pretend that interpretation, an Anglo-American idol, is Barthes's goal, but rather that his radical intertextuality forgoes the possibility of rigor in the discussion of individual texts, so much so that to attempt such a rigorous discussion, he must retrench on the theory. The theory nonetheless has a real heuristic or at least iconoclastic value in unsettling customary ideas about the author, the work, and the representation of reality.

The second path, that of using intertextuality to achieve greater interpretive certainty, has been taken by the writer who has used intertextuality most effectively in his practical criticism, Michael Riffaterre.[11] Like Barthes, he stresses the central role of the reader, defining the literary phenomenon as "not only the text, but also its reader and all of the reader's possible reactions to the text" (*Text* 3). Like both Barthes and Kristeva, he is profoundly interested in semiotics. Although he has sometimes been called a structuralist, this label is deceptive, for he believes that the only significant structure in a literary work is that which the reader can perceive. He rejects the structuralist's search for a deep grammar in literature, and he rejects as well the notion that all literary works of a given type share the same structure. For Riffaterre, the structure of a work is generated by the expansion of a single word or sentence, which he calls the "matrix" of the work. Although several works may share the same matrix, the structure that results from the transformation of this matrix into a poem or novel is unique. The analysis of structure, then, must attend to the specifics of the individual text, not to the matrix that several works may share. Riffaterre practices, in effect, a textual semiotics. The literary analysis must be "absolutely obedient to the text," by which he means the elements in a text "that we are obliged to perceive" (*Text* 6).

This textual semiotics leads Riffaterre to emphasize stylistic units different from those analyzed by traditional linguistics. Like Kristeva, who wants to bracket "the question of semantic sequences" so that she "can bring out the *logical practice* organizing them, thus proceeding at a *suprasegmental* level" (*Desire* 37); like Bakhtin, who employs a "translinguistics" in order to alter the unit of linguistic analysis; or like Barthes, who fractures the text of *Sarrasine* into arbitrary "units of reading" he calls "lexias" (*S/Z* 13), Riffaterre insists that "the stylistic unit cannot be confused with the units obtained through normal segmentation, to wit, words and phrases" (*Text* 7). One of the characteristic gestures of a textualizing criticism, it seems, is to revise one's customary ways of segmenting the literary artifact. As a spatializing technique, intertextuality itself might be seen as a radical resegmenting of literature, allowing a reading of the words of one text as "part" of another text in a single unit of meaning.

If Riffaterre's theory resembles the poststructural in its emphasis on the reader and on a textualized semiotics, it differs from poststructuralism, as we have said, in its insistence on a determinate conception of the literary artifact, one that rejects the dispersal of meanings through an infinite system of interlocking codes. Ambiguity, obscurity, undecidability, indeterminacy, unreadability, ungrammaticality — all of these exist only as a stage in the reading process and serve to alert the reader to the presence of an intertext that will resolve the work's difficulties. Riffaterre is adamant on this point. Intertextuality acts as a "constraint upon reading (as a set of restrictions upon the reader's freedom, as a guide for him in his interpreting)" ("Syllepsis" 628). There is only one correct reading, and the intertextual method will unfailingly direct the wise reader to *"the* proper interpretation,"* barring absentmindedness ("Interpretation and Undecidability" 227). Talk of restricting the reader's freedom, controlling interpretation, guiding one to *the* proper view of a text seems far removed from the plural, infinitely circulating texts of Kristeva and Barthes, but the potential was there from the beginning.

The example of Riffaterre dramatizes the logical independence of intertextuality from many poststructuralist assumptions, even among those who do not write cultural criticism. With less focus on the historical specificity of an utterance than Marxists or new historicists, for instance, Jonathan Culler argues for the constraining power of intertextuality, although not so absolutely as does Riffaterre. In "Presupposition and Intertextuality," Culler suggests that we consider intertextuality in terms of two kind of presuppositions, those inherent in the logic of a sentence ("Have you stoppped cheating on tests?") and those inherent in the pragmatics of a sentence ("Once upon a time there was a beautiful princess."), in that every utterance presupposes an appropriate situation. The practical virtue of Culler's proposal is that it limits the set of intertexts for an interpretation to those that are either logically or pragmatically suggested by the text one is studying (resolving one of the problems with Barthes's method), without excluding the anonymous, already read discourse of the social text, which is usually ignored in influence studies. An implicit consequence of this proposal is to restore a degree of certainty to the act of interpretation, although this certainty is a function not of "moments of authority and points of origin" ("Presupposition" 117) but of the reader's awareness of conventions, both linguistic and literary. Culler's concept of convention, here as elsewhere in his work, serves as a check on the endless play of signification. As he says in another essay, describing his version of a textualized semiotics: "Because literary works do have meaning for readers, semiotics undertakes to describe the systems of convention responsible for those meanings" ("Pursuit" 38-39).

In Riffaterre's own more elaborate scheme, determinate interpretation arises from the special two-stage process of reading that a literary work demands. The first stage is a naive, "mimetic" reading, in which "words signify through their one-to-one relationship with nonverbal referents" ("Syllepsis" 625). This mimetic reading yields what he calls the "meaning" of a work, the linear, word-by-word decoding of the message in accordance with an assumption that language is referential, that words relate directly to things. In the course of this reading, however, one encounters "ungrammaticalities"—difficulties, obscurities, undecidable moments, figurative language—any wording so unacceptable in a mimetic context that it prompts one to look elsewhere for the "significance" of the work, which emerges only in a second or "retroactive" stage of reading. The mistake of believing that a work's meaning can be indeterminate or undecidable, according to Riffaterre, is the result of taking as final, indeed permanent, a transitory stage in the reading process ("Interpretation and Undecidability" 227-28, 230, 239). As he puts it in the conclusion of *Semiotics of Poetry:* "any ungrammaticality within the poem is a sign of grammaticality elsewhere. . . . The poetic sign has two faces: textually ungrammatical, intertextually grammatical; displaced and distorted in the mimesis system, but in the semiotic grid appropriate and rightly placed" (164-65).

Culler has charged Riffaterre with inconsistently claiming that the reader's interpretation is strictly determined by the semiotic grid while asserting that all previous commentators have misread the poem ("Riffaterre" 94-95).[12] The issue of conflicting interpretations must trouble any theory that insists so strenuously that a single reading is not only correct but unavoidable. More important still is the question of "linguistic competence." According to Riffaterre, the ability to recognize the gaps and hurdles of a work as ungrammatical are part of every reader's linguistic competence. "Interpretation, therefore, does not need much philology or erudition." Solving the puzzle of a literary text is not a special talent, to be cultivated by long years of training, but a skill within the reach of "the most ordinary reader"; the interpreter "is only a more conscious reader" ("Interpretation and Descriptive Poetry" 236, 238). Yet his own interpretations of poems and novels are full of learned allusions and draw on an encyclopedic command of French and English literatures.

The issue of linguistic competence recalls a more troubling problem, that of literary canons. Whose competence is at stake? Which works make up the customary knowledge of a typical reader? Riffaterre is really talking not about "linguistic" competence, which is something that one absorbs unconsciously, like the deep grammar of a language, but about "literary" competence, "the reader's familiarity with the descriptive systems, with themes, with his society's mythologies, and above all with other texts" (*Semiotics* 5). Riffaterre's concept is akin to E. D. Hirsch's "cultural literacy," and both authors employ their ideas to similar ends — the development of the proper climate for validity in interpretation. The notion of literary competence, of course, introduces a highly variable factor into what is supposed to be a universally available interpretation, the effect of the differences of class, race, gender, and cultural heritage.

The third path, that of putting intertextuality at the service of political and historical projects, has become identified with two schools, *Rezeptionsästhetik* and critics associated with Michel Foucault. The former has tried to chart historical development by looking at the ways the intertextual connections that a text evokes change over time. Its leading proponents, Hans Robert Jauss and Wolfgang Iser, do not rely extensively on the term intertextuality, but their investigations into continuity and change employ related notions. Jauss's Gadamerian notion of the "horizon of expectations" that a reader brings to a work resembles intertextuality, because the reader's horizon is constructed by an inherited system of norms and conventions. To the study of this intertextual field, however, Jauss's reception criticism adds a historical dimension by tracing the ways different readers' horizons diverge from one another over time. "Literature and art only obtain a history," Jauss writes, "when the succession of works is mediated not only through the producing subject but also through the consuming subject" (15). Iser's reader-response criticism employs a similar intertextual concept, the notion of the "repertoire of the text," a repertoire that exists only in the reader and is activated by "references to earlier works, or to social and historical norms, or to the whole culture from which the text has emerged" (69). In some ways, though, Iser's treatment of historical process is closer to Kristeva's than to Jauss's, for change enters his system not through alterations in the reader but through the way new writing shatters or conforms to the existing repertoire.

Foucault's path leads toward exactly those "differences" that Riffaterre's theory elided — race, class, and in its more recent manifestations, gender.[13]

As early as 1978, Edward Said advocated a Foucauldian rather than Derridean conception of textuality, because the former makes the "text assume its affiliation with institutions, offices, agencies, classes, academies, corporations, groups, guilds, ideologically defined parties and professions" (701). By the mid-eighties Foucault's political vision of intertextuality had become a crucial premise for those critics who wanted to focus on the ways that the social saturates the literary object.

Foucault's conception of intertextuality emphasizes the role of both discursive and nondiscursive formations — such as institutions, professions, and disciplines — in shaping what can be known and, more radically, what can count as "true." Unlike Barthes and Derrida, with their boundless visions of textuality, Foucault attends to the forces that restrict the free circulation of the text. Although every text possesses countless points of intersection with other texts, these connections situate a work within existing networks of power, simultanously creating and disciplining the text's ability to signify. Foucault insists that we analyze the role of power in the production of textuality and of textuality in the production of power. This entails looking closely at those social and political institutions by which subjects are subjected, enabled and regulated in forming textual meaning. In one of his most widely read essays, "What Is an Author?" he examines the regulative function of the author's name, which is a social, economic, and legal construct that limits the proliferation of meaning through its power to classify texts according to genre, group them as parts of a single oeuvre, grant them a particular status, and mark off their boundaries. The author "is a certain functional principle by which, in our culture, one limits, excludes, and chooses; in short, by which one impedes the free circulation, the free manipulation, the free composition, decomposition, and recomposition of fiction" (159). In other works he examines the subject's positioning in and by scientific, medical, penal, psychiatric, and psychosexual discourses. All these projects promote an awareness of the way intertextual networks shape not only our understanding of language but also our existence as social and political subjects.

In "The Discourse on Language" Foucault outlines how his alternative model of textuality would challenge the "traditional history of ideas" (230). In the past "one sought the point of creation, the unity of a work, of a period or a theme, one looked also for the mark of individual originality and the infinite wealth of hidden meaning" (230). This traditional operation involved the kind of procedures we have associated with influence criticism. Foucault's work, by contrast, seeks the "introduction, into the very roots of thought, of notions of *chance, discontinuity* and *materiality*" (231, italics in original). This program, whether or not explicitly derived from Foucault, has set the agenda for historicist inquiries ranging from Fredric Jameson's investigations into the "political unconscious" of forms and genres to Rachel Blau DuPlessis' feminist examination of literary conventions as social "scripts" (2); from new historicist treatments of subversion and containment[14] to the oppositional criticism of gays, lesbians, and peoples of color.

Foucault's program is explicitly invoked by the black critic Houston Baker, who grounds his treatment of African-American literature in a Foucauldian version of intertextuality. Baker argues that "ideological analyses may be as decidedly intertextual as, say, analyses of the relationship between Afro-American vernacular expression and more sophisticated forms of verbal art" (3). In support of this contention, he looks at blues as both code and force, both intertextual network and ideological script. Baker calls this double relation the "matrix" of African-American culture. "The matrix is a point of ceaseless input and output, a web of intersecting, crisscrossing impulses always in productive transit. Afro-American blues constitute such a vibrant network. . . . They are the multiplex, enabling *script* in which Afro-American cultural discourse is inscribed" (3–4).

With this last example, we reach the same stage in our argument where we ended our discussion of influence: the adoption and occasional critique of such terms by oppositional criticisms. Just as Annette Kolodny thought that feminist theorists must revise Bloom's notion of influence, feminists and critics of color have begun to rethink the notion of intertextuality. Barbara Johnson, for example, focuses on the poems of Mallarmé in order to demonstrate how "questions of gender might enrich, complicate, and even subvert the underlying paradigms of intertextuality theory" (124). Mallarmé himself attempts to displace the image of the silenced woman that he had inherited from a rich intertextual network, and in doing so, to give a voice to the place of her silence. But "the revaluation of the *figure* of the woman by a male author cannot substitute for the actual participation of women in the literary conversation. Mallarmé may be able to speak from the place of the silenced woman, but as long as *he* is occupying it, the silence that is broken in theory is maintained in reality" (Johnson 131). Conseqently, Johnson juxtaposes poems by Anne Sexton and Lucille Clifton that show that the "intertextual house has many mansions, and each 'New Thing' can teach us to rewrite its history all over again from the beginning" (133). Her article—and others like it—have taken an important step, and her work demonstrates again the close connection of our topic to a renewed practice of literary history.

As an empowering image for feminists, however, Johnson's "intertextual house" may not be as effective as Nancy Miller's figure of "women weaving" (an image that recurs in Friedman's contribution to this volume). In "Arachnologies," Miller emphasizes the figure who spins—the spider, the lacemaker, the woman at her loom — rather than the abstract network of relations that emerges from so much intertextual theory. Intertextuality becomes an activity, one centered in an embodied and gendered agent, not a shifting field of references. Miller's revision of the concept to include a principle of agency participates in a project — both political and historical in nature — that claims the allegiance of many of the authors in this volume.

IV

The essays in this volume pose questions about influence and intertextuality within the context of a renewed interest in historical approaches to literature. They extend and complement rather than look back to the definitions that make up this history of the two terms. Part II continues the approach of the Introduction with four papers that devote themselves fully to theory. Jay Clayton, in the first of them, weaves a series of reflections, questions, and evocations about a group of nineteenth-century British texts that represent infant death. He reintroduces in a new register, that of a reader's lifeworld, many of the literary and textual issues raised by our topic. Next, Tilottama Rajan uses the example of Blake to examine whether intertextuality is the "historical" element within poststructuralism. In the third, A. N. Doane rethinks fundamental editorial problems for Old English texts in the light of contemporary theories of orality and intertextuality. Finally, Eric Rothstein asks how influence and intertextuality can be brought together so that one can imagine a discursive space in which differing literary histories can coexist and respond to one another.

Part III turns to essays that employ readings of particular texts to further the project of the volume. Susan Stanford Friedman's essay on the (re)birth of the author focuses on a topic of importance to most of the contributors in the volume: the idea of agency. Rothstein ended the prior section by arguing that a concept of agency may be necessary for any historical inquiry. One who tries to explain a text diachronically needs to treat it as the result of actions, not only of random or patterned events, and actions imply agency. In this section, agency generally resides in an author. The essays center on one or two authors, and they rarely do so to make those authors disappear into mere figures for our legibility. Friedman suggests that this emphasis on the agency of authors represents a characteristically American redefinition of intertextuality, not a naive misunderstanding of French theory. One consequence of such a redefinition is that firm boundaries between influence and intertextuality tend to dissolve.

Thomas Schaub's study of John Barth's *End of the Road,* however, finds reasons to maintain some boundaries, contrasting intertextuality and allusion, which is a broader conception of influence. He discusses the novel from without, treating cold war writing as an intertext that serves as metalanguage for our reading of Barth and novel as cultural products; his parallel discussion of the novel from within takes Barth as agent, a cultural *bricoleur* who strategically employs allusion to set up his own metalanguage around the fictional lives of his characters. A radically different angle appears in Lynn Keller's account of Marianne Moore's "Marriage." Keller stresses Moore's feminist staging of a conflict between a great, gray paternal line of influence and a more open, less gender-bound, egalitarian flux of intertextuality. Here the choice of the intertextual becomes authorial strategy, one that displays agency through Moore's very act of willed disappearance into a pastiche of impersonality. Conversely, Cyrena Pondrom points to the claim of influence as an equally feminist strategy of Edith Sitwell's, acting to forward a new canon rather than to baffle an old one. For both Pondrom and Keller, the claim (or repudiation) of influence is itself an intertextual act, a way of putting a simple label on complex relations; but to invoke that act *as* an act is to return to some notion of agency, thereby to the discourse of influence.

Other questions arise when "influence" and "intertextuality" encounter the literary history of times before readers began to prize originality itself. Is "influence" anachronistic when there is no conceptual ground upon or against which it can stand as figure? Is it useless when there is no material ground either, in a culture that does not care about individual authorship and accurate textual transmission, and in which the historiography of literature is not practiced? Under these circumstances, how useful (that is, how loose or tautological) is "intertextuality"? Like Doane's paper in the previous section, Andrew Weiner's essay here considers such issues. Through a discussion of Shakespeare, Sidney, and Spenser, Weiner proposes a category of remaking. He demotes the acute sense of past and present that underlies the discourse of influence, while he at the same time retains an ideal of conscious craft.

Other essays, such as Jeffrey Steele's exploration of Margaret Fuller's psychological life and Friedman's peeling away of the layers of James Joyce's repression, move questions of motive into the play of the un- and preconscious, a half-light of agency where influence and intertextuality might swim together. Both of these essays lead one to ask how far differences in degrees of awareness make up much of at least one working distinction between influence and intertextuality. Any given text, of course, filters its substance from the intertextual, and the process of filtration lends itself to the language of influence. An influential work, presumably, is one that changes the components of the intertext and their relative weighting. With a definition like this in mind, William Andrews shows how Nat Turner's rebellion, turned into a text by Thomas Gray's account, created conditions out of which a revised image of African Americans emerged, at once recognizing and remastering the personal force that Turner had so surprisingly, to Southerners, exhibited. Turner "alters the discursive space" of the representation of African Americans, even if his text did not influence white writers. Similar issues, more tangled as to ascriptions of agency because of ways in which one normally thinks of biography, come into play in Betsy Draine's exploration of Jean Rhys's *Quartet*, "some of" which, Rhys confided, "was lived of course." To understand the selections made from an intertext, Draine points out, one needs a notion very like that of influence, as one does to read the intertext of Rhys's relationships and her accounts of them vis-à-vis other, differently motivated accounts of the "same" events.

It is only appropriate that we conclude this overview of the volume's contents, as we concluded our surveys of "influence" and "intertextuality," with some remarks on the way gender issues have come to be mapped onto the terms. In fully half the twelve essays, gender difference becomes an important theme. In Steele's essay, influence emerges as a kind of allegorical figure for the Father, intertextuality for the Mother. Keller, Pondrom, and Draine each see a woman author's relation to intertextuality in strategic terms, as part of the struggle to make a place for women in a male literary history. Friedman uses intertextual study as a way to recover the mother in Joyce's work, a figure whose repression she argues was a crucial step in the construction of male modernist fiction. Finally, Clayton discusses the representation of women whose acts as solitary female agents translate them, in life and literature, into figures of shared suffering.

NOTES

1 Protests against this method are no recent development; an article published by R. E. Neil Dodge of the University of Wisconsin in *Modern Philology* in 1911 was titled "A Sermon on Source-hunting."
2 For an account of this illustrative debate, which spanned the years 1934–68, see Morris (16–20).
3 The bibliography on this topic includes articles by Dodge, Craig, Clark, Taylor, Stallman, Block, and Guillén. Some versions of intertextuality would make this hotly debated topic irrelevant, since if a resemblance or parallel is seen as inhering in the mind of the reader in the first place, then one does not need to worry about whether the author really read, remembered, and imitated a specific precursor.
4 The centrality of the artistic subject to an understanding of literature has remained a leitmotif of Hassan's criticism from the fifties to the present. His

contribution to a special issue of *Contemporary Literature* titled "Contemporary Literature and Contemporary Theory" defends the continued importance of a pragmatic notion of subjectivity even to criticism within the poststructuralist vein.

5 Of the many treatments of Bloom's theory, two that might be singled out for special notice are those by Lentricchia (318–46) and O'Hara.

6 For a discussion of avant-garde literature as allusive and thereby both original and intertextual, see Jenny (271–78).

7 An illuminating example of intertextual analysis used with an evaluative force appears in Umberto Eco's treatment of the movie *Casablanca* as an archetype. Eco also illustrates how intertextuality, unlike influence, can be used to talk about "references" to works that are chronologically later than the text being studied: "*Casablanca* is a cult movie precisely because all the archetypes are there, because each actor repeats a part played on other occasions, and because human beings live not 'real' life but life as sterotypically portrayed in previous films. *Casablanca* carries the sense of déjà vu to such a degree that the addressee is ready to see in it what happened after it as well. It is not until *To Have and Have Not* that Bogey plays the role of the Hemingway hero, but here he appears 'already' loaded with Hemingwayesque connotations simply because Rick fought in Spain. . . . Two clichés make us laugh but a hundred clichés move us because we sense dimly that the clichés are talking among themselves, celebrating a reunion. . . . What *Casablanca* does unconsciously, other movies will do with extreme intertextual awareness, assuming also that the addressee is equally aware of their purposes. These are 'postmodern' movies, where the quotation of the topos is recognized as the only way to cope with the burden of our filmic encyclopedic expertise" (208–9).

8 Indeed, one can argue that the "spatial form" that Eliot himself and his associates pioneered helps constitute the intertextual: *The Waste Land,* for example, compresses into a single space of readerly and narrative consciousness fragments of "high" and demotic texts from many times, putting them on one synchronic plane. Eliot's tradition, always exerted at the present, is systemic rather than historical, just as is Eliot's allusiveness.

9 See Culler's lucid discussion of this Derridean procedure in *On Deconstruction* (134–56).

10 Todorov does not distinguish between Kristeva's presentation of Bakhtin and Bakhtin's own views, but Todorov's account of Bakhtin thoroughly supports the distinctions we have drawn here. Todorov emphasizes that Bakhtinian "intertextuality" belongs to discourse not language and that it is evidence of the presence of a speaking subject. Except for his conflation of the dialogic with intertextuality, Todorov (60–74) provides a useful digest of Bakhtinian ideas that anticipated intertextuality.

11 The most useful introduction to Riffaterre's system is Culler's "Riffaterre and the Semiotics of Poetry." Frow clarifies the definition of two of Riffaterre's technical terms, "matrix" and "hypogram." Freadman is helpful in placing Riffaterre's work on the theoretical scene, and Hartman has responded to

Riffaterre's reading of Wordsworth's "Yew-Trees," insisting on a more historical and author-centered understanding.

12 Riffaterre has responded to Culler by saying that commentators recognize the same ungrammaticalities that he finds, but they look to the real world or to the sociolect for the answer and hence miss the intertextual clue to the work's significance ("Making" 57). This answer does not fully respond to the problem. If the intertextual clues are always "obvious to the reader, since they are part of his linguistic competence" and the reader "is therefore under strict guidance and control as he fills in the gaps and solves the puzzle" (*Semiotics* 165), then why is not every reader guided to look beyond the mimetic reading for the answer?

13 Foucault's neglect of gender issues has often been noted (see the essays collected in Diamond and Quinby). Historicist criticism in the eighties has generally attempted to correct this lacuna in Foucault's project, so much as to prompt wits to suggest that historicist critics should begin hyphenating race-class-gender.

14 A full account of the emergence of historicist criticisms in the eighties would distinguish the "influence" of Raymond Williams on British cultural materialism from that of Foucault on American new historicism, and would attend to the modifications introduced into both programs by critics such as Stephen Greenblatt, Louis Montrose, Jonathan Dollimore, Alan Liu, and others. It would also discriminate the various strains of new historicist work emerging around Renaissance, romantic, and American studies. The clearest treatment of the difference between cultural materialism and new historicism may be found in Dollimore. An excellent discussion of the difference between Renaissance and romantic new historicism appears in Liu.

WORKS CITED

Abrams, M. H. "How to Do Things with Texts." *Partisan Review* 46 (1979): 565–80.

Bailey, Nathan. *Universal Etymological English Dictionary.*

Baker, Houston A., Jr. *Blues, Ideology, and Afro-American Literature: A Vernacular Theory.* Chicago: Chicago UP, 1984.

Bakhtin, Mikhail M. *The Dialogic Imagination.* Ed. Michael Holquist. Trans. Caryl Emerson and Michael Holquist. Austin: U of Texas P, 1981.

Barthes, Roland. "The Death of the Author." In *Image-Music-Text* 142–48. Trans. Stephen Heath. New York: Hill and Wang, 1977.

Barthes, Roland. "From Work to Text." In *Image-Music-Text* 155–64.

Barthes, Roland. *S/Z.* Trans. Richard Miller. New York: Hill and Wang, 1974.

Bate, W. Jackson. *The Burden of the Past and the English Poet.* Cambridge: Harvard UP, 1970.

Baxandall, Michael. *Patterns of Intention: On the Historical Explanation of Pictures.* New Haven and London: Yale UP, 1985.

Block, Haskell. "The Concept of Influence in Comparative Literature." *Yearbook of Comparative and General Literature* 7 (1958): 30–36.

Bloom, Harold. *The Anxiety of Influence: A Theory of Poetry.* New York: Oxford UP, 1973.

Bloom, Harold. *A Map of Misreading.* New York: Oxford UP, 1975.

Clark, David Lee. "What Was Shelley's Indebtedness to Keats?" *PMLA* 56 (1941): 479–97.

Craig, Hardin. "Shakespeare and Wilson's *Arte of Rhetorique,* An Inquiry into the Criteria for Determining Sources." *Studies in Philology* 28 (1931): 618–30.

Culler, Jonathan. "In Pursuit of Signs." In *The Pursuit of Signs: Semiotics, Literature, Deconstruction* 18–43. Ithaca: Cornell UP, 1981.

Culler, Jonathan. *On Deconstruction: Theory and Criticism after Structuralism.* Ithaca: Cornell UP, 1982.

Culler, Jonathan. "Presupposition and Intertextuality." In *The Pursuit of Signs* 100–118.

Culler, Jonathan. "Riffaterre and the Semiotics of Poetry." In *The Pursuit of Signs* 80–99.

Culler, Jonathan. *Structuralist Poetics: Structuralism, Linguistics, and the Study of Literature.* Ithaca, NY: Cornell UP, 1975.

Curtius, Ernst Robert. *European Literature and the Latin Middle Ages.* Trans. Willard R. Trask. New York: Harper Torchbooks, 1963.

Danto, Arthur C. "Artworks and Real Things." In *Aesthetics Today,* rev. ed., ed. Morris Philipson and Paul G. Gudel, 322–36. New York and Scarborough, Ont.: NAL, 1980.

Danto, Arthur C. *The Transfiguration of the Commonplace: A Philosophy of Art.* Cambridge and London: Harvard UP, 1981.

Derrida, Jacques. *Of Grammatology.* Trans. Gayatri Chakravorty Spivak. Baltimore: Johns Hopkins UP, 1976.

Diamond, Irene, and Lee Quinby, eds. *Feminism and Foucault: Reflections on Resistance.* Boston: Northeastern UP, 1988.

Dodge, R. E. Neil. "A Sermon on Source-Hunting." *Modern Philology* 9 (1911): 211–23.

Dollimore, Jonathan. "Introduction: Shakespeare, Cultural Materialism and the New Historicism." In *Political Shakespeare: New Essays in Cultural Materialism,* ed. Jonathan Dollimore and Alan Sinfield. Manchester: Manchester UP, 1985.

DuPlessis, Rachel Blau. *Writing beyond the Ending: Narrative Strategies of Twentieth-Century Women Writers.* Bloomington: Indiana UP, 1985.

Eco, Umberto. "Casablanca: Cult Movies and Intertextual Collage." In *Travels in Hyperreality,* trans. William Weaver. San Diego: Harcourt Brace Jovanovich, 1986.

Foucault, Michel. "The Discourse on Language." Appendix in *The Archaeology of Knowledge and the Discourse on Language,* trans. A. M. Sheridan Smith. New York: Harper & Row, 1972.

Foucault, Michel. "What Is an Author?" Revised version. Trans. Josué V. Harari.

In *Textual Strategies: Perspectivies in Post-Structuralist Criticism,* ed. Josué V. Harari, 141–60. Ithaca, NY: Cornell UP, 1979.

Freadman, Anne. *"Riffaterra Cognita:* A Late Contribution to the Formalism Debate." *SubStance* 42 (1983).

Friedman, Susan Stanford. "'I go where I love': An Intertextual Study of H. D. and Adrienne Rich." *Signs* 9 (1983): 228–45.

Frow, John. "Intertextuality." In *Marxism and Literary History* 125–69. Cambridge: Harvard UP, 1986.

Frye, Northrop. *Anatomy of Criticism: Four Essays.* Princeton: Princeton UP, 1957.

Guillén, Claudio. "The Aesthetics of Influence Studies in Comparative Literature." In *Proceedings of the Second Congress of the International Comparative Literature Association,* ed. Werner P. Friederich, 1:175–92. 2 vols. Chapel Hill: U of North Carolina P, 1959.

Hartman, Geoffrey. "The Use and Abuse of Structural Analysis: Riffaterre's Interpretation of Wordsworth's 'Yew-Trees.'" *NLH* 7 (1975): 165–89.

Hassan, Ihab H. "The Problem of Influence in Literary History: Notes Towards a Definition." *Journal of Aesthetics and Art Criticism* 14 (1955): 66–76.

Hassan, Ihab H. "Quest for the Subject: The Self in Literature." Special Issue, "Contemporary Literature and Contemporary Theory," ed. Jay Clayton and Betsy Draine. *Contemporary Literature* 29 (1988): 420–37.

Hermerén, Göran. *Influence in Art and Literature.* Princeton: Princeton UP, 1975.

Iser, Wolfgang. *The Act of Reading: A Theory of Aesthetic Response.* Baltimore: Johns Hopkins UP, 1978.

Jameson, Fredric. *The Political Unconscious: Narrative as a Socially Symbolic Act.* Ithaca: Cornell UP, 1981.

Jauss, Hans Robert. "Literary History as a Challenge to Literary Theory." In *Toward an Aesthetic of Reception,* trans. Timothy Bahti, 3–45. Minneapolis: U of Minnesota P, 1982.

Jenny, Laurent. "La stratégie de la forme." *Poétique* 27 (1976): 257–81.

Johnson, Barbara. "Les Fleurs du Mal Arme: Some Reflections on Intertextuality." In *A World of Difference* 116–33. Baltimore: Johns Hopkins UP, 1987.

Kolodny, Annette. "A Map for Rereading: Gender and the Interpretation of Literary Texts." In *The New Feminist Criticism: Essays on Women, Literature, and Theory,* ed. Elaine Showalter, 46–62. New York: Pantheon, 1985.

Kristeva, Julia. *Desire in Language: A Semiotic Approach to Literature and Art.* Ed. Leon S. Roudiez. Trans. Thomas Gora, Alice Jardine, and Leon S. Roudiez. New York: Columbia UP, 1980.

Kristeva, Julia. *Revolution in Poetic Language.* Trans. Margaret Waller. New York: Columbia UP, 1984.

Lentricchia, Frank. *After the New Criticism.* Chicago: U of Chicago P, 1980.

Liu, Alan. Review of *Wordsworth's Historical Imagination: The Poetry of Displacement,* by David Simpson. *Wordsworth Circle* 19 (1988): 172–81.

McKerrow, Ronald B. *Review of English Studies* 1 (1925): 362–63.

Miller, Nancy. "Arachnologies: The Woman, the Text, and the Critic." In *Subject to Change: Reading Feminist Writing* 77–101. New York: Columbia UP, 1988.

Morris, Wesley. *Toward a New Historicism.* Princeton: Princeton UP, 1972.

O'Hara, Daniel T. "The Genius of Irony: Nietzsche in Bloom." In *The Romance of Interpretation: Visionary Criticism from Pater to de Man* 55–92. New York: Columbia UP, 1985.

Rich, Adrienne. "When We Dead Awaken: Writing as Re-Vision." *College English* 34 (1972): 18–30.

Riffaterre, Michael. "Interpretation and Descriptive Poetry: A Reading of Wordsworth's 'Yew-Trees.'" *NLH* 4 (1973): 229–56.

Riffaterre, Michael. "Interpretation and Undecidability." *NLH* 12 (1981): 227–42.

Riffaterre, Michael. "The Making of the Text." In *Identity of the Literary Text,* ed. Mario J. Valds and Owen Miller, 54–70. Toronto: U of Toronto P, 1985.

Riffaterre, Michael. *Semiotics of Poetry.* Bloomington: Indiana UP, 1978.

Riffaterre, Michael. "Syllepsis." *Critical Inquiry* 6 (1980): 625–38.

Riffaterre, Michael. *Text Production.* Trans. Terese Lyons. New York: Columbia UP, 1983.

Said, Edward W. "The Problem of Textuality: Two Exemplary Positions." *Critical Inquiry* 4 (1978): 673–714.

Smith, Barbara. "Toward a Black Feminist Criticism." In The *New Feminist Criticism: Essays on Women, Literature, and Theory,* ed. Elaine Showalter, 168–85. New York: Pantheon, 1985.

Spacks, Patricia Meyer. Introduction to *The Author in His Work: Essays on a Problem in Criticism,* ed. Louis L. Martz and Aubrey Williams. New Haven and London: Yale UP, 1978.

Stallman, R. W. "The Scholar's Net: Literary Sources." *College English* 17 (1955): 20–27.

Taylor, George C. "Montaigne-Shakespeare and the Deadly Parallel." *Philological Quarterly* 22 (1943): 330–38.

Todorov, Tzvetan. *Mikhail Bakhtin: The Dialogical Principle.* Trans. Wlad Godzich. Minneapolis: U of Minnesota P, 1984.

Walker, Alice. *In Search of Our Mothers' Gardens.* San Diego: Harcourt Brace Jovanovich, 1983.

Wellek, René. "The Concept of Evolution in Literary History." 1956. In *Concepts of Criticism* 37–53. New Haven: Yale UP, 1963.

Wimsatt, W. K., Jr., and Monroe C. Beardsley. "The Affective Fallacy" and "The Intentional Fallacy." Rpt. in W. K. Wimsatt, Jr., *The Verbal Icon: Studies in the Meaning of Poetry.* Lexington: U of Kentucky P, 1954.

CHAPTER 2

The Alphabet of Suffering: Effie Deans, Tess Durbeyfield, Martha Ray, and Hetty Sorrel

JAY CLAYTON

1. Anxiety. Thomas Hardy is anxious about the influence of George Eliot. When *Far from the Madding Crowd* begins running in *Cornhill Magazine,* critics speculate that it is the work of his more famous predecessor. In his review of the published novel, Henry James calls it an imitation of Eliot's rustic manner and discusses the "difference between original and imitative talent" (James 1044). Hardy remains troubled by this comparison. Many years later, in his autobiography, he writes defensively about his relation with the older novelist, hinting that he has not read her extensively and that he values her more as a thinker than as storyteller of rural life. Perhaps, he conjectures, his reading of Comte has given them a common philosophical vocabulary (*Life* 100). But of course it is not their shared terminology that provokes the comparison but their common talent for recording "ale-house and kitchen-fire conversations among simple-minded rustics" (James 1043). Moreover, Hardy has read *Adam Bede,* extracts of which appear in his *Literary Notebooks* (2:458).

Is Hardy's defensiveness enough to justify speculations—along lines suggested by Harold Bloom's *Anxiety of Influence*—that Hardy's fiction was shaped by his uneasy relation with Eliot? Can we speak of one of Hardy's later novels, *Tess of the d'Urbervilles,* as a *clinamen* or swerve, in which a precursor's novel, in this case *Adam Bede,* is rewritten and crucially revised, in order to correct the admired model at the place where that work went astray? If so, should we also think of Hardy as struggling with Eliot's precursor, the Scott who wrote *The Heart of Midlothian?* or with one of that author's most important precursors, the Wordsworth of "The Thorn"? Once the chain of influence extends beyond one link, should we not begin to talk of intertextuality rather than influence?

2. Babies. A child is born to an unwed mother, the birth hidden from the light of day, and the infant dies. Tess, who is open enough about her baby when she lives at home amid her fellow laborers, conceals his brief existence from Angel Clare until after their marriage. Hetty Sorrel leaves home in search of her seducer before the evidence of her pregnancy becomes visible; even when she is on trial for the murder of her child, she continues to deny ever having given birth. Effie Deans successfully hides her condition for the entire course of the pregnancy; the secrecy in which she gives birth is the principal fact that weighs against her when she is on trial for infanticide. Madge Wildfire, Scott's madwoman, has an illegitimate child, born in secrecy, and this child is murdered as well. Martha Ray, a maiden seduced in Wordsworth's "The Thorn," is supposed to have delivered her baby on a lonely mountain ridge and buried it there.

The women in these novels suffer terribly because of their babies, and because of the cruel social prohibitions that surround their babies' births. Suffering drives Effie mad for a time, Madge forever. "Oh misery! oh misery! / Oh woe is me! oh misery!" is Martha Ray's demented cry, a wail that finds an echo in Madge's "Wae's me! wae's me! wae's me!" (*Heart* 289).[1] Hetty, in her turn, is reduced to a hunted animal, who shrinks in fear from the people who love her. Tess, whose unbaptized baby is denied a grave in the churchyard, is forced to leave her family and home.

Suffering with others, Eliot tells us, teaches a strong soul the rudiments of sympathy. Her hero, Adam, learns "the alphabet of it" (*AB* 214) when his father dies, but Hetty's suffering soon teaches him chapter and verse.

3. Conventions. The suffering of an abandoned woman is so common in eighteenth- and early-nineteenth-century literature that its conventionality perhaps argues against a direct line of influence running from Wordsworth through Scott to Eliot then Hardy. Mary Jacobus finds this motif not only traditional but often associated with thorn trees: "The commonest of all literary associations for a thorn tree were illegitimate birth and child-murder. In Langhorne's *Country Justice,* it is under a thorn that the pitying robber finds the body of an unmarried mother with her new-born child . . . and in Richard Merry's *Pains of Memory* (1796), a remorseful seducer recalls: 'There on the chilly grass the babe was born, / Beneath that bending solitary thorn.' The Scots ballad known as 'The Cruel Mother' shows how traditional the association would have been: 'And there she's lean'd her back to a thorn, / Oh, and alas-a-day! Oh, and alas-a-day! /

And there she has her baby born'" (241–42). Wordsworth first uses a thorn in his early fragment "The Three Graves," a poem heavily influenced by Burger's "Des Pfarrers Tochter von Taubenhain," translated by Wordsworth's friend William Taylor as "The Lass of Fair Wone" (Jacobus 224–28). Burger's poem, which has also been cited as a source for "The Thorn," is another tale of illegitimacy and infanticide.

The conventionality of the association has been used to argue that Martha Ray never had a baby, that the story repeated by the credulous narrator is a folk response to the striking image of a thorn tree. When Scott has the imprisoned Effie compare herself to "the bonny bit thorn" (*Heart* 204), once lovely with flowers, now trodden under foot, or when late in the novel, Effie writes that her hollow laughter is like "the idle crackling of thorns" (*Heart* 455), the metaphors come from that common stock of images that is the heart of conventions. Traditional associations, too, seem to lie behind Lisbeth Bede's dream that her husband should be buried beneath the "White Thorn" (*AB* 60). Hardy makes only passing references to thorns, but he stresses the conventional nature of Tess's situation by having her rustic companions sing a ballad about an abandoned woman (*Tess* 142).

The conventionality of a motif works against the kind of influence study that depends on tracing parallels, but the argument for influence can be made using other kinds of evidence. Hardy's reading of *Adam Bede* has already been documented. He also refers repeatedly to Wordsworth, quoting from his poetry several times in *Tess*.[2] Hardy professes to be no admirer of Scott's novels but alludes to his work frequently.[3] Eliot begins *Adam Bede* with an epigraph from Wordsworth, and Arthur Donnithorne gives a copy of *Lyrical Ballads,* the volume in which "The Thorn" appeared, as a present to his godfather. Scott, whose novels introduced her to writing fiction (Haight 7), remains a favorite with her throughout life. She had read most of his novels by the age of thirteen; she refers to *The Heart of Midlothian* in "The Natural History of German Life" (Eliot, *Essays* 279), a piece often connected with the composition of *Adam Bede;* and Lewes gave her an edition of the Waverley Novels in 1860, calling them the "works of her longest-venerated and best-loved Romancist" (Haight 319). Scott's reading of the relevant Wordsworth poem is clear from a remark Scott makes in the novel itself. The grave of Madge Wildfire's infant is described as "a variegated hillock of wild flowers and moss, such as the poet of Grasmere has described in his verses on the Thorn" (*Heart* 297).

In effect, we find a double determination of the motif, one traditional and anonymous, part of every author's storehouse of images, the other traceable to specific literary sources. How do we weigh one determination in relation to the other? Does the case for a literary source, once established, override a motif's traditional roots, causing us to ignore its conventionality from that point onward? Such has been the bias of most influence studies: finding a canonical origin for a motif seems to carry more prestige than locating a nexus of traditional associations. One wonders why. Either determination — literary or traditional — lessens an artist's claim to originality.

If the existence of conventions works against certain kinds of influence study, it forms an essential part of most claims about intertextuality. The anonymous and the traditional make up the intertextual web, just as much as do allusions to canonical texts. Perhaps the double determination of our motif could best be addressed by combining the assumptions of influence study with those of intertextuality. This is a convenient solution, although it ignores the many ways in which the assumptions of the two approaches conflict. But perhaps one could make such a compromise workable by specifying at each point in the analysis which assumptions were operative and which were being temporarily suspended. This strategy, however, would entail the admission that both sets of assumptions — rival beliefs about subjectivity, agency, originality, language, canons, and more — were detachable, heuristic positions rather than fundamental principles.

4. Desire. In all three novels women suffer because male sexual desire capitalizes on class distinctions. Tess is forced to submit to Alec d'Urberville's unwanted attentions because of her dependent state: "she was more pliable under his hands than a mere companionship would have made her, owing to her unavoidable dependence upon his mother" (*Tess* 104). When Alec asks her why she has said nothing if his lovemaking offended her, she can only answer: "You know very well why. Because I cannot help myself here" (*Tess* 114). Their first sexual encounter would today be categorized as a sexual assault, but Hardy emphasizes the class element involved: "Doubtless some of Tess d'Urberville's mailed ancestors rollicking home from a fray had dealt the same measure even more ruthlessly towards peasant girls of their time" (*Tess* 119).

Although Arthur Donnithorne does not assault Hetty, the power differential between the handsome heir of the manor and a seventeen-year-old dairymaid is extreme. In today's terms, this is a case of sexual exploitation, not rape, but that does not cause Adam to take a lighter view of the crime: "You think little o' doing what may damage other folks," Adam says angrily, "so as you get your bit o' trifling, as means nothing" (*AB* 306). In Scott's novel the distance between George Staunton, eldest son of a wealthy English clergyman, and the innocent servant lass, Effie, is equally great, even when his identity is hid behind the name of Gentleman

George Robertson, the highwayman. He eventually marries Effie, but she is not the first pretty servant he has seduced: he had a child by Madge Wildfire when she was still a maid in his father's house.

The desires of the women differ markedly from those of the men. Tess feels nothing at all for Alec. She is numb, passively obedient, only marveling to herself at how he has mastered her. Desire plays virtually no role in her behavior at this period. She is driven reluctantly from one act to the next by other people's demands. Effie and Hetty are full of desires, but their urges are still not sexual in nature. These women long for finery, luxuries, money, and status. Scott hints that "self-conceit and obstinacy" (*Heart* 98) had more to do with Effie's pregnancy than desire for George Staunton. Their actual marriage is joyless enough, whereas Effie's appetite for fine clothes and polite company never diminishes. Hetty, too, thinks only of becoming a fashionable lady, of white stockings, earrings, Nottingham lace, and perfume, not of Arthur Donnithorne himself; and her principal pleasure in these fantasies lies in reflecting on how Mary Burge will envy her. Acquisitive and competitive, such desire is thoroughly conditioned by society, more so even than sexual longing. What she wants is entirely mediated by her economic and social position; she has no desire of her own, only the shopworn dreams common to her class. To a certain extent, this is true of everyone: our dreams are all mediated by our social posiion. But when that position is as humble as Hetty's, the consequences of social mediation become intensified. Hetty is doubly vulnerable—as a woman and as a member of her class—to exploitation by a man of rank and fortune.

Eliot takes pains to render not only the mediated objects of Hetty's desire but also its exact tenor and tone. Her longings are "vague, atmospheric, . . . producing a pleasant narcotic effect, making her tread the ground and go about her work in a sort of dream, unconscious of weight or effort, and showing her all things through a soft, liquid veil" (*AB* 100). The very formlessness of her desire conveys the extent of Hetty's vulnerability. She is lulled, drugged by her own dreams, surrounded by a soft, liquid veil. She is made passive by her own desire. The desire of a man in Arthur's position leads him to act. Although it may conflict with his conscious intentions (as it does in fact in Arthur's case), desire still works as a motive for such a figure, providing a causal explanation for the events that follow. By contrast, Hetty's desire prevents her from acting. Moving about in a narcotic haze, she ceases to be a subject. She waits expectantly for her future to unfold, both before and after the seduction. "There was no knowing what would come, since this strange entrancing delight had come" (*AB* 137). The delight itself unfits her for action; the delight entrances, in a literal sense. "How could she but have thought that her whole lot was go-

ing to change, and that to-morrow some still more bewildering joy would
befall her?" (*AB* 137). For a woman in Hetty's position, joy befalls and
bewilders, but it does not lead to action. Only suffering will have that effect.

Critics have often accused Eliot of condescending to Hetty, occasionally going so far as to suggest that Eliot's jealousy of attractive women
causes her to be unsympathetic to this kind of character. The sexism of
such accusations is gross, especially since Eliot's criticism of Hetty participates in an important strand of feminist thinking. Cora Kaplan notes
that as far back as Mary Wollstonecraft many feminist writers have deni-
grated female desire, because they see it as a trap that will prevent women
from achieving independence. Wollstonecraft is harsh on sensuality in
women, for she regards it as a "danger first of all to women themselves,
whose potential and independence were initially stifled and broken by an
apprenticeship to pleasure, which induced psychic and social dependency"
(Kaplan 156–57). Eliot picks up on exactly this train of thought in an
article on Wollstonecraft and Margaret Fuller written four years before
Adam Bede. Eliot quotes approvingly a long passage from *A Vindication
of the Rights of Woman* in which Wollstonecraft argues for the education
of women by pointing to the damage done to men by the "childish passions and selfish vanity" of uneducated women (Wollstonecraft, quoted
in Eliot, *Essays* 202).

One of the functions of identifying intellectual contexts, such as the
context Wollstonecraft provides for Eliot's attitude toward desire, is count-
ering the impression that an attitude or motif is solely the product of an
author's personal bias, in this case Eliot's supposed prejudice against attractive women. Does it matter whether such a context is phrased in terms
of influence or intertextuality? If one's interest is merely in the interpretive
question, the answer is no. However established, the context helps to explain Eliot's view of Hetty. But if one wants to connect Eliot with an eclectic tradition of feminist inquiry, extending from the eighteenth century to
our own day and including women writers from diverse backgrounds and
with conflicting programs, then an intertextual perspective has advantages.

Kaplan maintains that Wollstonecraft's model of the female psyche continues to play a major role in some contemporary feminist debates. This
model sees women as incapable of combining intellectual, sexual, and
maternal impulses in the same being, as if these impulses were "in competition for a fixed psychic space" (158). Eliot's contrast between Hetty
and Dinah follows a similar logic. In the chapter "The Two Bed-Chambers,"
Eliot juxtaposes Hetty, suffused with desire, "her cheeks flushed and her
eyes glistening" (*AB* 161), with another image of womanhood, that of the
praying Dinah, sitting "perfectly still, with her hands crossed on her lap,
and the pale light resting on her calm face" (*AB* 159). In the former image

there is no room even for maternal feelings (see *AB* 156), much less spiritual or rational concerns, as if the presence of desire precluded all other modes of being. With the help of Kaplan's article, we can see Wollstonecraft and Eliot as engaged in an intertextual dialogue not only with one another but with many feminists of our own day.

5. Eliot. George Eliot informs us that she got the idea for *Adam Bede,* not from reading *The Heart of Midlothian,* "The Thorn," or *The Rights of Woman,* but from an actual case of female suffering. Eliot's Methodist aunt told the novelist how she "had visited a condemned criminal, a very ignorant girl who had murdered her child and refused to confess — how she had stayed with her praying, through the night and how the poor creature at last broke out into tears, and confessed her crime" (Eliot, *Letters* 2:502). The author bases the character of Dinah on her recollections of her aunt, but she changes details such as Dinah's physical description and her style of preaching. Adam, too, comes in part from recollections of her father, "but Adam is not my father any more than Dinah is my aunt. Indeed, there is not a single *portrait* in 'Adam Bede'; only the suggestions of experience wrought up into new combinations" (*Letters* 2:503). Other aspects of the novel, such as Adam's marriage to Dinah and the fight between Adam and Arthur, are suggested by Eliot's companion George Henry Lewes.

6. Fields. A symbolic geography of pleasure and suffering organizes all three novels. Scott contrasts England's fertile lowlands with Scotland's windswept highlands. Eliot juxtaposes Hayslope's rich farmland and Stonyshire's bleak hills. Hardy opposes the oozing lushness of the Vale of Froom to the exposed chalky heights of Flintcomb-Ash. Such contrasts make the landscape eloquent, and one recognizes this eloquence as one of the distinctive features of the rural tradition in English literature.

What is the status of this contrast? We might view it as (1) a borrowing from or allusion to specific works in the rural tradition; (2) derived from independent observations of actual landscapes; (3) a conventional feature in all nature writing; (4) a fundamental building block of the human imagination, an archetype; (5) a rhetorical figure, antithesis, the mark of division, of opposition itself. Only the first two of these alternatives require the author as agent, and only the first is related to the theory of influence, narrowly conceived. Each of the others could function in an intertextual account of the rural novel. The final alternative, however, is the most radically intertextual. It relates the contrast not merely to similar depictions of the landscape but to other symbolic oppositions, from whatever sphere: economics (rich/poor), gender (male/female), biology (young/old; life/death), or the formal (inside/outside; container/contained).

As an *intratextual* practice, such comparisons are a feature of almost all interpretive methods from New Criticism onwards: we routinely relate diverse symbolic systems within a single work in order to produce a coherent account of that work's meaning. Only when the comparison is extended beyond the bounds of a work does the method become controversial. As an intertextual practice, such comparisons erase the author as controlling subject and suggest instead that meaning is dependent upon a restricted economy of substitutions. The eloquence of the fields — that innocent-seeming antithesis — becomes a reflex of all the hierarchical oppositions that structure our lives.

7. Genre. The hierarchy of genres plays a crucial role in two of the most important contemporary theories of influence and intertextuality. On the one hand, Harold Bloom distinguishes poetry from all other kinds of writing, arguing that the essential features of what he calls influence apply only to poets. On the other hand, Mikhail Bakhtin explains his intertextual notion of dialogism as a special virtue of the novel.

For Bloom, less privileged genres such as the novel are relevant to his theory of influence only to the extent that they can be said to contain "poetry" within them, because Bloom eliminates from consideration everything that is not unique to poetry: "By 'poetic influence,' I do not mean the transmission of ideas and images from earlier to later poets. . . . Ideas and images belong to discursiveness and to history, and are scarcely unique to poetry" (*Anxiety* 71). The realms of discursiveness and history, of course, are of great concern to the novel — Bakhtin would say a necessary part of any definition of the novel.

For Bakhtin, the novel, even more than the epic, is the genre that best illustrates intertextuality. Novelization, in fact, is his name for what happens to a work or a genre when it becomes intertextual. This process involves the mixing of diverse languages, of words drawn not only from other texts but from other realms of discourse. In particular, the novel mixes language from nonliterary genres — from the realms of discursiveness and history — with language from literary genres. The radically intertextual nature of the novel stems from its "special relationship with extraliterary genres, with the genres of everyday life and with ideological genres. . . . in later stages of its development the novel makes wide and substantial use of letters, diaries, confessions, the forms and methods of rhetoric associated with recently established courts and so forth" (Bakhtin 33).

There are a rich multiplicity of sources for the common motifs in Scott, Eliot, and Hardy, only some of which have yet been mentioned: traditional ballads, folklore, other works of fiction and drama, newspaper accounts of infanticide, broadsides of criminals' confessions, court records, historical archives, scientific works, popular science articles, religious tracts, scholarly works of history and social theory, philosophy, personal reminiscences, advice from friends, letters from informants, firsthand observations, and more. Although this multiplicity does not make influence criticism superfluous, it does suggest that an intertextual approach can deal both more flexibly and more comprehensively with issues of filiation surrounding the novel. There is a more radical conclusion as well. Just as much as the novel stems from an intertextual network, the theory of intertextuality may stem from the novel. The novel, that is, may be responsible for our modern sense that writing itself is intertextual. From this perspective, the genre's typical subject matter — its focus on manners, morals, class, race, gender, and the constituents of the self — may prefigure intertextuality's emphasis on the role of anonymous cultural codes in writing. The novel's lack of decorum, its willingness to mix all levels of style, may look forward to the democratic character of intertextuality. And the novel's formal inclusiveness — its incorporation of history, biography, diaries, letters, court proceedings, and other nonliterary forms — may prepare the way for the anticanonical impulse within intertextuality.

8. Hardy. Rich as are Hardy's written sources, many striking features of *Tess* are nonetheless drawn from life. The name of Talbothays dairy is taken from a farm that belonged to his father. The idea of a great family in decline comes from stories about his own family: when he was young, his mother pointed to a common man and said "he represented what was once the leading branch of the family. So we go down, down, down" (Hardy, *Life* 224). Hardy witnesses pretty girls dancing on the green at Sturminster Newton. He bases Marian, one of the dairymaids at Talbothays, on a "pink and plump damsel" who was a pupil in a Sunday school class he taught, "one of the few portraits from life in his works" (*Life* 30). From his first wife he gets the idea of having Tess put on the jewels Angel gives her on the first night of their honeymoon (*Life* 250). As a boy, he sees a man hanged from the vantage of a distant hill: "The sun behind his back shone straight on the white stone facade of the gaol, the gallows upon it, and the form of the murderer in white fustian, the executioner and officials in dark clothing. . . . He seemed alone on the heath with the hanged man; and he crept homeward wishing he had not been so curious. It was the second and last execution he witnessed, the first having been that of a woman two or three years earlier, when he stood close to the gallows" (*Life* 33).

9. Infanticide. Child murder has been a frequent practice in every society, in the West as well as the Orient, from the dawn of history up until nearly the present day. During antiquity, infanticide was a widely accepted method of population control. Children who were born with any defect, who cried excessively or too little, who exceeded the number of desired children, or who simply had the misfortune to be female when a male was wanted were generally killed, most often by abandonment.[4] The historical literature is full of gruesome descriptions of babies who are thrown down the privy, onto dung heaps, in ditches, into ponds, down wells; who have their throats cut, are smothered or hanged; who are plastered up in walls, potted in jars, exposed on hills; who are fed unhealthy concoctions; who are battered, flung about the room, or dropped from windows. Laws against infanticide are a relatively recent phenomenon, the first in England dating only from 1623 (Hanawalt 10). This statute, however, gives unprecedented powers to the state, making infanticide the only crime in which the accused is presumed guilty unless proven innocent. Because it was so difficult to establish that a mother had murdered her child, concealment of its birth was regarded as presumptive evidence of intent to murder. Conviction resulted in the death sentence. Effie Deans is condemned under a similar Scottish law when she can produce neither a living baby nor a person to whom she has confided her pregnancy. By the second half of the eighteenth century, this statute was being widely excoriated for its severity. Throughout the century, it was only irregularly enforced, and when a case did come to trial, juries often returned votes of innocence in open defiance of the evidence (Malcolmson 197). The law was ultimately repealed in 1803.

Infanticide is a prominent topic in eighteenth-century newspapers, literature, social criticism, and political debate. "Newspapers were particularly prone to dwell on the lurid details of infanticide: the discoveries of mutilated bodies, the corpses in the Thames, the remains which were turned up by dogs and swine. Some observers gave the impression of an endemic situation" (Malcolmson 189–90). In Germany, infanticide is a favorite theme of the Sturm und Drang period, a literature Wordsworth, Scott, and Eliot knew well. "Between the 1760s and the 1780s dozens of essays, treatises and dramatic writings dealt with infanticide in some form or other; in fact, almost every significant literary figure of the period referred to it at some point in his writings, and a few works, such as H. L. Wagner's *The Child-Murderess* (1775) and Schiller's poem *The Infanticide* (1781), used it as a central literary theme" (Malcolmson 189). In *The Heart of Midlothian,* which is set in the first half of the eighteenth century, there are two infanticides, and in *Adam Bede,* set at the end of the eighteenth century, there is another; Martha Ray in "The Thorn" (1798) would have been guilty of infanticide, whether her child were born dead or not, under the presumptive evidence of the statute.

Scott, Eliot, and Wordsworth capture the typical profile of the eighteenth-century child murderer in remarkable detail. Babies were almost always killed by women, generally the baby's mother. These women were usually unmarried. When another person was involved, it was usually the mother of the pregnant woman (as happens in the case of Madge Wildfire's baby). The mothers were typically from the poor or working classes. The great majority were servant maids (as are Madge, Effie, and Hetty).[5] The sex of the baby was generally not a factor at this period (the babies of Effie, Hetty, and Tess are male; the sex of Madge's child is unspecified). The motive was almost always to save one's reputation, which for servant maids was a matter of economic necessity. Frequently the child was abandoned out of confusion or panic rather than from a premeditated intent to murder.[6]

10. Journeys. The most memorable feature of *The Heart of Midlothian* is Jeanie Deans's journey from Edinburgh to London. Traveling alone and mostly on foot, she covers twenty miles a day, sometimes more. At first she walks barefoot and with her native tartan screen over her head, but the taunts of strangers soon drive her to change her dress and to put on her only pair of shoes. But she cannot change her accent, which brings down on her countless "jests and gibes, couched in a worse *patois* by far than her own" (*Heart* 272). In addition to rudeness, she experiences loneliness, fatigue, and the threat of robbery, sexual assault, and murder.

Equally memorable are two chapters in *Adam Bede,* "The Journey in Hope" and "The Journey in Despair." Hetty, far advanced in pregnancy, sets off alone both to find Arthur and to hide her condition. On the road she is tormented by shame, loneliness, and fear. From the first she is prey to the unwelcome advances of strangers. As one unfortunate accident after another turns her trip into a disaster, she is reduced to traveling on foot, with no place to sleep at night and little money for food, an object of scorn and suspicion to many of the people she meets. In a weary, semiconscious state, she searches for a place to die, for a low, dark pool in which she might drown herself. Her journey ends in a stranger's house where she gives birth to her baby. The next day she leaves surreptitiously and makes her way to a field where she abandons her infant under a bush.

If the idea of Hetty's journey was influenced at all by *The Heart of Midlothian,* the motif has been "transposed" from Jeanie, the sister of the woman who got in trouble, to Hetty, the pregnant woman herself. In *Tess* there are no journeys directly related to Tess's pregnancy. But she does take a long weary trip on foot eight months after her husband Angel has abandoned her. This trip is memorable too, both because of the hardships of the road and because of her near brush with rape. Hardy, who is more open about sexual matters than his predecessors, makes explicit the dangers of sexual assault that a single woman of her class encounters on a journey. "Among the difficulties of her lonely position not the least was the attention she excited by her appearance, a certain bearing of distinction, which she had caught from Clare, being superadded to her natural attractiveness" (*Tess* 349–50). On the road near Chalk-Newton, she meets a man who knows of her past and whose suggestive remarks make her take to her heels. She spends a horrible night hiding under some holly bushes in the woods. This incident so frightens her that she changes into her worst field-gown and cuts her eyebrows off with scissors. "Thus Tess walks on; a figure which is part of the landscape: a fieldwoman pure and simple, in winter guise" (*Tess* 355).

11. Kine. The immemorial image of Hardy's fieldwoman obtains added credibility from the novel's richly various portrayal of women at work. We see them performing daily chores, laboring at a hayrick, grubbing swedes in a field; most memorably, we see them at work in a dairy farm, driving in the cows or on their stools milking. For contemporary reviewers, nothing stood out so vividly as the scenes at Talbothays dairy. One perhaps forgets that the scenes in Mrs. Poyser's dairy were also crucial to the high reputation *Adam Bede* enjoyed throughout the nineteenth century.[7] The dairies in both novels serve as a counterpoint to the stories of unrelenting misery. They are cool, pure spaces, and they establish their own timeless rhythm of recurrence: "Nothing in the picture moved but Old Pretty's tail and Tess's pink hands, the latter so gently as to be a rhythmic pulsation only, as if they were obeying a reflex stimulus, like a beating heart" (*Tess* 208). It is poignant to encounter such comforting images of milking in novels about mothers who have lost their children.

Doubtless few readers have had reason to notice that Jeanie Deans is a dairymaid, who is uncommonly fond of her familiar "kye." But Scott makes the link between motherhood and dairy cattle explicit, twice referring to Jeanie's cows as her "milky mothers" (*Heart* 252, 434). In Scott the dairy represents not only the peaceful routine of rural life, as it does in Eliot and Hardy, but also the practicality of its mistress. Model housekeeper and skilled dairy manager, Jeanie Deans looks forward to Mrs. Poyser as much as to Dinah Morris.

12. Linearity. If the diurnal round of labor, the recurrent tasks of life in the fields, imparts to these works a steady, rhythmic pulse, then are we justified in abandoning, at least in part, the linear logic of argument? Can we find sanction for the alogic of this alphabetic arrangement in our response to the timeless patterns that the novels evoke? Labor in the fields, the suffering of women, motherhood, madness, and death. What order would arguments impose?

13. Mad mothers. Wordsworth has a poem, which in the first edition of *Lyrical Ballads* is titled "The Mad Mother," about an abandoned woman whose only hold on reality is the baby at her breast: "Suck, little babe, oh suck again! / It cools my blood; it cools my brain" (lines 31–32). The same motif appears in "The Thorn," when one of the old farmers of the neighborhood maintains "That in her womb the infant wrought / About its mother's heart, and brought / Her senses back again" (lines 150–52).

In Scott, Madge Wildfire's rationality returns fitfully when she speaks of her lost child. Judith Wilt interprets this motif, as well as Madge's mother's inability to kill the man she once nursed, as evidence of a "nearly fail-safe psychic system," which equates motherhood and female identity, so that "even in the most brutalized masculinized woman . . . 'motherhood' is the last fragment of female identity to go" (132–33). Paradoxically, the loss of rationality can convey the same message. Madge blames her madness on the death of her baby, whom her mother killed and buried: "I think she buried my best wits with it, for I have never been just mysell since" (*Heart* 300). Locating such a "natural" cause for Madge's insanity surely serves the interests of society in having mothers devote themselves to their children.

But perhaps the system is not entirely "fail-safe." A subversive reason for the madness of mothers can be discovered in Scott's novel, and in Eliot's as well. The trauma of giving birth in these books is so severe as to produce a form of temporary insanity, a "madness" in which women contemplate or commit the crime of infanticide. Effie, who protests that she could never have killed her child when "in her perfect senses," admits that she cannot answer for "what bad thoughts the Enemy might put into her brain when she was out of herself" (*Heart* 225). After her labor Hetty has a "strange look with her eyes" (*AB* 443) and is described by the man who discovers her child's corpse as looking "a bit crazy" (*AB* 444). The novels suggest that more than physical pain drives these women to distraction, that immense psychological pressures contribute to their condition. It is society, of course, with its religious, economic, and social sanctions, that produces this psychological pressure; it is society that produces the "mad mothers" that kill children. The same "psychic system" that strives to identify women with motherhood can also create a murderous insanity.

14. Networks. In intertextuality "the networks are many and interact, without any one of them being able to surpass the rest; this text is a galaxy of signifiers, not a structure of signifieds; it has no beginning; it is reversible; we gain access to it by several entrances, none of which can be authoritatively declared to be the main one" (Barthes 5).

Can we respond to such a network without privileging one structure over another, without locating a beginning, drawing a line through the maze, giving priority to one particular entrance? Will some arbitrary order suffice, one that reverses or scrambles ordinary chronology, one with twenty-six entrances, the earliest of which chronologically (Wordsworth) comes near the very end? Not if it dramatizes the priority of influence by reminding the reader of an earlier alphabet, Barthes's *Pleasure of the Text*.

15. Openness. The intertextual network is "open" in a way that the relation of influence is not. Influence is unidirectional, flowing from an earlier to a later author, whereas intertextuality establishes a flexible relation among texts. The itinerary of the reader, which is shaped by individual interests and experiences, determines the "direction" of the relation, and that direction can change over time as the reader develops new interests and accumulates further experience. Conscious and unconscious desires, literary training, religious background, nationality, familiarity with popular culture, class, gender, race, the accidents of everyday life, world-historical events — these are some of the variables that determine the connections the intertextual reader draws among texts.

When I see Adam working through the night on a coffin I think of Cash making the coffin in *As I Lay Dying*. The plants in the garden at Talbothays, which rub against Tess's hands and arms staining her skin, remind me of the wet sticky vegetation and stinging nettles that Birkin rubs against his skin in *Women in Love*. The night Tess spends under a holly bush recalls to me Jane Eyre's night on the heath after she has fled from Rochester; Tess is frightened by wounded birds, thrashing in the underbrush, and Brontë compares Jane to "a bird with both wings broken," thrashing "its shattered pinions" on the ground (328). Tess asleep on the altar at Stonehenge evokes for me the scene at Stonehenge in Frances Burney's *The Wanderer,* and both together bring to mind Wordsworth's imagery of Druidical sacrifice in *Salisbury Plain*. Robert McAlmon, one of the American expatriates in Paris during the 1920s, describes killing rabbits in a way that makes me think of the reapers in *Tess* stoning the huddled rabbits and field mice. Other images of rural laborers in that novel evoke Wordsworth's "Solitary Reaper," the gleaners singing hymns in Gaskell's *Cousin Phillis,* Millet's luminous painting of fieldworkers praying, *L'Angelus,* and a movie by Terence Malick, *Days of Heaven*.

16. Punishment. Images of women suffering may intersect with a virtually infinite network of cultural texts, but these three novels share a relatively unusual form of misery: women being punished for capital crimes. Effie is condemned to hang for the murder of her child. Although her punishment is commuted to fourteen years of banishment after Jeanie's appeal to the Queen, Scott presents the sentencing in sensational detail, even appending a long footnote on the institution in Scottish law of that gothic figure, the Doomster. If Effie is spared from the gallows, Scott will not deny the reader the spectacle of a woman hanging. Effie's death is displaced onto the more deserving figure of Meg Murdockson, whose execution on a hill near Penrith in northern England is made only more horrid by being described from a distance. A connection that enriches Scott's text for contemporary readers, but which Scott himself could not have known, is that the environs of Penrith is where Wordsworth frightened himself by stumbling upon the ruins of a gibbet-mast when a boy, sometime around 1775 (*Prelude,* lines 225–47).

Hetty, too, is condemned to hang for the crime of infanticide, and her sentence is also commuted to banishment at the last possible moment. Misled by *Midlothian* or by an uncharacteristic streak of sentimentality, Eliot vitiates much of the novel's talk about the inescapable consequences of one's deeds by rescuing Hetty from the gallows. Hardy makes no such mistake. The final scene of *Tess* describes the heroine's execution, which Angel and Tess's sister watch from a distant hill. The motif of distance reproduces the execution Hardy witnessed as a boy, but it also resonates strangely with Scott's description of Meg Murdockson's hanging.

17. Quarry. Eliot called one of her notebooks, in which she recorded the fruits of her research into the background of her novels, a "quarry" (Kitchel). Her quarry — and the other notebooks — demonstrates a remarkable passion for historical accuracy. She researched in painstaking detail many elements that seem utterly "natural" to the reader, an organic part of the living world the fiction creates. In *Adam Bede* many of Adam's attitudes and mannerisms are taken directly from Samuel Smiles's *The Life of George Stephenson: Railway Engineer* (Eliot, *Writer's Notebook* 30). John Wesley's ideas and preaching style, drawn from Southey's *Life of Wesley,* inform the portrait of Dinah Morris, perhaps more fully than Eliot's memory of her aunt *(Writer's Notebook* 24–27). The novelist took details of turn-of-the-century fashion from F. W. Fairholt's *Costume in England: A History of Dress from the Earliest Period till the Close of the Eighteenth Century (Writer's Notebook* 28). She carefully researched what the weather was like on specific days during July and August of 1799 and borrowed some folksy wisdom about clouds from Henry Stephens' *The Book of the Farm (Writer's Notebook* 30–31, 32–34). Arthur's coming of age party is modeled on one for John Henry, duke of Rutland, that was reported in the *Gentleman's Magazine* of January 1799; that magazine also served as a source for information about the life and habits of rural

curates at that period *(Writer's Notebook* 29, 31–32). Adam's expertise as
a manager of the woods on the Donnithorne property was worked up
from a number of curious volumes, including Selby's *A History of British
Forest Trees,* Strutt's *Sylva Britannica, or Portraits of Forest Trees, Distinguished for their Antiquity, Magnitude, or Beauty,* Gilpin's *Remarks
on Forest Scenery,* and Loudon's *Trees and Shrubs of Britain (Writer's
Notebook* 34–35).

Some of the details from Eliot's quarry establish a relationship with a
prior author that one might term "influence," whereas other details do
not. No one would ever speak of Eliot's being influenced by a book on
clouds or by textbooks on forestry. But it is conceivable to talk about
Southey's *Life of Wesley* as having influenced Eliot's conception of Dinah.
Is influence, then, a word reserved for major effects? Does intertextuality—
leaving its theoretical implications aside—have a place as a more comprehensive term than influence simply because it is receptive to all forms
of textual transmission, however trivial?

Hardy kept a notebook similar to Eliot's quarry, Wordsworth drew on
his sister's journal, and Scott researched the legal and historical facts that
appear in his fiction. What is the status of such research in imaginative
works? Clearly, it enhances the realism, reinforcing through factual accuracy the feeling of actuality generated by other conventional features
of nineteenth-century realism: probable plots, linear time schemes, par-
ticularized characters, recognizable settings, and prominent narrators. Accurate notation of details of climate, dress, manners, etc., are referential,
in the sense that they refer the reader directly to the external world. But
their success as realism depends upon dissembling their referentiality in
another sense, their status as references to other texts rather than to some
nondiscursive realm. Realism depends, in this case, upon both the existence and the occlusion of intertextuality.

18. Reference. Most theories of intertextuality, in turn, dismiss the importance of external reference. Michael Riffaterre speaks of the "referential fallacy" and repudiates "the firm belief of language users in nonverbal
reference, their assumption that words mean by referring to a reality without the pale of language, to objects that exist in themselves before they
become signs" (227–28). For Riffaterre, literary meanings are always and
only intertextual. "The text refers not to objects outside of itself, but to
an intertext. The words of the text signify not by referring to things, but
by presupposing other texts" (228). Barthes, too, denies the possibility of
reference to a reality beyond the intertextual network. Literature refers
"not from a language to a referent but from one code to another" (55).

Curiously, Bloom's version of influence dismisses nonliterary references just as decisively. To interpret a poem, according to Bloom, is not to elucidate its subject, not to discuss what the work is "about," but to look at its connections with other poems. "To study what poems are about is to interpret their outside relationships. . . . To interpret a poem, necessarily you interpret its difference from other poems" (*Map* 75). As Bloom puts it in *The Anxiety of Influence,* "The meaning of a poem can only be another poem" (94).

Both these visions of literature stand at odds with many writers' sense that they are responding to a world outside of textuality. Writers speak of being true to their subject, of capturing reality, of evoking a way of life. We have seen that both Eliot and Hardy are conscious of drawing elements of their fiction from their own life and family background. Riffaterre would assert that these writers, in believing that their works refer to a nonliterary world, are victims of a mistaken conception of language. Bloom would assert that the aspect of their works that is about the nonliterary world is simply inessential, ephemeral, not a part of what makes a poem poetic. The claim that literature does not refer beyond the realm of textuality is not susceptible to empirical verification. It is an example of "theory" at its purest. We cannot leave theoretical implications aside, as was suggested in the prior section, because the very conceptions of intertextuality and of Bloom's radical form of influence are dependent for their "truth" upon their participation in a particular discursive field, the domain of theory.

19. Scott. As a historical novelist, Scott certainly intends his account of the Porteous riot and of Jeanie Deans's journey to refer to actual events. Scott bases the tale of Jeanie Deans on the story of a woman named Helen Walker, whose sister was tried for infanticide and found guilty because Helen would not compromise her religious scruples by testifying falsely that her sister had made any preparations for delivery or had intimated the pregnancy in any way. When her sister was found guilty, Helen made the same journey on foot to London to see the Queen that Jeanie undertakes in the novel. Scott recounts the story of Helen Walker in the Introduction to the 1830 edition of *The Heart of Midlothian.* He also explains how he learned of her tale through an anonymous letter sent by a woman who had met Helen Walker when she was seventy or eighty years old. In a Postscript to the Introduction he adds what particulars of Helen Walker's life he has been able to discover through subsequent research.

20. Transposition. Kristeva's term signifies the strange mutations a motif undergoes when it is transposed from one text to another. An intertextual relation, according to Kristeva, involves not merely a reference to another text but the "absorption and transformation" (66) of that text. The sisters in Scott, Effie and Jeanie, become the cousins, Hetty and Dinah, in *Adam Bede*. Whereas the suffering is divided in Scott's tale between Effie, who loses her illegitimate child and is condemned to hang, and Jeanie, who endures the cruel hardships of the journey, Hetty unites the suffering of both women in one character. Hardy takes Hetty's tale, which formed only a part of the story of Adam's life, and turns it into the central subject of *Tess*. Instead of murdering her child, who dies of natural causes, Tess murders her child's father. The passionate commitment to nonconforming religious sects, which plays a prominent role in all three novels, moves from Jeanie and her father, Davie Deans, to Dinah Morris, to the seducer in Hardy's novel, Alec d'Urberville.

Cumulatively, the transpositions have a strange power. There is an uncanniness in the repetition, the ebb and flow, the mutation and unexpected return of motifs. The intertextual network creates its own disturbing effects, a dimension missing from any discrete text. But can one part of the network ever be read in isolation from the others? The transpositions leave their mark on the individual texts, even for the reader who is ignorant of other parts of the web, for the reader may sense strange distortions, "ungrammaticalities" as Riffaterre puts it (230), that are the result of the unknown relation. Each text is haunted by the others, the earlier by the later, the later by the earlier. This uncanny afterlife constitutes, in part, the felt life of each text. Intertextuality is a ghost effect.

21. Uncanny. The uncanny incidents that abound in the texts of Wordsworth, Scott, Eliot, and Hardy may be thought of as the representational correlative or "instantiation" of the uncanniness that pervades the intertextual network. In Wordsworth's "The Thorn," the narrator's encounter in a storm on the mountain's height with what looks like the form of Martha Ray is strikingly uncanny, as are the incidents of the willow wand and the story of Hetty's grim journey in *Adam Bede*.[8] Scott's novel is full of gothic episodes that at times rise to an uncanny power, particularly Jeanie's rendezvous with Effie's seducer at Muschat's cairn, the "ominous and unhallowed spot" (*Heart* 151) where a man had once murdered his wife. In *Tess* the sleepwalking incident, during which Angel lays Tess down in a coffin, the scene of Alec forcing Tess to swear on the "Cross-in-Hand" where legend held that a criminal had been buried, and the episode of Tess's capture on the altar of the Druids, all possess the mark of uncanniness.

22. Victims. So much suffering, so many victims, yet the list is still not complete. Madge Wildfire, who perhaps least deserves her unhappy fate, meets one of the most horrible ends imaginable. After her mother's hanging, Madge is turned upon by the crowd who have gathered to watch. She is harried across a wide field, the crowd's taunts driving her into ever more mad gyrations. They "came up from the place of execution, grouping themselves with many a yell of delight around a tall female fantastically dressed, who was dancing, leaping, and bounding in the midst of them" (*Heart* 392). As it happens, Jeanie Deans observes this senseless cruelty from the window of a carriage drawn up nearby. While the carriage drives off, she can hear both the "hoarse roar" of the mob and the "screams of the unfortunate victim" (*Heart* 393). Madge is ducked in a muddy pool so cruelly that she later dies of her injuries, all for the "crimes" of madness and of being her mother's daughter.

In a note Scott observes that the character of the "poor maniac" was taken from that of a real woman known as Feckless Fannie, a beggar who traveled all over Scotland and northern England between the years 1767 and 1775 (*Heart* 533). She too was murdered by a crowd, whose mockery of her peculiar dress and manner escalated into an assault, which ended with her stoning. Curiously enough, Scott uses this note as an occasion to ward off suspicions that his novel was influenced by sources in literature rather than in reality. He suggests that the idea of returning to an infant's grave came from the story of Feckless Fannie, rather than from "The Thorn" by Wordsworth, which he mentioned earlier, and he confesses to another anxiety as well: "In attempting to introduce such a character into fiction, the author felt the risk of encountering a comparison with the Maria of Sterne" (*Heart* 536). The final effect of this note, however, is to impress the reader with the pervasiveness of violence toward women.

23. Wordsworth. Despite the numerous literary sources, the actual composition of "The Thorn" is prompted by the sight of a stunted thorn encountered on a walk Wordsworth took with Dorothy on March 19, 1798. In the notes that Wordsworth dictated to Isabella Fenwick, he says that the poem "arose out of my observing, on the ridge of Quantock Hill, on a Stormy day, a thorn which I had often passed in calm and bright weather without noticing it. I said to myself, 'Cannot I by some invention do as much to make this Thorn prominently an impressive object as the storm has made it to my eyes at this moment?'" (290). The poet may have taken the name of Martha Ray from the mother of one of his friends, Basil Montagu. Wordsworth may have been reminded of her name, however, not by her grandchild, little Basil Montagu, who was the Wordsworths' ward at Alfoxden, but by reading the notorious story of her murder by a jealous lover in Erasmus Darwin's *Zoonomia, or the Laws of Organic Life,* which the poet read sometime around March 13, 1798 (Averill 166–68).

24. Xenophobia. Just the year before, during the invasion scares of 1797, Wordsworth, Dorothy, and little Basil had been the victims of xenophobia. The arrival of these strangers in the neighborhood of Alfoxden excited so much turmoil that a local doctor wrote to the Home Secretary about "a very suspicious business concerning an emigrant family, who have contrived to get possession of a Mansion House" (quoted in Moorman 1:329). The way Wordsworth and his friends went tramping about the countryside, asking questions and taking down notes, seemed troubling enough to the Home Office for a spy to be assigned to report on the poet's movements.[9] Wordsworth's poems at this period exhibit his sensitivity to the issue of prejudice against outsiders, the fear and distrust that greet anyone who is different from those around him. In poems such as "The Female Vagrant," "Goody Blake and Harry Gill," the discharged soldier passage of *The Prelude,* and of course, "The Mad Mother" and "The Thorn," abandoned women, the poor, and the infirm become objects of suspicion—their poverty and pain make them aliens in their own land.

Scott is sensitive to a more literal form of xenophobia, the prejudice that confronts all Scots when they travel in the south. We have mentioned the abuse Jeanie's accent and clothes provoke on the road to London (and the unwelcome attention that Hetty and Tess excite during their journeys as well). Feckless Fannie also could be seen as a victim of xenophobia. But Madge suffers the most for her alien appearance. A member of the mob that kills her makes explicit the role that xenophobia plays in the violent outbreak: "Shame the country should be harried wi' Scotch witches and Scotch bitches this gate—but I say hang and drown" (*Heart* 391).

This last comment causes one to notice the prominence of women in these accounts. If fear of difference lies at the root of this disease, then the difference of gender must be counted as one of its most virulent sources.

25. Years. Is it the unchanging nature of female suffering that brings together works so widely separated in time? Spanning nearly a century, written in two different countries, in various genres, and by members of both sexes, these four literary works share more than our theories can easily accommodate. A word like "influence" is unavoidable, for we need something to register the determined engagement, as well as the anxious evasion, of these authors vis-à-vis their precursors; "tradition" too seems important—the commitment to a complex but shared cultural heritage is manifest; "convention" provides some help as well, for the many reasons we have mentioned; terms that we have not explored, such as "topos," "allusion," "context," or "motif," could certainly be of service; and "intertextuality" gives us a method for drawing still more comprehensive maps of affiliation. But something escapes all our theories, that which is different and that which remains the same. The years fall away, and they come back again to haunt us.

26. Zones. Influence suggests a line of descent, a steady progress down through the years, facilitating the creation of coherent literary histories. Intertextuality suggests not a line or a progress but multiple, overlapping, occasionally conflicting zones of force. Is literary history still possible when intertextuality offers ways to challenge our concepts of both "literature" and "history"? One would think so, for every text exists within specific fields of power, and these fields may be observed and charted. Literary history, within an intertextual frame, becomes situating a text within the zones of force that alter and are altered by it. Such histories, however, can no longer pretend to be universal. One must look for different zones, of varying sizes and shapes, depending on one's purpose for undertaking the inquiry. These histories must be acknowledged to be partial and specific — oriented to particular tasks, with particular readers in mind. We must still spell out the exact zones of our suffering. We cannot abandon our alphabets entirely.

NOTES

I wish to thank Keith Callis for sharing his knowledge of Hardy sources, and Laurence Lerner and Eric Rothstein for their careful comments on early drafts of this essay.

1 *The Heart of Midlothian* will be cited in the text as *Heart. Adam Bede* and *Tess of the d'Urbervilles* will be cited as *AB* and *Tess* respectively. Wordsworth's poetry is quoted from the first edition of *Lyrical Ballads,* the one Scott would have known and that Arthur Donnithorne gives to his godfather in *Adam Bede.*

2 For the most complete account of Hardy's extensive borrowings from Wordsworth, see Casagrande, who concludes: "Hardy relied upon Wordsworth throughout his career, not just in his early years. In particular, Wordsworth's 'Ode: Intimations of Immortality,' generally thought of as an isolated target of Hardy's satire in *Tess* (1891), was for Hardy, as for many other Victorians, a life-long touchstone — in personal affairs as well as in his poetry, fiction and criticism. Finally, it is clear that Hardy developed his own poetic, especially in the 1890s, with conscious reference to the author of the Preface to *Lyrical Ballads*" (211). Casagrande also notes that Hardy seems to allude to "The Thorn" in one of his earliest poems, "Domicilium," a work that Hardy himself characterizes as "some Wordsworthian lines" (Casagrande 211).

3 A list of Hardy's allusions to Scott may be found in Pinion (211-13). Hardy took the epigraph for his first novel from Scott and praised *The Bride of Lam-*

mermoor as the only example of an "almost perfect specimen of form" (*Literary Notebooks* 1:365).

4   For the history of infanticide, see Langer and deMause (25–32). Scholars differ over the social acceptability of infanticide. Those who think it socially acceptable in many societies include Ariès (128), deMause, and Piers. Contemporary ethicists have relied on the evidence of these researchers to argue that the current Western taboo against infanticide is parochial and that the killing of newborns with birth defects is ethically permissible (Tooley 309–22; Kuhse and Singer 98–117). The specious character of this argument is effectively demonstrated by Post. Other historians contend that the prevalence of child death in earlier societies does not necessarily mean that infanticide was widely condoned. Boswell, for example, writes of the practice of exposure in antiquity: "Parents intended to offer the child up—to the kindness of strangers, to the mercy of the gods, to public welfare, to a better fate (than the natal parent could offer), or simply to his chances. . . . *Expositio* was an *alternative* to infanticide" (13). Historians who have made similar cases for other historical periods include Hanawalt (Middle Ages), Helmholtz, Wrightson (Renaissance), and Pollock (modern period).

5   Malcolmson writes: "It is now well known that, with a relatively late age of marriage in the seventeenth and eighteenth centuries, a large number of women were employed in service during a significant portion of their potentially child-bearing years; indeed, it may be that at any given time in the eighteenth century as many as half of the unmarried women between the ages of about sixteen and twenty-five were living-in servants—chamber maids, scullery maids, cooks, dairy maids and the like. It is not surprising, then, that they appeared so prominently in infanticide cases" (202).

6   This profile is drawn from Malcolmson's survey of 350 reported infanticides in eighteenth-century England (192, 200, 202–3).

7   The first sustained comparison of *Tess of the d'Urbervilles* and *Adam Bede,* published in the *Quarterly Review* in 1904, begins by noticing the prominence that dairy farming plays in both books: "It may be that for a long time Mr. Hardy delayed to depict a rural dairy in order to avoid direct comparison with the author of *Adam Bede.* Truly, no little courage was required to intrude upon a scene over which the indomitable Mrs. Poyser reigned" (Cox 360). In addition to the parallel with *Adam Bede,* a resemblance has been traced between the dairy in *Tess* and one in Emile Zola's *Abbé Mouret's Transgressions,* a book which Hardy read in 1886 or 1887 (Hardy, *Literary Notebooks* 2:571).

8   For a more complete account of the uncanniness of these episodes, as well as a discussion of the role of repetition in narrative in producing the effect of the uncanny, see Clayton (109–17, 152–56).

9   Alan Liu recounts another near-violent encounter with xenophobia, as well as examples of Wordsworth's own xenophobia, that occured during the poet's visit to Wales in 1793 (58–60).

WORKS CITED

Ariès, Philippe. *Centuries of Childhood: A Social History of Family Life.* Trans. Robert Baldick. New York: Knopf, 1962.

Averill, James H. *Wordsworth and the Poetry of Human Suffering.* Ithaca: Cornell UP, 1980.

Bakhtin, Mikhail M. *The Dialogic Imagination.* Ed. Michael Holquist. Trans. Caryl Emerson and Michael Holquist. Austin: U of Texas P, 1981.

Barthes, Roland. *S/Z.* Trans. Richard Miller. New York: Hill and Wang, 1974.

Bloom, Harold. *The Anxiety of Influence: A Theory of Poetry.* Oxford: Oxford UP, 1973.

Bloom, Harold. *A Map of Misreading.* Oxford: Oxford UP, 1975.

Boswell, John Eastburn. *"Expositio* and *Oblatio:* The Abandonment of Children and the Ancient and Medieval Family." *American Historical Review* 89 (1984): 10-33.

Brontë, Charlotte. *Jane Eyre.* Ed. Margaret Smith. Oxford: Oxford UP, 1980.

Casagrande, Peter J. "Hardy's Wordsworth: A Record and Commentary." *English Literature in Transition* 20 (1977): 210-37.

Clayton, Jay. *Romantic Vision and the Novel.* Cambridge: Cambridge UP, 1987.

Cox, R. G. *Thomas Hardy: The Critical Heritage.* New York: Barnes & Noble, 1970.

DeMause, Lloyd. "The Evolution of Childhood." In *The History of Childhood,* ed. DeMause, 1-74. New York: Psychohistory Press, 1974.

Eliot, George. *Adam Bede.* Ed. Gordon S. Haight. San Francisco: Rinehart, 1948.

Eliot, George. *Essays of George Eliot.* Ed. Thomas Pinney. London: Routledge and Kegan Paul, 1963.

Eliot, George. *The George Eliot Letters.* Ed. Gordon S. Haight. 9 vols. New Haven: Yale UP, 1954-55.

Eliot, George. *A Writer's Notebook, 1854-1879, and Uncollected Writings.* Ed. Joseph Wiesenfarth. Charlottesville: UP of Virginia, 1981.

Haight, Gordon S. *George Eliot: A Biography.* Oxford: Oxford UP, 1968.

Hanawalt, Barbara A. "Childrearing among the Lower Classes of Late Medieval England." *Journal of Interdisciplinary History* 8 (1977): 1-22.

Hardy, Thomas. *The Life and Work of Thomas Hardy.* Ed. Michael Millgate. Athens: U of Georgia UP, 1985.

Hardy, Thomas. *The Literary Notebooks of Thomas Hardy.* Ed. Lennart A. Bjork. 2 Vols. New York: New York UP, 1985.

Hardy, Thomas. *Tess of the d'Urbervilles.* Harmondsworth: Penguin Books, 1978.

Helmholtz, R. H. "Infanticide in the Province of Canterbury during the Fifteenth Century." *History of Childhood Quarterly* 2 (1975): 379-90.

Jacobus, Mary. *Tradition and Experiment in Wordsworth's "Lyrical Ballads" (1798).* Oxford: Clarendon P, 1976.

James, Henry. "Thomas Hardy." *Literary Criticism: Essays on Literature, American Writers, English Writers.* Ed. Leon Edel. New York: The Library of America, 1984.

Kaplan, Cora. "Pandora's Box: Subjectivity, Class and Sexuality in Socialist Feminist Criticism." In *Making a Difference: Feminist Literary Criticism,* ed. Gayle Greene and Coppelia Kahn, 146–76. London: Methuen, 1985.

Kitchel, Anna Theresa, ed. *George Eliot's Quarry for "Middlemarch."* Berkeley: U of California P, 1950.

Kuhse, Helga, and Peter Singer. *Should the Baby Live? The Problem of Handicapped Infants.* Oxford: Oxford UP, 1985.

Kristeva, Julia. *Desire in Language: A Semiotic Approach to Literature and Art.* Ed. Leon S. Roudiez. Trans. Thomas Gora, Alice Jardine, and Leon S. Roudiez. New York: Columbia UP, 1980.

Langer, William L. "Infanticide: A Historical Survey." *History of Childhood Quarterly* 1 (1974): 353–65.

Liu, Alan. "Wordsworth and Subversion, 1793–1804: Trying Cultural Criticism." *Yale Journal of Criticism* 2 (1989): 55–100.

Malcolmson, R. W. "Infanticide in the Eighteenth Century." In *Crime in England: 1550–1800,* ed. J. S. Cockburn, 187–209. Princeton: Princeton UP, 1977.

Moorman, Mary. *William Wordsworth: A Biography.* 2 vols. London: Oxford UP, 1968.

Piers, Maria W. *Infanticide.* New York: Norton, 1978.

Pinion, F. B. *A Hardy Companion: A Guide to the Works of Thomas Hardy and Their Background.* New York: St. Martin's, 1968.

Pollock, Linda A. *Forgotten Children: Parent-Child Relations from 1500 to 1900.* Cambridge: Cambridge UP, 1983.

Post, Stephen G. "History, Infanticide, and Imperiled Newborns." *Hastings Center Report* 18.4 (1988): 14–17.

Riffaterre, Michael. "Interpretation and Undecidability." *NLH* 12 (1981): 227–42.

Scott, Walter. *The Heart of Midlothian.* Ed. Claire Lamont. Oxford: Oxford UP, 1982.

Tooley, Michael. *Abortion and Infanticide.* Oxford: Clarendon P, 1983.

Wilt, Judith. *Secret Leaves: The Novels of Walter Scott.* Chicago: U of Chicago P, 1985.

Wordsworth, William, and Samuel Taylor Coleridge. *Lyrical Ballads: The text of the 1798 edition with the additional 1800 poems and the Prefaces.* Ed. R. L. Brett and A. R. Jones. London: Methuen, 1965.

Wrightson, Keith. "Infanticide in Early Seventeenth-Century England." *Local Population Studies* 15 (1975): 10–21.

CHAPTER 3

Intertextuality and the Subject of Reading/Writing

TILOTTAMA RAJAN

In recent years the idea of intertextuality has increasingly replaced that of influence as a way of describing the status of texts within a tradition. As we shall go on to suggest, there are certain texts that are constructed according to an aesthetics of intertextuality so as to disestablish themselves as sources of influence. But the provenance of the term is actually much wider, describing as it does not simply a quality of texts but a practice of reading that is applied even to texts that construct themselves as originating or transmitting influence. Influence and intertextuality can therefore be seen restrictively as ways of describing certain kinds of texts. But they can also be approached more broadly as cultural categories that describe the way we relate text and reader, and thus the way we conceive of texts within a cultural hermeneutic that causes them to participate in the "self"-formation of the reader or of the writer considered as her own reader. The trope of influence enacts this hermeneutic in relatively conservative ways. Affiliating itself with a history of ideas criticism, it allows the parent work the status of a transcendental signified that precedes its perpetuation through filial texts or readings. In some sense intertextuality will always remain (to use Kristeva's term) the "transposition" of influence into a critical terminology rewritten by deconstruction, and thus a way of preserving the position of the text as resource if not as source. It is not, in other words, a synonym for poststructuralism but rather a transposition of poststructuralism into literary history. At the same time the concept of intertextuality makes the source of influence into a text that is already within a chain of textual substitutions. In so doing it radically reconceives the hierarchical model of literary history as a sequence of repetitive confirmations in which authority is protected from any inscription in its own

61

uture, without substituting for it a discontinuous model in which a later text can claim a revolutionary autonomy from any inscription in its past.

This paper will not focus on the obvious differences between influence and intertextuality, but will be concerned with the latter concept as the site of a theoretical exchange between poststructuralism and reader-response theory, and with the consequences of such an exchange for the place of the subject (writer or reader) in relation to textuality. Perhaps the most straightforward way to approach the concept of intertextuality is to suggest that it extends to the consideration of texts (and potentially to the problems of reading and ideology) the radical implications of a post-Saussurean theory of the sign. Derrida himself makes the connection to a diacritical concept of language in an interview conducted, interestingly enough, with Julia Kristeva:

> no element can function as a sign without referring to another element which itself is not simply present. This interweaving results in each "element" . . . being constituted on the basis of the trace within it of other elements of the chain or system. This interweaving, this textile, is the *text* produced only in the transformation of another text. Nothing, . . . is anywhere ever simply present or absent. There are only, everywhere, differences and traces of traces.[1]

Like the notion that there are no positive terms in language, the idea that the text does not contain a meaning but possesses it only in relation to other texts can be taken in very different directions. Michael Riffaterre follows Saussurean semiotics in assuming that paradigmatic and syntagmatic relations serve to clarify rather than to disseminate the meaning of the individual text, marking the fact that an ungrammaticality within the text is a sign of "grammaticality elsewhere, that is, of belonging in another system."[2] Intertextuality for him is part of a process of encoding and decoding. But the diacritical structure of the text can be interpreted much more deconstructively, so that the deautonomizing of the text challenges its positive authority, its very ability to posit. Intertextuality has not actually been a term much used by American poststructuralists, and the reason is probably that the Yale School does *not* deautonomize the text. While focusing on a kind of "intratextuality," a play of differences within the text that results in its positions being always already textual, de Man and his followers make literature into the most "refined mode of deconstruction"[3] and thus reinforce the canonical status of the individual work, or at least of the category "literature." Where they do not do so, their rigorously philosophical style, which suspends the text between figure and referent but which is not self-interrupting, claims for the critic the authority to posit the text as a site of aporias. Vincent Leitch has, however, given intertextuality a deconstructive genealogy in the work of Joseph Riddel.

Riddel's work is inter- rather than intratextual in that it absorbs the text into other texts:

> The resident earlier texts open out the present text to an uncontrollable play of historical predecessors. The predecessor-texts themselves operate intertextually, meaning that no first, pure, or original text ever can or did rule over or delimit the historical oscillations at play in texts. Thus all texts appear doubled: they are uncontrollably permeated with previous texts. . . . The forces of intertextuality, in Riddel's view, fundamentally infiltrate the operations of the sign, disallowing any notion of pure or nonintertextual textuality.[4]

It is, however, debatable whether Riddel's is really a theory of intertextuality and whether such a theory is possible within the framework of poststructuralism. Inscribing the text within other texts, the deconstructive version of intertextuality is still a way of relating *literary* texts. Thus as Leitch (unwittingly) concedes, it "merges intertextuality with textuality,"[5] in effect reducing the former to the latter, in a formalism of Literature if not of the individual text.

It is thus to Julia Kristeva that we turn for a concept of intertextuality that desynonymizes it from difference or dialogism. What distinguishes Kristeva is her definition of intertextuality as the transposition of one sign system into another, such that the new signifying system may be produced with different "signifying material"[6] and thus does not have to occur entirely within language. This notion of transposition as the intersection of different material as well as textual surfaces allows Kristeva to see intertextuality as the mutual displacement of the literary and the historical or social by each other. Intertextuality, according to her, "situates the text within history and society, which are then seen as texts read by the writer, and into which he inserts himself by rewriting them."[7] This intersection of material surfaces produces a dynamic textualization of social structures that we might otherwise take as given, while also making textuality a force rather than simply a trace structure. The breaching of formalism that Kristeva effects is of course present in Bakhtin's work, which is concerned with authorial discourse as an intersubjective construction, dialogically situated in relation to other social discourses that it struggles to rewrite even as it is displaced by them. Denying the distinction of other Russian Formalists between ordinary and poetic language, Bakhtin does on one level describe the transposition of one kind of signifying material into another. But what we do not find in him (although he also does not preclude it) is a vocabulary that suggests how the resulting instability can be ideologically productive. Bakhtin is more concerned with how dialogism dehomogenizes the literary work than with the reinsertion of the transformational complex thus produced in the social text that deautonomizes it. It should be clear also how intertextuality differs from the "intratextuality" practiced by the Yale School, which creates an intersection of textual surfaces that blurs the boundary between outside and inside, or between reference and figure, largely to absorb the outside into the inside. Distinguishing Barthes from the (post)structuralist legacy of a language conceived as negativity because it allows for no positive terms, Kristeva notes that in his work "this negativity reaches the edge of a positivity because it operates within language and the subject," within a "signifying materiality" that "stops the movement of absolute negativity."[8]

The (dis)placement of difference in history, then, is what distinguishes intertextuality from a deconstruction whose lineage has tended to be (post)-structuralist rather than Bakhtinian. But as the ambiguity of Derrida's formulation suggests, intertextuality may be a logical development of difference beyond what David Carroll calls the "ultratextuality," the postformalism to which its practitioners on this side of the Atlantic have seemed to confine it. For Derrida speaks not simply of the suspension of textual identity by the aporia of the trace, but also of the text produced only in the transformation of another text, in other words of a productivity of the trace. Earlier in the same interview he calls into question the possibility of "translation," a concept analogous in its confirmative structure to influence and to reading conceived passively as the reproduction of the text:

for the notion of translation we would have to substitute a notion of transformation: a regulated transformation of one language by another, of one text by another. We will never have, and in fact never have had, to do with some "transport" of pure signifieds from one language to another, or within one and the same language, that the signifying instrument would leave virgin and untouched.[9]

In questioning a philological concept of translation as that which confers constative status on the prior text Derrida, it is worth noting, does not simply make translation the site for a deconstruction of the work as a transcendental signified anterior to writing (as the object of translation precedes and governs its translation). He also characterizes this deconstruction as a "transformation," as the production of a further text through the mutual textualizing of "original" and "translation" in a process that inscribes each in the language of the other. We are close here to Kristeva's concept of intertextuality as the "transposition of one (or several) sign-systems into another" so as to produce thereby "a new articulation of the thetic — of enunciative and denotative positionality."[10] We are close, in other words, not simply to intertextuality as the decentering of the sign, but also to a reconception of decentering as part of a continuous revolution at the site of language that makes writing a work of ideological transformation.

Transformation is not the replacement of an already existing system by a new one, for intertextuality is precisely the site of our recognition that signifying systems have no positive authority because they are transformational surfaces in which writing is simultaneously a rereading of itself. A literary structure, according to Kristeva, "does not simply *exist* but is generated in relation to *another* structure."[11] That intertextuality produces the ideology of the text and that of its reading as a transformational surface is evident in Kristeva's definition of transposition as a process that brings about a new articulation of enunciative and denotative positionality. Describing the subject of discourse (or of the *énonciation*) and the meaning of the text as positionalities, she suggests that the position taken by the writer and the content of the text are effects of its language rather than autonomous entities. These positionalities, in turn, do not have the stability they might possess in structuralist accounts of the text, because the text itself is always in transit to something else. While "transposition" implies the carrying over of an already existing system into a new context, the point is rather that what is carried over is already the product of transposition, of an intersection of ideological surfaces. The nonidentity of what is carried over causes any attempt to reproduce the existing system to occur as transposition rather than translation, while any attempt to change it is itself subject to further transposition.

We must not, however, take too positive a view of the revolution in poetic language generated by intertextuality. Negativity remains crucial to intertextuality, which is best defined as a dynamics of negativity. The dynamic element arises from the fact that Kristeva places negativity in a circuit of social exchanges. Bakhtin, according to her, does not see dialogue only as language assumed by a subject; he sees it, rather, as "a *writing* where one reads the *other* (with no allusion to Freud). . . . as both subjectivity and communication, or better, as intertextuality."[12] The negation of reality by its character as writing, and of writing by its character as reading, is thus given a positive thrust by the fact that negation is an attempt to understand the other as a resistance to the thetic and enunciative position of the subject. On the other hand the negative element of intertextuality arises from its chiasmic structure as a process in which writer and social text (and potentially writer and reader) mutually read each other. The text, according to Kristeva, is a "reading of the anterior literary corpus," the "absorption and transformation" of another text.[13] But it also thwarts the linearity of such transformation by inserting the writer into the texts he rewrites. Not all texts are governed by an explicit intention on the part of the writer to rewrite an anterior corpus—a point to which we shall return. But the refraction of the text's transformative energy, which has the effect of marking its historicity, is endemic to its

conception (whether by the writer or by the reader) as an intertext rather
than as an autonomous work. Or to put it differently, the inscription of
the material within the textual, which we have described as a dynamic textualization of social structures, is also recursive, aporetic, because it inscribes the materiality even of the revolutionary text's intervention in history within signifying systems that it has displaced but not overturned.

This account of intertextuality as a process that shows negativity as productive because it operates in the subject and in the language of events
would seem logically to assume the presence of the reader as an element
in the intertextual process. Kristeva's failure to include any discussion of
the reader raises several problems, and one is uncertain about whether it
is an oversight or is symptomatic of a residual ahistoricism in poststructuralism. One problem is that without an account of different readings
history remains an abstract category, little more than a synonym for relativity. Another problem is that the absence of a reader makes it difficult
to construct that bridge between textuality and history that seems the goal
of Kristeva's theory. For the transposition of the material into the textual
must be balanced by a reinsertion of the textual into the material if negativity is to be rendered dynamic. Kristeva does to some extent absorb the
reader into the writer who "rereads" an anterior literary or social corpus
by liberating the semiotic potential (to use her term) within the symbolic
order. But because of the chiasmic structure of intertextuality, which re-
inscribes the writer in what he reads, such reading will tend to slip back
into absolute negativity if we do not posit a further articulation of the
enunciative and denotative positionalities generated in the initial inter-
transposition of writer and social text. Of necessity this further articulation must be produced by the transposition of the text into the experience
of the reader, or more accurately by a triadic interchange among the writer,
the anterior social or literary corpus, and the later reader who is able not
only to situate the text in its own historicity but to read or write beyond
it. In other words the purely dyadic interchange between writer and social
text risks lapsing into a textualization of the historical. Despite the differences between dialogism and aporia, one senses similar dangers in Bakhtin who, in contrast to Volosinov, often seems to textualize ordinary language by contextualizing the literary in the social text. Yet Kristeva, like
Bakhtin, presumably does not intend to dispossess intertextuality of its
material force, given her description of it as an interchange between subjectivity and communication.

In expanding on Kristeva's discussion therefore we shall suggest that intertextuality functions along two axes. Though the first of these has not
been described with any degree of theoretical detail, the ways in which it
operates are clear enough from the work of Kristeva and Barthes. On the

horizontal level of an author's own textual network or that of his circle, individual texts can be seen as intertexts that transcode certain thematic matrices that therefore do not emerge undialogically from any single text. Sometimes the individual text may be structurally segmented in such a way as to further dehomogenize the text by breaking it up into parts which transcode each other along paradigmatic or syntagmatic axes. Thus in Blake, whose deployment of intertextuality I have discussed elsewhere,[14] the preludium to *Europe* (spoken by the shadowy female) and the preface in which "Blake" meets the fairy are different versions on a paradigmatic axis of a scene of origination or creativity that stages the feasibility of a revolution in how we perceive the world. The prophecy itself then repeats the concept of perceptual revolution as historical revolution, and develops it on the syntagmatic axis of a narrative describing eighteen hundred years of European history.

The horizontal level operates exclusively as an interchange between the text and contemporaneous writings (not necessarily literary). But in addition the text also functions vertically in relation to previous and future history, and it is here that it becomes necessary to posit a reader who will effect the transposition of the horizontal into the vertical. Kristeva introduces what we shall call the vertical dimension of intertextuality in describing history and society as "texts read by the writer, and into which he inserts himself by rewriting them."[15] Part of this dimension is the tacit or explicit reviewing of an anterior social canon through its transposition into a medium whose textuality submits it to semiological analysis and ideological dismantling. But another aspect of the vertical dimension is the reinsertion of the writer's own scripts in that text which calls them into being and also marks their limits and complicities. For the description of the writer as "inserting" himself into what he rewrites builds into intertextuality a certain reflexiveness that makes all writing the site of its own reading. We can argue that this reflexiveness is intrinsic to textuality and does not have to be part of the writer's intention. Nevertheless it is hard to see how the transformational and reflexive potential of textuality can be brought out without the presence of a subject position which will facilitate a new articulation of the thetic. That position may be provided by the "writer" who has constructed his work intertextually so as to make available in the text a "reading function" that allows for a shift in enunciative and denotative positionality—in other words for movement beyond what the text says. In such a case the writer would not so much become his own reader as provide, through the kind of form he uses, for rereadings of his "position" whose possibility he foresees without predicting their details. But Kristeva's failure to deal with the problem of intention leaves unexplored how a text that reproduces rather than questions the social text is to generate something more than a passive reading that reinstalls the text as influence and source. In other words, for mimesis to be perceived as transposition, for transposition not to be naturalized as mimesis, it seems necessary to hypothesize a *reader* so as to produce a new receptive positionality that will allow for a different articulation of the thetic.

There are reasons why a conception of the text as productivity requires us to posit this reader as an extratextual subject, even in cases where the text consciously inscribes itself as a reading. For such a text can reread the anterior corpus and can situate its own reading, but in order to make this situatedness dialectical it is necessary that transposition also be conceived as a communicative transfer to a subsequent reader. The positing of a reader, as we have suggested, is also a corollary of Kristeva's failure to negotiate the problem of intention. Because she assumes that intertextuality is a function of writing rather than reading (or more precisely because she does not raise the problem at all), Kristeva does not distinguish between two kinds of texts: those that are "passively" and those that are "actively" intertextual. Certain texts actually construct themselves intertextually. They may thematize intertextuality so as to make it their operative mode, as Blake does in *The Marriage of Heaven and Hell*. There pietism and Puritanism are exposed as semiotic practices, in such a way that the reduction of influences like Swedenborg and Milton to texts makes it impossible to reinstall "Blake" as an influence not subject to his own critique of the concept. Alternatively they may mark the fact of intertextuality on a formal level by an internal segmentation that demimeticizes content by making it an effect of structure. Blake constructs his early texts out of brief segments that can be ordered in more than one way. By composing them in modular parts that do not so much unfold into each other as reflect on each other, he ruptures the sense of the text as an organism necessary to naturalize its content. Moreover, by oversignifying the part in relation to the whole, he makes us aware of how the whole that we construct is assembled out of texts that are always part(ial).

We shall return briefly to such writings and to the question of whether attributing intertextuality to a conscious intention does not reinstall the autonomous subject that intertextuality claims to put under erasure. But the more common case is of a text that is passively intertextual. In imitating historical and social "realities" such a text tacitly defamiliarizes both them and itself, such that the space between reality and mimesis becomes a space in which we can see the text as a reading and the object of its reading as itself a text. Despite the mimetic claims of such texts, their transposition of a material into a textual signifying system causes history and society to emerge as "texts read by the writer," and thus creates that internal distantiation within ideology that has been described by theorists like Macherey and Althusser, and that clearly informs Kristeva's concept of intertextuality. The text that constructs itself intertextually obviously facilitates its own rereading. But the passively intertextual work can be seen as such only by a historically and culturally different reader who situates what claims to be an autonomous representation of reality on the horizontal and vertical axes of its own intertextuality.

If the inclusion of the reader seems necessary to a more complete theory of intertextuality, there is also the question of what such theoretical intertextualization does to the more traditional versions of hermeneutics and reader-response theory. However they conceive the text, such theories have not attributed to reading any significant degree of reflexiveness: in other words they have not made the reader subject to textuality or historicity, assuming instead that he is an autonomous subject. But if writing and reading exist on a transformational continuum, the reader will himself be subject to rereading, to further articulations of the thetic generated by his inscription in the text. For the text has already been invested with what we have called a "reading function," whether it be associated with the writer or with the reader. We can approach the consequences of an intertextual theory of reading from two directions. There is first of all the problem raised by the crossing of reader-response theory with some form of (post)structuralism: the problem of whether the reader is a self (phenomenological or social) or is a (trans)position generated in language. But if we grant the validity of the latter there is also the second question of whether intertextuality is not still compatible with some kind of theory of the subject — a question inevitably raised by the transposition of poststructuralism into reader-response theory, and by the very nature of intertextuality as a transposition of difference into history. In order to explore such questions we must recall our earlier distinction between the reader as person and the reader as a function: between a given reader and the receptive positionality that his or her existence allows to emerge in the text. This distinction is significantly different from the one made by the Konstanz school between "explicit" and "implicit" readers. For the term "receptive positionality" withholds from the extratextual reader any intratextual hypostasis of her reading in the form of a person, an implied reader, produced by a dialectic between differing horizons of expectation in which she subsumes her identity as "explicit" reader into the more complex identity of "implied" reader. The term suggests a semiotic structure rather than a semantic content. In other words the reading function in the text is not to be identified with the reader who generates it, being a subject position that can be occupied in different ways by different readers or by the same reader at different points. Available for occupation by other readers, it is therefore a site at which the individual reading becomes dialogized. Nor, in the case of the consciously intertextual work, is the reading function to be identified with the writer who envisions an implied reader. Thus reading does not result in a mastering of textuality, nor in the identity of the reader with her reading. Rather the positionality of any given reading disclosed by its transposition into the text introduces a space between the subject and her position that makes the particular reading a "state" (in Blake's sense of that term): something that we transit without becoming identified with it. Having occupied this position the individual reader experiences the double structure of subjectivity. She grasps the positionality of her consciousness of herself as a subject; in other words she comes to read herself as a product of certain social structures. And she makes this determination by structure the site of a certain freedom, in that the perception of positionality is a hermeneutic act, part of the self-understanding of the subject-in-process.

We can sum up this discussion by suggesting that what is generated by the intertextual process is not a "reader" so much as a "lector," an equivalent to what Kristeva calls the "writer" as opposed to the "author" and to what Barthes terms the "scriptor." For the reflexiveness of intertextuality requires a process in which not simply is textuality reappropriated to material use through its transposition into the life of someone outside the text, but also the realities in which we as readers participate are resituated as ideologies by their transposition into the text. But the very terms "scriptor" and "lector," while designating writer and reader as subjects of language, do nevertheless designate them as subjects. While a phrase like "enunciative positionality" is purely linguistic, words like lector and scriptor inhabit the threshold between a structuralism that figures the subject as an effect of language and a social phenomenology that allows subject and structure to be at least coexistent. Kristeva herself seems ambivalent about the existence of a subject, since she refers to a "writer" who "inserts" himself into an anterior corpus, thereby implying the existence of the writer as someone different from this corpus: someone whose identity as a subject both precedes or exceeds and is the product of the corpus. For her description suggests that the writer is conscious of himself as a subject before and apart from his insertion of himself into the corpus, but also that the corpus is "anterior" to him. Indeed without a notion of the subject as the difference between self and structure it would be impossible to make the Lacanian dyad of the imaginary (self) and the symbolic (structure) dialectical, by positing some kind of resistance to determination by the symbolic. In general Kristeva locates this resistance in the "semiotic," a presocial order of drives and pulsions associated with the mother's body and surviving in language only in the negative form of gaps, silences, and contradictions. It is unclear whether her discussion of intertextuality allows this resistance to operate in more conscious and positive ways, through the "writer," or through "rewriting" as a potential of textuality articulated by the reader. In other words it is unclear whether the concept of intertextuality transposes the category of the semiotic from the presocial to the social, from the maternal body to culture, so as to effect some kind of mediation between the semiotic and the symbolic that will bring the former into being as a political unconscious and not simply a pre-oedipal *chora*. But if Kristeva's theory does not allow for such mediation, there remains a problem we have raised before: the problem of how a resistance conceived only as negativity can become a "productivity" without some kind of intervention, some transposition of the subject into textuality. Or to put it differently, there remains the problem of how to mobilize the semiotic without hypothesizing some kind of agency.

For our part, therefore, we shall assume that the lector is a subject, but that this subject is intentional in structure: able to posit but unable to ground anything except as an intent of consciousness. The concept of intentionality as developed by Sartre and the early de Man[16] complicates the binary distinction between phenomenology and deconstruction made canonical by Derrida, in opposing consciousness not to language but to the world of objects, and in thus calling into question not the phenomenological positing of a subject but the naive realism that gives this subject the stability of a thing. To this earlier notion of consciousness as linguistic in the sense of "mental" or "ideal" we can now add a more specific awareness of the subject as textual and cultural. Aligning consciousness with language, a more complex theory of intentionality would thus posit a consciousness that precedes its insertion into a specific text, but whose awareness of itself as constructed by metaphors and metonymies is potentiated through its transposition into a signifying material (that of the text) which foregrounds its own metaphorical construction.

The birth of the lector through the transposition of reader into text generates an awareness of the historicity and not just of the textuality of writing/reading. Influence involves a transference in which the reader, under the guise of confirming the authority of the source, also engages in a process of self-confirmation. To see influence as a text by reading intertextually is to become aware of the cultural transferences that structure "literary history." Intertextual reading can therefore be defined as a practice that shows the text as inscribed in its history, so as to make interpretation into a scene of self-reading the effect of which is also to inscribe us in our own history. Like the writer who inserts himself into an anterior (social) text by rewriting it, the lector by a dialectical reduplication thus inserts her own scripts in the literary text by rereading it. We turn to Kierkegaard's term "dialectical reduplication" because it both anticipates and refigures Kristeva's concept of transposition. A dialectical reduplication involves a translation from one mode into another, for instance from theory into practice or from life into text. The word "translation" is of course inadequate except in its Derridean sense, since what Kierkgaard has in mind is a process that shifts rather than repeats: a repetition that doubles, that defers/differs from what it reduplicates.[17] But if the notion of translation from one signifying material into another anticipates Kristeva, there are of course differences. Kierkegaard introduces his concept as part of a self-reflection that implies an existential commitment, and he does so on the assumption that complete erasure of the subject is an ethical abdication.[18] Dialectical reduplication therefore implies a subject who situates herself through a transposition that *engages* theory in life, or "life" in self-reflection; and it indicates, moreover, that this doubling treads a thin line between self-cancellation and productivity or dialectic. Palimpsestically (or intertextually) combining the linguistic term "transposition" with the Kierkegaardian term, we arrive at a concept of intertextual reading that retains the existentially situated subject but sees it as intergenerated with language, and thus as socially dialogized and not simply as self-reflexive.

Our discussion of the reader as subject brings us back to a problem earlier raised: that of the writer as subject of his own intertextuality. We can explore this problem by raising two related questions. To what extent is the author subject to intertextuality, and conversely, to what extent is it necessary to restore a sense of the writer as a subject in order to make intertextuality not a synonym for pure difference, but the transposition of difference into history? What holds true for the lector also holds true for the writer: not the least for the writer who constructs his work intertextually. As reader-response theory risks merely replacing the authority of the text with a logocentrism of the reading process, so too there can be certain dangers in simply replacing the autonomy of the text with an intertextuality intended by the author. Such a move might reinstall a personified Text as source and origin. It could allow the text to become "agent, author, and master of différance," not by achieving what Derrida calls an "in-*different* being [that] precedes *différance* and spacing,"[19] but rather by becoming the very embodiment of difference. The characterization of the text as pure difference is a new kind of essentialism in that the text is now identical with itself by virtue of not differing from its difference, by virtue of being in-different to the achievement of identity. Or to restate the problem, "difference" becomes a positive term, emancipated from being a diacritical effect of identity.

The elision of history that results from a celebration of pure difference is evident in Barthes's account of intertextuality as involving a shift of emphasis from author to reader:

a text is made up of multiple writings, drawn from many cultures and entering into mutual relations of dialogue, parody, contestation, but there is one place where this multiplicity is focused and that place is the reader, not, as was hitherto said, the author. The reader is the space on which all the quotations that make up a writing are inscribed without any of them being lost; a text's unity lies not in its origin but in its destination. Yet this destination cannot any longer be personal: the reader is without history, biography, psychology.[20]

In effect the death of the author has also become the disappearance of the reader, in a description of heteroglossia that is curiously without material density. The renunciation of the authorial subject requires, by a kind of symmetry, that the "reader" be conceived impersonally. But as a result, he or she is little more than a receptacle. Even more disturbing is a kind of transcendentalism in the description of the reader: as the site of an absolute difference, he or she becomes a figure for totality, "the space on which *all* the quotations that make up a writing are inscribed without any of them being lost." Recovering "in a *single* field *all* the traces" (my emphasis) that make up the text, the reader occupies no particular perspective and cannot be situated. This emancipation from history is evident in the fact that the reader exists not in time but in a "space" that has achieved temporal simultaneity and thus is beyond dialectic. Conceiving of literature simply as "writing" rather than as the writing of a specific subject, Barthes necessarily makes reading a process that happens nowhere and to no one.

It is in order to avoid this evaporation of history that we must, for instance, specify a "Blake," a historical subject about whose intentions it is possible to speak. "Intention," however, should not be understood in the sense (assumed by the New Criticism) of the desire to posit an author transcendent to writing or to the text. It should be taken in its phenomenological sense of an "intent of consciousness" refracted by the difference between language and its object. "Subject" likewise should be understood both in the sense of an interiority, and in the Althusserian sense of being "subject to the law." What Barthes's essay reveals with reference to the reader is that one cannot make writer or reader subject to intertextuality without constructing them as subjects, and that the effacement of the subject is also the avoidance of history in a difference without material specificity. In the case of the passively intertextual work it is the reader who must construct the writer as subject in the double sense suggested above. But in cases where intertextuality is consciously deployed, it is not therefore possible to see the writer as reconverting textuality into authority, except through a transference on the part of the critic. Recognizing that the cultural scene is overdetermined, composed by competing discourses, someone like Blake constructs his work intertextually not to transcend his histor-

ical situation, but rather to write himself into it. He clears a space for
his own position precisely by inscribing it in a text whose construction
makes writing and reading a mirror of their own cultural production.

NOTES

1 Jacques Derrida, *Positions*, trans. Alan Bass (Chicago: U of Chicago P, 1981),
   26.
2 Michael Riffaterre, *Semiotics of Poetry* (Bloomington: Indiana UP, 1978),
   164–65.
3 Paul de Man, *Allegories of Reading: Figural Language in Rousseau, Nietzsche,
   Rilke, and Proust* (New Haven: Yale UP, 1979), 17.
4 Vincent Leitch, *Deconstructive Criticism: An Advanced Introduction* (New
   York: Columbia UP, 1983), 98.
5 Ibid.
6 Julia Kristeva, *Revolution in Poetic Language*, trans. Margaret Waller (New
   York: Columbia UP, 1984), 59.
7 Julia Kristeva, *Desire in Language: A Semiotic Approach to Literature and
   Art* (New York: Columbia UP, 1980), 65.
8 Ibid. 108.
9 Derrida, *Positions* 20.
10 Kristeva, *Revolution* 59–60.
11 Kristeva, *Desire* 64–65.
12 Ibid. 68.
13 Ibid. 69, 66.
14 See Tilottama Rajan, *The Supplement of Reading: Figures of Understanding
   in Romantic Theory and Practice* (Ithaca: Cornell UP, 1990), 197–276.
15 Kristeva, *Desire* 65.
16 Jean-Paul Sartre, *Imagination: A Psychological Critique*, trans. Forrest Williams (Ann Arbor: U of Michigan P, 1972), 131–33; Paul de Man, "The Intentional Structure of the Romantic Image," *The Rhetoric of Romanticism* (New
   York: Columbia UP, 1984), 6.
17 Søren Kierkegaard, *The Point of View for My Work as an Author*, trans. Walter Lowrie (New York: Harper and Row, 1962), 17.
18 Ibid. 44–45.
19 Derrida, *Positions* 28.
20 Roland Barthes, *Image-Music-Text*, trans. Stephen Heath (New York: Hill and
   Wang, 1977), 148.

CHAPTER 4

Oral Texts, Intertexts, and Intratexts: Editing Old English

A.N. DOANE

For nearly forty years, scholars concerned with Old English literary documents have had either to consider or deliberately overlook the concept of orality, and still the field has not come to terms with orality as a formative element in the texts it studies. Investigations of formula and theme in Old English poetry abound (see Foley's *Bibliography*). There is a small but promising new current of "ethnographic" studies looking at the society that produced putatively oral texts.[1] But most studies have been naively "textual" in the sense that the *voice* of orality has not been heard as strongly as might be hoped, nor have the *texts* that focus the debate been editorially reconsidered from the point of view of their possible oral production and consequent voicing. Those scholars most productive in the field of orality per se have shown little interest in textual matters and the problems of the deep literacy and textualization implicit in criticism,[2] while those scholars expressly concerned with textuality have more often than not been openly hostile to oral theory. Meanwhile, the contests about orality have taken place and continue to take place over a corpus formed on the assumption that Old English texts are *only* writing, with single authors (even if unknown) and definite, intended meanings (even if irecoverable). Old English textual studies have so far developed no systematic way of dealing with the traditional production and motility of texts (*mouvance*) influenced by orality.[3]

This essay attempts to address the relation of orality, textuality, and intertext and the implications of these notions for editorial methods in Old English. In particular it wants to consider the problematics of *the production of oral texts*, an ambiguous phrase which refers equally to the primary setting (a setting of genuine orality, of speaking or singing), the secondary setting (the making of chirographs that descend from oral production), and the tertiary setting (the making of edited, printed texts from chirographs putatively related to oral production).

This essay criticizes editorial methods usually applied to Old English poetic texts preserved in unique copies because these methods are intertextual. Intertextuality is used in this essay to mean the editors' ability to refer outside a given text as it appears in a manuscript to two intertextual resources: a primary intertext or "hypertext" constructed from a wide variety of Old English sources as a concordance; and a secondary intertext consisting of all previous editorial conjectures about a given text. Intertextuality bestows upon the editor the ability to make selections of variant "readings" where the actual manuscript tradition of particular texts provides no basis for such choice, where there are, in fact, no variants. These intertexts, one an inexhaustible idealized "primary" intertextual reservoir, the other a limited secondary intertextual grid, take the place, in the case of *unici*, of the actual *traditio* or *paradosis* that exists for texts preserved in several copies. But these normalizing editorial resources are normal neither to the speaking person nor to the medieval vernacular scribe. Nevertheless, the editor searches for and claims to find the "ideal," "intended," or "virtual" text via the intertexts and tends to close off any approach to the voices, shifting from performance to performance, within the text, the "actual" text as it appears, what I will call later the "intratext." The position brought forward here is that in the face of the radical motility of the oral text, edited texts derived from oral performative situations neither can achieve nor ought to attempt the monumentality, intertextuality, and virtuality implied in the concept of the "definitive edition." I will argue that the "oral written text" in its edited versions ought rather to suggest and allow for the variety of forms possible in a field of voiced production *without necessarily choosing between them*,[4] at the same time that the definiteness and specificity of individual performative situations (of which a manuscript is an instance) are respected.

Two implications for the development of a new editorial praxis involving putatively oral texts will emerge. The first is that an editor of a medieval text has to make an informed, principled, definite, and declared decision about a given text's relation to writing and orality. For many or most vernacular medieval texts the assumption of oral origin is no more prodigious than that it is written in origin, as Clanchy and Stock have amply demonstrated. If a decision is made to edit a text as an oral text, other procedures must be used than if it had been assumed to be written. The second implication is that a more direct and subtle presentation of chirographic evidence has to be developed. Accent marks, notations, spacing, sectional divisions, diacritics, spelling, hesitations, broken syntax, phonic repetitions supplemental to "formal" metrical demands, corrections, notations, and any other cues and clues that may be present in a chirograph must be treated seriously and represented in an edition rather than being stripped away or sedimented out, because these supply the most direct evidence for conditions of production, performance, and audibility. The argument will claim that *performative factors*, actual chirographically produced marks (individual, ad hoc, and difficult of interpretation as they may be), rather than printed, standardized symbols, are the very traces that the oralist claims to be and ought to be looking for. Paying attention to such marks may mean that an editor will have to give up the idea of the "definitive" edition in Old English in order to produce a "definite" edition, an edition that will reflect a single performative situation, rather than a virtual text.

I. THE SCENE OF ORALITY

Most utterances are oral, and in some cultures all are oral. In most cultures some systematic aspects of the natural orality of speech are isolated, foregrounded, conventionalized, and associated with special kinds of speaking in specific situations. On certain well-marked occasions a specially knowledgeable or privileged speaker may thus shape utterance consciously according to formal demands that are added to those of the ordinary language in order to connect with an audience possessing a continuum of relevant aural experience and able in various ways to judge the kind of speech taking place.

Such language use — proverbs, jokes and riddles, songs, genealogies, prayers, challenges, tales, myths, epics, to mention only the most familiar — is located within but marked as apart from the ordinary flow of everyday language. In its original settings it includes besides the phonemic string we call "text" all the concomitants of spoken language and performance: intonations, special pronunciations, melody, musical accompaniment, facial expressions, somatic gestures, special times or seasons for speaking, not to mention the ambience created by the entire bodily presence of the living speaker and of a living audience. In its functions oral poetry has a force that is always dispersed and weakened by purely textual dissemination. Daniel Biebuyck captures the immediacy of the oral poetic ambience in his description of the Mwindo epic of the Congo:

Functionally the epic is many things: entertainment, moralization, and explanation of causes, and an interpretation of existing customs; it is a paideia.

. . . It is music, rhythm, song, dance, movement, dramatic entertainment. It is feasting and gift-giving (those who present the gifts dance and gesticulate). It is group solidarity and mass participation. For the bard himself, the act of narrating the story has religious significance. . . . The narrator believes he will find in his songs the force that Mwindo himself, the hero of the epic, derives from them. (Biebuyck and Kahombo, cited by Opland 83)

The communication itself has a special status, different from that of ordinary language, both in the nature of its formulism and in its use; everyone normally involved in such special oral exchanges is aware of the differences. While it cannot spatially separate itself from the flow of generalized experience, as a written text does, and cannot aurally excerpt itself from the sounds preceding, following, or surrounding it, the "performative situation," as I will call it, is clearly marked off as a moment of unusual time. "Grandpa, tell me a story" is the archetypical marker of performative time, while Tedlock (298) notes how in a Zuni household it takes a few minutes for the "normal chaos" of everyday to reestablish itself in the "wake" of the story.

Even in a purely oral setting, or primary oral culture,[5] such language calls attention to itself *as* language and is made up of more or less predetermined, more or less flexible, more or less everyday language elements that conform themselves to familiar and expected genres and contents. We may thus, in spite of Ong's elaborate objections (13–14), be justified in speaking of an "oral text." An oral text is an oral utterance that has internal formal features differentiating it from ordinary language, generic features understood and recognized by both speaker and hearers, and markers at beginning and ending that separate it from the aural flow around it. The paramount difference between the oral text and the written text is that the former cannot, so long as it is entirely oral, be glimpsed as a fixed object. Not that in their "natural" condition primary oral texts fail to be preserved — indeed, preservation is of the essence of oral texts — but they are preserved only by means of "oral memory" and consequent reperformances. The oral text is latent in the head of everyone who knows the discourse, and its mode of existence is passing and recurrence, "the preservation of tradition by the constant recreation of it" (Lord 29).

If we can speak of an "oral text," then we are obliged to consider what the terms "author" and "intention" might mean in relation to orality. Oral texts are of course "traditional" in the sense that they are "handed down" from the past, that is, from past performances, and oral verbal artists are keenly aware of this aspect of their work. But they are not aware of the tradition in the same way an outside literate observer is.[6] To the illiterate singer the tradition is not a diachrony — the sense of the past tends to be "homeostatic," that is, flat, one-dimensional, given, constantly reasserting itself as a reflection of the present (Ong 46–49), hence constantly changing in detail in order that it need never confront change as such. The past is as the poet speaks it to be with the assent of his audience. As Paul Zumthor has suggestively put it, we must reverse the valence of Derrida's phrase, and recognize the oral poet's *vouloir-dire*, not as *Bedeutung*, but as, in actuality, "the wish to speak."[7]

Nevertheless the past is not felt as something created by the speaker; the poet is the bearer of a past that is a common possession of all the persons active as poets or audience within a given tradition. A poet who distorts the common sense of the "past," of the "true," will be "censored," in that his version of things will not be carried on within the tradition (Jakobson and Bogatyrev 91). Moreover, what a poet might be able to say about "long ago" in a given performative situation is determined by the particular precipitate from the real historical past that has accumulated in him as bearer of the tradition up to the particular instant of performance. A speaker hasn't the means, let alone the will, to violate his own ontogeny or that of his audience. The intention of the traditional oral performer is to "tell the truth" as he and his audience have always understood it: within the resources of his language that leaves him free to invent considerable detail and to connect the performance to his present audience.[8] Intentional changes take place during the transmission of the tradition, but they are expressions of "an insistent, conservative urge for preservation of an essential idea" (Lord 120). Paradoxically, from the protean multiformity of oral-traditional texts emerges the formulaic and thematic redundancy arising from many retellings of the same thing that both reduces the role of intentionality without extinguishing it and eliminates the element of indeterminacy that is associated with written texts that always repeat the same words, allowing and even requiring a multitude of interpretations.[9]

At certain discrete historical moments a culture that has adopted writing as a privileged or as a secondary mode for the production and preservation of texts may form an "interface" (Goody 78ff.) with a primary(ily) oral culture or with an oral strain of culture within itself. An interface is the moment when the oral text and the technology of literacy are capable of penetrating and interpreting each other. The result of these encounters is the gradual undermining of the oral culture by the power of writing and literacy. Once it comes into contact with writing, the orality of oral cultures tends to bifurcate into written traces, the products of high formulism being replaced by the power of writing, and into ordinary language which is not considered worth preserving in writing. At the same time, during these interfacial moments (moments which may last for months, years, centuries — even millennia, as in the case of India), many performative situations may migrate into written residue. These "oral-residual texts"[10] are always particular reflexes of specific, individual historical encounters at the oral/written interface and constitute the body of the various "oral literatures" available for study in contemporary lettered culture.

At the immediate level of function the work at the interface in situations where electronic means of recording are not available has been thought to be able to take place in three ways: by a speaker dictating directly to a scribe, by an oral poet writing down his own lines as he pronounces them, and by a literate poet who is familiar with a particular oral tradition imitating or interacting with the produce of oral-traditional performative situations by literary means. Lord has discussed all three methods in *The Singer of Tales*. Dictation is well attested in various situations and was used frequently by Lord and Parry themselves in their fieldwork in Yugoslavia. While poorer poets tended to become confused by the slowing-down of the natural process of composition, Lord found that the better poets could make longer, more elaborated poems by this method because length was not constrained by audience factors (128). He supposes that the length and excellence of the Homeric poems are attributable to their being "oral dictated texts" (149).

The second situation, where a literate poet dictates to himself, is attested by Lord (129), who considers that it produces more or less normal "oral dictated texts" of an inferior type. But all such texts Lord knows of were the nonspontaneous product of the encounter between a (rare) traditional poet who as it happened could write and a collector who made the demand for self-dictation. However, the possibility of this type of text must be kept in mind in relation to medieval texts written at an interface where the traditional culture was not yet marginalized and might be intent on merging its products with writing, which still bore the marks of the magic and sacral (since the kind of writing encountered would normally be Bibles and service books). Even before *The Singer of Tales* appeared, Magoun (460) had supposed that Cynewulf composed his poems by this method.

The third type of interfacial text has an oral style but is not the product of a direct oral performative situation. Lord (135–36) notes the existence in Yugoslavia from the eighteenth century of literary texts in the style of oral songs—texts that were always written, never spoken—that were taken as genuine folk art in the pre-Romantic period. Lord considers this type a "literary imposture" that is of little interest in the study of oral poetry. Yet this type is of great potential importance in the study of medieval orality, for such a type truly hangs balanced between two worlds, recalling orality and imagining new horizons within literacy. Doubtless many old texts having an oral style (e.g., *The Heliand, Genesis B,* the Old English Chronicle poems) are of this type and they provide an interesting basis for comparison of the oral and the nonoral type of text within the same cultural/linguistic context.

In this paper I am proposing a fourth model: reperformance. Whenever scribes who are part of the oral traditional culture write or copy traditional oral works, they do not merely mechanically hand them down; they rehear them, "mouth" them, "reperform" them in the act of writing in such a way that the text may change but remain authentic, just as a completely oral poet's text changes from performance to performance without losing authenticity. A textualist perspective will show scribally reperformed texts to have a different textual form from their "originals," but these texts reperformed in their writing will be new originals in that the forms they draw from will be from the same sources and conform to the same canon as completely oral texts.[11]

Now, in oral traditional performative situations, the text is not a fixed form of words, but, in John Miles Foley's conception, a "multiform," a limited number of grammatical patterns, "a supersegmental latticework," certain "rhythmical predispositions," with some morphological stability (Foley, "Limits" 121–22). Thus the formula can be seen as the dynamic means of structuring texts that directs the traditional audience in its participation in the structuring of the performative situation, for composition and reception are simultaneous in the oral text (Bäuml 36).

Once the oral text is written down its relation to the audience changes somewhat but not entirely. A true interfacial text is one produced in a milieu where the oral tradition is still alive and productive, one whose intended/actual audience (in an oral milieu the two are coterminous), whether literate or illiterate, is conversant with the tradition and capable of receiving the "oral text" *as* an oral audience, not just aurally, but critically, with a traditional understanding of the meanings and functions of traditional language, formulas, and themes. As Bäuml has argued: "the written formulaic text inescapably refers the receiver to the oral-formulaic tradition, provided only that he is familiar with its attributes. In referring to the oral tradition, the written text fictionalizes it" (43). The audience may have to "fictionalize" the text in the sense that it has to imagine the original unlettered singer behind the (aural or visual) reading or reciting, but it does not have to fictionalize an oral situation, with which it will, by definition, be familiar. Further, it fictionalizes by not reducing oral text features to matters of "style." It accepts them as evidence of genuine oral production.

In fictionalizing such a text the oral audience is able to grapple with it as a living imaginative entity. It might be said that any literary work has to be fictionalized before it is capable of being received, for fictionalization is simply the natural way of receiving fictions, that is, stories. The "fiction" operative within the natural oral audience is the "truth" of the story to the community receiving the text. "Truth," a word that is used frequently in oral performances, apparently refers not to an ontological or referential concept of truth, but to "validity," the validation of the stance of the story by bringing it into line with the stance of its audience. Goody (151) tells how when he at last was allowed to hear "the most secret of all the performances," the Funeral Bagre, and was told, "now you know all," what he heard was "almost nonsense from the semantic point of view."

In some societies, the "same" story has different endings for male and female audiences in order to keep them "true." Cognitively, the oral story is, in its telling, always a double action, the telling of a telling preceding those ancient deeds that made all the tellings possible. In other words, the oral performance is in its essence a pattern of indefinite regression to an originary event that can never be imagined outside of the present action/telling (Vance 381).

The fiction operative for the semiliterate audience of secondary orality, the audiences within the oral/written interface, is that the text, now in writing, whether derived from a real oral performative situation or a feigned one, is oral and stems from telling and action, not from writing or imagination. The truth of the orality of the text resides not in some ethnographic or literary category outside the text, but within the text, in its voice. In these interfacial performative situations, whether the text comes from a reciter who has memorized a written text in oral style, or from an oral poet who has written his own, or from the document descending from an orally dictated performance, the reception will be aural or at least within the reach of aural memory, and the response will be to the intratext. There will be no need for an audience to reconstruct a performative situation, since either they will be in it (the text will be performed orally, even if memorized from a book) or it will be familiar from other truly oral occasions, even when the reading is private. When Lord, working from the modern literate perspective, encounters the eighteenth-century poet Andrija Kačić-Miošić, he thinks of this text as a counterfeit and puts it to one side of the question (Lord 135–36). But an oral audience, receiving such a text, would not distinguish it fundamentally from other oral texts, but accept it in a spirit of orality.

Much medieval vernacular literature, particularly from the earlier periods, the eighth through the tenth centuries in England and the eleventh and twelfth in Germany and France, is writing produced at the oral interface (Stock 79–87 et passim). In these periods orality and literacy interpenetrated in complex, shifting, and unpredictable ways. Literacy had power and prestige far beyond the numbers of people who could actually read or write, while orality was the normal mode of doing business, attesting to contracts, and even of making documents. Oral/aural transmission remained the primary mode by which audiences received literary works, even textualized, written ones (Clanchy 210–13). The oral products and modes that dominated these interfacial periods can only be apprehended by us at all because at some point writing invaded orally, textualizing the phenomena. But at the same time, in ways that are obscure to us, orality invaded writing, "oralizing" and destabilizing the written words. Moreover, because medieval "oral written texts" are always chirographically produced, the distinction between oral and written is not so sharp as it appears at first to members of a print culture.[12]

II. THE SCENE OF (HAND) WRITING

Chirographs[13] are writing, of course, and as such have assumed the spatial form and fixity that mark all texts. But they differ from modern printed texts (and even modern chirographs—influenced by print just as literate speech is) in many ways that make them resemble oral texts more than printed ones. Chirographs are, like oral utterances, somatic—they are not separated from the body in the moment of their production and they continue to show traces of the body that produced them (forms of handwriting, individualistic layouts, idiosyncratic phonetic arrangements, ad hoc decorations, accidental marks and errors). They are "performative productions" by which a relatively valuable or rare skill (that of the scribe) is brought to bear in a direct communicative link with a reading or hearing audience that cannot or does not write for itself, in many cases a specific individual or corporate audience (though we in many or most cases do not know who these audiences were). That is, to turn Walter Ong's famous dictum around, the chirographer's audience is *not* "always a fiction."

As a performer, the scribe may be seen as analogous to the "singer" of oral culture. Like the singer, the chirographer takes the traditional material, in his case a pre-text in either written or oral form, and makes a "fresh event."[14] Like a traditional singer, a medieval scribe is usually in immediate contact with the community or individuals for which the writing is being done. Like singers, chirographers tend to be concerned not with exact repetition of words but with the transmission of a traditional, already received message. The concern is not with the distance of the message—its alterity—but with the closeness of the expectations of the audience. The scribe transcribes, for example, Dan Boethius to an audience that has made it clear why it needs the message and seldom cares to separate the "real" words of the sixth-century "auctor" from all the comments and glosses that have invaded the text since.[15] He copies a text that begins "Augustinus ait" (medieval manuscripts seldom have textualizing titles or labels) and listens to what the text says, pronouncing it with his lips, feeling it through his arm. Like a conversationalist, or like a "singer of tales," he delivers the "straight truth," very often not the exact words, still less the exact spelling, lineation, decoration of the visual material standing before him.

And in many cases the material is not visual but aural, for it may be dictated either by speaking composer or by a reader pronouncing the manuscript to be transcribed, that is voiced from one scribe's chirographic production to another's. When an "auctor" dictates his words to a secretarial scribe and then reads them over, he cannot say that the scribe has not written them exactly, for the dictated words have vanished and only the written ones remain. All he can say is that he doesn't like this or that expression or this or that meaning and must negotiate further writing with the writer. In a chirographic culture there can be no fixed authorial intention, because the author's intention is always mediated by a scribal intention.

Chirographs further resemble speaking in that they cannot conceal mistakes and can be interrupted. When a speaker (whether an ordinary conversationalist or a singer of tales) misspeaks, the misspoken words cannot be taken back; they can only be "repaired," that is, transfigured by a modulated respeaking (Goodwin): two utterances comment on each other in the memory of the audience even as both pass away. A chirographer's "mistakes" do not even pass away into thin air — the variants remain visible and comment on each other: on parchment even an erasure usually remains legible in ordinary or special light (and even if illegible the *fact* of the erasure is always evident), while quite often alternative writings will continue to exist as coequals in subsequent copies. And in a chirograph other hands may interrupt the scribal discourse by "correcting," commenting, or glossing, asserting their own uncertain authority over the wavering text.

In short, the fixity of a chirographic text is not at all like the fixity of a modern printed text. Our ideology of literacy tells us that the printed text stays exactly the same whether it represents the first or five-millionth copy, whether it occurs in a first edition or a ninth, whether it is found in an overhead transparency or a quotation in a printed book of different title, whether it is on a computer screen or in a handwritten copy. All the changes "behind" the printed text seem to take place in secret, in "drafts," that are erased and forgotten once the text reaches its intended final home on the page. Changes after printing are authorized by some recognized faculty, such as the original author, the publisher, or a scholarly editor; other changes are merely "misprints." The printed text, though always apprehended in some physical, visual manifestation, does not exist in its individual forms, but in an idealized space that is independent of the individual page before us, which is seen only as a disposable matrix for the enduring text. We do not say "the book says," "the paper says"; we say "Ong says," "Clanchy says," but we refer not to real speech ("Augustinus ait") but to idealized visual forms. The printed text as text "stays the same" because it has, in most cases, countless physical manifestations that confirm one another and no one of which, even if different from other through some happenstance, can affect the ideal text. The modern text is a radically immaterial object.[16]

The chirographic text, on the other hand, has no existence other than a material one. Each manuscript is utterly unique, in both what it is and what it contains. Each has its own textual and historical value, its own text to bring, its own story to tell.[17] The body of the manuscript is from the bodies of sheep or calves—you can see the pores and hairs—no two pages were alike even before they were written on. The letters have been laboriously traced with a portion of a bird's body with the visible residue of earth, water, and fire. Unlike typeset letters, which exist before the writing, chirographic script comes into being with a somatic gesture, like speech, at the instant of articulation (Ong 121–22). The physical characteristics of the writing surface—holes, blemishes—determine somewhat the display of the writing.

And the chirograph is intimately connected to human bodies: the lips spoke to the ears that instructed the eyes that guided the hand and fingers that inscribed these physical marks. If the lips misspeak or the hand miswrite, a razor (erasor) may scrape away part of the epidermis. And then again it may not. A manuscript is not just indifferent technologized text-bearing surface but also a three-dimensional object demanding attention in its own right, presenting depth and color as well as extension and contrast. A manuscript page is an immediate record not just of what was in the pre-text and its history, but of all the performative acts that ever physically inscribed, manipulated, mutilated, or distorted the writing surface itself. Finally, the pre-text itself is not an idealized text either, but another manuscript, with all the partiality and peculiarity of a chirograph—whether on wax or parchment—if it is not the voice itself. For, as Clanchy notes:

The commonest way of committing words to writing was by dictating to a scribe. "Reading and dictating" were ordinarily coupled together, not "reading and writing," the skill of writing a letter in proper form was the "art of dictation" (ars dictaminis), a branch of rhetoric. Writing was distinguished from composition because putting a pen to parchment was an art itself. Even when an author declares that he is writing something, he may in fact be using the term metaphorically. (97)

In practice, it is necessary to make a distinction between more and less "oral" chirographs. Less oral are most manuscripts containing Latin texts, which imply deep literacy from their beginnings, and those containing very old texts of oral origin copied in a tradition of writing that has long since separated from the living oral tradition—Latin rhetorical texts, Homer in medieval Byzantine manuscripts, etc.—these texts had entered into scholastic traditions that separate them from immediate orality.[18] More oral are chirographs of vernacular "oral-type" texts that represent a still living or vestigal orality integral to the chirographic culture that produced the documents. Behind their production is doubtless a still oral imperative and an audience still aware of the pertinent oral tradition to be factored into the reception of such texts. We may say that the former type of chirographs are relatively more textlike in their responsibility to visual forms and fixed forms of words. The latter are more unique, voiced, immediate, more like "fresh events."

To move by way of example to the group of texts with which this project is primarily concerned, it cannot be entirely accidents of transmission that texts which on other grounds have been accepted in the past thirty years as in some way or another products or oral tradition are at the same time almost always texts occurring in only one copy.[19] The few Old English exceptions, *Daniel/Azarias, Soul and Body, Solomon and Saturn*, exist in several independent versions, as if the product of different performative situations.[20] The same is true in other oral traditions: the *Cid* is unique to one manuscript and the *Chanson de Roland* occurs in many unique and distinct versions.[21] Moreover, these same texts appear almost invariably in manuscripts that entirely fail to put them in context, that is, there is no literary or historical message around them. Voiced poems, where poem, poet, and audience are implicated in a specific situation, do not need explanation. In contrast, literary texts not only tend to occur in multiple copies (in spite of the accidents of long and casual transmission), they tend to occur in specified "literary" contexts, however imperfectly realized, because texts separated from speakers and performance need explanations. Germanic examples exist: Bede's story of Caedmon, Otfrid's prefaces in Latin and German, above all, the Old Saxon *Heliand* (ninth century), a Gospel harmony in traditional-type alliterative verse, which occurs in five closely related fragmentary copies and is associated with a sparse but nevertheless explanatory text about the circumstances of its origins.[22] The reason that there is one isolated witness to *Beowulf* and five witnesses and a relatively elaborate background to the *Heliand* is unlikely to be that the latter was more popular (it is a poem created by royal fiat, not popular tradition), or that Germany was kinder to vernacular manuscripts than England.[23] The explanation would seem to lie rather in the origins of the texts themselves. The *Heliand* is a literary work, concocted by learned compilers in a monastery imitating a residual orality at the same time that they were undertaking the daring project of raising a vernacular text to literary, even biblical, status. It exists in multiple accurate copies because it arises from a tradition of writing, not speaking, and from the beginning was meant to be transmitted by pen and ink. Old English poetry, on the other hand, is for the most part writing at the interface. That it is writing at all is accidental, extrinsic to its main existence in ongoing oral traditions; hence it was never intended to feed into a lineage of writing.

There are exceptions which test the rule: examples of Old English texts that are indubitably of oral origin and yet that have entered fully into a tradition of writing. The so-called *Death Song* of Bede, a five-line meditation on the swiftness of death, extant in at least twenty-nine copies as an inset in the *Epistola Cuthberti de obitu Bedae*, has in essence become part of the Latin work.[24] Even more instructive are the circumstances surrounding the writing of Caedmon's *Hymn*, extant in seventeen copies. Twelve copies are in the form of an appended gloss to the Latin version of the *Hymn* that Bede presents in his *Historia ecclesiastica*, a Latin book existing in hundreds of copies throughout Europe. In it, Bede tells the story of the lay brother Caedmon who could not produce the traditional oral songs he was expected to sing when the harp was passed to him at the beer drinking. One night Caedmon was visited by an angel who urged him to make an impromptu verse on the Creation. In the morning he repeated it to the abbess and it was written down. Bede tells this not as an explanation of the origin of Christian verse, as is often said, but because it is a miracle. In his text he shows forth Caedmon's poem not in the barbaric oral babble in which it was spoken, for the oral fact had no meaning for Bede in this context, but in carefully phrased Latin clausulae giving an exact sense-by-sense translation, an unprecedented case of the more prestigious language appropriating truth from the lesser. This Latin version is always very carefully copied, with the punctuation of the clausulae clearly and correctly marked (O'Keeffe 17–18). Shortly after Bede's death, about 737, a scribe in an Anglo-Saxon foundation on the continent copied the *Historia ecclesiastica*[25] and included in the margin, next to Bede's Latin version, the English text of the *Hymn*; it would seem that this miraculous text already had its own textual tradition and was circulated separately from Bede's account. It was already becoming not an oral text, not even a text at all, but a relic.[26] Indeed, in the latest copies its function within the Latin text is purely iconic, for it is copied in an English house in the fourteenth century[27] and in Cologne in the fifteenth[28] by scribes who could hardly have understood a word of the Old English text, as the mistakes in their writing show. It is a text that, once wrested from its oral setting and "set in" a Latin text, partakes entirely of the latter's literate connections, even though it has become illegible. It has become, like texts and relics, and unlike performative situations, indefinitely replicable in the "same" form. On the other hand, the other five copies, appearing as an integral part of the late-ninth-century Old English translation of the *Historia,* show a textual multiformity that, as O'Keeffe has shown with great probability, is directly related to their more "oralistic" vernacular environment.[29]

III. EDITORIAL INTERLUDES

The perplexing question "what is an oral text?" begins to run into its equally perplexing counterpart: "what is a text?" It is undeniable that for us to confront the absent present of orality we have to apprehend it in terms of the present absences we call texts. And these texts are not given, they are made by editors as well as poets. Therefore, we have to move beyond an idealized meditation on performative situations to the problem of the production of texts that will stand for prior performative situations; that is, we have to face the truth about the present (scholarly) performative situation. It is a question that has become submerged however in the longstanding ideologies of the "critical edition."

What is the status of an "oral written text"? In its manuscript state is it a record or a score, or both? It is certain that it does not have the same status as a text that had its origin "in writing." If a record, it is a product of voice, of a voiced performative situation; its origin is not text but voice, and its destination is as a visual trace of a material event that once existed in a different register. The record/text that results is the product of a writer listening to an outer voice—his own or another's—rather than an inner one. Thus meaning is intertwined with two intentions, that of the instigator of the text, the speaker, and that of the designator, the writer, in a process that is less cooperative than it is mutually interventionist.[30]

But the written text may also be a score, meant to engender other voiced productions. As such it will be a more textualized object in its own right because subject to elaborated visible intervention (phonic, diacritical, etc.). The latter is the product of a third intention, that of a "scorer" (who will always be a later intervener than the "recorder" even if the same person), and a fourth, the performer of this score, who will have to add another layer of interpretive intention in order to translate the text back into voice. And these subsequent performances, theoretically, feed into further recordings, ad infinitum.

The story of Caedmon is again instructive here. In Bede's Latin version, the focus is on the content of the song and its miraculous effect on the audience: "[Caedmon] learned all he could by listening [to Bible verses recited to him], and then, memorizing it and ruminating over it, like some clean animal chewing the cud, he turned it into the most melodious verse: and it sounded so sweet as he recited it that his teachers became in turn his audience" (Cassidy & Ringler 131). The Anglo-Saxon translator, working in a context closer to orality than Bede's though two hundred years later, seems to have been more sensitive to the exact nature of the changes that would have been made in the traverse from Bible to Caedmon and back to Caedmon's auditors: "and his song and his leoð wæron swa wynsume to gehyranne, þætte seolfan his lareowas æt his muðe wreoton and leornodon" (and his song and music were so delightful to hear, that even his teachers wrote down the words from his lips and memorized them). Auditors become learners and a further performance is implied.

Historically, editors of old texts have represented their editions as records (as in "the Anglo-Saxon Poetic Records"). Yet they are not records of what presents itself in the manuscripts, but the records of what the collectivity of modern editors have decided the original poets must have written. My position is that the latter is something not only indeterminable, but, in the case of many Old English poetic texts, something that never did nor could have existed. It would be truer to the status of these texts to present them as something *scored for the voice.* Yet this might lead to the conclusion that the editor of a text that is thought to derive from an oral situation has to discover the complex interaction of layers of written production alternating with layers of speaking and audition. But this is an archeological task for which there are no tools and no evidence. For oral texts, and, a fortiori, for oral written texts, the only method that can make sense while respecting the nature of oral events is to take *each "textual" manifestation of orality as the manifestation of the whole tradition at that point.* Just as an oral event is concrete and unique, its text must also be regarded as concrete and unique. The editor cannot project back to a virtual or intended text. Nor can he make a claim for a "definitive edition."

The problematics apply not only to "oral written texts," of course. The issues in relation to the editing of modern printed texts have recently been ventilated by Jerome McGann in *A Critique of Modern Textual Criticism.* McGann is concerned to unveil the hegemonic ideologies of editorial criticism. For him, the two crucial issues are the doctrines of "authorial autonomy" and "final intentions." McGann takes the dominant modern editorial methods to task because they suppress the actual "social formations" that collaborated in a systematic way to produce the work (that is, author, copyists, publisher's agents and editors, audience, reviewers). Rather, the dominant method for the editing of printed works, a method associated with the name of Fredson Bowers, privileges those versions of a work "closest to the author," the author's last draft or "fair copy" if such is available, over the first or other printed edition because drafts should reveal an author's "final intentions" better than a version that has been "corrupted" (especially in its "accidentals — spelling and punctuation) by publisher's agents and printinghouse styles.

McGann sees this tendency as a transference of the "Lachmannian principles" of biblical and classical editorship into the editing of modern texts. With ancient texts the problem is to bridge the gaps in a fragmentary transmission by building a stemma of interrelated recensions in order to get back as close as possible to a hypothetical common original (McGann 15–22).[31] The stemmatic model proceeds by finding common error and by "a process of subtraction" of error (McGann 15). It naturally therefore concentrates on "corruption": indeed, according to a good handbook on the editing of classical texts, the editor is a "pathologist of texts" (West 57). As a derived version of stemmatics, the Bowers method also tends to see the normal processes associated with print publication as "corruption" that deflects the autonomous author from his final intention. "In this view, the textual critic is urged to produce an edition which most nearly reflects the author's autonomously generated text, and the critical editor will seek this goal even if that text is not one which the author published or could have had published" (McGann 42).

Nevertheless, a definitive or final edition must be an idealized text, a text that always projects one stage further than the evidence that is present. That is, no single actual text, even an author's carefully corrected fair copy, is actually "the" document, the perfect one. In the case of the classical editor the original is always something lost, and in the Bowers model the text is always something one step beyond any preserved, actual text. The critic of old texts builds the stemma to reconstruct the predecessor texts that are supposed to be closer to some document that once actually existed. Stemmatic editors always posit a gap between the original and the apex of the stemma, the "archetype," which is as far back as the evidence can take one (in the case of classical Latin texts this is usually a hypothetical Carolingian minuscule manuscript, centuries later than the original).[32] The totality of the evidence for transmission, that is, all the manuscripts that make up the tradition of the work, diffused over a closed or open stemma, is the "paradosis."[33] The situation of the modern textual critic is not so different: "because this textual critic actually possesses the 'lost originals' which the classical critic is forced to hypothesize, his concept of an ideal text reveals itself to be – paradoxically – a pure abstraction . . . " (McGann 57). The critical editor of modern texts produces an entirely new text that never existed before he set to work. And he does this in the face of the plethora of textual evidence that typically confronts the editor of a modern printed work. Indeed he does it because of this superabundance of evidence, for as McGann demonstrates, the more textual evidence there is for a text the harder that text is to establish.

McGann posits a model that calls the epistemology of the virtual or ideal text into question. In this model there may be a number of author's originals none of which were prepared for publication, as is actually the case for many poems of Byron. These are the situations that test the norm, for in them, the issue of intention becomes moot, the poem never having proved its intention before an intended audience. In such cases, says McGann, we cannot speak of the author's final intentions but only of the latest manuscript state of the work:

At this point we should be able to see the theoretical importance of these texts for criticism. They are peculiarly significant because they reveal the paradox im plicit in the concept of authorial intention. In their earliest "completed" forms these texts remain more or less wholly under the author's control, yet as a class they are texts for which the editorial concept of intention has no meaning. These texts show, in other words, that the concept of authorial intention only comes into force for criticism when (paradoxically) the artist's work begins to engage with social structures and functions. The fully authoritative text is therefore always one which has been socially produced; as a result, the critical standard for what constitutes authoritativeness cannot rest with the author and his intentions alone. (75)

In other words, intention is always something transmitted. If there is no social setting, no receiver (and in a print culture that must include the publisher and its agents), there can be no transmission, hence no intention.

What becomes of the text when it has no *paradosis* and no author, that is, when we are dealing with traditional texts stemming from oral tradition that exist in unique manuscripts?

An oral written text, even when (even though) it occurs in a unique manuscript, is typically treated by a modern editor in a stemmatic way. That is, although there is only one manuscript and that manuscript must therefore be equivalent to both the archetype and the paradosis, the editor proceeds as if there were evidence for a diachronic stemma (that is, manuscripts of higher descent than the one present) and for a synchronic paradosis (that is, other extant manuscript witnesses). The stemma is represented by conjectural readings accepted into the edited text and the paradosis by the comparative display of the readings of other modern editors. With this armature the modern editor professes to present a form of the text closer to the author's original intention than that manifest in the manuscript. In other words, precisely as a result of lack of other evidence, the editor of the oral written text tends to behave like the editor of modern texts who, contemplating the variety of authorially generated material, seeks the author's intention.

Moreover, editors of "oral written texts" treat their materials as transmissions of words written rather than as words uttered. Something was written, which is a reflection, accurate or corrupt, of something written before (and before . . .), of something meant to be written. But the oral written text requires an entirely different model. Even if a particular oral written text does descend through a rather long series of written transmissions, as almost certainly the poems in the Junius Manuscript do, they do not "stem" back to something written, but to something said. The thing said, whatever it was, itself stems not from something intended by an author, but from something inherent in the oral tradition. That is, the sayer, speaker, poet does not draw primarily from an intentional meaning that takes conscious verbal form before being spoken, but from a poetic *langue* of which the particular spoken form is the *parole*. Even more than the modern text, what the performance/text "means" depends on the total context of its production. In the case of medieval texts, there is usually no information about reception except evidence that is in the manuscript itself, its "accidentals," evidence that, oddly, editors of medieval texts generally disregard.

From the standpoint of virtuality, any given "oral written text" might have existed in numberless similar versions, not connected stemmatically by means of derivation from a common original, or laterally, as corruptions of one another, but in parallel careers of transmission. The performative situations of oral tradition radiate numberless "oral texts" from a generative core. We can be sure, for example, that the unrecorded performances of *Roland* would have filled many thousands of volumes beyond Mortier's ten. Normally, performative situations never involve writing; the tradition remains alive, is remembered, changes slowly, and dies, like a star, in response to the energies of its generation and radiation. It is likely that many or most of the preserved manuscripts of Old English poems represent rare and unique performances presented to specific and unique audiences; moreover, they are likely produced by aural transmission or at least in an atmosphere where aural habits predominate over visual ones. As such, therefore, each copy of a putatively oral text ought to require a separate edition as a distinct version.[34] This is the actual editorial case, for practical reasons, with the Yugoslav epics in the Parry collection: the known conditions of their performance, which attest to the historical reality of each performative situation, prevent the search for redactions or virtual texts. Each performance is itself a text (and there are more than fifteen thousand of them in the collection!).

When a particular performance is written down by one means or another, the scribe (whether he is "the" poet or not) is an active participant in the total performative situation; what he writes in the first instance is not what he sees (though a stemmatics of seeing may grow up from a particular oral written text) but what he hears. As a critical member of the audience who is as conversant with the oral tradition as any member of a traditional oral audience, he is able to discriminate between a poet's misspeaking (that is, misenunciating, since we cannot speak of individual intentions) and true speaking, that is, the words as they conform to the rhythmic, morphological, phonetic, and semiotic demands of the system of oral poetry. Even in the case of a scribe copying already written oral written texts, he is still a functioning member of the oral audience and records what he sees as he "hears" it in terms of a traditional performance (although of course in these cases visual factors enter in). The scribe is the productive and critical component of the performative situation, the crucial part of the "social formation" that makes it possible for oral written texts to be produced in the first place. The text he writes cannot represent what the "author" intended to say, since speaking is an activity that does not reveal its intentions except in its sonic manifestations, its already-having-happenedness. The scribe can only record what was said, though he can go beyond this to "reperform" any segment of the performance as he recopies. Any conscious modifications by an oral traditional scribe will themselves be elements drawn from the tradition and will represent a reperformance, though of a new type. The scribe is our link with a performative tradition that guarantees the authenticity of the intention. We cannot speak of intention until we take the scribe into account. He is analogous to McGann's publisher's agents in the model of the printed work.

Thus emerge two salient problems in the editing of old texts commonly accepted as oral in origin: intention versus audition and the implications of this opposition for editorial praxis. Traditionally, editors of old texts take the written status of the document for granted, hence assume the relevance of authorial intention, even if they commonly regard it as irrecoverable. But if the text stems from or represents actual audited performance (record) or performance meant to be audited (score), then in some way that has yet to be worked out, the editor must respond to this auditory factor for the understanding and interpretation of the oral performance and its presentation in a permanent textualized form.

Therefore the unspoken process of editing oral written texts by analogy with methods that might apply to texts that were always written and which do have an original writer needs to be critiqued. *Oral texts do not descend*, except secondarily in written copies subsequent to the living oral tradition from which they stem (as in the essentially Latin copying tradition of Caedmon's *Hymn*). *Each oral written text is a fresh event.* In an interfacial situation, scribes writing traditional oral texts either directly from a full performance, or copying texts derived from them, rehear and reperform them as part of their writing. Therefore the communications model of decay occurring between each act of transmission which is the basis of stemmatic textual criticism does not apply with full force. This does not mean that in practice a traditional scribe writing or copying an oral text might not radically mishear or mechanically miswrite, but it does mean that *evidence of scribal change does not in and of itself constitute corruption nor does it imply a less "authorized" text.*

Therefore, theoretically (and paradoxically) the editing of an "oral written" text ought to be less problematical than the editing of an always written text. For whatever the state of the evidence for it, unlike the text that descends through a written tradition, the oral text ought to have only one layer of production, the latest, since it is a fresh event, a reperformance springing as authentically from the oral tradition as any of its congeners. The editor of the oral text should be seeking not the "virtual," "ideal," or "intended" text of one originary author, but the form of the text he has before him. The pre-text is not another text but the oral event, the performative situation itself, *and that is what he is looking at.* Every changed form of an oral text, however minor or deliberate, is not further evidence for the virtual text, as in a stemma, but another text. The proper editorial question would seem to be not "what did the author intend to write?" or even "what did the author write and by what courses did that writing assume the form it has in this text?" The proper question, it would seem, is "what did the audience (the scribe) hear on a given occasion (from his own voice or that of another) and what in the event led him to write it this way?" The oral text should be concentrating not on evidence for corruption away from a previous text, but on evidence concerning the oral event at hand, that is on *evidence of voicing within performance.* It would seem that if an editor could satisfactorily identify voicing cues in oral written texts (manuscripts), then a "translation" via a system of transcription could be worked out that would give an accurate textualizing of the oral performance in terms not only of phonemic but of phonetic features.

How this might be done is a practical question requiring the empirical scrutiny of all the extant internal and external documentary evidence within a given tradition bearing on the orality of that tradition.

IV. INTERTEXTS, ORAL-FORMULAICS, AND EDITORS

Intertextual modes of approaching and criticizing texts are a deeply literate practice. Merely to speak of "the song of Beowulf," for example, is to appeal to an intertext, that is, to refer to something already written and to hypothesize about forms unknown but assumed to have existed, in a way and to a degree that was impossible for the oral poet. Although in his narration of the return of the warriors from Grendel's mere, the singer of *Beowulf* tries to define a *sið Beowulfes,* he is incapable of making the requisite intertextual generalization literates take for granted and instead *tells a story,* a story about Sigmund the dragon slayer (*Beowulf* 869b–875). As literates we take this story as an intertextual allusion to the story of "Beowulf the dragon slayer." But the poet doesn't seem to know how to allude; he only knows how to tell a story and is forced to give a full court treatment of Sigmund's adventures because he knows that the final adventure of Beowulf is out of place in his narrative about the beginning of Beowulf's fame.

One would suppose that scholars concerned with oral poetry would modify their concepts of intertextuality, but that is not necessarily the case. When we go to the founding text of oral-formulaics, Albert B. Lord's *Singer of Tales,* we can see that, even though nobody better understands the precise workings of specific oral cultures or has done more to bring an understanding of orality to the scholarly world, the method and ideology remain intertextual rather than contextual; a scene of writing, not a performative situation, is still the fundamental background once Lord begins to talk about texts, as opposed to their ethnographic background.

In his chapter "The Formula," Lord adopts the abstract definition of "formula" propounded by his master, Milman Parry, apropos Homeric verse: a formula is "a group of words which is regularly employed under the same metrical conditions to express a given essential idea" (Parry 13). The problem is how to get from this highly abstract predication, which contains the literate concepts "word," "regularity of use," meter," "a thought separated from its thinker," to an understanding of the specific practices of unlettered Yugoslavian bards of the twentieth century who were the objects of Parry's and Lord's fieldwork.[35]

Lord begins by reminding us that formulas are not dead residue, merely things to be collected and applied to textual analysis (30). Formulas are the product of specific moments of performance and exist in the singer's head; they are "the offspring of the marriage of thought and sung verse" (Lord 31). As such they are very fluid, their mysterious origin being similar to the origin, production, and nature of all natural language. Formulas, Lord says, are not at all "so mechanical" as their schematization and categorizing would make them appear (35):

When we speak a language, our native language, we do not repeat words and phrases that we have memorized consciously, but the words and sentences emerge from habitual usage. This is true of the singer of tales working in his specialized grammar. He does not "memorize" formulas, any more than we as children "memorize" language. (36)

He goes on in the next paragraph: "If we analyze oral epic texts that are recorded from actual performance rather than texts taken from dictation and normalized to some extent, we can observe the oral poetic language in its pure state, with its irregularities and abnormalities arising from usage. Then it is clear that the style is not really so mechanical as its systematization seems to imply" (36). Suddenly, "not so mechanical" is identified with grammatical irregularities and dialectal and metrical deviation. That is, what is not mechanical are the "accidentals" of performance, performance that is associated with "irregularity" and "deviancy." What is "regular," "undeviant," but also "mechanical" are the formulas themselves as they appear in texts. But all that can be preserved, or rather, all that is preserved for study are, on the one hand, a huge collection of sound recordings in the Milman Parry Collection of Oral Literature at Harvard, and on the other, the edited texts of *Serbocroatian Heroic Songs* by Parry and Lord (and similar edited collections). In other words, we have the mass of irregular deviant raw material on one side and the texts bringing regularity, order, and mechanization on the other.

This separation becomes more evident as the chapter proceeds. Lord warns, "Were [the young singer] *merely* to learn the phrases and lines from his predecessors, acquiring thus a stock of them, which he would then shuffle about and mechanically put together in juxtaposition as inviolable, fixed units, he would, I am convinced, never become a singer" (37). Yet the processes of a scribe's composition are described less and less as the rarefied operations of natural language and more and more as the compiling and abstracting of the editor, as when Lord is meditating on how a boy learns to make a song: "There are two ways in which a [formulaic] phrase is produced; one is by remembering it, the other is through creating it by analogy with other phrases. . . . The remembered phrase may have been a formula in the other singer's songs, but it is not a formula for our singer until its regular use in his songs is established" (43). "Establishing a formula" is really the project that Lord, not any singer, is engaged in.[36] In the next pages Lord shows the formulaicity of specific (printed) texts by searching for similar or identical phrases in the songs of the same singers and matching them to lines of the text under examination. He finds it significant "that there is no line or part of a line that did not fit into some formulaic pattern" (47). This feat, however, is accomplished, not by the singer, and not by the analyst considering the psycholinguistic bases of formula production, but rather by "mechanical" concordance of phrases.

The matching of similar verses to find formulas was first applied by Parry to the texts of Homer; later Parry and Lord used the same method when studying living Yugoslavian poetry that was empirically known to be oral in order to show that it resembled Homeric poetry in the nature and pervasiveness of its formulism. The Yugoslav poetry was formulaic, as shown by the analysis of the texts it produced, and it was reasonable to show that the formulism was the means oral poets used in order to compose. Applying a similar analysis to Homeric texts, Lord and Parry assumed that a high degree of formulism implied oral composition.[37] The Homeric "proof" via formulism was then extended by Magoun and others to Old English. The analogical use of empirical evidence, on the one side beginning with contemporary ethnographic evidence, on the other beginning with written texts, deeply implicated oral-formulism in textuality, though that was the opposite of its avowed purpose. It puts the oral-formulist literally "out of the field" and into the play of intertextuality, into a use and attitude of textuality that is very close to that of traditional textualists, that is, editors.

Moving from oral-formulaic theory to the theory that governs the making of texts, we see that the editorial intertext, a product of seeing, not hearing, also appeals to a hypertextualized body of formulas, now fully represented in the case of Old English poetry by Bessinger's computer-generated concordance (1978). Such formulas are the haphazard residue of what has already been said and written down, collected, and preserved to the present day in a handful of Anglo-Saxon manuscripts produced from the eighth to the twelfth century. This body of work is the intertextual reservoir from which an editor may draw in the criticism of existing textual forms. When chirographic texts are preserved in two or more manuscripts (very rare in the case of Old English poetic texts), "variants" — genuine choices between readings — occur, at the least, wherever two extant documents present a divergence within the same slot. The editor notices difference, the deviation from what has been collected, and makes the text "prove itself" against a "more informed" judgment. But in the case of the unique text the editor finds an intertextual variant in the concordance, that is from some other slot. The editor always tends to pull an oral text in toward what has been "written" elsewhere. Thus the editing of oral texts is made to conform to the traditional practices of classical stemmatics; however, it must cut out of the picture the actual "tradition" being edited, which is the result not of a stemma but of productive language, the operations of voice, and what is meant ("the offspring of the marriage of thought and sung verse").

In the case of unique Old English manuscripts, the editors use previous editors' intertextual contributions to construct a replacement for the paradosis of stemmatically constructed texts. They rely on conjectural emendations resulting from an intertextual powwow between the editors of a given text, emendations which constitute its now textualized "tradition," and on hypervisual (i.e., paleographical) speculations, overlaid with metrical and grammatical rules, topped off by indefinable canons of "experience and taste." They search for an authorial intention which classical stemmatics does not claim to be able to reach while denigrating the scribal work which is the interface between the chirographic text and the tradition. What do other texts say in similar places? what are the technical faults of the place? what might it better mean? what have other editors done that can be surpassed? Such are the questions of the Old English editor filled with *Konjekturfreudigkeit.*[38]

Though modern editors have tended to be more conservative, i.e., resistant to emendation, than those of two generations ago, the standard text of Old Engish poetry, "The Anglo-Saxon Poetic Records" (*ASPR*), published in six volumes between 1931 and 1953, reflects, especially in the earlier volumes edited by G. P. Krapp, the older approach that allows frequent emendation on the grounds that present manuscripts, have diminished authority because of their postulated distance from (written) originals. *ASPR* further valorizes a tradition of disenabling the

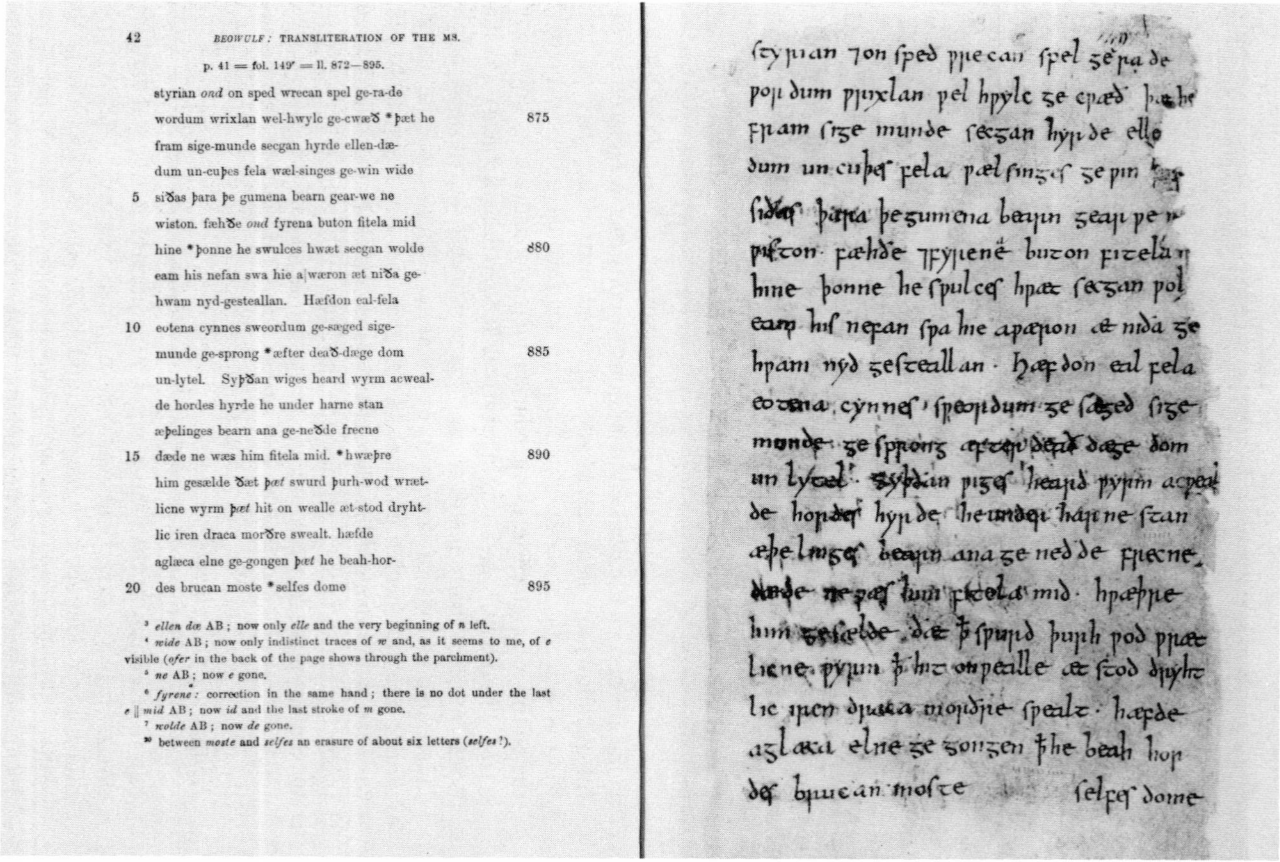

42   BEOWULF: TRANSLITERATION OF THE MS.
p. 41 = fol. 149ᵛ = ll. 872-895.

styrian ¹ond on spel wrecan spel ge·ra·do
wordum wrixlan wel·hwylc ge·cwæð *þæt he
fram sige·munde secgan hyrde ellen·da·
dum un·cuþes fela wæl·singes ge·win wide   875

siðas þara þe gumena bearn gear·we ne
wiston. fahðe ²ond fyrena buton fitela mid
hine *þonne he swulces hwæt secgan wolde
eam his nefan swa hie a|waron æt niða ge·
hwam nyd·gesteallan. Hæfdon eal·fela   880

eotena cynnes sweordum ge·sæged sige·
munde ge·sprong *æfter deaðdæge dom
un|lytel. Syððan wigs hearll wyrm acweal-
de hordes hyrde he under harne stan
æþelinges bearn ana ge·neðle frecne   885

dæde ne wæs him fitela mid. *hwæþre
him gesælde ðæt þæt swurd þurh·wod wrætlicne wyrm þæt hit on wealle æt·stod dryhtlic iren draca morðre swealt. hæfde
agleca elne go·gongen þæt he beah·hor-   890

des bruican moste *selfes dome   895

¹ ellen dæ AB; now only elle and the very beginning of n left.
² wide (æfer in the back of the page shows through the parchment).
³ ne AB; now e gone.
⁴ fyrena: correction in the same hand; there is no dot under the last
⁵ mid AB; now id and the last stroke of m gone.
⁶ wolde AB; now de gone.
¹⁰ between moste and selfes an erasure of about six letters (selfes?).

Figure 1. From Zupitza's *Beowulf*. Copyright Oxford University Press. Used by permission

swylce geong manig   of gomenwaþe
855 fram mere modge   mearum ridan,
beornas on blancum.   Ðær wæs Beowulfes
mærðo mæned;   monig oft gecwæð
þætte suð ne norð   be sæm tweonum
ofer eormengrund   oþer nænig
860 under swegles begong   selra nære
rondhæbbendra,   rices wyrðra.
Ne hie huru winedrihten   wiht ne logon,
glædne Hroðgar,   ac þæt wæs god cyning.
Hwilum heaþorofe   hleapan leton,
865 on geflit faran   fealwe mearas
ðær him foldwegas   fægere þuhton,
cystum cuðe.   Hwilum cyninges þegn,
guma gilphlæden,   gidda gemyndig,
se ðe ealfela   ealdgesegena
870 worn gemunde,   word oþer fand
soðe gebunden;   secg eft ongan
sið Beowulfes   snyttrum styrian
ond on sped wrecan   spel gerade,
wordum wrixlan.   Welhwylc gecwæð
875 þæt he fram Sigemundes   secgan hyrde
ellendædum,   uncuþes fela,
Wælsinges gewin,   wide siðas,
þara þe gumena bearn   gearwe ne wiston,
fæhðe ond fyrena,   buton Fitela mid hine,
880 þonne he swulces hwæt   secgan wolde,
eam his nefan,   swa hie a wæron
æt niða gehwam   nydgesteallan;
hæfdon ealfela   eotena cynnes
sweordum gesæged.   Sigemunde gesprong
885 æfter deaðdæge   dom unlytel,
syþðan wiges heard   wyrm acwealde,
hordes hyrde.   He under harne stan,
æþelinges bearn,   ana geneðde

867 cuðe] cuð e with r erased between ð and e   875 Sigemundes] sige munde
879 fyrena] fyrene with a written above the final e by the same hand

frecne dæde,   ne wæs him Fitela mid.
890 Hwæþre him gesælde   ðæt þæt swurd þurhwod
wrætlicne wyrm,   þæt hit on wealle ætstod,
dryhtlic iren;   draca morðre swealt.
Hæfde aglæca   elne gegongen
þæt he beahhordes   brucan moste
895 selfes dome;   sæbat gehleod,
bær on bearm scipes   beorhte frætwa,
Wælses eafera.   Wyrm hat gemealt.
Se wæs wreccena   wide mærost
ofer werþeode,   wigendra hleo,
900 ellendædum   (he þæs ær onðah),
siðða Heremodes   hild sweðrode,
eafoð ond ellen.   He mid Eotenum wearð
on feonda geweald   forð forlacen,
snude forsended.   Hine sorhwylmas
905 lemede to lange;   he his leodum wearð,
eallum æþelingum   to aldorceare;
swylce oft bemearn   ærran mælum
swiðferþes sið   snotor ceorl monig,
se þe him bealwa   to bote gelyfde,
910 þæt þæt ðeodnes bearn   geþeon scolde,
fæderæþelum onfon,   folc gehealdan,
hord ond hleoburh,   hæleþa rice,
? Scyldinga.   He þær eallum wearð,
mæg Higelaces,   manna cynne,
915 freondum gefægra;   hine fyren onwod.
Hwilum flitende   fealwe stræte
mearum mæton.   Ða wæs morgenleoht
scofen ond scynded.   Eode scealc monig
swiðhicgende   to sele þam hean
920 searowundor seon;   swylce self cyning
of bryðbure,   beahhorda weard,
tryddode tirfæst   getrume micle,
cystum gecyþed,   ond his cwen mid him
medostigge mæt   mægþa hose.

894 moste] An erasure of about six letters after this word   902 eafoð] earfoð

Figure 2. From Dobbie's *Beowulf.* Copyright Columbia University Press. Used by permission.

manuscript by printing at the end of each volume an elaborate micro-
history of each emendation, so that the whole weight of modern tradition appears against the manuscript evidence.[39] Of all scholarly editions *ASPR* is the one that most completely textualizes and decon-
textualizes the text because it reduces all poems, whatever their manuscript source or appearance, to the same clean format, removing all
nonphonemic features and replacing any manuscript rhetorical markers with modern conventional punctuation, bringing the text, now
reduced utterly to the pure phonemic string, into conformity with
modern textual expectations. The scene of orality and handwriting have
nearly disappeared.

It is thus ironic that the *ASPR* edition has become, in combination with
J. B. Bessinger's computer-generated concordance based on it, near-scripture
to workers in oral-formulaics. Although the text was produced in an atmosphere entirely unconcerned with orality (*ASPR* falls exactly between
Milman Parry's first publications working the theory out and F. P. Magoun's influential introduction of Parry's ideas to the field of Old English),
it has formed the basis of nearly all oral studies in Old English. The whole
oral-formulaic project of the past thirty years has been dealing with a body
of hypertextualized manifestations of the evidence, "clean" emended texts
and the supertext provided by Bessinger (himself a leading oral-formulist). This reified oral-formulaic textual material is thus about as far as it
could be from oral production imagined as voicings in a specific socio-
historical situation.

To produce a "clean" text like the *ASPR*, not only has an editor to resolve phonemic difficulties by resorting to the phonemic supertext but also
to strip the text of its "accidentals," that is, all those marks which are peculiar to chirographic textuality. The nature of this work is strikingly graphed
in a comparison of Zupitza's version of *Beowulf* with Dobbie's in volume
4 of *ASPR*. On every opening of Zupitza's work appears a photograph of
the manuscript and, facing it, Zupitza's transcription of what he "sees"
translated into the machine-produced deindividualized marks of modern
typography. For instance, on the lefthand side of the sample opening (Figure 1: Zupitza and Davis 42), not only do we see a blur of peculiar chirographic letter forms, no two exactly alike and many of them ambiguous
in themselves, we also see very irregular spacing between words; evidence
of hesitations and erasures; and evidence of later changes by the same
hand (not to mention incidental bleedthroughs and fire damage). Zupitza's
transcription strips out the chirographic features, not by accident, but
deliberately, changing the immediate chirographic evidence into a visual
text of a kind familiar to a modern audience. The text has been shifted
radically from one productive basis to another, totally different and unknown to the first. Those chirographic elements that have no significance

in a modern textual system are discarded altogether, even if they might have some phonic significance (e.g., evidence of fast or slow writing, hesitation, spacing). Those elements which seem to have a bearing on the phonemic string are not lost altogether, but fall to the bottom of the page, depositions against the authority of the manuscript.[40]

Looking at Dobbie's critical edition of the same portion of the text (Figure 2) we see that the processing of the original performative situation has gone much further. The line arrangement of the manuscript is gone, entirely replaced by an idealized lineation based on a modern reconstruction of metrics. The metrical signifiers, however, have only a negative valence, for they do not profess to determine a phonic performance but only operate as a check on false phonemic and morphological "readings." Even such manuscript "accidentals" as Zupitza preserved, numbered divisions within the poem, capitalization and punctuation, have disappeared from Dobbie's edition without trace, replaced by a fully modern system of paragraphing, capitalization, and punctuation. Zupitza's deposit of forms has been distilled and purified so that only those that have a clear bearing on the phonemic string remain at the bottom of the page. A glance at the notes again (see my endnote 39) would show that the interest has shifted much more to what is not there, and to alternative readings and meanings. Moreover, whatever the manuscript source, and whatever the peculiarities of a given textual situation, *ASPR* (and most modern critical editions) reduce them all to a uniform format.[41] The chirograph, an authentic residue physically linking us historically and imaginatively to a real performative situation sometime in the past, has been put as far out of sight as possible, and entirely out of ear, and its place taken by an idealized and standardized text form in a pantheon of collected virtualized texts that have all been reduced in exactly the same manner.[42]

It is therefore probably right to say that in the production of Old English editions from unique manuscripts, W. W. Greg's rule about the relation of accidentals to substantives has been reversed: that is, accidentals are systematically passed over and allowed to drop entirely from sight (and hence from discussion), or they are reinterpreted as substantives and then tenaciously maintained.[43] The synchronic system of accidentals and phonic signals that the chirograph presents is passed over, usually in silence, in favor of a modern synchrony of markings valorizing a rhetoric of silent, individualized reading. On the other hand, the elements that are taken to be of diachronic significance, that is, those which are thought to relate to and possibly descend from a virtualized stemma, that is, the phonemic string and what is taken to be the diachronic phonetic system as manifested by orthography (Greg's substantives), are taken extremely seriously, carefully preserved, commented on, and emended with a great amount of debate and scholarly display. In other words, many of those synchronic elements that the performer (conceived of here as a combinative tension of "poet and scribe") and audience would have most attended to, the sounds and the scribal rhetorical markings, are deliberately dispensed with, and those that the original performer and audience could hardly have been aware of are featured.[44] The scribe's performance is replaced by editorial conjectures that become the equivalent of the *paradosis*, lost or never-existent textual variants, while the stemma itself is made to appeal to the hypothetical earlier stages of the language itself.

Even though all this may be necessary in the case of very old texts, it produces the paradoxical result that these editors, in their concern for earlier and hypothetical stages of their text, and by failing to take principled account of their own rhetorical symbols, "accidentally" produce the alibi of a new oralization, based on private or implicit concepts of modern rhetoric.[45]

V. THE ORAL INTRATEXT

There are many mentions of song and singing in various Anglo-Saxon sources. There is only one that gives us a hint of what a performative situation actually might have *sounded* like. In the Twelfth Canon of the Council of Clofeshoh (747), priests are commanded: "ut . . . saecularium poetarum modo in ecclesia non garriant, ne tragico sono sacrorum verborum compositionem ac distinctionem corrumpant vel confundant" (that they are not to babble in church in the style of worldly poets lest their "tragic" ["histrionic"] sounds confuse the composition and articulation of the sacred words) (cited by Opland 141–42). Evidently the style of delivery of oral vernacular poetry, at least in the opinion of some eighth-century English prelates, was rushed and overly dramatic, in sharp contrast to the plainness and dignity and fully composed meaning of the Latin liturgy (itself an oral form, as we are often led to forget). Vernacular poetry seems to have given the canonist an impression of sound before sense. This is confirmed by the references to poetry within Anglo-Saxon poetry itself, where the music seems stressed over meaning. Thus, the song of the Creation in *Beowulf* is first and foremost a *sweet sound* ("swutol sang scopes," line 90) that irritates and provokes Grendel. Its "sense" — the glories of the Creation in Genesis — is in fact immediately contradicted in the text, which in a few lines tells us that the Danes (presumably that would include their poet) are hopelessly heathen and do not know the true God.

In a context where voice is so predominant over meaning, is it appropriate to speak of "oral intertexts?" At first sight it would seem that primary oral art is absolutely intertextual since it always has a relation to a preexisting body of "texts." This vast pre-text, the formulaic stock, visible to us in the Bessinger concordance, could be thought of in the Derridean sense as the grammatological writing that must precede the individualized, material, interiorized/exteriorized speech acts of the oral artist. But the relation of productive speech to this precedent material is of something generated, not something to be referred to. Rather than intertextual relations to a pre-text, we might rather conceive of an infratext, the invisible structuration that organizes any actual manifestation of speech, the prespoken, always drawn from deep structural recesses of the mind and always recursive, unified within the flow of the voice. Written intertexts appear as contradictions, "complementary homologues" (Riffaterre 143), interdictions, with a valence of alterity and figuration, whether allegoric or ironic.

The oral poet and his audience do not splinter their consciousness between texts during performance: rather all the manifestations of *parole* that come into the performance join into a single act of resonation. While to the literary observer, the always/already observed oral performance can be related back to "tradition" and hence presents a figure of foreseeability, to the oral poet and audience, the tradition exists only as a present speaking, a dynamic interchange between speaker and receiver, that "finds support in the foreseeable"[46] but is not "forespeakable" and does not reduce itself to a figure. The poet and the audience are captivated by the absolute presentness of the act that binds all previous performances to the one at hand. Written texts push back to the past, to past performances recorded in *other places*; the reader extrapolates from one textual place to another; under the pressure of reading the text seems to exfoliate. Oral performances push forward and inward, pouring the tradition into the present with a somatic gesture, urging the heroic and sententious *langue* into real experience that absorbs all other experiences at the moment of production and then is gone.

The dialectic between productive past and producing present, between tradition and poet, creates an intratext that must be understood in terms of its own wholeness and uniqueness. No two (re)statements (even if verbally identical) remain the same in the dynamic of two different performative situations.[47] The oral text, not inscribed in the voice, but borne on it, as Zumthor says, comes and goes, is never fixed and never finished. It can be resumed at any time and gives therefore an illusion of infinite repeatability but is never the same (the written text is always "the same"). The actual forms oral texts will take reflect the cultural and commemorative purpose of the concrete event actualized by the poet in a dynamic "interlocutory" relation with the audience.

At the same time, the interface between oral production and writing produces a text that is certainly subject to a different kind of reading, for in the interface the performative situation moves, as Ngal (339) puts it, from "potentiality" to "overdetermination," or in Zumthor's phrase, from "voice" to "text." The oral text is stretched out, "tortured" (pace Derrida, *Gram-*

matology 106 et passim) and what existed as the reverberation of many voices from the past in a single present one, an audible metaphor for all performances, becomes a visible palimpsest, which can further, under the scrutiny of intertextual readings, become a metonymized array of textual elements.

The oral performative situation builds on the past unconsciously, does not usurp its meaning from other texts, does not reflect on an effort of bridging time; hence the tradition is unreflexive, malleable, and productive. Conscious intertextuality binds a text to the meanings of another, brings it to a redoubled consciousness of itself. As Zumthor says, "reflection opens the doors of history," hence also of conscious intertextuality.

Archaic societies possess a greater capacity for absorbing individual contributions and blending them into more or less constraining customs[;] the enlargement of the network of communications and the diffusion of writing, coupled with the subsequent establishment of a regime assuring writing its preeminence, contribute to the weakening of people's memories and to an acceleration in the rhythms of transmission: a contradiction henceforth inscribed in the language itself and in its relation to the body. Thus we find the emergence of new social roles: the intellectual, the poet, the "author." (Zumthor, "Impossible Closure" 33)

The latter categories of textual producers respond not to the socially immediate situation in which they must perform and which will immediately receive the performance, but to a future performance, always deferred, in both its production and its reception.

Zumthor characterizes the double problematic of the oral texts:

. . . nothing authorizes us to take [medieval texts] as simple recordings of spoken words—that is to say, to jump, by metaphor and as if it were of no great consequence, from the mode of our sensory perception of it to another mode. . . .

. . . "medieval texts" present us with nothing but an empty form that is without a doubt profoundly distorted from what was, in another sensorimotor context, the whole potential of the spoken word. All questions regarding the oral quality of poetry of that period remain subordinate to this general fact. ("The Text and the Voice" 70)

Yet, in spite of Zumthor's pessimism, or because of it, it is now the responsibility of those of us trying to recapture the specific nature of oral literature to become the oral text's interlocutor, to imagine the difference that voice in performance makes, to put as much work into the imagining of voice—the informing and unifying material element of oral texts—as we habitually put into the imagining of intertextual signification. This is not an easy, perhaps not even a possible task, in the sense that we can aspire to philological exactitude or definitiveness. Real voice is always already lost, and real text remains. But it is an effort that must be tried in the face of the current recognition of the oral nature of certain large classes of medieval texts as well as in the face of new uncertainties about the nature of textuality itself. The primary impulsion toward this activity (I do not say search) will be the realization that to continue to do otherwise merely heightens the sense of the emptiness of the textual forms, their lack of "meaning" outside of intertextual constructs that seem arbitrary insofar as they are based entirely on the individual experience of each critic who tries to construct such meanings.

NOTES

1 Especially the work of Jeff Opland.
2 Foley has a tentative discussion of some of these matters in "Tradition-dependent and -independent Features in Oral Literature."
3 The concept of *mouvance*, now pervasive in the study of early French texts, has not yet penetrated the Old English scene. *Mouvance* has been defined by Paul Zumthor this way: "that character of a work which—to the extent that we can consider something to be a work before the era of the printed book—results from a quasi abstraction, insofar as those concrete texts which constitute the work's real existence present through the play of variants and reworkings something like a ceaseless vibration and a fundamental instability" (*Essai de poétique médiévale* 507).
4 On the binarism of editorial logic see Patterson (84–89).
5 "Primary orality" is the term Walter J. Ong applies to cultures "totally untouched by any knowledge of writing or print" (11). Such cultures are virtually nonexistent today and are rare in any setting we are likely to know anything about, even in medieval Europe, since to know about them attests to their already being "tainted" by some influence of writing.
6 "For the ethnologists of the present-day contextualist school, the term [tradition] refers to a scientific construction more than to a cultural product and the discourse one uses to speak of it proceeds from an ideology which functions according to categories developed in our own social sphere" (Zumthor, "Impossible Closure" 31).
7 See Zumthor ("Impossible Closure" 25), who silently alludes to Derrida's *La voix et le phénomène* (17ff.).
8 For instance, Tedlock (291) relates how a Zuni storyteller "slips out of the story" to connect an obscene detail of this story to his daughter-in-law who has just left the room and how her overheard giggle animates the rest of the audience.
9 "It is one function of formula (and the theme) to increase the semantic redundancy of the text and thus to decrease its indeterminacy, the possibilities of its interpretation. This decrease in indeterminacy, which is brought about by

the use of traditional stereotypes, lexical as well as thematic, vouchsafes the conservation of tradition in the production of the 'message' of the text and in its reception. Associated with this reduction of indeterminacy is the function of the formula in directing the participation of the audience in the performance, that is, in the production of the text, for composition and reception meet in the oral performance" (Bäuml, "Medieval Texts" 36–37).

10 The term is derived from Ong's concept of residual orality in traditional cultures, ones in which although writing is known, the forms of utterances and the processes informing thought remain largely oral.

11 Curschmann speaks of the multiple oral interference in written texts by subsequent orality, of "constant debate between competing versions . . . in either written or oral form" (74), of the symbiosis between orality and literacy in relation to texts like the *Nibelungenlied*.

12 There are occasional insignificant exceptions — medieval texts that have been preserved in early prints whose manuscript sources have perished, e.g., *Finnesburh Fragment, Battle of Maldon*, and *Rune Poem*. These texts require special treatment of the source material.

13 I follow Ong's distinction of "chirograph" from its Latin equivalent "manuscript." As used here, the former implies the activity and results of handwriting; the latter implies particular textual products.

14 I borrow the phrase from a conversation with Deborah Brandt.

15 See the notes on Chaucer's text of Boethius and his treatment of it by Ralph Hanna III and Traugott Lawler in the *Riverside Chaucer* (1003–5). Certainly Chaucer is in general more "lettered" and textual in his approach to writing than poets of earlier periods, but residual orality still plays a major part in his practice and in his fictions.

16 Jay Clayton has called to my attention Walter Benjamin's similar remarks about modern methods of reproduction that allow infinite replication and dissemination of visual art objects. But whereas, according to Benjamin, mechanically reproduced paintings, sculptures, etc., have diminished authenticity compared with the original, the authenticity (and authority) of texts is enhanced by mechanical reproduction because since the age of print texts exist apart from a particular physical matrix. Hence texts, to use Benjamin's term, have no "aura." A *manuscript*, on the other hand, has an aura because it is a unique physical object. See Benjamin, "The Work of Art in the Age of Mechanical Reproduction," especially 221–22.

17 It is true that as literacy and literate modes of thinking penetrated further and further into the European mentality, chirographs tended to become more regularized and suited to the visual needs of an autonomous, individualized reader (Parkes). Up to about the twelfth century, however, chirographic writing was much determined by what was heard, or what was pronounced by the lips of a scribe, with legibility and visual convenience being a secondary factor at best. In fine manuscripts, calligraphy as a visual design takes precedence over legibility. In vernacular manuscripts particularly, visual arrangements tend to be ad hoc, eccentric, and different from copy to copy.

18 Haymes (21–23) stresses, perhaps overstresses, the Latin, clerical atmosphere

that must have pervaded all writing, even in the vernacular, during the interfacial periods of transition from lay illiteracy to literacy in the German twelfth century.

19 Fry (292) notes this fact too, and attributes it to the memorial nature of oral poetry: many manuscripts of this type of text were not called for because their contents were normally preserved by memory and transmitted by speaking.

20 Jabbour (182–90) analyzes all the Old English poetry remaining in more than one copy. Three groups emerge: (1) short, ecclesiastical poems (translations of Latin hymns, etc.) amounting to 1,360 lines which are certainly entirely scribal in composition and transmision; (2) those texts like *Soul and Body* that must involve memorial, oral transmission; and (3) *Bede's Death Song* and Caedmon's *Hymn,* which were oral and have been appropriated by a scribal tradition. See p. 87.

21 The many different versions are brought together in the ten-volume edition by Mortier.

22 The *Praefatio* and *Versus* printed from an unknown manuscript in 1562, probably yet another lost copy of the *Heliand* (see Hannemann), tell us that Louis the Pious (d. 842) commissioned Old and New Testament poetry in the Saxon tongue. Even if this document is a later forgery (i.e., from the later ninth century), it is certainly old and shows the prevalent attitude to the "literary" text, one known primarily as writing rather than voice.

23 Rather the reverse is true; there is very little early German vernacular poetry left to us compared with the relative copiousness of Old English verse. As for the *Heliand*'s fate: two fragments were found bound into sixteenth-century printed books, one is preserved in the blank spaces of an early-ninth-century calendar, and one—the most complete copy—was made and preserved in England from the late tenth century!

24 Chickering shows how the death scene of Bede is a series of dictations of oral statements—both in English and Latin—into writing, followed by a further, more composed, rewriting.

25 University Library, Cambridge, Kk.v.16, "The Moore Bede," fol. 128b.

26 O'Keeffe, marshaling the evidence of all the Old English versions appended to the Latin text of the *Historia,* concludes: "Caedmon's *Hymn* in the *Historia ecclesiastica* became textual fairly early, that is, became a *written* poem in a relatively modern sense" (14).

27 Trinity College, Cambridge, R.5.22, fol. 32b.

28 Bibliothèque Nationale, Paris, Cod. Lat. 5237, fol. 72b.

29 "When we examine the variations in these five records of the West-Saxon version, we see . . . evidence of a fluid transmission . . . somewhere between the formula-defined process which is an oral poem and the graph-bound object which is a text. We see a reading activity reflected in these scribal variants which is formula-dependent, in that the variants observe metrical and alliterative constraints, and which is context-defined, in that the variants produced arise within a field of possibilities generated within a context of expectations. . . . Variance in an oral tradition is made inevitable by the subjectivity of the speaker (and hearer) but is constrained by impersonal meter and allitera-

tion. The writing of a poem acts as a very powerful constraint on variance, and in the face of such constraint, the presence of variance argues an equally powerful pull from the oral" O'Keeffe (15–16).

30   We are talking of the textual situations stemming from orality or near-orality; compare Havelock's speculative description of the analogous dynamic relation of poet and audience in the primary oral situation: "The minstrel recited the tradition; and the audience listened, repeated, and recalled and so absorbed it. But the minstrel recited effectively only as he re-enacted the doings and sayings of heroes and made them his own, a process which can be described in reverse as making himself 'resemble' them in endless succession. He sank his personality in his performance. His audience in turn would remember only as they entered effectively and sympathetically into what he was saying and this in turn meant that they became his servants and submitted to his spell. As they did this, they engaged also in a re-enactment of the tradition with lips, larynx, and limbs, and with the whole apparatus of the unconscious nervous system. The pattern of behaviour in artist and audience was therefore in some important respects identical. It can be described mechanically as a continual repeating of rhythmic doings. Psychologically it is an act of personal commitment, of total engagement and of emotional identification" (159–60).

31   Needless to say, Lachmann and his followers did not take seriously the orality of ancient texts, but regarded them as written from the beginning and only written. Oral versions existing "behind" or "alongside" these written texts might be brought in as explanatory factors in this or that place, but they were not considered part of the text or productive of it. The text begins only when it is written down. For example, Lachmann could posit productive "Lieder" out of which the *Nibelungenlied* was stitched, but he conceived of them as written or fixed texts of a certain type. He could also posit three "redactions" of this epic, the product of three acts of writing, all of which were somehow related to a "virtual" text. The virtual text is not an "Ur-text," an earlier, more primitive version (though such were indeed thought to have existed), but an unobtainable "perfect" version that the editor seeks out of all the extant textual variants.

32   "Since all that we know of it is ultimately derived from extant manuscripts, the original can have no characteristics not found in some at least of the extant manuscripts. The original, therefore, must be presumed to be the last version of the text produced before copying of the extant manuscripts and their ancestors began. Any number of lost versions may intervene between it and the author's original, which is forever out of our reach.

"Well known as such statements about the nature of the original may be, they are still necessary since they close the door to much speculative tampering with texts. If the author's original is out of our reach, how much further out of our reach the author's intention — what he meant to write, but did not — must be!" Hill (75–76).

33   The paradosis is "a rather imprecise but convenient term meaning 'the data furnished by the transmission, reduced to essentials'" West (53).

34   This is in fact the procedure of Mortier, the editor of *Roland*, simply because

the preserved versions are so different. It is also the way one could imagine proceeding with the many radically differing manuscripts of the *Nibelungenlied* or *Piers Plowman* (both titles covering collections of texts that, although certainly more written than oral, are radically implicated in orality because of their performative nature and susceptibility to "mouvance"). Yet the editors of both these traditions have held to the concept of "redactions," that is, written defractions of a virtual text that is unrecoverable in its unity.

35 In an interesting ethnographic chapter of *The Singer of Tales*, "Singers: Performance and Training" (17–29), Lord demonstrates how the Serbo-Croatian singers interviewed had little or no conception of "word," "line," "formula," or any other of the textual terminology that literates take for granted.

36 At times Lord embeds the aural/oral in the vocabulary of the visual/textual, as in this remarkable passage: "If a singer sings a song many times the underlinings, as in Zogić's case, will be many, but this will not be the case with a song infrequently sung. One obtains thus a photograph of the individual singer's reliance on habitual association of lines and of the degree to which habit has tended to stabilize, without fixing or petrifying, passages of varying length"(60).

37 Lutz has shown how the "oral-formulaic theory" is in reality two theories: a primary theory of observed oral performances that states that a high degree of formulism is evidence that formulism is a necessary means for oral composition; and a secondary theory of written texts that states that a high degree of formulism in a preexisting written text whose mode of composition is not observable is evidence that the work was orally composed.

38 The high point of conjectural emendation as a positive force in Old English textual criticism was reached early in this century among German editors, particularly F. Holthausen and M. Trautmann, as a result of Sievers' analysis of Old English meter which allowed confident emendation *metri causa*. Typically, Holthausen and Trautmann would find cause to emend in almost every line, and they were by no means alone. Anglo-American practice has tended to be more conservative although the most powerful statement on behalf of free emendation and the power of modern editorial tools over Old English unique texts is Sisam. For an excellent history of Old English editorial practice see Stanley.

39 Just a few examples from Dobbie's textual notes to *Beowulf (ASPR*, Vol. 4) will illustrate the point (both examples relate to places in the text provided as Figure 2):

868 gilphlæden] Not "covered with glory, renowned," as Klaeber, Mod. Phil. III, 456, translated it, but rather "laden with glorious words" (Chambers, note), "stored with glorious deeds" (Bryan, JEGPh. XIX, 85). Then *gilphlæden* is synonymous with *gidda gemyndig*. Trautmann emended unnecessarily to *gliwhlæden*.

875 Sigemundes] So Grein, Ettmüller, Wülker, Holder, Socin, and later edd., except Chambers and von Schaubert, who retain the dative *Sigemunde*. Chambers translates, "concerning Sigemund, concerning his deeds of valour." Malone, Engl Studies XV, 150, would retain *Sigemunde* and take *ellendædum* as a dative of accompaniment, "with mighty deeds." But the emendation is slight, particularly in view of the following *s-*, and gives a more probable reading.

Such ameliorative words as "the emendation is slight," "a more probable reading," "not . . . but rather" do not prevent the cumulative effect: a vast intertextual network is established that infuses the poem with voices and meanings that neither the poet nor his audience might have heard or understood. Dobbie's notes occupy more than 150 closely printed pages of intertextual commentary against a poem occupying 106 pages of loosely printed text, and of course Dobbie's notes are just the tip of the intertextual iceberg in which *our Beowulf* is preserved when the whole modern tradition of 150 years is taken into account.

40   In fact, as Kiernan has shown, Zupitza's "word-processing" has become the basis of all modern *Beowulf* texts, virtually (in all senses) replacing the manuscript itself. Editors after Zupitza conduct an argument between what Zupitza "saw" and what they "see" using the photo as their arbitrator.

41   The first five volumes of *ASPR* are each editions of the poems in a single manuscript. A uniform format seems therefore "natural." But the assumption is deconstructed by the nature of Volume 6, the "Minor Poems," the texts of which stem from many different manuscripts. The editor, E. V. K. Dobbie, tries to preserve the uniformity of his format, which he inherited from the beginner of the series, G. P. Krapp, and with which he was by no means happy (*ASPR* 4: v–vi) by, e.g., ignoring the prose context of the poems of the *Anglo-Saxon Chronicle;* yet when he edits the so-called Metrical Charms, he is forced to include prose passages that are embedded in the "poetic" part of the text.

42   But see Gollancz and Mackie's Exeter Book, Lumby's edition of CCC 201 poems, and my own edition of *Genesis A* for attempts to give some impression within the confines of a printed edition of what the manuscript looks like.

43   "Since, then, it is only on grounds of expediency, and in consequence either of philological ignorance or of linguistic circumstances, that we select a particular original as our copy-text, I suggest that it is only in the matter of accidentals that we are bound (within reason) to follow it, and that in respect of substantive readings we have exactly the same liberty (obligation) of choice as has a classical editor, or as we should have were it a modernized text that we were preparing" (Greg 22).

44   One of the greatest of modern conservative editors established the following "rule": "Where there is reason to think that the spelling or the dialectical form has been tampered with, I do not try to restore the original, such a task being at once too uncertain and too far-reaching. But where there is reason to think that the scribe has departed from the wording and grammatical construction of his original, and that this can be restored with tolerable certainty, I do so" (Chambers xxvi).

45   For example, the rhetoric of the day produced late-nineteenth-century German editions that were very heavily punctuated in a manner that attempted to produce an artificial sense of hypotaxis, while more modern — and particularly Anglo-American — editions tend to favor relatively light punctuation and parataxis. Both can't be right in relation to virtuality.

46 "As a traditional and external fact, the oral text is foreseeable; as a literary fact (poetic, individual experience, etc.), the produced oral text has an internal finality that finds support in the foreseeable" (Ngal 337).

47 As Ngal (336–39) puts it from his Derridean perspective: "The great natural events such as birth, initiation, marriage, death, mourning, by the intimate reverberations that they cause, often given rise to rereadings of oral archaic texts (proverbs, fixed expressions, maxims, prayers, etc.) that one would be wrong to consider as simple literal retellings, as simple repetitions of the commentary. It is really a matter of actualizations that re-create, that are something other than a simple reproduction. Rereading is therefore production in the strongest sense of the term, ie., production of new knowledge."

WORKS CITED

Bäuml, Franz H. "Medieval Texts and the Two Theories of Oral-Formulaic Composition: A Proposal for a Third Theory." *New Literary History* 16 (1984): 31–39.

Benjamin, Walter. "The Work of Art in the Age of Mechanical Reproduction." In *Illuminations: Essays and Reflections*, ed. Hannah Arendt, trans. Harry Zohn, 217–51. New York: Schocken, 1985.

Bessinger, J. B., Jr., et al. *A Concordance to the Anglo-Saxon Poetic Records.* Ithaca: Cornell UP, 1978.

Biebuyck, Daniel, and Kahombo C. Mateene, ed. and trans. *The Mwindo Epic.* Berkeley and Los Angeles: U of California P, 1969.

Cassidy, Frederic G., and Richard N. Ringler. *Bright's Old English Grammar and Reader.* 3d ed. New York: Holt, Rinehart, and Winston, 1971.

Chambers, R. W. *Beowulf with the Finnsburg Fragment.* Cambridge: Cambridge UP, 1914.

Chaucer, Geoffrey. *The Riverside Chaucer.* 3d ed. Ed. Larry D. Benson. Boston: Houghton Mifflin, 1987.

Chickering, Howell D. "Some Contexts for Bede's *Death Song.*" *PMLA* 91 (1976): 91–100.

Clanchy, M. T. *From Memory to Written Record: England 1066–1307.* London: Edward Arnold, 1979.

Curschmann, Michael. "The Concept of the Oral Formula as an Impediment to Our Understanding of Medieval Oral Poetry." *Medievalia & Humanistica* 8 (1977): 63–76.

Derrida, Jacques. *Of Grammatology.* Trans. Gayatri Chakravorty Spivak. Baltimore and London: Johns Hopkins UP, 1976.

Derrida, Jacques. *La voix et le phénomène.* Paris: Presses universitaires de France, 1967.

Doane, A. N. *Genesis A: A New Edition.* Madison and London: U of Wisconsin P, 1978.

Foley, John Miles. "*Beowulf* and Traditional Narrative Song: The Potential and Limits of Comparison." *Old English Literature in Context: Ten Essays*, ed. John D. Niles, 117–36. Woodbridge, Suffolk: D. S. Brewer, 1980.

Foley, John Miles. *Oral-Formulaic Theory and Research: An Introduction and Annotated Bibliography.* New York and London: Garland, 1985.

Foley, John Miles. "Tradition-dependent and -independent Features in Oral Literature: A Comparative View of the Formula." In *Oral Traditional Literature: A Festschrift for Albert Bates Lord*, ed. Foley, 262–81. Columbus: Slavica, 1981.

Fry, Donald K. "The Memory of Caedmon." In *Oral Traditional Literature: A Festschrift for Albert Bates Lord*, ed. J. M. Foley, 282–93. Columbus: Slavica, 1981.

Gollancz, Sir Israel, and William S. Mackie. *The Exeter Book.* 2 vols. Early English Text Society, o.s. 104, 194. London: Paul, Trench, and Truebner, 1895; Oxford: Oxford UP, 1934.

Goodwin, Charles. *Conversational Organization: Interaction between Speakers and Hearers.* New York: Academic, 1981.

Goody, Jack. *The Interface between the Written and the Oral.* Cambridge: Cambridge UP, 1987.

Greg, W. W. "The Rationale of the Copy-Text." *Studies in Bibliography* 3 (1950): 19–36.

Hannemann, Kurt. "Die Lösung des Rätsels der Herkunft der Heliandpraefatio." In *Der Heliand*, ed. Jürgen Eichhoff and Irmengard Rauch, 1–13. Wege der Forschung 321. Darmstadt: Wissenschaftliche Buchgesellschaft, 1973.

Havelock, Eric. *Preface to Plato* Cambridge: Belknap, 1963.

Haymes, Edward R. *The Nibelungenlied: History and Interpretation.* Urbana: U of Illinois P, 1986.

Hill, Archibald A. "Some Postulates for Distributional Study of Texts." *Studies in Bibliography* 3 (1950): 63–95.

Jabbour, Alan. "Memorial Transmission in Old English Poetry." *Chaucer Review* 3 (1967): 174–90.

Jakobson, Roman, and Petr Bogatyrev. "On the Boundary between Studies of Folklore and Literature." In *Readings in Russian Poetics: Formalist and Structuralist Views*, ed. Ladislaw Matejka and Krystyna Pomorska, 91–93. Cambridge and London: MIT Press, 1971.

Kiernan, Kevin. *Beowulf and the Beowulf Manuscript.* New Brunswick: Rutgers UP, 1981.

Krapp, George Philip, and Elliott Van Kirk Dobbie. *The Anglo-Saxon Poetic Records.* 6 vols. New York: Columbia UP, 1931–53.

Lord, Albert B. *The Singer of Tales.* New York: Atheneum, 1965.

Lumby, J. R. *Be domes daege, De die judicii, an Old English Version of the Latin Poem ascribed to Bede; Edited (with other short poems) from the Unique Manuscript in the Library of Corpus Christi College, Cambridge.* Early English Text Society, o.s. 65. London: Truebner, 1876.

Lutz, Hans Dieter. "Zur Formelhaftigkeit mittelhochdeutscher Texte und zur 'theory of oral-formulaic composition.'" *Deutsche Vierteljahrsschrift für Literaturwissenschaft und Geistesgeschichte* 48 (1974): 432–47.

McGann, Jerome J. *A Critique of Modern Textual Criticism.* Chicago: U of Chicago P, 1983.

Magoun, Francis P. "The Oral-Formulaic Character of Anglo-Saxon Narrative Poetry." *Speculum* 28 (1953): 446–67.

Mortier, Raoul. *Les Textes de la Chanson de Roland.* 10 vols. Paris: La Geste Francor, 1940–44.

Ngal, M. a M. "Literary Creation in Oral Civilizations." *New Literary History* 8 (1976–77): 335–43.

O'Keeffe, Katherine O'Brien. "Orality and the Developing Text of Caedmon's *Hymn.*" *Speculum* 62 (1987): 1–20.

Ong, Walter J. *Orality and Literacy: The Technologizing of the Word.* New York: Methuen, 1982.

Opland, Jeff. *Anglo-Saxon Oral Poetry: A Study of the Traditions.* New Haven: Yale UP, 1980.

Parkes, M. B. "The Influence of the Concepts of *Ordinatio* and *Compilatio* on the Development of the Book." In *Medieval Learning and Literature; Essays Presented to Richard William Hunt,* ed. J. J. G. Alexander and M. T. Gibson, 115–41. Oxford: Oxford UP, 1976.

Parry, Milman. *The Making of Homeric Verse: The Collected Writings of Milman Parry.* Ed. Adam Parry. Oxford: Oxford UP, 1971.

Patterson, Lee. "The Logic of Textual Criticism and the Way of Genius: The Kane-Donaldson *Piers Plowman* in Historical Perspective." In *Negotiating the Past: The Historical Understanding of Medieval Literature* 77–114. Madison and London: U of Wisconsin P, 1987.

Riffaterre, Michael. "Intertextual Representation: On Mimesis as Interpretive Discourse." *Critical Inquiry* 11 (1984): 141–62.

Sisam, Kenneth. "Notes on Old English Poetry: The Authority of Old English Poetical Manuscripts." *Review of English Studies* 22 (1946): 257–68.

Stanley, E. G. "Unideal Principles of Editing Old English Verse." *Proceedings of the British Academy* 70 (1984): 231–73.

Stock, Brian. *The Implications of Literacy: Written Language and Models of Interpretation in the Eleventh and Twelfth Centuries.* Princeton: Princeton UP, 1983.

Tedlock, Dennis. *The Spoken Word and the Work of Interpretation.* Philadelphia: U of Pennsylvania P, 1983.

Vance, Eugene. "Roland and the Poetics of Memory." *Textual Strategies: Perspectives in Post-Structuralist Criticism,* ed. Josué V. Harari, 374–403. Ithaca: Cornell UP, 1979.

West, Martin L. *Textual Criticism and Editorial Technique Applicable to Greek and Latin Texts.* Stuttgart: Teubner, 1973.

Zumthor, Paul. *Essai de poétique médiévale.* Paris: Editions du Seuil, 1972.

Zumthor, Paul. "The Impossible Closure of the Oral Text." *Yale French Studies* 67 (1984): 25–42.

Zumthor, Paul. "The Text and the Voice." *New Literary History* 16 (1984): 67–92.

Zupitza, Julius, and Norman Davis. *Beowulf: Reproduced in Facsimile from the Unique Manuscript, British Museum MS. Cotton Vitellius A. xv.* 2d ed. Early English Text Society 245 [orig. ed., o.s. 77, 1882]. London: Oxford UP, 1959.

CHAPTER 5

Diversity and Change
in Literary Histories

ERIC ROTHSTEIN

Michel Foucault: "Develop . . . thought . . . by proliferation, juxtaposition, and disjunction, and not by subdivision and pyramidal hierarchization. . . . Prefer what is positive and multiple: difference over uniformity, flows over unities, mobile arrangements over systems. Believe that what is productive is not sedentary but nomadic."

Foucault's maxims come from his preface launching Deleuze and Guattari's *Anti-Oedipus*, and, through posthumous citation in a translator's preface, also launching Deleuze's launching of Foucault, *Foucault* (xlii). Influence? Intertextuality? In any case, an example of continuity both inside and outside what Foucault says, that continuity is a case of diversity and change. The discourse that Foucault thinks unproductive, one of uniform and systematic hierarchies, divides the continuous from the discontinuous. It is made up of fixities: people and texts that are largely autonomous, categories, isms, cunning Hegelian abstractions. In short, it is a world of expressive agents; call its operating principle Influence. Most of us studying literary history inherited such a world. Students still receive its (brumma)gems as their intellectual bequest.

In opposition, writers like Foucault turned to the world of structures; call its operating principle Intertextuality. As "the first completely positivist historian," in the celebratory words of his colleague at the Collège de France, Paul Veyne (204; see Foucault, *Archaeology* 125, 234), Foucault discarded causal explanations and entities. Agents, such as Descartes, Cuvier, and Bentham, became only their roles; and pseudo-agents, like the Zeitgeist or Society, disappeared. Having thus approximated what he took to be truth, he then had to replace the banished criteria of meaning. To accomplish this as a positivist, Foucault insisted in the early *The Order of Things* on an equivalent to a "covering law," a general rule in accord with which one can explain specifics as instances. The episteme, historical and systemic, served him as that rule, through which to spy a succession of "discursive formations" in a societal continuum. It is the Same to which the seemingly different discourses of an "age" can be referred, thus shifting the metaphysical burden of totality from the authoritarian reign of a Zeitgeist or "Age of" or "ism" to the pervasive bureaucracy of a *langue*.

Such a scheme, unfortunately, can accommodate neither change nor diversity. The interface between covering laws, the change from one episteme to another, remains inexplicable. One can see only morphë and metamorphosis, "as if," in Foucault's words, "time existed only in the vacant moment of rupture, in that white, paradoxically atemporal crack in which one sudden formulation replaces another" (*Archaeology* 166). As a system, moreover, the episteme is still more absolute than the Zeitgeist and its kin that commanded the universe during the nineteenth century. Even with a loosening of this method (see *Archaeology* 173-77), the early Foucault could not, besides, address the moral issues that are naughty for positivists to address at all, but that progressively gripped him. Some respect for the agent as moral focus underlies *Discipline and Punish* — and the hortatory tone of the quotation with which I began — and blossoms for the Foucault who declared in the early eighties that "a system of constraint becomes truly intolerable when the individuals who are affected by it don't have the means of modifying it" (*Politics* 294). Here diversity and change reappear along with the empowerable agents whom Foucault's moral convictions required. "Modifying" supposes purposive action, therefore causal relationships such as Foucault had once slighted; and suddenly his practice of criticism breaks from the earlier limits, limits that no one would accept in waging other affairs of life, such as buying a car, engaging in politics, or reading a novel.

Drawing on the lessons of recent theory, I shall try to systematize a pragmatic literary historiography, allying myself with those scholars and critics who have returned to the study of historical agents: people and texts. While it emphasizes the social, intersubjective nature of acts, such a historiography does not assimilate purpose and action ("Influence") to behavioral events and systemic interplay ("Intertextuality"). It assumes that we need to be able to "say significantly that a thing doesn't simply happen to us, but that we *do* it" (Wittgenstein, *Philosophical* sec. 159). What I hope to sketch from these beginnings is a literary-historical theory that can accommodate practices broadly shared within the discipline. Literary historians who share it share a framework for setting forth different positions. With this in mind, I have been eager to attend to the needs of those who have positions to advocate and those who pursue immediately disinterested, intellectual ends in accord with applying the evidentiary logic of "history." Recent critical theory has shown how dyed with interest the disinterested is likely to be, and has thereby implicitly emphasized the need for a theory that accommodates both groups. For those who subscribe to the schema of change I shall offer, such a theory has the greatest likelihood of representing a path to change.

Still, I do not offer the sketch because I wish (let alone hope) to convert everyone's practice. If one's theory ought to do what one wants it to do, a theory with the bias of mine will discontent behaviorists, Platonists, those who would discard linear discourse, polemicists making their points through hyperbole and deliberate outrage, practitioners of corrective guerrilla warfare through stressing the -graphy in "historiography," writing as a means of doing and undoing, and, no doubt, many others. Some of them have causes that I applaud. Their practices and theories may well have greater likelihoods than mine of changing the social environment to which literary historians must adapt. I offer my sketch, then, not to convert but to encourage them: I believe that for diverse practices to thrive, they need to be situated as to what they can and cannot do, they need to be understood in broadly shared terms, and they need to have their assumptions made explicit. The more broadly shared, "communicatively rational" practices, as Habermas calls them, also need to have the best case made for them, to have on show what they can do within a mode of explanation that promotes diversity of interests and saps imperial consensus.

I. INDIVIDUALS

I have several reasons, practical rather than ontological, for framing my hypothesis in terms of agents, of people and texts.

Anthony Giddens: "The constitution of agents and structures [is] not two independently given sets of phenomena, a dualism, but represent a duality." (25)

1. Because we talk about all sorts of social interactions with reference to agents, I suggest, we can use agent-terms to explain any social phenomena. Even for large-scale phenomena, agents may be seen as acting out structure intertextually. Given this flexibility of choice, I would continue to use them as the (re)identifiable counters, persisting through time, that any kind of history needs. For literary history these counters have been people and texts, which can be discriminated from one another in a matrix of time and space better than structures can. They have more visibility and immanence than other possible entities. They are also familiar from everyday use, so that to employ them is to couch one's conceptual work in terms very much like those of one's family, business, and social life.

Ease of use gives these terms, as one would expect, a high degree of operative definition that lets them serve well in many "language games."

Mikhail Bakhtin: "Everything that pertains to me enters my consciousness, beginning with my name, from the external world through the mouths of others . . . , with their intonation, in their emotional and value-assigning tonality." (138)

2. It follows that both people and texts are at least in principle usefully open to analysis as social constructs. As older historians allowed and newer ones have usefully trumpeted, authors and readers are culturally produced producers of texts, sharing a common pool of desires, beliefs, and practices, as well as having the power of agency. In and beyond the level of ethographical variation, of heredity and instinct, people are people-produced through the human practices and values that they encounter. Such an environment determines, even overdetermines, what someone will do, how a text will be understood. It also underdetermines these things, of course, since as a natural entity, a person does have heredity, a text does have constraints of transmission. To understand the specifics of diversity and change, one needs to understand how these forces from outside the social environment enter it and become objectified within it, helping resolve people's emotional and value-assigning tonalities into this form rather than that or that.

Equally important for a discussion of change is that the environment always underdetermines actions, as opposed to behavior. As entities defined in part by their tendency to act in certain ways, people and texts have an indeterminacy capable of making and shaping the new. The process of social life makes each person act as an "independent and creative initiator of fundamentally unpredictable actions" in the process of change, as Habermas says (in discussing G. H. Mead). So with diversity. "The very structure of linguistic intersubjectivity forces the actor"—that is, each of us in social life—"to be *himself* even in norm-conformative behavior" (2:100, 59). Therefore agents are the locale of the new. Not only are their acts unpredictable from the generative structures that make them possible and meaningful, including introspective claims about intention, but these acts are retrodictable (seen in hindsight as necessary) only up to the level of plausibility, verisimilitude. An explanation of why a physical object did what it did depends on causal fact, but an explanation of why someone did what she or he did depends on likely strategies involving ends, means, and values. No wonder intertextual theorists, craving the forbidden principle of agency, sneak back a notion of strategic action at some level in the psyche. As many versions of intertext translate influence into an impersonal register, so these displaced versions of strategy impersonalize action into strategic behavior: Freudianisms, the demands of the body, the workings of an ideology that now leads to conscious craftiness and now to involuntary, un- or semi-witting possession, as by an invasion of body snatchers who are always already there.

Although people are "programmed" by the Other, then, one cannot even statistically predict what will emerge from a complex social system by summing up what goes into it. The variables, "parts" in the system, are too many, indeterminate, and diverse, including values, logics, procedures, and weighing of contingencies as well as things. At the nonstatistical level, a reader produces new meanings despite being a product of social norms. How, after all, is a given person "programmed"? Here are some ways: he or she receives genetic dispositions, receives facts and judgments, receives general procedures with which to handle information, receives goals to aim for as best he or she can, receives values (for example, logic, prudence, moral values, consideration for others, ego boosting) that prescribe paths to follow. "Programming" implies something unified, but in this mare's nest of formal, efficient, final, and material causes, an unhabitual situation is bound to lay many puzzles, contradictions, questions of proportion and decorum. A real person, unlike a machine, will then address these problems with unpredictably selective, distorted recall, riddled by crosstalk.

Paradoxically, then, to conform in simple societies may lead to conformity but to conform in complex societies — that is, to make relational sense of a medley of inherited dispositions, rules, goals, and injunctions — drives one toward the reorderings and transformations that we call creativity, an isthmus between reductiveness and confusion. I think it a mistake to treat more complex societies as byzantine versions of "traditionalistic" communities, which have single theoretical frameworks that contain their diversity (Horton 222–24), very much like Kuhnian paradigms or Foucauldian epistemes. Besides, because programming in Western societies is multiple, the most useful ideology for them is to insist on choice and freedom. Even as an illusion, social approval of these ideals boosts their exercise, and not necessarily in an illusionary, trivial, or bounded way. Finally, I should say, one can more easily "imagine" new wholes and "as if" situations through thought experiments when the means of encountering experience, the means of decoding, are flexible and various. The greater the interpretative demands of a society, the more incentive to offer a variety of social examples and a maximum of social leeway, thereby radically attenuating the unitary force of "programmed." The reader in modern America or Europe can be, and I would say *is* and *must be*, a conscious, competent, and responsible agent of meaning production, while at the same time the product of social norms. And this "modern" goes far back in time, I won't speculate how far.

Maurice Merleau-Ponty: "Properly human acts—the act of speech, of work, the act of clothing oneself, for example—have no significance in their own right. They are understood in reference to the aims of life." (163)

3. The terms of agency—people and texts—have great practical advantages for literary history, including precision, an explanatory scope equal to that of any other terms, and a special aptitude for the study of diversity and change. As Merleau-Ponty indicates, they have other virtues as well. The focus on people as readers and writers recognizes that literary histories serve other people, their readers. This class of reader, maybe unlike Houyhnhnms or angels, is anthropocentric. That is why Merleau-Ponty here does not need Derridean reins to slow the old gray nag of absolute illusion. Derrida's critique—"I don't destroy the subject, I situate it" (271)—does not apply, I think, to a judgment deriving from our existential sense of ourselves, of our selves, as acting subjects. For such judgments, Derrida's own principle deconstructs, or turns itself inside out, in that any subject—the "I" to whom Derrida refers in his sentence, for example—acts as a reference point for cognizing states of affairs. One can situate a subject only by bracketing the very function it so indispensably serves, which is the function of situating the world and, in it and out of it, a self. Why perform the Derridean bracketing maneuver and not its reverse? Surely the subject has as much claim to situate the world as the world has to situate the subject, for though the definition of selves is mostly an artifact of our culture, the fact of selves (subjects who act) is not: all animals behave quite elaborately on the basis, it seems, of their clear, natural distinctions between themselves and an environment that may supply or threaten them. Among us rational bipeds the self seems to be a universal postulate, as Mauss notes previous to his historicizing of "self": "In no way do I maintain that there has ever been a tribe, a language, in which the term 'I,' 'me' . . . has never existed, or that it has not expressed something clearly represented. . . . there has never existed a human being who has not been aware, not only of his body, but also at the same time of his individuality, both spiritual and physical" (2–3).

Logic falters in legitimating a hierarchy in which the perspective of the I is devalued in favor of another, the me. Even if one grants for the sake of argument that the I is legible only in terms of the me, that the subject is constituted through its capacity to be an object, the (compromised) perspective of the I continues to differ radically from the impersonal of the me. For example, a historical description in personal terms can refer to a sense of purpose, Merleau-Ponty's "aims of life," while no nonanthropomorphic historical description can; and we people are inclined to make purpose a central idea in our notions of causation. Understanding at this existential level does not demand a total image of the self. Nor does it demand a sharp line between semiotic competency and other kinds. It calls for a grasp of certain dispositions and capacities within which the self can act, as my dog Tony knows how far he can jump and how another spaniel he meets is likely to act. As "can act" implies, the I represents the uncertainty that choice entails.

From this perspective, let me repeat, the self is not being reified, as some intertextualists would charge, but is rather the ground for the phenomena to be explained, action and thought. "Giving grounds . . . comes to an end; — but the end is not certain propositions' striking us immediately as true, i.e.[,] it is not a kind of *seeing* on our part; it is our *acting*. . . . If the true is what is grounded, then the ground is not *true*, nor yet false." After all, "Somewhere we must be finished with justification, and then there remains the proposition that *this* is how we calculate" (Wittgenstein, *On Certainty* 204–5, 212).[1] So needful is the axiom of the self that to interrogate it is in some ways to reinforce its power: I suspect that the more we accept lessons about our ignorance of ourselves — that is, our ids, our blindly firing neurons, our unremembered traumas, and our indoctrinations — the more willing we are to accept as "natural" the areas of ignorance in the strategic-action model. When in doubt here, we opt for more belief by faith, not more skepticism. As an alternative or complement to poststructuralist critiques, then, the constitutive fact of the existential "I" guarantees that persons (that is, individual people) are objects needed by literary history. And where "I" is, there "me" will also be.

Jürgen Habermas: "[In aesthetic judgments,] grounds or reasons serve to guide perception and to make the authenticity of a work so evident that this aesthetic experience can itself become a rational motive for accepting the corresponding standards of value." (1:20)

4. The model of 3 accommodates a form of explanations by influence: to be influenced here is for an agent to be alert, always strategically, sometimes consciously, to certain select elements from the intertext of her or his personal experience. In this sense, no text is influenced, only authors. The inverse is that authors qua authors influence others only through texts; texts influence people. Their version of agency is value. In literary history, a text or its parts act insofar as they have value, centrally but not exclusively value in terms of aesthetic judgment. Literary texts often fail to act because they fail cognitive or moral tests at some historical moment, but such tests have usually been less exacting, hence less discriminating, than the aesthetic ones applied at those same moments. Habermas' criterion suggests why: though many novels, plays, and poems at a given time share cognitive and moral values, few achieve that inner sense of the Real, of the valid-upon-perception, that I take evident "authenticity" to signal.[2]

If aesthetic value depends upon an appeal to the "authenticity of a work," one is committed either to include those works, individual texts, as historical objects or to write literary history that slights aesthetic value. But such value is the main reason why one wants to read literary works or, presumably, to read about them, and the main reason why people have read them in the past. Their cultural significance makes so little sense without terms of value (as well as vice versa) that one can hardly talk of matters other than value, such as the process of literary production, without understanding aesthetic issues in the same depth as one understands their ethical or cognitive counterparts. For another reason, moreover, literary history especially seems to need texts as individuals. Because they appear in literary history as "monuments," not simply as "documents," texts provide—and historically have provided—the arenas within which people can discern the patterns and ambivalences in "the play of the signifier," such as, in accord with many current notions of "literariness," distinguishes a specifically literary emphasis within a reading practice. For this reason, one cannot, without reducing explanatory range, merely dissolve such texts into a lumpy potage of textuality. In that the qualitative distinctions made between texts, aesthetic and intentional, underlie their effect on the production and reception of other texts, moreover, these distinctions, I think, are needed to relate textual production and reception.

The distinctions in my 3 and 4, of course, do not allow one to collapse the categories "person" and "text" by treating persons as texts. Some writers give a new twist to automation by having manufactured entities ("texts") take over the jobs of humans on the grounds that humans too are manufactured. Textualizing persons was once desirable as a way to invert and mock the anthropomorphizing (or fetishizing) of texts. Now that it no longer shocks, however, I think the time has come to acknowledge its inadequacy. For one thing, this textualizing sets up an unwarranted hierarchy in which one set of social practices, those grounded (or groundable) in an existential sense of self—what I tried to evoke with Merleau-Ponty and my dog Tony—get slighted in favor of another set, those grounded in social conditioning, the technology of "nurture," as that term used to be opposed to "nature" in psychologists' debates. To take people as a basic type has a philosophical claim equal to that of taking texts or textuality as a basic type. Furthermore, to treat persons as texts or intertextual nodes is also to conflate behavior with action. As I shall argue, to do so creates trouble in explaining emergence, how the unpredicted and unpredictable new comes out of the old. Within the system of textuality, then, human agency plays a crucial role. Finally, treating people as texts is not even economical. Persons are too complex to specify intertextually, so that to treat them as persons is more economical than any alternative. As Jeremy

Campbell writes, "A complete description of a simple automaton, von Neumann said, would be simpler than the automaton itself. A complete description of a very complicated automaton, on the other hand, would be more complicated than the automaton. In fact, the automaton would be its own simplest description" (257). For these reasons, an economical, satisfying historical scheme should include both persons and texts.

II. INFORMATION

What does one need so as to conceive the process of change? First, one needs a plausible way of envisioning how novelty, hence change, can take place through actors — texts or people — who are largely creatures of their society; second, a rationale for such agents to produce novel works and ideas; and third, a regulating principle to pattern the changes. People act or behave within an elastic, open repertoire of social practices. From this standpoint, I shall argue, one can envision how the new comes into being through the activity of information processing, at a level of freedom that allows choice among given alternatives and, for people, an additional power to create nongiven resolutions. Information theory lets one discuss the likelihood of change but not the nature of that change, which is agent-centered, nor can it describe change in terms of an existential perspective. Therefore, to talk about the nature of change and its personal production, I would like to borrow the two notions of *schema-and-correction* and of *satisficing*, and to use a third, that of *habitus*, for joining the self and its environment. I will argue that the rationale for change exists in the very fact of social heterogeneity, so that novelty spawns more novelty, as well as in the force of a consumer system that demands new products (including ideas) and new mastery over the resources of the world (see Lyotard 45–53). Here the new may be the recycled or the trivially new, as with "new" detergents, but even that kind of novelty encourages as well as substitutes for the really new. In no way except in short-term Darwinian survival value, of course, need change be for the better.

In borrowing these notions I suppose that pattern derives, first, from the social context in which the new products are uttered, and second, from being produced and interpreted by people with limited capacities, time, articulation of desire, and expectations. By refusing to acknowledge these contexts of practice, much theorizing falls prey to "a certain philosophical disease," in which one tries to show the invalidity of a procedure by overextending its principles, "to continue talking where one should stop." A deconstruction can always be induced if one "keeps on extending concepts past the points where they continue to make sense" (Wheeler 244–45; Wittgenstein, *Remarks* 2: sec. 402). But someone who brackets the conditions of the concepts' actual employment gains only the right to attack idealist versions of them, which are never worth defending.

Warren Weaver: In information theory "the word information relates not so much to what you *do* say, as to what you *could* say. That is, information is a measure of your freedom of choice." (17)

At a system level, therefore, information is a measure of the probability of novelty and change. At the level of the agent's possibilities, what Weaver calls "your freedom of choice," appears something that we laypeople call information, which combines novelty with meaning. New data come in but are accompanied by or infused with old, familiar data, material already known and assimilated into patterns of meaning. In information theory, the data anchored in previous knowledge are called "redundant" because one already knows them, though they are crucial for making sense of those perceived as new. Messages perceived as entirely new are gibberish; messages entirely redundant are boring; the proper mix of novelty and redundancy provides learning. Thus one grasps sequences of English words through knowing that some orderings are more likely than others and some so unlikely (that is, so new and strange) that they do not carry meaning at all until one recuperates them with techniques developed for modern poetry or decoding spy messages. One learns these rules by experience, repetition of prior patterns. Because it has been assimilated into patterns, redundant information establishes rule-based constraints that operate at the level of probability.

For the utterances that make up texts, sources of redundancy and meaning include the contractual structures of everyday life, how by implied consent people speak to each other. These contractual structures comprise speech acts (cf. the remarks in the Introduction to this volume about Jonathan Culler's treatment of presuppositions as meaning constraints), genres, and — a very important area of redundancy — inferences about influence and intentionality. The range of interpretative options left when the constraints have been recognized provides the possibility of novelty, of reordering, recombining, reimagining, adding, and synthesizing. Material previously otherwise understood is integrated anew so as to build on past meaning (that is to say, on meaning) and to create new meaning. While information theory has to do with cognitive learning, I believe that the same principles apply to ethical and aesthetic learning. The reinforcing, the comfortable, the phatic, the tried and true — these are needed redundancies that make change possible. Their capacity to bore people is measured by the degree to which change actually occurs, but any society that has a cultural history must have changed, so that redundancy must have palled some of the time.

From the Saussurean principle that *parole*, not *langue*, initiates change, one can infer that theories of neither influence nor intertextuality can explain change if they look backward to system, to the codified up-till-now which is the lair of redundancy. (That is one of the things wrong with isms, which are *langues*.) Similarly with a given message, containing information: in system-bound theories, the area of freedom and options can appear only as that of indeterminacy. If one sets aside the system-bound theories in favor of agent-based ones, however, the pattern is different: through making do (what Herbert Simon calls "satisficing") or turning a blind eye to certain textual options, readers always disambiguate, though some of the time with more assurance than at another, just as when choosing new shoes, say. The textual meaning may always be deferred, but in practice meaning is always "presencing" itself (let us enheidegger it as *Dasinn*). In reading, ambiguity itself, indeterminacy itself, is a disambiguation which readers choose, when they do, as a specific aesthetic or philosophical option preferable for its "richness" or titillatingly "disturbing" quality or superior "realism." The choice is quite determinate though the possibility of choosing it nowadays is socially provided as an option — surely not, in most nonacademic circles, as a demand. The creation of determinate meaning in taking a passage in *The Winter's Tale* as ambiguous or *Paradise Lost* as indeterminate represents the emergence of the novel from the previously known. One needs "to distinguish between an indeterminate text and a quite determinate textual act, which explores tensions that arise from attempting to interpret complex events by simple thematic categories or an insufficient typological grammar" (Altieri 231).[3] "The Lady and the Tiger" is quite determinate although the outcome of the story it relates remains undetermined.

To understand that story or *The Winter's Tale* or *Paradise Lost* involves a series of determining choices along fault lines to which one is disposed in the construction of the text, of the self, and of interpretive methods; and those choices are made till making more seems unnecessary or undesirable. This process of guided choice, an exclusion of possibilities, leads to the constitution of the "work" out of its signs; the same process also leads to the dissolution of the work into an intertext made up of crystals of meaning, that is, what one remembers as "meaningful": this little group of words, this recurrent image, this arrangement of characters, this gesture, this way of solving a problem. In the process of converting text into intertext, what one remembers is liable to dismemberment. The "classic" is a term of degree for texts that keep up their double life — as works and as aggregates of intertextual crystals — for the longest time. I see this general procedure going on with all experience as it is received, understood, and returned for reuse to the storehouse of redundancy.

E. H. Gombrich: "[T]he very process of perception is based on the same rhythm that we found governing the process of representation: the rhythm of schema and correction. It is a rhythm which presupposes constant activity on our part in making guesses and modifying them in the light of our experience. Wherever this test meets with an obstacle, we abandon the guess and try again." (271–72)

Writing in the late 1950s, Gombrich adapted insights from information theory to his discussion of individual perception and representation. For him — and I agree — one makes sense of experience by analogy with past experience, by hypotheses of assimilation (x is like a) which one then checks against the evidence (x does[n't] share trait t with a). A great value of Gombrich's way of describing this tentative process of learning by trial and error with an open schema is that it supersedes, I think, the *huis clos* of the hermeneutic circle, with its paradoxes and credulity. Induction, before Gombrich's philosophical mentor Popper redefined it as the search for falsifying instances, was thought to be a search for confirmations, which in the hermeneutic circle means the fit of whole and parts. By Gombrich's and Popper's method, though, perception and representation appear to be a continual challenge to the past forms that are entertained as possible analogues, therefore provisionally, heuristically. Experience, then, is continuous, as the new is understood by its resemblance to the old, but also keeps opening out with a keen eye for difference. By the way one attains to it, understanding requires a search for novelty.

Because I agree with Wollheim (258–60) that the term "schema" is imprecise in Gombrich, and because I do not want to suggest that one conceives of objects as unified (such as Gombrich's own debt to Gestalt psychology prompts him to do), I will drop "schema-and-correction" for, more simply, "analogizing." One defines a text by postulating an idiom (a "language game") for it and then testing and changing that idiom by comparing the parts of the text with analogues to them, to see if and how they conform to usage established in past experience. How far one takes the comparison varies as one's purposes vary: if one wants to identify a tree as a tree, a tree as an oak, a tree as the old oak on which the kids' swings swung, one pursues the comparison in different ways and to different extents. So with literary texts; so with attitudes and ideas. Therefore, texts with complex uses often require several analogues or analogues of different sorts. A reader, in turn, needs a large, subtle reading competence with its range of probable options and nuances, its skill with (in the broad sense) grammar and syntax and idiom, because in relating the text to its analogue(s), the nature and degree of resemblance or variance are important, not simply the fact of resemblance or variance.

My method here is what Lakatos calls "sophisticated falsificationism," according to which one scraps an old theory only when the bit of contrary evidence can be incorporated into a new one. "The honesty" of this method, he writes, "demand[s] that one should try to look at things from different points of view, to put forward new theories which anticipate novel facts, and to reject theories which have been superseded by more powerful ones" (38). To place something new in relation to previous categories, both conscious or parts of tacit knowledge; to create something new, an act that takes its sense from previous categories; to interpret texts; to solve problems—these all require variants of the same procedure of making hypotheses and testing so as to modify them. My proposal, then, will be that the way one makes sense of the world, through analogies, is also the way conceptual change occurs. If one accepts this version of the way the new is produced, by culturally produced producers such as people, questions still remain: when does one stop? how does the historian envision a historical process from these actions in time? I propose that "satisficing" sets the stopping rule and that bodies of dispositions, what Pierre Bourdieu calls "habitus"—the Latin singular and the plural of the word have the same form—offer a way of deriving a historical process. As I have been doing, I will try to describe what I mean in terms of individual rather than intersubjective, negotiable action, both for reasons already stated and for another, empirical one: reading and writing literature are typically carried on by people in mental private, withdrawn into their individuated, though socially saturated, minds.

Herbert Simon: "[H]owever adaptive the behavior of organisms in learning and choice situations, this adaptiveness falls far short of the ideal of 'maximizing' postulated in economic theory. Evidently, organisms adapt well enough to 'satisfice'; they do not, in general, 'optimize.'" (261)

To satisfice is to achieve a resolution that both suffices and satisfies at some level of adequacy. What satisfices depends on the desires, capacities, expectations, beliefs, and available time of the "organism," whereas to maximize or optimize is to get the most from the material at hand. (One might say that satisficing is a kind of optimizing, doing what one can or what one needs to within a given situation of available time, space, energy, memory, etc.) Reading and writing, I am sure my own and I believe others' as well, are processes of satisficing: even when I am in the cordoned-off time of aesthetic contemplation, with every inclination to optimize *The Wings of the Dove* which I hold, I magnify some things and slight others, register causes here and neglect them there, and remain willing to accept my maimed James rather than read with that analytic perseverance that decades of academic training have asked me to value and taught me to make my own. From satisficing, one can draw a stopping rule for the process of analogizing: a reader stops when understanding seems comfortable. "What happens is not that this symbol cannot be further interpreted, but: I do no interpreting. I do not interpret, because I feel at home in the present picture" (Wittgenstein, *Zettel* 43). This at-homeness is sooner for a casual or hurried or naive or conventional or dogmatic reader than for, well, naturally, than for *us*; but in reading as in all the rest of life, we too need to stop somewhere.

The text as a historical object represents a set of historical options, produced by reading practices (literary and more general social competences, options for making analogies, degrees of satisficing), and in that sense is indeterminate. What about other senses? If the text is ahistorical, perhaps in others too; but historically, no — if the reader is a social artifact, as structuralist and poststructuralist writers maintain, surely so is a text, and the constraints on the one also apply to the other (see Lentricchia 143). If people historically — whether by "nature" or "nurture" — have tendencies to behave in certain ways and not in others, so should texts. Without anthropomorphizing texts or textualizing people, I think, one can argue that both are socially produced producers with consequent similarities. No doubt for some purposes texts are "just" marks on the page, and with equal justice their readers are "just" batches of organic molecules. But these adjustments to the way we usually see things, these severe and knowing reductions, carry no privilege as really real. Since we comprehend all our experience as part of some variety of semiosis, there is nothing special about words that exempts them from historicity or exempts anything else from the need for interpretation or, if one warms to it, from radical indeterminacy. As I have said, I believe that people reading novels or their grocer's motives, even their politicians' motives, rarely choose radical indeterminacy as the determinate consequence of their reading; the option of overplural knowing is most of the time kept squirreled away till lack of other suitable nourishment makes one drag it out, and that is because for performing the tasks of life it is not itself a very nourishing option.

As much as anything else, then, literary texts enter the world with a set of dispositions to render meaning. These govern their interaction with their environment. Such a habitus, to use Bourdieu's term for such a set of dispositions, responds to an assemblage of contemporaneous demands and constraints. It does so through interaction with an environment of readers who embody most, not all, of these demands and constraints and who also bring new ones that try the adequacy of the habitus. Specific readers with specific interests and competences explore how the text is interpretable, how far and how usefully its dispositions to act (by being read, that is) can be kept in play. This scheme implies that the whole of the text need not fit situations any more than somebody's dispositions to act need to be tightly coherent with each other, and that a really adaptable text, say *Paradise Lost*, which can remain a social producer for a long time, is one that lends itself at least to powerful partial readings of strikingly different sorts. The power makes a reader more eager to pass over or accommodate the incongruous parts of the text, that is, to save the desirable whole by satisficing.

To put this another way, a text seen as a historical utterance represents, like any other historical action, a response to interests, and in the sense that an unsatisfied interest is tantamount to a problem, a text presents solutions to immediate problems. Some of these problems emerge from the audience and author and some from the inner logic of the medium. Some are thematic, some formal or representational or ethical. If a text puts forth excellent solutions to problems thought important, one will overlook its faults and anomalies. Since most problems change over time, the likelihood of textual benefit—of an old text's solving updated or new problems—shrinks and so people become less lenient toward faults and anomalies (the perception of which also, of course, changes). Historical reading tries to restore textual benefit by making the importance of the old problems reappear, even some that the author and her audience were unaware of. Long-lasting works provide such highly acceptable solutions (often through having them canonized, therefore not retested) and/or such a variety of good solutions to recurrent problems that they continue to earn leniency. Because people often have an interest in returning to the familiar or the venerable, long-lasting works even develop a peculiar status from having aged in public. This acquired value is often much prized, oddly, by scholars whose tenets otherwise ban readings that exceed authorial intention.

From the procedures of satisficing, one can imagine the way in which texts enter literary history. Hans Robert Jauss has argued incisively, through his history and practical criticism, for artworks in dialogue with their publics, both therefore changing. I would complement his stress on the monumental work, a system of meaning, with another, in which texts become historical resources only in deformations that often make previous analytic rigor on the integral text useless. Let me hasten to say that such rigor is invaluable in pointing to the text as an achievement of a person or of intertextual confluence, and in establishing certain dispositions or tendencies that help one understand how that text is likely to be read. The rigorously read text also shows a historical mode in detailed operation. But an actual text, which enters history as a constrained entity, remains in history not only in its rereadings as a whole but also, and mainly, as it is disassembled and diffused, misremembered, stolen from, and abused. A text exerts most influence by entering the intertextual, by giving up its integrity; its moments of greatest agency involve the splitting of what one might call the textual "self." The modes of textual appropriation are usually the best guide one has to text reception, and text reception is the best guide to what constitutes "redundancy," the already processed repertoire through which the new begins to mean, through which one finds analogues with which one can understand the new.

In writing literary history, one can isolate probable ways in which a given text becomes "redundant," therefore useful for understanding what is newer than it: for example, a text typifies itself, it collocates elements, and it puts various logics into operation. It typifies itself in making itself a public phenomenon, an object or presence to be commented on as such. One thinks of the importance for Stoppard of the canonical status of *Hamlet, Waiting for Godot, Six Characters in Search of an Author,* and *The Mousetrap*; for Milton of Virgil and Ariosto; for Bunyan of the Bible. Measures of self-typification are popularity, staying in the repertoire, proper-naming or its equivalents in later works. A text collocates by establishing or reinforcing an association of ideas or a paradigm of how some problem can be solved — *Paradise Lost*'s making blank verse sublime; *An Essay on Criticism*'s making a quotable quip; *To the Lighthouse*'s making *boeuf en daube* an act of social resolution (or sham or dearly purchased social resolution — the reader's reading determines what the paradigm solves). Collocations are likely to be what authors, sometimes readers, can make peculiarly their own; and so one measures the collocative force of a text by how much future texts beckon it into dialogue with them. Conversely, a text puts various logics into operation by extending tendencies from previous works, not always works of the same genre or in the same discipline. Thus one can speak of novels moving to incorporate more and more "realism" or more and more sense of time as Bergsonian *durée*; one can propose that poststructuralist aporia logically extends an existentialist complex of which an important element, the idea of human freedom, has been called into doubt. One measures textual logics by asking how a given work augments a historical sequence by change or reinforcement, asking where vector lines drawn through the work and its predecessors point.

Everything that I have said about texts, of course, can also be said of people when they are textualized. They too can be seen and — which is here the same thing — see themselves in these behavioral terms of their being responded to, or of their public status and presence (physically, legally, by repute . . .), or of the various values they represent. In addition, as reflective agents, people look at their roles in creating response, personal presence, and values somewhat differently. They create history differently from texts, as one can see when the intertextual terms of Bourdieu's idea of "habitus" are made to reappear as the terms of agency. Then one has not only a greatly elaborated version of choosing among already offered options but also the freedom to create something new and consequential, something deliberately emergent.

Pierre Bourdieu: "The structures constitutive of a particular type of environment produce *habitus*, systems of durable, transposable *dispositions*, structured structures predisposed to function as structuring structures, that is, as principles of the generation and structuring of practices and representations which can be objectively 'regulated' and 'regular' without in any way being the product of obedience to rules, objectively adapted to their goals without presupposing a conscious aiming at ends or an express mastery of the operations necessary to attain them and, being all this, collectively orchestrated without being the product of the orchestrating action of a conductor." (*Outline* 72)

In other words, as social productions, people also have redundancy. (I do not believe that this is the only reason they have it.) This redundancy is "personality," "character," "style," or, in Bourdieu's broader, more aseptic term, "habitus." I prefer to translate his engineering description ("structures . . . produce . . . structured structures") back into the commonsense language of agency: people as actors develop in early life a set of dispositions toward action. Ideals as well as exigencies pattern these dispositions, as people shape themselves not only for instrumental success but also for the fulfillment of different roles with ethical and expressive value. As long as a person can make his or her habitus satisfice, he or she sticks to it come anything short of hell or high water. In brief, the habitus constitutes a person's character with regard to practice: "that would be in character for her." As with this meaning of "character," a term that links identities with predictions, somebody's habitus may be quite coherent or loosely tied, for one's typical milieus — home, work, school, tennis court, inauguration ball, barroom — need not call for or even tolerate similar behavior.

Whereas Bourdieu employs "habitus" as a single engine for action, so that one's "discourse continuously feeds off itself like a train bringing along its own rails," and each "*trouvaille* appears as the simple unearthing, at once accidental and irresistible, of a buried possibility," impressive "as much by [its] retrospective necessity as by [its] novelty" (*Outline* 79), I would stress its contingency, not its necessity. I would stress the options for the cuisine of self-feeding, the options for the laying of rails, the options for the spadework of unearthing. In saying this I am explicitly rejecting the present possibility of a science of behavior in accord with which one can figure out what options will be taken. And this follows from my agent-oriented sense of habitus, just as it followed earlier from an agent-oriented approach to social programming. The more diverse and open the society in which someone grows up, the more variously that person — say, an author or reader — can embody her habitus. She will find more variety to which she must adapt; she will find greater autonomy of idioms in which to gain competency for action, greater specialization of response, and therefore a greater range of behaviors which she will register as her own, "in character" for her, and charged with positive value. He will find greater social acceptance for his different behaviors, so as to supply him with continued validation of the self. He will find greater pragmatism, so that he will have more options as to the methods he takes to achieve his ends, even if the ends are part of an orthodoxy. In the West (and elsewhere) she will find a society where "the very conditions that make possible the state's existence call into play, and depend upon, mechanisms that run counter to state power" (Giddens 315).

That she will also find a society in which values sometimes gain general force regardless of the age group where they originate reinforces another source of diversity: in modern societies, people of different ages differ because of change, because they have started to grow up in and adapt to different general social environments. Therefore one not only has options at any one moment, one also has a change in the number, quality, and mix of options as time goes on. If one couples this formulation with the principle of habitus, diversity and heterogeneity produce historical change. The more heterogeneity in society, the more likely social change becomes, as people try to accommodate conflicting social demands in ways that suit their own dispositions; and the more likely short-run change is, the more likely long-run change becomes, since a younger person, developing under conditions different from those of even his slight elders, learns a habitus different from theirs.

Traditional societies, with a harmony or long-established accommodation of social demands, insure stability by keying the definition of persons to set social roles. In contrast, a society open to rapid change makes much of individual freedom, producing a category (call it "self") that stresses personal consciousness, rather than one of prefigured roles (Mauss's word is "personnage"; see Mauss 4–12; for another terminology, see Rorty 78–98). The "invention of liberty" during the eighteenth century, a time of the most daring and startling creativity in Western cultural history, is not only evidence of change but also its source (Starobinski 10–11, 41). In this process of differentiation, the "self" as socially narrated has been not only progressively embellished (with rights, with psychological density, with ideals of "realizing" or "fulfilling" that which is proper to it) but also stripped down to an operator that creates or assembles its own experience. Such a double production of the "self" implies a social emphasis on choice among options governed by general, generative rules for action, rather than on prescribed behavioral patterns. Through this procedure, as the idea of the "self" has changed little by little, the habitus of a person has formed around broadening notions of one's resources and opportunities.

This hypothesis, I suggest, like the argument about social programming above, allows for the creation of novelty, therefore diversity and change, through the continuous process of adapting to conflicts in demands and constraints. In modern societies, the process of creating novelty is over-determined in that novelty itself is typically demanded in various kinds of utterance, literary works included. Self-interest and the weakening of traditional authority (which is to say, a long redefining of self-interest) produce this demand: people will read or listen to something only if they expect doing so to bring a benefit, and one such benefit — its weight differs in different situations and societies — comes from the new, through which one is enlightened, surprised, given to feel personal rapport with the speaker or writer, and so forth. As Quine notes, the increasingly positive value of the words "wonderful" and "admirable," together with their "Romance and German cognates," "bespeaks a general tendency to prize surprise" (6). An increasing desire for the new is marked by the rise of an "early modern" category, boredom, to denote the lack of it. The weakening of traditional authority and self-interest (which is to say, a long redefining of authority) produce this desire: when people have to adapt to faster-changing circumstances and choose among multiplying options, when they have to earn "their rights by virtue of their powers, rather than have their powers defined by their rights" (Rorty 88), they increasingly look for new information to show them and tell them about the field of possibilities. New literature, with its "as if," at once informs and, through the aesthetic involvement (whether contemplation or the satisfaction of desire) that has become cardinal in aesthetic theory over the last three hundred years, temporarily displaces — by complaisance — the problems of choice and adaptation.[4]

To ease the way for the new, a process of what Bakhtin calls "novelization" has since the mid-seventeenth century made literature more heterogeneous, as different voices enter it and claim their rights of reorganizing the common space. Over the same time, representational content and traditional forms have lost their patents on structuring literature. Their successors, formalist and process-oriented modes, evade familiar definition and exercise constraints therefore less publicly visible. "We cannot exercise power," said Foucault about our society above all, "except through the production of truth. . . . Power . . . institutionalises, professionalises, and rewards its pursuit. In the last analysis, we must produce truth as we must produce wealth" ("Two Lectures" 93). Nowadays more than ever, oppositional critics, conservatives, and libertarians are all the employees of "power," properly understood: that is why in academia so many of us work Nibelung-like to forge novelty (for "truth" is socially ratified novelty or information), and why those who do not mine themselves and their books for public print are thought to be slackers.

III. INSTEAD OF ISMS

Salman Rushdie: "How does newness come into the world? How is it born? Of what fusions, translations, conjoinings is it made?" (8)

How? Through diversity, I have ventured. Newness is a translation of multiple injunctions and ends; of puzzlement, partial transmission, and faulty recollection; of myriad, small discontinuities in history.[5] Most literary historians, however, like history only if they can lump it. They design to suppress differences, using entities whose raison d'être is to normalize and reduce multiplicity. Isms are best for this, but when reified or put on the level of *langue*, some generic terms, like "the novel," also imperil the description of heterogeneity and change. I mean, of course, the use of these terms, not their mention: one does not imperil anything by referring to others' labels, such as Jung's collective unconscious (unless one believes in it), Kingsley's muscular Christianity, Lewis' vorticism, or the way Barrett Browning thought about "the sonnet." Using the terms oneself is something else. For scholars, such simple tales appeal to a wish that deep down, order exists, and that the discomfiting confusion of the past need not permanently disturb us, overburdened and unsure of rapport with that which we study. In the classroom, successful pigeonholing helps keepers of knowledge hatch more of themselves within the corporate institutions to which they owe and rebelliously give their allegiance: "In place of practical schemes of classification, which are always partial and linked to practical contexts, [the school system] puts explicit, standardized taxonomies, fixed once and for all in the form of synoptic schemas or dualistic typologies (e.g., 'classical'/'romantic'), which are expressly inculcated and therefore conserved in the memory as knowledge that can be reproduced in virtually identical form by all the agents subjected to its action" (Bourdieu, *Distinction* 67).

Bourdieu helps explain in social terms why the appeal of canonic "periods," or other well-entrenched, reified universals, outweighs commitments to particulars and diversity. Imposed as a means of uniform knowledge, a typology of "periods," for example, enacts — as influence or intertext or both? — in the heads of twentieth-century students the single-mindedness that is claimed to mark the thinking of the past. When these students ascend to the professoriat, they find history imitating their own stock ways of thinking about it, for those who misremember the past are condemned to make it repeat them. In keeping with these social as well as personal interests, then, influence-based and intertextual readings of culture alike have tended to reify their texts as lawlike structures and have had to resist the multiplicity logically implicit in their assumptions. Witness the flurry of studies asking what Romanticism was instead of if it was or if there

was an it in the first place. The argument here applies to both heterogeneity and change, both of which are sacrificed by the territorial specialist in some "period" and by the Young Turk, also no doubt a specialist,
who values the discontinuous (or revolutionary) and the marginal (or limi-
nal), thus a past that metamorphoses, not changes. In such work, the intertextual merely becomes a Weberian "iron cage" of impersonalized influence. Thus reflexive reflections on "modernism" and "postmodernism"
rework old-fashioned emanations from the canon and "the age" into hegemonic structures, on which trapped natives ring changes.

Ism-ism comes in two brands, both bad for one's health. The Platonic
brand, packaged with ideas of influence, looks like this: "The historian
searches the possibilities of history to understand its elements and its
qualities," Ira Wade announces, "but his ultimate goal is the apprehension
of its inner reality, what is often called the spirit of the age. . . . The historian of ideas is always seeking a dominant idea" (xvii–xviii). Thus the
visible — selected similarities among some seventeenth-century poems —
can be explained by "discovering" an occult energy, "Neoclassicism." Body
is filled with soul. Soul in turn gets body when one reifies spectral Ages
and isms. If in personal life Me dialectically begets Not-Me, then in cultural history the same old, easy habit of thought generates a Spirit for the
Age to poise against the Mind of the Author. Instead of a heterogeneous
field of constraints, requisite for action, then, appears a single Zeitgeist
that takes on human standing: "the Middle Ages believed . . . "; "the teach-
ings of Modernism." Given this agonistic mode, one can stage historical
change, if one likes, as a battle of self and society or of visionary heroism,
Chaucer setting sail from the homely Middle Ages to plant his gonfalon
on the New World shores of the Renaissance. Other scenarios beside the
agon of periods depict the violation or "subversion" of genres or other
abstract entities. Periods and isms are only the most deliciously absolute
such creatures — the loosest, baggiest, and most blindly voracious.

The Aristotelian brand, with a broader market share, takes the "period"
as "a time-section dominated by a set of [empirically discovered] literary
norms . . . whose introduction, spread, diversification, integration, decay,
and disappearance can be traced" (Wellek 484).[6] The scientific flourish of
this method relies on the shaky hunch that one set of norms need dominate or that dominant norms need form a set or, in fact, that norms retain
a traceable identity. A modern scholar who tracks down norms (rather
than makes use of models useful for local knowledge) ipso facto endorses
an assimilationist agenda. By now we have had enough analyses of such
pairs as normal/pathological and normal/deviant — by Foucault, by Can-
guilhem — to make clear the willfulness and the danger of such an agenda.

A rule at cross-purposes with Wade and Wellek might be this: in doing literary history, never use an uneliminable, irreplaceable term except for agents. "To define is to eliminate," Quine helpfully points out: "Availability of the definiens renders the definiendum dispensable, save perhaps as a convenience" (44). Once an ism is eliminable, it loses its thinglike status and the definition that replaces it becomes open to historical testing.[7] Some very convenient generic terms or terms such as "mass culture," "women's writing," "oppositional criticism," and so forth can best be understood and analyzed as practice, like "driving a car" or "giving a public lecture."[8] One need not generalize when discussing such terms, though one does need to analogize, perceive "family resemblances." Isms, however, seem to be for some reason (it varies) irreducible to shared notions of practice, and staunch in their encouragement to generalize. So as to serve as criteria of exclusivity, they invite definition, but they must also seem to exceed it and its threat to mark them as mere conveniences. In that way the isms embezzle and control the rich inexhaustibility that really belongs to historical facts by sheer diversity and to agents, like people and texts, by their indeterminate potential for change. The definable, hence eliminable, categories I shall propose for literary history lack this charm of interpretative excess.

Jean-François Lyotard: "A self does not amount to much, but no self is an island; each exists in a fabric of relations that is now more complex and mobile than ever before. . . . one is always located at a post through which various kinds of messages pass. No one, not even the least privileged among us, is ever entirely powerless over the messages that traverse and position him at the post of sender, addressee, or referent." (15)

To indicate what might in practice replace isms, perhaps I first should try to replace the "two basic representational models," as Lyotard says (11), that have wooed and won so many for so long. One outworn model is holistic, from likenesses to machines, organisms, and systems; the other, antagonistic, the drama of class struggle and negations. To the totalities of both models, I prefer a relational dispersion, along the lines of Lyotard's "fabric of relations." Lyotard's description implies a self situated in multiple "fabrics," and fabrics, too, of variable consistencies, variable densities, variable capacities to change as the selves exercise power at their "posts." One way of imaging this condition is through the metaphor of populations as I define the term below. For the historian, envisioning a population is not a falsifiable hypothesis but an instrument to be fine-tuned so as to be most useful for the descriptive tasks one wants it to aid.

Ernst Mayr: "Th[e] uniqueness of biological individuals means that we must approach groups of biological entities in a very different spirit from the way we deal with groups of identical inorganic entities. This is the basic meaning of population thinking. The differences between biological individuals are real, while the mean values which we may calculate in the comparison of groups of individuals (species, for example) are man-made inferences." (46)

Thus one can make provisional groupings within an urban community by speaking of "the Greek-American population of Cleveland," "the population of men between 21 and 44 in the fourth income quintile," "the population of lodge members." As elements of commentary and analysis, such groupings are all pragmatic, instruments with limits instead of falsifiable knowledge: one isolates them only because one wants to do something via the categories they represent, such as estimate the market for retsina and souvlaki, explain a high crime rate, or discover why only 3 percent of positions in upper management are held by women. Population groups have system-like, probabilistic coherences: their members have a greater than random likelihood to have similar values, tastes, and marital practices. Each individual has the possibility of altering the group by shifting its concerns and dynamics. Within a larger society, these groups may overlap but need not. They define that society as a community, therefore, through discontinuous superimposed patterns. Of course some of the patterns will seem more important or natural than others (color and straightness of hair versus a tendency to myopia), but here, as usually, nature is culture: to a great extent the groups define the society as a community by illustrating what the society thinks important or natural, its preferred and influential knots. Myopia outweighs skin color for Bausch & Lomb. Since literary historians are social products, the populations they single out will respond to their (that is, to parts of their society's) interests: that is what lets them talk with one another and what requires that they never (mis)take the groups they see as "realer" and more "natural" than the groups they do not.

Conversely, as is crucial for a hypothesis like mine, one can always treat the same phenomena from the standpoint of individuals with multiple strands reaching out, multiple affiliations — Andy Koropoulos, age 37, member of the Elks — rather than from that of system. Each strand, in other words, represents at least one hypothetical population to which a given individual might belong. Looked at this way, the community is defined by a network of allegiances. Because the strands tie individuals, to include them in the metaphor is to allow it to represent individual action, choice, intention, distinction, as well as the system. An emphasis on strands may call population bounds into question, and an emphasis on populations may call into question the range of options and distinctions open to a given individual. To use both aspects certainly underscores the multiple demands for which historical explanation should account, and forbids its simply making "minor" works into Context — i.e., system-produced phenomena — for transcendent "major" works taken as free individuals. Everything is dividual or not, depending on what you want to use it for. (I have argued that persons and texts are necessary "individuals" of literary history, but neither in my language nor in common speech does that mean that they are elementary, unanalyzable.) To use both strands and populations, too, suggests the provisionality of both, the looseness of their systematicity. To keep their lack of ideal totality and their degree of regulatory force in mind, I suggest that strands and populations are best defined in terms of a core of acknowledged members, often with more dubious members around these.

Richard Miller: "[C]oncepts such as that of a number and of a work of art [are each] based on a core of elementary varieties, extended to further cases by rational but unpredictable processes of discovery and criticism. . . . [A] representational but non-trompe l'oeil easel painting, made for contemplation, and a statue of a person, slightly stylized but not enormously so, and made for contemplation are elementary varieties of works of art. People who deny the title to Pollock drip paintings but give it to Vermeers are philistine or ill-informed, but have the concept. Someone who grants the title to a Pollock but, without visual flaw or critical argument, asks, 'Why does anyone call *that* a work of art?' faced with a Vermeer, has a potentially interesting but rather different concept from that of a work of art." (74–75)

To recognize that literary-historical terms have this form is not only to encourage replacing the isms with sets that make less claim to being "real," it is also to get rid of the silly solemnities that genre disputes produce: "Is *Moll Flanders* picaresque?" "Is *Alkestis* a tragedy?" Such questions could be rethought, "In what relation does Work A stand to the core works of picaresque (tragedy), and why ask?" One reason to ask, of course, it that the extension of any term, even its core, changes because of such questions, and they thus are a means of precise definition. A heuristic of population and strand groups patterned around points of reference ("the body of blank-verse poetry"; "texts that imitate Horace's *Ars poetica*") could bring such definition to literary history. It would not matter whether one's categories had sharp boundaries — "men between 21 and 44" is sharply bounded, "Greek-Americans" much less so. Once again, the better defined the groups as functions of an argument, the less chance such artifacts have of passing as "natural," thus occluding the politics of their use.

Precisely because populations in the common or my figurative sense are defined by cores or samples, the groups of objects they are taken to denote have the capacity to change: once one decides one wants to examine Victorian lyric poems, or aesthetic reactions to evolutionary thought, or the post-"Romantic" elegiac strain ("Romantic" here names a self-styled movement, not a supposed period), a population appears with some assured members and some dubious ones; the nature, interrelationships, and affiliations of these members and the ratio of assured members to dubious ones alter as one analyzes an earlier or later cross-section.[9] In this way, the concept "population" can represent a mixture of continuity and change within a group constituted as an object of interest. Ethnic populations, for example, typically change over time in degree of influence, size, coherence, and relative difference from other populations, and the core conception — what is taken consensually as a sample — thereby changes. Those changes produce others, in that the status of a population typically helps define the habitus of each of its contemporaneous members. Since at any given time the population has a variety of members — by age, class, education, familial structure — who have been formed in accord with different demands and constraints, one can *talk* about change within it. A history, then, can discuss these populations with certain ends in mind and treat them as more than mere aggregates, without, however, granting them an exclusive or value-normative status or an inner essence. Strands too change as they pass through different populations — think of the history of a *topos* — and they signal the diversity of demands on the members of a population. From these properties of populations and strands, I can pass to my final point, proposing a method that will allow one to explore them. That would make possible the kind of questions to which the isms responded, heuristic questions involving the logic of a mode or genre or style or turn of mind, in addition to simple empirical labors such as cataloguing the traits of actual satires or novels or gongoristic poems or idealizations of womanhood.

"Exemplification and expression," says Nelson Goodman, "though running in the opposite direction from denotation — that is, from the symbol to a literal or metaphorical feature of it instead of to something the symbol applies to — are no less symbolic referential functions and instruments of worldmaking" (12). Exemplification and denotation are combined in a homeomorphic model, in other words, a model that serves as a schematization or class representative of a population.[10] Such a model is an intertext that displays and, just as important, interconnects core concepts defining a population and that denotes traits of the population's members. For some purposes the model may be a real member of a population: Horace's *Ars poetica*, seen as a sample of a mode, might act as the model in terms of which one can assess the range of its imitators. In that case, one is talking not about the actual verse epistle written in about 20 B.C., give or take a half dozen years, but about a conceptual diagram of it to pick out salient operations: Horace's poem as model is an intertext for comprehending Horace's poem as text along with others. *AP*-model displays features and interconnections that one finds in *AP*-text (say, ones that are of interest for relating the text to other Latin epistles, or other examples of similar verse style, or expressions of dramatic theory) but neglects what does not fit in its system, whatever that system is — it is dictated by the use to which it will be put.

For different purposes, one might want to construct an ideal model, perhaps by working out a specimen that incorporates the whole system of traits one wants to show in operation, or perhaps by developing a set of possibilities in a kind of verbal diagram. For still other purposes, finally, one might codify a number of actual works into a set to achieve a sensitive enough instrument to calibrate a conceptual space. This last method allows one to isolate invariables and traits that vary over time, and to make sense of structural transformations. Its apparent advantages make it among the most common of literary-historical methods, but it also is one of the most perilous. When, for example, two novels of the 1840s, two of the 1860s, and two of the 1880s are used to chart changes over those years, the novels chosen must be convertible into types (or tokens of hypothetical types), and what then happens to their inconvenient, idiosyncratic parts? A safer course would be to make the hypothetical types, the ideal models, explicit and to show how the two novels of each decade resemble and differ from the rationalized form exhibited in these models. Procrustes and his cutler would weep, but that is quite all right.

Clearly, the sort of model I have in mind differs in conception and function from that familiar to literary critics from Barthes's early essay "The Structuralist Activity": a simulacrum or imitation of a functional system made in order to render that system intelligible. My kind of model imitates nothing, but presents both resemblance and difference. In shaping one's model, one strives not for likeness but for heuristic benefits in response to the questions one wants answered. Similarly, just as the model is shaped in terms of the critic's problems and solutions, so the models themselves operate in terms of the reader's, the source of her or his literary interest. They embody a group of options for solving problems that within its social idiom the text creates, such as, for example, fulfilling the expectations of a sonnet, avoiding cognitive dissonance, resolving a pattern, or awaking titillating unease through suspense or ambiguity. They also embody options for solving problems that readers bring to the text, readers who crave having their patriotic fervor stirred in wartime, the patterns of their social relations made understandable, their hearts warmed, their inchoate feelings given voice (cf. Jauss 146). My kind of model, then, emphasizes agency, the reader's purposes in being interested in the text and, I should add, the reader's inferences about the writer's intention. It describes "functions" differently from Barthes's, and historicizes them, for problems and solutions have being only in given historical situations.[11]

Rather than the Barthesian form, my models use the principle of comparison that I have adapted from Gombrich. In analogizing one searches for resemblances and differences, the parts of various travel voyages and utopian fictions and visiting-naïf narratives that let one make sense of *Gulliver's Travels*. Analogues are explanatory. In the use of the model, one makes up a gauging analogue. That is, one imagines a schematic intertext, an artifact in which each detail is rationalized, purposive, connected in logic and/or idiom to the others. Then one measures the interrelations of real texts by using the model as a gauge by which to situate members of a population (cf. Wittgenstein, *Philosophical* sec. 131). These population members do not express, employ, or embody the model, but more or less resemble it. Because the model as conceived is an ideal system (machine, interrelated whole), it acts as a rational economy in which the texts to a greater or lesser extent share. But each text itself has many traits that do not appear in the model, affiliations that the model cannot register, and so the text remains open despite its disposition to be understood in certain ways. If one accepts not only the openness of historically disposed texts and agents but also the principle that general terms (like the isms and their kin) apply only on the level of the critic's construction, the model, then one can embark upon explaining cultural change without regard to the spectral howls of pseudo-individuals — concepts or movements or tendencies — stranded on the historiographical shore.

W. S. Gilbert: "But it *does* put you out / When a person says, 'Oh, / I have known that old joke from my cradle!'" (475)

"You" want diversity and change in your wit; so does the "person"; so do I — and why, then, do I come up with the old punch line of texts and persons? I have borrowed from others' theory and practice far too much for me to claim a new Kuhnian paradigm here (even if I believed in such things). If, however, my synthetic hypothesis were to be taken as a guide, supported by its apparatus of analogizing, habitus, satisficing, populations and strands, models — if this schema were to be taken as a guide, it would not only rationalize, it would also correct the old schemas in ways that can be usefully believed or disbelieved. To describe human beings as at once programmed and productive, for a start, turns influence into a form of intertextuality and vice versa.

(1) Its stress on the reader as a correcting and satisficing figure foregrounds a reader's current motives so as to encourage a desire-based or interest-based criticism. By "desire-based criticism" I do not mean something Lawrentian, but rather a mode of analysis that treats readers as acting purposively to satisfy interests, even if they do not quite know what interests. Plainly, such a criticism does not curl a lip at works that cater

to readers' wishes and smile on those that flout or legislate them. The means for analyzing mass and high culture are likely to be continuous with each other, and differences will depend on elaborated and subtle distinctions among audiences and their typical interests. (2) Its stress on model-making, on heuristic intertexts around which works are differentiated, asks for a new clarity of definition (and clarifies what "clarity of definition" might plausibly mean) and shows how to achieve it. (3) Its scheme of the way that change takes place makes "revolutions" and smooth continuity alike improbable. It opposes any idea of culture as a kind of determinism and change like genetic mutation. Continuity here is not in forward movement but always in going back, retrospect upon possibilities, on facts, problems, and heuristics. (4) It emphasizes *use*: people and texts are its individuals not because they represent hard data, as in one way of thinking they do, but because they are irreplaceable instruments. Understandings and explanations satisfice because they are keyed to certain uses. The historical meaning of something is given by what it does within a process of change. A generalization is not an essence or a truth to be falsified but a specific pragmatic tool, useful for gauging differences as well as resemblances among acts and options. Different artworks too have different uses, the validity of which is not encompassed by what has traditionally been taken as aesthetics. Terms of value, such as "sublime" or "serious," assign an artwork to its use(s). (5) It highlights an active repertory of works, intertexts, and options at given historical moments; it also highlights an active repertory of "selves" coexisting but socially constructed under different conditions. It thereby ties the rate and breadth of cultural change to the sociopolitical world. Indeed, like much contemporary reasoning it partakes—in a vigorously upside-down, anti-essentialist way—of "the essential thing about metaphysics: it obliterates the distinction between factual and conceptual investigations" (Wittgenstein, *Zettel* 458).

NOTES

I should like to acknowledge with gratitude the careful reading and help of Elizabeth Hirsh, Allen Hunter, Alan Liu, and Nicholas Rand, in addition to that of my fellow contributors to this volume.

1   Followers of Popper would protest that we never need justify, but rather try to falsify, and that the "proposition [that] remains" needs to be open to falsification (see Radnitzky and Bartley 208–10, 295–97). For my purposes, Wittgenstein's "justification" applies to the way one explains one's ideas to oneself and others, and Popper's "falsification" applies to the setting of limits and uses to what Wittgenstein would call "forms of life"—the "I-perspective" has

its uses, the "me-perspective" its. That is why, as a Popperian would say, both have evolved as part of our cognitive apparatus.

2   Inasmuch as Habermas' "authenticity" assumes the material presence of objects, I should note that by "texts," I mean the sets of symbols whose integrity is implicit in the concepts of plagiarism or forgery. If persons are to be viewed as texts, the concept of impersonation should be added. To the extent that legal notions of literary work and of person function reasonably well, involving — as does the factuality of all facts — stipulations within a discourse, one can rely pretty heavily on the terms; and in real life no one does without them. Of course texts and plagiarism do not apply in the same way in largely oral cultures, as Doane points out in this volume. Nor, in some cultures, may persons and impersonation. I intend to posit logical distinctions here, not ethnohistorical ones, and I recognize that they will have different utility for different kinds of cultural or even literary history.

3   Altieri's whole discussion of indeterminacy (214-37), as well as his explorations of "competency," "use," and "performance," are among the most illuminating I know.

4   Wuthnow's scheme of change and heterogeneity, more sophisticated than mine here, uses not only historically linear trends, such as I have invoked, but also recurrent historical patterns; see in particular chap. 7, "The Moral Basis of Cultural Change."

5   Some of these discontinuities would count as "artistic revolutions" for Clignet. His intriguing, post-Kuhnian (if Clignet had cited him, Lakatosian) scheme turns on nonhegemonic novelties that change the configuration of an artistic field by force of dramatic entrance, through highly visible protagonists and/or new controversies.

6   With regard to Wellek's own defense of "Romanticism," Jackson attacks "the idea that literary periods have an identifiable character that distinguishes them from other literary periods[, a] belief . . . so widespread as almost to constitute a critical axiom" (118); and he proposes the "general rule" that "the more active the critical effort to generalize about a literary period has been, the greater the handicap to historical criticism" (125), the act of trying "to read past works of literature in the way in which they were read when new" (3).

7   Jameson insists that "periodization and its categories, which are certainly in crisis today, . . . seem to be as indispensable as they are unsatisfactory for any kind of work in cultural study" (28). One might argue that they are unsatisfactory in large part *because* they seem indispensable, hence real. Disposable categories, like cartons for one's milk or subdirectories on one's hard disk, would bear less burden, be less real, therefore be less in crisis, be more satisfactory.

8   The means of analysis would be those that "intuitionist" speech-act theories have developed, calling on an infinitely graded typology of utterances (see Pratt 86, 201-10), or better, those developed by Erving Goffman for "the naturalistic study of . . . the forms and occasions of face-to-face interaction" (162). Shared notions of practice, not ontologized isms, help Goffman define the legibility of self-presentation.

9 Again, in practice this decision is taken by a real person, hence a creature of a real society, so that the "decision" does not — as well as does — result from free choice. For reasons of brevity, I represent as a rational practice what everyone who does historical work knows to be a good deal more complex.

10 For a short discussion of different model types, see Bhaskar.

11 Frances Kavenik and I have tried to exemplify such a model in our book on Carolean comedy.

WORKS CITED

Altieri, Charles. *Act and Quality: A Theory of Literary Meaning and Humanistic Understanding.* Amherst: U of Massachusetts P, 1981.

Bakhtin, Mikhail. *Speech Genres and Other Late Essays.* Trans. Vern W. McGee. Ed. Caryl Emerson and Michael Holquist. Austin: U of Texas P, 1986.

Barthes, Roland. "The Structuralist Activity." Trans. Richard Howard. *Partisan Review* 34 (Winter 1967): 82–88.

Bhaskar, Roy. "Models." In *Dictionary of the History of Science*, ed. W. F. Bynum, E. J. Browne, and Roy Porter, 272–74. Princeton: Princeton UP, 1981.

Bourdieu, Pierre. *Distinction: A Social Critique of the Judgement of Taste.* 1979. Trans. Richard Nice. Cambridge: Harvard UP, 1984.

Bourdieu, Pierre. *Outline of a Theory of Practice.* 1972. Trans. Richard Nice. Cambridge: Cambridge UP, 1977.

Campbell, Jeremy. *Grammatical Man: Information, Entropy, Language, and Life.* New York: Simon & Schuster, 1982.

Clignet, Remi. *The Structure of Artistic Revolutions.* Philadelphia: U of Pennsylvania P, 1985.

Deleuze, Gilles. *Foucault.* 1986. Trans. Seán Hand. Minneapolis: U of Minnesota P, 1988.

Derrida, Jacques. "Structure, Sign, and Play in the Discourse of the Human Sciences." In *The Structuralist Controversy: The Languages of Criticism and the Sciences of Man*, ed. Richard Macksey and Eugenio Donato. 1970; rpt. Baltimore: Johns Hopkins UP, 1972.

Foucault, Michel. *The Archaeology of Knowledge and The Discourse on Language.* 1969, 1971. Trans. A. M. Sheridan Smith (1972) and Rupert Sawyer (1971). Rpt. New York: Harper & Row, 1976.

Foucault, Michel. *The Order of Things: An Archaeology of the Human Sciences.* 1966. New York: Random House, Vintage, 1973.

Foucault, Michel. *Politics, Philosophy, Culture: Interviews and Other Writings, 1977–1984.* Trans. Alan Sheridan and others. New York and London: Routledge, 1988.

Foucault, Michel. "Two Lectures." 1976. In *Power/Knowledge: Selected Interviews and Other Writings, 1972–1977*, ed. Colin Gordon, 78–108. New York: Pantheon, 1980.

Giddens, Anthony. *The Constitution of Society: Outline of the Theory of Structuration*. Berkeley and Los Angeles: U of California P, 1984.

Gilbert, W. S. *The Yeomen of the Guard*. In *The Annotated Gilbert and Sullivan*, ed. Ian Bradley, 2: 411–515. Harmondsworth: Penguin, 1984.

Goffman, Erving. *Forms of Talk*. Philadelphia: U of Pennsylvania P, 1981.

Gombrich, E. H. *Art and Illusion: A Study in the Psychology of Pictorial Representation*. Bollingen Ser. 35.5. New York: Pantheon, 1960.

Goodman, Nelson. *Ways of Worldmaking*. Indianapolis: Hackett, 1978.

Habermas, Jürgen. *The Theory of Communicative Action*. 1981. Vol. 1: *Reason and the Rationalization of Society*. Vol. 2: *Lifeworld and System: A Critique of Functionalist Reason*. Trans. Thomas McCarthy. Boston: Beacon Press, 1984, 1987.

Horton, Robin. "Tradition and Modernity Revisited." In *Rationality and Relativism*, ed. Martin Hollis and Steven Lukes, 201–60. Cambridge: MIT, 1982.

Jackson, J. R. de J. *Historical Criticism and the Meaning of Texts*. London and New York: Routledge, 1989.

Jameson, Fredric. *The Political Unconscious: Narrative as a Socially Symbolic Act*. Ithaca: Cornell UP, 1981.

Jauss, Hans Robert. *Toward an Aesthetic of Reception*. Trans. Timothy Bahti. Brighton: Harvester, 1982.

Lakatos, Imre. *The Methodology of Scientific Research Programmes*. Vol. 1 of *Philosophical Papers*. Ed. John Worrall and Gregory Currie. Cambridge: Cambridge UP, 1978.

Lentricchia, Frank. *After the New Criticism*. Chicago: U of Chicago P, 1980.

Lyotard, Jean-François. *The Postmodern Condition: A Report on Knowledge*. 1979. Trans. Geoff Bennington and Brian Massumi. Minneapolis: U of Minnesota P, 1984.

Mauss, Marcel. "A Category of the Human Mind: The Notion of Person; the Notion of Self." 1938. Trans. W. D. Halls. In *The Category of the Person: Anthropology, Philosophy, History*, ed. Michael Carrithers, Steven Collins, and Steven Lukes, 1–25. Cambridge: Cambridge UP, 1985.

Mayr, Ernst. *The Growth of Biological Thought: Diversity, Evolution, and Inheritance*. Cambridge: Belknap P of Harvard UP, 1982.

Merleau-Ponty, Maurice. *The Structure of Behavior*. 1942. Trans. Alden L. Fisher. 1963; rpt. Pittsburgh: Duquesne UP, 1983.

Miller, Richard W. *Fact and Method: Explanation, Confirmation and Reality in the Natural and the Social Sciences*. Princeton: Princeton UP, 1987.

Pratt, Mary Louise. *Toward a Speech Act Theory of Literary Discourse*. Bloomington: Indiana UP, 1977.

Quine, W. V. *Quiddities: An Intermittently Philosophical Dictionary*. Cambridge: Belknap P of Harvard UP, 1987.

Radnitzky, Gerard, and W. W. Bartley III. *Evolutionary Epistemology, Rationality, and the Sociology of Knowledge*. La Salle, Illinois: Open Court, 1987.

Rorty, Amélie Oksenberg. *Mind in Action: Essays in the Philosophy of Mind*. Boston: Beacon, 1988.

Rothstein, Eric, and Frances M. Kavenik. *The Designs of Carolean Comedy*. Carbondale and Edwardsville: Southern Illinois UP, 1988.

Rushdie, Salman. *The Satanic Verses*. Harmondsworth, Mx.: Viking, 1988.

Simon, Herbert A. *Models of Man, Social and Rational*. New York: John Wiley & Sons, 1957.

Starobinski, Jean. *The Invention of Liberty, 1700–1789*. Geneva: Skira, 1964.

Veyne, Paul. *"Comment on écrit l'histoire" suivi de "Foucault révolutionne l'histoire."* 1971, 1978. Paris: Seuil, 1979.

Wade, Ira O. *The Intellectual Origins of the French Enlightenment*. Princeton: Princeton UP, 1971.

Weaver, Warren. "The Mathematics of Communication." 1949. Rpt. in *Science and Literature: New Lenses for Criticism*, ed. Edward M. Jennings. Garden City, New York: Doubleday (Anchor), 1970.

Wellek, René. "Periodization in Literary History." In *Dictionary of the History of Ideas: Studies of Selected Pivotal Ideas*, ed. Philip P. Weiner, 3: 481–86. 5 vols. New York: Scribners, 1973.

Wheeler, Samuel C., III. "Wittgenstein as Conservative Deconstructor." *NLH* 19 (1988): 239–58.

Wittgenstein, Ludwig. *On Certainty*. 1969. Ed. G. E. M. Anscombe and G. H. von Wright. Trans. Denis Paul and G. E. M. Anscombe. Rpt. New York: Harper & Row, 1972.

Wittgenstein, Ludwig. *Philosophical Investigations*. Trans. G. E. M. Anscombe. Oxford: Basil Blackwell, 1958.

Wittgenstein, Ludwig. *Remarks on the Philosophy of Psychology*. Vol. 2. Ed. G. H. von Wright and Heikki Nyman. Trans. C. G. Luckhardt and M. A. E. Aue. Chicago: U of Chicago P, 1980.

Wittgenstein, Ludwig. *Zettel*. Ed. G. E. M. Anscombe and G. H. von Wright. Trans. G. E. M. Anscombe. Berkeley and Los Angeles: U of California P, 1967.

Wollheim, Richard. "Art and Illusion." In *Aesthetics in the Modern World*, ed. Harold Osborne, 235–63. New York: Weybright and Talley, 1968.

Wuthnow, Robert. *Meaning and Moral Order: Explorations in Cultural Analysis*. Berkeley, Los Angeles, and London: U of California P, 1987.

CHAPTER 6

Weavings: Intertextuality and the (Re)Birth of the Author

SUSAN STANFORD FRIEDMAN

Does the "birth" of intertextuality as a critical term insist upon the "death" of influence as its conceptual precursor? Is the "death" of the author as writer the precondition for the "birth" of the critic as reader? In the evolution of critical discourse since Julia Kristeva coined the term "intertextualité" in 1966 and Roland Barthes proclaimed the "death of the author" in 1968, these two questions have been entwined, indeed knotted together. I want to explore the politics and psychodynamics of their knotting, to unravel their strands in historically specific terms, and to determine their influence on and intertextual transformations in the American critical scene, where "the author" and the correlative concept of agency insistently return. An intertextual reading of James Joyce's texts featuring Stephen Dedalus will suggest how the "death" and "(re)birth" of the "author" in critical debates enact a subtextual struggle between the desire to repress woman as speaking subject and women's persistent return to claim the position of agency.

I. INTERTEXTUALITY'S ANXIETY OF INFLUENCE

In this volume, the terms "influence" and "intertextuality" become at times personifications of a diachronic conflict between generations or a synchronic confrontation between European and American modes of analysis. Battles are often personified because a contest between systems is hard to visualize, to narrate, without actors moving as focal points in the ritual dance of confrontation. But this anthropomorphizing is not as figurative as it at first seems. For, it is people-as-actors (authors, writers) who voice theories, even if they don't originate them. No matter how much we problematize "writers," "authors," and even "people" who occupy historical time and geographical space, a theorist's text has a moment when it was not yet written, then a moment when it was. The writer makes that transition from the not-yet-written to the written happen. The writer is not just a figure, a trope as ideological construct. A "subject" already exists before he or she is reconstituted (again) in a text. That subject sets in motion and plays some part in the textual process of his or her own re-making.

"Intertextualité" "happened" when Kristeva introduced the term in 1966 under the guise of bringing Mikhail Bakhtin to the attention of theorists in France, first in "Word, Dialogue, and Novel" (1966) and then in "The Bounded Text" (1966–67), essays she wrote shortly after arriving in Paris from her native Bulgaria.[1] Feminist critics might readily recognize the gender inflection of Kristeva's self-authorizing strategy, one she uses often: to propose her own theories, she presents a "reading" of some (male) precursor or fellow writer, a re-reading in which her attribution of ideas to a male master screens the introduction of her own ideas. This "misreading," to invoke Harold Bloom's term, does not eliminate the other, but rather borrows his authority from the position of disciple.[2] Intertextuality was paradoxically born under the guise of influence.

The concept of intertextuality that Kristeva initiated proposes the text as a dynamic site in which relational processes and practices are the focus of analysis instead of static structures and products. The "literary word," she writes in "Word, Dialogue, and Novel," is "an *intersection of textual surfaces* rather than a point (a fixed meaning), as a dialogue among several writings" (*Desire* 65). Developing Bakhtin's spatialization of literary language, she argues that "each word (text) is an intersection of word (texts) where at least one other word (text) can be read" (66). "Any text," she continues, "is constructed as a mosaic of quotations, any text is the absorption and transformation of another. The notion of *intertextuality* replaces that of intersubjectivity, and a poetic language is read as at least double" (66).

There are always other words in a word, other texts in a text. Kristeva calls this a "translinguistic" doubleness (or "ambivalence") that "situates the text within history and society, which are then seen as texts read by the writer, and into which he inserts himself by rewriting them" (69, 65). The writer is first a reader of cultural texts; writing is always re-writing in the ceaseless construction of "history and society's" intersecting textual surfaces. Rejecting the New Critical principle of textual autonomy, Kristeva suggests that the reading of texts is the interpretation of their translinguistic doubleness, the infinite regress of tracing the other words in the word, the cultural texts in the literary text.

Less tied to an exposition of Bakhtin, the concluding sections of "Word, Dialogue, and Novel" effectively eliminate the writer from the analysis of intertextuality and anticipate the knot that ties intertextuality with the death of the author. In the earlier sections of the essay, the writer, as the "writing subject," is presented as one of the three intersecting coordinates of a text, along with the "addressee" (reader) and "exterior texts" (65, 74). As an agent, the "writer" acts to "insert himself" into history by rewriting his intertexts. But as Kristeva slides into a presentation of her own ideas in the final sections of the essay, this active writer vanishes into the concept of intertextual "anonymity." The "dialogism" inherent in writing, she argues, involves the writer in the construction of his own absence. Split into the "writing subject" ("subject of utterance") and the "author" ("subject of enunciation"), the writer is "drawn in, and therefore reduced to a code, to a nonperson, to an *anonymity*":

> He becomes an anonymity, an absence, a blank space, thus permitting the structure to exist as such. At the very origin of narration, at the very moment when the writer appears, we experience nothingness. . . . On the basis of this anonymity, this zero where the author is situated, the *he/she* of the character is born. At a later stage, it will become a proper name (N). . . . In this coming-and-going movement between subject and other, between writer (W) and reader, the author is structured as a signifier and the text as a dialogue of two discourses. (74–75)

Writing transforms the "writer" into an "author," who is a "signifier," an emptiness in the text filled by a proper name, the site of intertextual dialogue. The birth of the "author" in Kristeva's formulation happens at the moment when the writer dies into the text.

Two years later in "The Death of the Author," Barthes similarly suggests that "writing is the destruction of every voice, of every point of origin. Writing is that neutral, composite, oblique space where our subject slips away, where all identity is lost, starting with the very identity of the body writing. . . . The voice loses its origin, the author enters into his own death" (142).[3] The "author" dies in Barthes's text in more ways than one. Like Kristeva, he sees the "author" or "writer" vanishing into the play of signifiers on the page. But additionally, Barthes regards the "author" as a construct of post-Renaissance humanism, individualism, and capitalism— a concept whose moment of death has come, along with the death of the symbolic order that produced it.[4] In the poststructuralist moment, we are privileged to witness the "death of the author" and the unveiling of the true nature of "writing"—that is, its purely linguistic, intertextual anonymity. Where Kristeva's concept of intertextuality invites the "translinguistic" analysis of cultural texts in literary texts, Barthes asserts that writing is "intransitive," language is nonreferential, signifiers refer only to other signifiers in the ceaseless play of signification, in the endless deferral of the signified.[5] Kristeva's link with Bakhtin means that her formulation of intertextuality maintains some tie, however tenuous, to the "translinguistic." But in Barthes's view, the "death of the author" allows for the birth of the "scriptor," the writer as a scribe through whom the multiplicity of anonymous texts can pass. For the "modern scriptor," "the hand, cut off from any voice, borne by a pure gesture of inscription (and not of expression), traces a field without origins—or which, at least, has no other origin than language itself, language which ceaselessly calls into question all origins" (146). Even more radically, the scriptor is "this immense dictionary," which, unlike "the Author," "no longer bears within him passions," since "life itself does no more than imitate the book, and the book itself is only a tissue of signs, an imitation that is lost, infinitely deferred" (147). While "the Author is thought to exist before it," like "a father to his child," the "modern scriptor is born simultaneously with the text, is in no way equipped with a being simultaneously preceding or exceeding the writing" (145).

The "death of the author"—and with "him," the death of origin, meaning, and referentiality—makes possible the transformation of "the work" into the "Text" and the "Text" as a performative site of engagement with other texts: in short, intertextuality.[6] "We know," he writes, "that a text is not a line of words releasing a single 'theological' meaning (the 'message' of the Author-God) but a multi-dimensional space in which a variety of writings, none of them original, blend and clash. The text is a tissue of quotations drawn from the innumerable centres of culture" (146).

For both Barthes and Kristeva, intertextuality posits the notion of a text which is a "mosaic" or "tissue" of quotation without quotation marks, without a preexistent author exercising agency in the construction of that text. Intertextuality is an "anonymous" and "impersonal" process of blending, clashing, and intersecting. Texts "blend and clash," not people. Supplanting the "he" or "she" of a preceding author, the "it" of a text engages in intertextual play. In "The Bounded Text," Kristeva refines the concept of intertextuality proposed in "Word, Dialogue, and Novel" to suggest the process of "intersection":

The ideologeme is the intersection of a given textual arrangement (a semiotic practice) [i.e., a text] with the utterances (sequences) that it either assimilates into its own space or to which it refers in the space of exterior texts (semiotic practices). The ideologeme is that intertextual function read as "materialized" at the different structural levels of each text, and which stretches along the entire length of its trajectory, giving it its historical and social coordinates. . . . The concept of text as ideologeme determines the very procedure of a semiotics that, by studying the text as intertextuality, considers it as such within (the text of) society and history. (*Desire* 36–37)

Note that "it" refers to and assimilates other texts, not the author or writer. Similarly, for Barthes, "It is language which speaks, not the author; to write is, through a requisite impersonality . . . to reach that point where only language acts, 'performs,' and not 'me'" (143). "A text," he writes, "is made of multiple writings, drawn from many cultures and entering into mutual relations of dialogue, parody, contestation" (148). For both Barthes and Kristeva, the text—an "it"—draws, makes, enters, and dialogues with its intertexts. The subject of these verbs is the anonymous, impersonal "it" that engages in intertextual play. This personification of the verb's subject—the one who performs the action—as the anonymous "it" is a necessary corollary to the "death of the author."

The birth of the text's "it"—the text-as-it—also introduces the concept of the text-as-psyche, subject to the psychodynamic laws of the psyche and accessible to interpretation through psychoanalysis.[7] The "death of the author" allows for the birth of the textual subject, the "it" or psyche that is constructed in and through the text. As corollary to Lacan's notion of the psyche-as-text, the text-as-psyche lays the foundation for Kristeva's psychoanalytic semiosis in *Revolution in Poetic Language* (1974). The intertextual play of a text, she argues in 1974, involves both synchronic and diachronic axes of desire, reaching across the boundary between the conscious and the unconscious in the adult psyche, reaching back from the adult present into the developmental stages of the past child. The textual subject acts out a dialectical interaction of "the Semiotic" and "the Symbolic" modes of discourse—on the one hand, the pre-oedipal babble of the maternal *chora*, and on the other, the oedipal (or post-oedipal) discourse of the paternal symbolic order. The text plays out the psychodynamics of the psyche. The critic, in turn, reads the text according to the principles of a psychoanalytic hermeneutic.

The concept of intertextuality as Kristeva and Barthes proposed it is not exempt from the psychodynamics that it posits. Refusing the influence of influence, intertextuality is a concept that denies its filiation to its precursor, influence. Both Barthes and Kristeva take considerable pains to separate intertextuality from influence. And within the context of the history of ideas, they are right in doing so. Intertextuality is not the same as influence; adapting various poststructuralist discourses, intertextuality introduces something "new" to the methodology of reading texts in relation to other texts. But within the context of intertextual studies, their insistence on difference appears overdetermined. Each invokes the psychologically loaded language of purity as they resist the contamination of intertextuality with its precursor. Barthes, for example, writes in "From Work to Text" (1971):

The intertextuality in which any text is apprehended, since it is itself the intertext of another text, cannot be identified with some *origin* of the text: to seek out the "sources," the "influences" of a work is to satisfy the myth of filiation; the quotations a text is made of are anonymous, irrecoverable, and yet *already read*: they are quotations without quotation marks. (*Rustle* 60)

Origin, filiation, author, sources, and influence occupy one position in Barthes's binary; absence of origin or filiation, anonymity, scriptor, and intertextuality constitute the valorized pole. Further, "influence" is associated with a prior methodology, "intertextuality" with the modern. In "From Work to Text," he refers to the "traditional notion" as Newtonian and implies that the contemporary view of the text as "methodological field" is an Einsteinian one (*Rustle* 57).

This analogy with the "old" and "new" science invokes the larger antihumanist project of poststructuralism in general. Although neither Barthes nor Kristeva directly addresses what they resist in the concept of influence, influence is tainted with its association with humanism, with the tyranny of the Author as a "person" to whom the text is reduced. "The *author*," Barthes writes in "The Death of the Author," "still reigns in histories of literature, biographies of writers, interviews, magazines, as in the very consciousness of men of letters. . . . The *explanation* of a work is always sought in the man or woman who produced it, as if it were always in the end . . . the voice of a single person, the *author* 'confiding' in us" (143). As an unquestioned presence in influence studies, the author and his or her inferred intention have been a focal point for research. Biography has traditionally been an important methodological tool in the study of influence, often essential to the documentation of the author's intention and knowledge of a precursor or preexisting source. Departing from the autonomy of the text posited by New Criticism, Barthes was nonetheless reinforcing New Criticism's separation of the text from its author. In overthrowing the tyranny of the author and the related biographical method, Barthes was fomenting rebellion against the prevailing methodologies of influence study.

Barthes's revolutionary rhetoric in "The Death of the Author" establishes an undercurrent of rebellion against the connotations of the word "influence," which have themselves influenced the study of literary influence. In medieval Latin, "influentia" means "to flow into" and includes an astrological dimension: "the supposed flowing or streaming from the stars or heavens of an etherial fluid acting on the character and destiny of men" (*OED*). By the eighteenth century, the English word "influence" had taken on the meaning it still carries today: "the exercise of personal power by human beings, figured as something of the same nature as astral influence. . . . The inflowing, immission, or infusion (*into* a person or thing) of any kind of divine, spiritual, moral, immaterial, or secret power or principle; . . . The exertion of action of which the operation is unseen or insensible (or perceptible only in its effect) by one person or thing upon another" (*OED*). "Influence" suggests a principle of causality in which one person (or thing) changes as a result of the action of an other, prior, more powerful force. It presumes a source, an origin, an agency that flows into or acts upon another. At work in the concept of influence is a hier-archical, subject-object binary in which one is the actor, while the other is the acted upon. Agency belongs to the originator; passive reception and transformation to the other. The process of influence is invisible, evident only "in its effects." As a word, influence is implicated in the rationalizing ideology of the conqueror, the colonizer, who envisions his influence as a hegemonic penetration of the conquered, the colonized.

As Jay Clayton and Eric Rothstein demonstrate in their introduction to this volume, the rise of influence studies is interwoven with the rise of the nation-state and imperialism. The year 1968 in France is synonymous with the intellectual overthrow of the ancien régime of humanism—with its tie to capitalism and imperialism—by the poststructural vanguard. Barthes's "murder" of the author in his 1968 essay is symptomatic of this larger in-tellectual revolution. Within the arena of literary studies, it represents the effort to sweep away the study of influence as a focal point for analysis.

As Kristeva makes clear in her later essay "Women's Time," she shared the intellectual barricades with Barthes in the attack on humanism. But her rejection of the author's tyranny along with the study of influence con-tains an inflection distinct from his, one based in gender and ethnic differ-ence. As a woman, Kristeva exists at the edge of phallocentric discourses, a historically specific position of marginality that makes her insertion into and against those discourses fundamentally different from Barthes's. As a Bulgarian, Kristeva is an expatriate whose homeland has been at the bor-ders of European culture and subject to the dominance of the Soviet Union. Trained in Russian Formalism, Kristeva brought a Bakhtinian form of antihumanism embedded in his concepts of dialogic and polyvo-cal texts to the attention of French intellectuals. Bakhtin's reading of nov-els as dialogic sites mixing different and often non-"literary" voices sug-gests that the position of the colonized or the marginalized is not a scene of passive reception, but rather one of active negotiation. Intertextuality was born of an anticolonialist resistance to the concept of hegemonic influ-ence. In adapting Bakhtin to her semiotic project, Kristeva eliminated the author as the agent of that negotiation, but her concept of intertextuality is nonetheless consistent with his notion of heteroglossia and the multi-plicity of voices in a literary work. Both, in stressing the text as a scene of dialectical and conflictual process, resist the principles of hegemony endemic to the word influence.

The antihumanist, anticolonial currents in Barthes's and Kristeva's resistance to the discourse of influence involve them, paradoxically, in a contradiction with the principles of intertextuality they espouse. The insistence on intertextuality's separation from influence is tantamount to asserting that intertextuality has its own origin. The birth of intertextuality out of the death of influence means a denial of an intertextual presence of the earlier in the later. Barthes and Kristeva refuse to have the discourse of the "author," "sources," "allusions," (etc.) clash, blend, or intersect with the discourse of anonymous intertextuality. Such a mixture would taint the purity of anonymity. The generational and organic (birth/death) metaphors that pervade Barthes's theoretical discussion of influence and intertextuality place him, as the advocate of intertextuality, in the place of the son who would displace the father by refusing to recognize the father's influence — the influence of influence on the generation of intertextuality.[8]

The denial of intertextuality's filiation with influence is matched by the refusal to have other people contaminate the concept with its precursor. In *Revolution and Poetic Language*, for example, Kristeva refers disdainfully to the "banal" (mis)understanding of her term, which leads her to attempt to substitute a new word for what she had meant by intertextuality:

The term inter-textuality denotes this transposition of one (or several) sign system(s) into another; but since this term has often been understood in the banal sense of "study of sources," we prefer the term *transposition* because it specifies that the passage from one signifying system to another demands a new articulation of the thetic — of enunciative and denotative positionality. (*Revolution* 59–60)

Kristeva's new definition of "inter-textuality" as "transposition of one (or several) sign system(s) into another" usefully clarifies the original intent of her term. But her redefinition may also be read as a desire for orthodoxy, for the purity of an idea. Her allusion to influence as a "study of sources" is a metonymic "mis-reading" (in Bloomian terms) of the methodology in influence studies, which is surely more complex than "the study of sources." This reductionism may in effect be a symptom of the desire to control the dissemination of intertextuality, to exert *influence* on the future use of an idea she authored.

The insistence of Kristeva's English editor, Leon S. Roudiez, on the fixed meaning of "intertextualité" intensifies the move toward orthodoxy present in her own clarification of what she meant by intertextuality:

INTERTEXTUALITY (*intertextualité*). This French word was *originally* [emphasis added] introduced by Kristeva and met with immediate success; it has since been much used and abused on both sides of the Atlantic. The concept, however, has been generally misunderstood. It has nothing to do with matters of influence of one writer upon another, or with the sources of a literary work; it does, on the

other hand, involve the components of a *textual system* such as the novel. . . . Any
SIGNIFYING PRACTICE . . . is a field (in the sense of space traversed by lines of force)
in which various signifying systems undergo such a transposition. (*Desire* 15)

Roudiez's disturbance at the "abuse" of Kristeva's term—authorized by
Kristeva's own disparaging remarks—reflects the wish for intellectual clarity and precision in terminology, but it also engages in a desire to maintain
a fixed meaning, a signified, for intertextuality. The concern for the purity
of Kristeva's concept—the critique of its "abuse"—insists upon the operation of influence in the dissemination of her concept in its *original* form
on "both sides of the Atlantic." Kristeva *authored* the term, which should
be used with the *meaning* she *intended*. I highlight these words, which are
either explicitly or implicitly present in Roudiez's glossary entry, to emphasize the irony of the discourse of anonymous intertextuality being pro-
moted within the discourse of influence.

My point is not to trap Kristeva in an inconsistency but rather to suggest
that the discourses of influence and intertextuality have not been and cannot
be kept pure, untainted by each other. Indeed, the attempt to do so undermines the important insight the concept of intertextuality has offered
to the analysis of the formation and dissemination of "new" critical terms.
From a poststructuralist perspective, nothing is really "new"; everything
is "already written," as Barthes writes in "From Work to Text" (*Rustle*). The
discourse of intertextuality blends and clashes with the discourse of influence; the "new" term contains within it a reference to and "quotations"
of the older term. The work of Barthes and Kristeva that promotes intertextuality is itself instructive. The discourse of influence, for example, occasionally slips back into Barthes's formulation. The paragraph in "The Death
of the Author" that articulates the anonymous blending and clashing of
tissued texts concludes with a clash of its own: "The writer can only imitate
a gesture that is always anterior, never original. His only power is to mix
writings, to counter the ones with the other" (146). Not an "it" in the text,
the writer, just for a moment in Barthes's text, is an actor, the subject of his
own verbs: to mix, to counter. Similarly, Kristeva's very use of Bakhtin to ex-
pound her theory of intertextuality embodies the principles of influence. Not
only is he the author of his ideas, as she presents him, but her text also
testifies to the authority of his influence on her. And as Jonathan Culler
points out in "Presupposition and Intertextuality," Kristeva often relies
heavily upon the methodologies of influence in her own intertextual studies,
as when, for example, in her discussion of Lautréamont's *Poésies* ("this
intertextual space which is the birthplace of poetry"), she insists that "in
order to compare the presupposed text with the text *Poésies II*, one needs
to determine what editions of Pascal, Vauvenargues, and La Rochefoucauld

Ducasse could have used, for the versions vary considerably from one edition to another."[9]

Conversely, the discourse of intertextuality was already implicit in the study of literary influences as a methodology. In point of fact, the study of influence in literary history has not been nearly so hierarchical or unidirectional as the etymology of the word "influence" might suggest. Since writers are infrequently clones of precursors, literary historians of influence have often focused as much on the agency of the receiver as on the agency of the originating "source." Writers seldom duplicate their influential precursor(s); rather, they often work within a certain framework established by other writers or generic conventions, but vary aspects of it in significant ways. The interesting question for the critic has been how the successor(s) adapted, assimilated, revised, transformed, altered, reshaped, or revised the precursor(s).[10] This dialogic element has probably been foregrounded in studies focused on the successor, while work on influential figures often emphasizes the power of the originator.[11] But both often implicitly or explicitly engage in an analysis of the process of adaptation, assimilation, revision, and transformation.

Already woven with the strands of influence, intertextuality flowed across the Atlantic into the discourses of American criticism as a major, shaping influence on literary history and theory from the mid-seventies until the present. But like any influential idea, it changed as it was assimilated and adapted within a different cultural and intellectual context. It met resistance to insistence that it remain in a pure, undiluted state. Rather than see such adaptation as an "abuse" or "misunderstanding" — a judgment that comes out of the narrowest influence paradigm — I would argue that intertextuality was woven into sets of divergent discourses, including threads of its precursor, influence, on this "side of the Atlantic." Adaptations of intertextuality have often refused orthodoxy and encouraged a multiplicity of interpretations that will not collapse the signifier "intertextuality" into a single signified controlled by an authoritative source, its originator. The joyous plurality of meanings exploding out of the "polyphonies and permutations" in the 1978 anthology *Intertextuality: New Perspectives in Criticism*, edited by Jeanine Parisier Plottel and Hanna Charney, may be one of the sources to which Roudiez alludes. Intertextuality itself, in this multifaceted volume, is a "textual system" which many different "lines of force" traverse, including many aspects of the discourse of influence.

The multiplicity of meanings on this "side of the Atlantic" has been symptomatic of a tendency in American intertextual criticism to ignore or refuse the "death of the author" as a precondition of intertextual readings. Jonathan Culler, perhaps the first critic to transpose intertextuality onto the American critical scene, did not at first connect the term with the "death of the author" in *Structural Poetics* (1975). Operating within the structuralist project of this book, intertextuality is introduced as Kristeva's term to explain how genre functions as a horizon of expectations in the minds of readers and writers (130–60). Later, in *The Pursuit of Signs* (1981), he identifies the range of meanings proliferating around the term intertextuality in the contrast of two extremes: the infinite, anonymous intertextuality of Barthes on the one hand and the finite, dyadic intertextuality of Bloom on the other. In spite of Bloom's title — *The Anxiety of Influence* — Culler places Bloom's work *within* the debates on intertextuality, not influence. While Barthes emphasizes the clash of texts, Culler writes, Bloom reintroduces "the person," the confrontation of authors battling in the oedipal rivalry of fathers and sons (100–118). Culler critiques both these extremes and proposes a definition of intertextuality that views each text in terms of "a prior body of discourse — other projects and thoughts which it implicitly or explicitly takes up, prolongs, cites, refutes, transforms" (101). The door is open for Culler's actor — the subject of his active verbs — to be the "it" of the text or a "he" or "she," the person of an author. The "death of the author" is not for Culler a precondition of intertextuality, but rather one among many forms that intertextuality may take.

Culler does not measure the distance between Barthes's impersonalism and Bloom's personalism in geographical terms such as French and American. Nor does he identify the openness of his fluid definition with American culture. But we might see reflected in his intertextual adaptation of the French term a historically specific intellectual and cultural difference between France and the United States. As part of the larger antihumanist project of French poststructuralism, the "death of the author" intrinsic to intertextuality in the French context partially reflects the fall-out from two massive wars fought on European soil in this century and the widespread sense among intellectuals that Western humanism is irredeemably bankrupt.[12] Existentialism, poststructuralism's immediate precursor on the French cultural scene, had valorized the "transcendental ego," the "I" whose leap into agency could be taken despite the meaninglessness of the universe. From Jacques Lacan and Luce Irigaray to Barthes, Kristeva, Foucault, and Jacques Derrida, poststructuralists rejected the transcendental ego (and its existentialist act) in favor of what they have perceived as a more radical transformation of Western phallo(go)centrism. The anonymity and death of the author in Kristeva and Barthes — central to their concept of intertextuality — are part of a general poststructuralist critique of the conventional (unified, authoritative, agenic) subject of Western humanism and existentialism.

In American culture, however, the euphoria of victory and the global power of the United States fostered the intensification of traditional American individualism, even among intellectuals. The year 1968, a watershed of radical activity in many parts of the world, was not the same in France and the United States, where Jean-Paul Sartre and existentialism were still quite popular in the New Left movement of the campuses. The cultural ideology of the Self—as individualistic, independent, self-reliant—is deeply rooted in American history and culture.[13] Groups who have been denied the agency and status of the individual for reasons of race, class, gender, religion, ethnicity, sexual preference (and so forth) have traditionally felt excluded from "the American Dream." Appropriation of the discourse of the Self, however redefined, has been and still is a central characteristic of cultural and political movements of the marginalized in the United States. Redefinitions of the Self to be (re)claimed have been critically important to these movements. Women, racial minorities, Jews, homosexuals and lesbians have in particular emphasized how the ideology of individualism has been central to the erasure and distortions of identity for those outside the white, male, Christian, heterosexual hegemony.[14] But nonetheless, the redefined and intersecting discourses of the Self, agency, authority, and identity have been a cornerstone of the cultural and political transformations of the past twenty years in the United States.

Adaptations of intertextuality on this "side of the Atlantic" reflect the cultural and historical difference between radicalism in France and the United States. The debate over the status of the "subject" or "self" in American feminist criticism highlights this difference and points to a different model of intertextuality, one in which the concept of the author's agency is central. Some American feminist critics influenced by French poststructuralism— such as Peggy Kamuf and Alice Jardine—agree with the antihumanist project of French poststructuralism and argue that feminist critics should recognize the radical possibilities that the "death of the author" and the "death of the Cartesian Subject" open up for women. Others—such as Barbara Christian, Elizabeth Fox-Genovese, and Nina Baym—resist the influence of French ideas about the self in favor of a criticism that is rooted in women's selves and experience portrayed in historically specific literatures.[15] Still others—especially Nancy K. Miller—adapt many aspects of French poststructuralist theory to a self-consciously identified American feminist project that claims subject status for women and explores the forms that the "female signature" (Miller's term) has taken in various traditions of women's writing.[16] Miller's debate with Kamuf in a 1982 special issue of *Diacritics* focused the confrontation between poststructuralism and American feminist criticism directly on the issue of whether "the death of the author" represents a radical or reactionary direction for feminists.

Miller's work is of particular importance to debates about what intertextuality means or should be allowed to mean. In "Arachnologies," she directly advocates a kind of gynocriticism (to echo Elaine Showalter's term for the study of women's writing) that she calls "arachnology." This method is a deliberate blending of Barthesian notions of the text as "textile" or "web" with a clashing American feminist insistence on the importance of the author. But where Barthes's text is an infinite web seemingly spinning itself, Miller insists on reintroducing the spider — as author, as subject, as agent, as gendered body, as producer of the text. American feminist critics, she writes in her debate with Kamuf, "may betray a naive faith in origins, humanism, and centrality," but they have importantly challenged "the confidence of humanistic discourse as universality" ("Text's Heroine" 52). She prefers this "naivety" to Foucauldian "indifference" or Barthesian "anonymity," because "only those who have it [status as subject] can play with not having it" (52). In "Changing the Subject: Authorship, Writing, and the Reader," she continues to advocate "the author" as central to feminist criticism:

The position that the Author is dead, and subjective agency along with him, does not necessarily work for women and prematurely forecloses the question of identity for them. Because women have not had the same historical relation of identity to origin, institution, production, that men have had, women have not (I think collectively) felt burdened by too much Self, Ego, Cogito, etc. . . . when the question of identity — the so-called crisis of the subject — is posed, as it generally is, within a textual model, that question is irreducibly complicated by the historical, political, and figurative body of the woman writer. ("Changing" 107)

Miller's feminist critical method involves weaving poststructuralist insights into textuality with a feminist insistence on examining "the historical, political, and figurative body of the woman writer." "Arachnology" examines the weaving of women's texts as they are interwoven with many other texts (female and male). The text as an intertextual weaving of other cultural and historical texts (the "already read") is assumed, but Miller refuses to accept the concept of anonymity that Barthes, Foucault, and Kristeva promote in their versions of intertextuality. "Arachnology," she writes, suggests a "theory of text production"; as a method of reading, it "is a critical positioning which reads *against* the weave of indifferentiation to discover the embodiment in writing of a gendered subjectivity; to recover within representation the emblems of its construction" ("Arachnologies" 272). In place of "the (new) monolith of anonymous textuality," Miller promotes "a political intertextuality," that is, a "positionality" that involves "placing oneself at a deliberately oblique (or textual) angle" ("Changing" 111). This political intertextuality "remains necessarily a form of negotiation with the dominant social text" ("Changing" 111). For Miller, women writers and readers are gendered subjects in history who partake of this "deliberately oblique," political intertextuality.[17]

Miller's "political intertextuality" offers a model, I want to argue, for reading the political in the textual and the intertextual not only in women's writing, but also in men's writing; not only in white writing, but also in the writing by people of color; not only in "first world," but also in "second world" and "third world" writing. To interpret the mark of the historical, political, and figurative body of the writer, we must separate the concept of intertextuality from the death of the author. Miller's model also suggests a way for understanding how many American critics—not just feminist critics—have responded to the discourse of intertextuality that flowed as an influential current out of French poststructuralist theory into the American scene. Not all, but many American critics—from Bloom to Miller—have refused to let the author die as they forged various intertextual methodologies. Kristeva, Barthes, and Foucault have deeply "influenced" the American critical scene, but what began as a unidirectional flow of ideas has become a multiplicity of "intertextual" revisions, grafts, and adaptations in the United States. The American discourse of intertextuality has refused a hierarchical model of influence in its dialogic interactions with the French discourse of intertextuality. Where in France the idea of intertextuality was interwoven with the death of the author, intertextuality in the United States has resisted the inevitability of this connection.[18] Certainly many American critics have used the term in its pure French form, but in general the transplanted concept has spread like a weed in American soil that resists the erasure of the writer.

This resistance to hegemonic influence in favor of a dialogic intertextuality on the American critical terrain paradoxically repeats the structure of Kristeva's dialogue with Bakhtin in the "birth" of intertextuality at the scene of influence. In "Word, Dialogue, and Novel," Kristeva introduced "intertextualité" as Bakhtin's idea. But in suppressing the idea of influence, intertextuality in effect allows Kristeva to erase the influence of her precursor to whom she is seemingly crediting the concept and from whom she borrows (masculine) authority. This complicated gendered interaction also enacts an unconscious narrative of colonial domination and resistance relevant to the reception of French intertextuality in the United States. Kristeva's antihumanist project contains distinctive strands colored by her status as a Bulgarian expatriate in Paris, the "political intertextuality" of Miller's "arachnology." As an Eastern European woman in France, Kristeva represents the position of the triply colonized: by nationality in relation to the Soviet Union and European cultural centers; by gender in relation to the male world of letters. And from this determinative "historical, political, and figurative" space, she formulated a concept of anonymous intertextuality that resisted the tyranny of Western, Eurocentric hegemony and the phallocentric authority of the "author" represented supremely by the concept and operation of influence. Bakhtin's concepts of dialogism and heteroglossia became the ground upon which she developed her resistance to his influence, the place from which she, with others, formulated the idea of intertextuality that suppressed the agency of the writer.

This gender-inflected narrative of colonization and resistance is *structurally* repeated in the story of intertextuality's introduction to and reception in the United States, even though the *content* of the term is altered. Reflecting its status as a former colony, American culture has often exhibited anxiety toward as well as resistance to European culture, especially its discourses of intellect and art. In turn, Europeans have often regarded Americans as intellectually "naive," "empirical," "pragmatic," likely at every turn to "water down" and abuse the ideas originating in the cultural centers of Europe. Freud's well-known disdain for American psychoanalysis is an important part of this history, in turn repeated in Roudiez's attempt to guard the purity of Kristeva's term. The unidirectional flow of poststructuralist ideas emanating from France has been met by an American discourse that mixes a postcolonial sense of inferiority with a "pragmatic" and "self-reliant" insistence on the "right" to interrogate, graft, and transform these influential ideas. Like Kristeva's dialogic adaptation of both Bakhtin and French antihumanism, American critical reception of intertextuality has itself largely resisted the concept in its "purest" French form and insisted on a dialogic weaving of intertextuality with a concern rooted in American history and culture for the agency of the author.

This overdetermined contest over the meaning of a word (intertextuality) in turn metonymically repeats the history of colonization and resistance in the evolution of language itself. American English, British English, and French occupy different places in the history of colonization, and consequently, in relation to the homogenous and heterogenous. In 1066, French conquered Anglo-Saxon, imposing its will, stratifying English society linguistically. As a language, English became increasingly an evolving, ever fluid site of dialogic blending and clashing of different linguistic threads. As the language of the conqueror, French in contrast evolved as a language more resistant to change than English.[19] In the seventeenth century, during a period of centralization around the monarchy and the national state, the French Academy was instituted, dedicated to the preservation of French in its pure form and to the prevention of contamination by rapid change and outside influences. Doubly colonized, the North American colonies and later the United States established a dialogic relationship with their mother tongue, assimilating Native American languages, as well as the languages of immigrants from all over the world. In relationship to British English and its partial parent French, American English is heteroglossic, polygot, multivoiced, and many-tongued—a language of the rebellious, postcolonial subject that refuses the orthodoxy of its precursor. In turn, as the United States has increasingly become a colonizing power within a twentieth-century frame, Standard American English attempts to impose an orthodoxy on the languages, dialects, and slang of the marginalized people who have provided it with its heteroglossic disruptions in relationship to European languages.[20]

Similarly, in relationship to the discourses of French critical theory, American critical discourses have often resisted the unidirectional flow of influential ideas from their former (direct and indirect) colonizers and insisted on an intertextual blending and clashing. At the forefront of this resistance have been critics like Miller who speak as and for the marginalized within the colonizing structures of the American academy. Reinstitution of the author and agency into poststructuralist discourses of textuality has been an essential component of the intertextual reformation of influential ideas flowing across the Atlantic.

II. INTERTEXTUALITY AND PSYCHOANALYSIS

Is the debate about the author and intertextuality psychologically, as well as historically, overdetermined? Psychoanalysis would suggest that the suppression of the author in poststructuralist discourses of intertextuality would lead to a return of the repressed. The debate about intertextuality, in other words, may have a "political unconscious" (to adapt Fredric Jameson's term), a narrative about the repression and insistent return of agency and the author within and through language. I want to explore this hidden psychodynamic by showing how it is rooted in the contestations about identity and the subject in modernism, poststructuralism's influential precursor. The case of Joyce—the making of his modernism—will suggest how the debate about the author in current critical discourse restages a gender-inflected conflict that took place in the formation of modernism. At stake in both stagings is the politics of identity as it intersects with textuality and agency. Intertextuality—and the place of the author within it—stands at the center, both substantively and methodologically, of these concerns. The return of the repressed in modernism, specifically the insistent return of women as subjects within the discourse of men, parallels, I want to suggest, the return of the author into the discourse of intertextuality.[21]

An intertextual reading of Joyce's multiple *Künstler* narratives shows that the making of his modernism involved (among other things) the transformation of woman from thinking and desiring subject into a signifier and object of male desire. In *Gynesis,* Alice Jardine argues that "modernity" (by which she means poststructuralism, not modernism) dismantles the Cartesian subject, the unitary "I" of Western humanism, through the discourses of desire in which WOMAN functions as signifier necessary to the production of male texts. I want to propose a psychopolitical hermeneutic that integrates the intertextuality implicit in Freud's method and explicit in Kristeva's to show that what Jardine means by "gynesis" was present in the formation of Joyce's modernism, and perhaps in the formation of (male) modernism in general. Specifically, the series of autobiographical texts Joyce wrote featuring Stephen Dedalus—*Stephen Hero, Portrait of the Artist as a Young Man,* and *Ulysses*—demonstrate the move from a nineteenth-century discourse of social realism, in which women, like men, feature as speaking subjects, to a modernist discourse in which woman functions as the signifier upon which the multiply split subjectivity of the male "I" depends.

Before turning to Joyce, however, I need to show how a psychoanalytic intertextuality can be used to read a series of closely related texts, in this case a "draft" (*Stephen Hero*), a "final" text (*Portrait*), and a text (*Ulysses*) that continues the narrative of its precursor (*Portrait*).[22] Freud's method of dream interpretation can be usefully adapted to reading such a textual series. Texts like Joyce's Dedalus narratives can be read intertextually, as distinct but intersecting texts whose points of connection and disconnection can be interpreted for what they reveal and conceal. Instead of reading them as autonomous or as inadequate "drafts" that teleologically lead up to the intended and fully realized "final" text, they can be read as distinct parts of a larger composite "text" whose parts are like the imperfectly erased layers of a palimpsest. Two aspects of Kristeva's formulation of dialogic intertextuality—texts as sites of linguistic intersection and texts as psyches exhibiting conscious and unconscious processes—supplement Freud's hermeneutic, to which I will add Miller's "political intertextuality." Like Miller, I will reintroduce the author as a writer situated in history into a discussion of (inter)textuality. Not only does the "signature" of the writer matter, but the (con)texts of a writer's biographical and historical record will be restored to the interpretive process. Some of the methodologies of influence studies will, in other words, be adapted to an intertextual project.

Freud's hermeneutic provides the essential outlines for an intertextual interpretation of the text-as-psyche. The "censor," according to Freud in *The Interpretation of Dreams,* is the personified force ("the psychical agency") that forbids the drive to pleasure. As internalized agent of the cultural ethos in the realm of necessity, the "censor" attempts, with only partial success, to silence the forbidden desires of the unconscious. The linguistic mechanisms of the dream-work — condensation, displacement, nonrational modes of representability, and secondary revision — accomplish a compromise between the desire to express and the need to repress what is forbidden (311–546). Functioning as a grammar of the unconscious, the dream-work distorts the latent wish just enough to "evade" the "censor." Freud himself likened the dream-work's negotiation between revealing and concealing to the delicate encoding of the political writer who must disguise dangerous content so as to fool the censor who works on behalf of the oppressive state: "The stricter the censorship, the more far-reaching will be the disguise and the more ingenious too may be the means employed for putting the reader on the scent of the true meaning" (*Interpretation* 176).

Freud's hermeneutic outlined in *Interpretation of Dreams* in turn fools the censor — undoes the repression of the psyche, and by extension the internalized suppression of the social order. Beginning in determinacy, his method ends in indeterminacy. The "overdetermination" of dreams necessitates their "overinterpretation." The multiple layers of manifest form and latent content require an infinite regress of interpretation that ultimately leads to the "unplumbable" spot, the dream's "navel . . . that is its point of contact with the unknown" (143). This metaphor for the knot in the dream-text suggests that the threshold of mystery is a point of contact with the maternal body, the irretrievable site of origins, as well as the origin of what is censored, what is disguised in the grammar of the dream-work. Ultimately, his figurative formulation suggests, the return of the repressed is the return of woman, of that mother/other, to him forever unknown, untranscribable, untranslatable.

Freud's method for "overinterpretation" is fundamentally intertextual. He rejects what he calls the "symbolic" method of dream interpretation which analyzes the dream as an autonomous unit with interrelating parts — a method that is strikingly consonant with the theory of art that Stephen Dedalus expounded in Joyce's *Stephen Hero* and *Portrait* and that New Criticism developed into a method. Freud proposes instead his psychoanalytic method, in which fragments of the dream become departure points into a labyrinth of associations that radiate without end into the dreamer's recent and distant past, the linguistic and visual artifacts of culture, and the events of history.

Freud also breaks down the autonomy of the dream-text by reading dreams in relation to other dreams, decoding a series of dreams as a composite text. In "consecutive dreams," one dream often "takes as its central point something that is only on the periphery of the other and *vice versa*" *(Interpretation* 563). Reading serial dreams requires an analysis of the gaps in each that can be filled in by the other — the traces of displacement, condensation, and secondary revision that can be deciphered by juxtaposing and superimposing the texts in the whole series. The resonances among the dreams — the consonances and dissonances — can themselves be read for clues to undo the work of the Censor. As he writes about dreams occurring in the same night:

The content of all dreams that occur during the same night forms part of the same whole. . . . successive dreams of this kind . . . may be giving expression to the same impulses in different material. If so, the first of these homologous dreams to occur is often the more distorted and timid, while the succeeding one will be more confident and distinct. (*Interpretation* 369)

This formulation of successive dreams anticipates Freud's concept of the repetition compulsion and transference. Repressed desires lead a person to "repeat" patterns of behavior as the person "transfers" the feelings from early childhood onto the contemporary adult scene. The analytic situation triggers the "transference": the analysand repeats with the analyst the patterns he or she once enacted with others. The goal of analysis, Freud believes, is to move the analysand from "repetition" to "remembering" by "working through" the transference. Once an adult can "remember" the past (in the full psychoanalytic sense of the term), he or she is no longer doomed to "repeat" it.[23]

Freud's intertextual hermeneutic and related concepts of transference are richly suggestive for literary analysis because writing, like dreams, can enact a negotiation between desire and repression in which linguistic disguise accomplishes a compromise between expression and suppression. When the novel is autobiographical, this negotiation — which may be conscious or unconscious — is further heightened. Like a palimpsest, both psyche and literary text are layered, with repressed elements erupting in disguised forms onto the manifest surface of consciousness, of a text. Adapting Kristeva's formulations of the text-as-psyche, critics such as Culler, Jameson, Shoshana Felman, and Michael Riffaterre further suggest that a text has an unconscious accessible to interpretation through a decoding of its linguistic traces and effects. For Culler and Felman, this textual unconscious is located in the interaction between reader and text, which they see as a scene of transference in which the reader "repeats" the complexes of the text. For Jameson and Riffaterre, the textual unconscious resides in the text, subject to the decoding of the reader, who occupies the authoritative position of the analyst. According to Riffaterre, the surface of a novel is narrative, but it has a lyric "sub-text," a "verbal unconscious" buried etymologically inside the manifest words of the text. For Jameson, texts have a "political unconscious," which he defines as the repressed narrative of class struggle which a Marxist hermeneutic can interpret (20). From another perspective, Culler suggests, "the literary unconscious is an authorial unconscious, an unconscious involved in the production of literature; and the notion is thus useful for raising questions about the relation between what gets into the work and what gets left out, and about the sorts of repression that may operate in the production of literature" ("Textual Self-Consciousness" 369).

All these approaches to the textual unconscious are useful for reading chains of related texts intertextually. The "draft" may contain elements that are repressed and transformed by the linguistic mechanisms analogous to the dream-work as the author revises the text. In becoming more "artful," the "final" version may indeed subject the "draft" to the process of linguistic encoding analogous to the production of a dream out of the forbidden desires restricted to the unconscious. In political terms, the repression of what is forbidden in the change from "draft" to "final" text may reflect the role of ideology as an internalized censor that allows the revelation of a given story only if it is concealed through the mechanisms of the dream-work. Existence of the "draft" potentially aids the interpretation of what is hidden in the "final" text. The earlier text may erupt into the gaps of the later text just as cultural and political rebellion disrupts the social order. Textual repression can reflect cultural and political oppression. Representing "the return of the repressed," the "draft" version may contain a powerful and forbidden critique of the social order reflected in the "final" text.

On the other hand, a chain of drafts and texts with the same characters invokes Freud's theory of serial dreams and repetition. Especially in autobiographical texts, *writing*, as well as reading, can be regarded as a scene of transference. Different "drafts" of a final text or texts in a series can be interpreted as "repetitions" in which the author is "working through" conflicts in an effort (conscious or unconscious) to move from "repetition" to "remembering." Within this context, the earlier "drafts" might well be the most repressed. Similarly, in a series of texts with the same character, the early text may be the most distorted or "timid," while the last text might represent the author's success in working through repetition to remembering.

I am suggesting, in other words, the necessity of reading a chain of related texts "both ways" — on the one hand refusing to regard the "final" text simply as the aesthetically superior and teleological endpoint of all the others; on the other hand, recognizing that repression can be present at the beginning as well as the end of the process. Rather than searching for the "authentic" or "intended" version, I want to regard all versions as part of a larger composite text whose parts remain distinct, yet interact according to a psycho/political dynamic to which we have some access with the help of Freud's theory of repression and grammar for the dream-work. These processes may be the result of conscious decisions on the part of the author or of unconscious negotiations of which the author was largely unaware. Sometimes these processes can be charted empirically by reading the "drafts" and "final" text as they intersect with texts in the biographical archive. At other times, they are traceable only through an interpretation of their effects in the texts at hand. But in either case, the critic needs a flexible concept of intertextuality that examines the clashing and blending of texts from the biographical, literary, and cultural records.

III. THE CASE OF JOYCE AND JOYCE AS CASE

Freud's hermeneutic, Kristeva's text-as-psyche, and Miller's "political intertextuality" are all useful for an intertextual reading of Joyce's three Dedalus narratives. *Stephen Hero* represents a portion of the unfinished draft for *Portrait* which Joyce apparently threw into the fire in disgust. Three hundred and eighty-three pages of the nearly one-thousand-page draft were saved and later published as *Stephen Hero* (1944). These pages narrate a number of the same episodes that appear in *Portrait*, but the differences between the texts are dramatic, often used to illustrate the transition from nineteenth-century narrative convention to modernism.[24] *Ulysses* is a continuation of *Portrait*, picking up the story after Stephen's return to Dublin from Paris because of his mother's final illness and death. Begun in February of 1904, not long after the death of Joyce's mother in August of 1903, *Stephen Hero* was abandoned in 1906. In 1908, after the birth of his second child, Joyce started a new draft of the Dedalus story, and between 1911 and 1914 he completed his third and final draft of *Portrait*. Appearing in serial form in *The Egoist* in 1914 and 1915, the book appeared in 1916 and concludes with inclusive dates that link *Stephen Hero* and *Portrait* together: "Dublin 1904 Trieste 1914." Begun in 1915, parts of *Ulysses* began to appear by 1918, with the first publication of the novel in 1922.

If we superimpose *Portrait* on top of *Stephen Hero*, *Portrait* reads like a dream-scape and primer of the modernist break with nineteenth-century fiction. In terms of Freud's grammar for the dream-work to a literary text, *Portrait* is a condensed, displaced, lyric, and symbolically restructured form of *Stephen Hero* — as is symptomatically evident in the change of his persona's name from "Daedalus" to "Dedalus."[25] What, then, is being repressed, censored, and disguised, and what does this tell us about the transition to modernism? The answer lies, I believe, in the issue of the mother and what she represents to Stephen. Freud's metaphor for the dream's knot as a navel is prophetic. *Portrait*'s modernist revision of *Stephen Hero* represents the silencing of the mother, the erasure of her subjectivity, and the creation of the m/other who exists for and in the discourse of the son who takes his place in the Symbolic Order of the Father.[26]

Censored out of *Portrait* is Stephen's confrontation in *Stephen Hero* with the Censor, the President who represents the paternal authority of the Irish Church that stifles the modern, the freethinking, and the creative. Significantly, Stephen's debate with the Censor follows a lengthy discussion of Ibsen with his mother. Stephen reads the paper he has written celebrating Ibsen as the spirit of the modern to his mother as she stands ironing. To his surprise, she likes the paper and asks to read Ibsen. At first, he imagines that all she wants is "to see whether I am reading dangerous authors or not" (85). But to his shock, she reveals that "Before I married your father I used to read a great deal. I used to take an interest in all kinds of new plays" (85). His father's distaste for such things led her to stop. "Well, you see, Stephen," she explains, "your father is not like you: he takes no interest in that sort of thing" (85). He is startled when she actually reads a group of plays "with great interest," and he suspiciously asks whether she thinks Ibsen is "immoral," writing about "subjects which, you think, should never be talked about?" Stephen tries, in other words, to put his mother in the position of the censor, a role she pointedly refuses. "Do you think these plays are unfit for people to read?" he asks. "No, I think they're magnificent plays," she answers. "And not immoral?" he repeats. "I think that Ibsen...has an extraordinary knowledge of human nature," she says (87).

In liking Ibsen, Stephen is his mother's child, not his father's. The role of moral censor which Stephen anticipated that his uneducated mother would play is actually acted out by her intellectual "superiors" — especially Father Dillon. Outside the college that does not admit women, outside the Jesuit educational system, Stephen's mother is free to respond to Ibsen. The "modern" toward which Stephen aspires is presented as a legacy from his mother, not his father, a "freethinking" that can be nurtured only beyond the reach of the Jesuit Censor.[27]

That Ibsen should be the playwright to introduce Stephen to the mother who knows, the mother who speaks, the mother who thinks outside the Jesuit hegemony is no arbitrary choice. Ibsen's women are powerful figures who insist on their status as human beings, as subjects in a patriarchal world that would confine them to what men desire them to be. Joyce himself wrote his brother in 1907 that Ibsen "was the only writer that ever persuaded me that women had a soul" (Ellmann 287). As with some of Ibsen's women, the potential for freedom that Stephen's mother represents is ultimately destroyed, in her case by the power of the Church and the authority she is willing to give it. His mother's defense of Ibsen is ironically followed in chapter 21 by her request for Stephen to perform his "Easter duty," which he refuses to do. In the context of her superiority to Father Dillon about Ibsen, her naive faith in the Church represents a betrayal of the "freethinking" to which her position as a woman privileges her. In refusing her request, Stephen remains true to the legacy she has betrayed for herself, but passed on to him.

In *Portrait*, the paper about Ibsen has vanished, along with the mother who knows and the father who censors. What remains is his mother's request that he perform his Easter duty and his ringing Non Serviam, displaced into the final chapter of *Portrait* and embedded in his last conversation with Cranly as the climactic preparation for his flight. And as Hélène Cixous points out, *Portrait* portrays words as Stephen's legacy from his father, while the body that he both desires and hates is his inheritance from his mother. As a secondary revision of *Stephen Hero*, *Portrait* reorders the *Bildung* narrative of development along classically oedipal lines. The mother is the figure from whom Stephen must separate, for whom he must repress and ultimately sublimate his desire.

Established in *Portrait*'s famous opening paragraph, the father is the storyteller, the impresario of words, while the maternal is associated with the "moocow," taste, smells, blossoms, music, nonsense syllables, and warm urine—a sort of Kristevan Semiotic (*Portrait* 7). Initiation as a youth, as Suzette Henke argues, means oscillating between desire for and loathing of the maternal body—in its pure form, the madonna; in its polluted form, the whore. Youth also means identification with the awesome power of the priest. Even when Stephen rejects the priesthood, he takes on the priest's authority in the secular domain of art. Stephen's birth as an artist in chapter V, however qualified through irony, nonetheless represents his identification with the legacy of the fathers exercising the authority of Logos. Within a Lacanian framework, Stephen's *Bildung* follows the expected pattern of the son who has come to take up his position within the Symbolic Order according to the Law of the Father. The endless deferral of his desire—first for his mother, then for E.C.—is what allows him to occupy the position of the Subject, the master of the signifier.[28]

The narrative of the mother who knows in *Stephen Hero* is the political unconscious of *Portrait*, censored out of the later text as Joyce forges the language of modernity. This transformation of the mother suggests that the development of Joyce's modernism—and perhaps the phenomenon of male modernism in general—involves the repression of the mother, of woman, as subject. In Lacanian terms, woman in *Portrait* exists as the position of castration—as the Other (m/other) who cannot speak, but whose function as signifier within the chain of signification in the Symbolic Order is essential. The constitution of Stephen as subject, in other words, depends upon the silence of the Other—the place occupied by women. While Lacan's concept of the subject in language is presented in universalist terms, I am suggesting that it is itself an extension of the modernism represented in Joyce's *Portrait*—the male modernism premised on the erasure of women's agency in language and women's reduction from subject to object in a male economy of desire.[29]

But what about "reading both ways"? Freud's concept of serial dreams, where the earliest ones are the most repressed, suggests that *Stephen Hero* may itself represent the operation of the Censor, while Joyce's later texts about Stephen may reflect his efforts to move from repetition to remembering. Joyce's mother, who died in August 1903, about four months after he was called home from Paris, is central to this succession of texts. I want to suggest that what governs Joyce's repetitions is an Orestes complex—the repressed fear that his break from his mother was indeed matricidal, that his glorious flight into the modern required killing his mother, an act that however necessary to his art paralyzed him with guilt.[30] Writing over and over again the story of Stephen represents for Joyce the exorcism of his mother's ghost and the search for expiation—to repeat, in other words, the movement of Aeschylus' *Oresteia*. Underlying the story of "Agenbit of inwit. Conscience," however, is the oedipal narrative of the son's ambivalent longing for and repulsion from the maternal body he has renounced and lost.[31]

Not until *Ulysses* was Joyce able to write overtly about his mother's death. But the chain of covert texts is like the series of dreams in which the first are the most "timid," while the last are the least censored. The absence of boundaries between dream-texts and other texts in Freud's hermeneutic further invites us to see the three Stephen texts in an even longer chain of texts linked to the death of Joyce's mother. First comes a highly coded poem called "Tilly" (written right after his mother's death, but not published until 1927), with its howl of unspecified grief connected with cows (Ellmann 136–37). The poem suggests in condensed and non-referential form some of the motifs that become associated with Stephen in later texts—particularly Stephen's ashplant and associations on maternal cows in *Portrait* and *Ulysses*. Next comes Joyce's autobiographical story "The Sisters," which he published on August 13, 1904 (the first anniversary of his mother's death) under the pseudonym "Stephen Daedalus." Then in January of 1904 Joyce wrote an "essay-narrative" entitled "Portrait of the Artist" about an unnamed Daedalus figure (Ellmann 172–73). "A Portrait of the Artist" comes closer to autobiographical origins in its brief allusion to the youth's refusal to take communion for the sake of his art, but lacks any reference to the youth's mother, her request, or her death. *Stephen Hero* (begun right after the essay was rejected by the journal *Dana*) and then *Portrait*, catalyzed by the birth of a child, both come closer to the forbidden material. They reproduce the mother's request and Stephen's refusal. But both repress the mother's illness and distort the sequence. *Stephen Hero* and *Portrait* displace Stephen's refusal of his mother's request that he perform his Easter duty to a scene *before* his flight to Paris, instead of after his return, when the event actually occurred. May Joyce's dying illness is absent from both texts. These displacements effectively repress any connection between the son's refusal and the mother's dying.

In *Ulysses*, Joyce finally wrote openly in a rectified sequence about his mother's dying request and his denial of her wishes. Curiously, the nightmare sequence in "Circe" presents the scene most directly. Once more Stephen's mother makes her request, once more Stephen refuses, and once more he "kills" her by declaring *"Non serviam!"* and swinging in a blind drunk with his ashplant at the chandelier (474–75). Stephen declares his independence from the Church—"The intellectual imagination! With me all or not at all." But the dramatic confrontation between mother and son suggests that it is at base his mother, not religion, that he must deny. Refusal of the Irish Church and State in *Ulysses* is unveiled in "Circe" as a flight from the maternal.

This flight from the maternal body is fueled by desire for it. For Stephen, the sea images the dual aspect of his mother and his feelings for her. She is both "a great sweet mother" and the green bile she vomits. Her arms enfold and suffocate. She is the place of life and death, the site of origin and end. She is the body that is both pure and polluted, a matrix of what is taboo—both desired and feared by the son. In Stephen's protean thoughts, the womb/tomb of the "unspeeched" maternal body calls him to kiss— forever fusing love and death, desire and loathing in a mother-son bond that binds and nourishes:

Bridebed, childbed, bed of death. . . . Mouth to her mouth's kiss.
His lips lipped and mouthed fleshless lips of air: mouth to her moomb. Oomb, allwombing tomb. His mouth moulded issuing breath, unspeeched: ooeeehah: roar of cataractic planets, globed, blazing, roaring wayawayawayawayaway. (40)

Stephen's theory about Hamlet is often read in relation to the theme of paternity, but this emphasis on the father-son relationship can also be interpreted as a screen for the incestuous mother-son matrix.

In relation to all the prior Stephen texts, *Ulysses* accomplishes what Stephen within the narrative of the novel could not. It "remembers" what *Stephen Hero* and *Portrait* disguised and "forgot." It names the pattern of repetition and confronts head-on the Medusa of longing, loathing, and guilt. In the transferential scene of writing, Joyce "works through" to "remember" what Stephen can only "repeat." In relation to Joyce's life — as we know it through other texts — *Stephen Hero, Portrait,* and *Ulysses* form a palimpsest in which each layer inscribes differently the author's attempt to deal with his mother's death, most especially her request and his refusal in April of 1903 that he perform his Easter duty — that is, that he confess and take communion.

Reading "both ways" with Joyce's various presentations of Stephen D(a)edalus appears to suggest two opposing views. From one perspective, *Portrait* and *Ulysses* are more repressed texts than *Stephen Hero* because in the later texts woman-as-subject has been erased and replaced by the woman who exists for the male subject as a crucial signifier in the chain of signification. From this perspective, *Stephen Hero* is the textual and political unconscious of *Portrait* and *Ulysses.* But from the perspective of writing as a scene of transference and potential "cure," *Stephen Hero* is more repressed than the later versions, especially *Ulysses.* Only after a series of textual repetitions can Joyce create a self-portrait that confronts the remorse, desire, and fear repressed after his mother's dying. *Ulysses* does not, of course, end the chain of textual repetitions. Even though Stephen does not appear as character in *Finnegans Wake*, the negotiations centered on the desire and loathing for the female body as constitutive of the writing subject — and language itself — is played out once again.

What remains constant, however, in reading the process of censorship both ways is the centrality of the mother. In both cases the creation of Joyce's modernist master-pieces depends upon the censorship of the mother who speaks and acts, the mother who negotiates some sort of agency in spite of and within the confinements of patriarchy. The making of Joyce's modernism, reflected in the composite "text" of *Stephen Hero, Portrait,* and *Ulysses*, leads us to ask broader questions about the formation of male modernism in general. Is the silencing of women as subjects a precondition for the artful voices of men? Is the dominant literary history of modernism a "case history" of (male) readers who have been transferentially captured by the complexes of texts like Joyce's *Portrait* and *Ulysses* in which women as subjects have been swallowed up into the productions and representations of male modernists? Like Joyce's Stephen texts, male modernism may have a textual and political unconscious censored by the Censor that Joyce himself censored out of his premodernist work in the making of modernism. Such hypotheses about male modernism raise related questions about women writers in the modernist period who assumed the agency of the author. How did they engage not only with the texts of their male counterparts who would read them as signifiers in a male economy of desire, but also with the psychopolitical dynamics of (self) censorship? If they, at times, represent the textual and political unconscious of male modernism, what has been repressed in their writing?

IV. JOYCE, KRISTEVA, AND INTERTEXTUALITY

Such questions, which ultimately attempt to theorize literary history and historicize literary theory, must wait for an extended study. But the case of Joyce in the making of modernism contributes to debates about inter- textuality in the poststructuralist period in several ways. First, the psycho/ political hermeneutic I have proposed for reading Joyce's textual series is itself an example of an intertextual methodology that weaves together a number of different concepts of intertextuality, along with aspects of in- fluence studies. Kristeva's (intertextual) adaptation of psychoanalysis to reading textual practices suggests ways to trace the effects of repression in a textual series by the same author. Culler/Felman/Riffaterre's (inter- textual) adaptation of Freud and Kristeva provides a mechanism for reading the unconscious text hidden within the conscious one. Jameson's (intertex- tual) adaptation of psychoanalysis suggests a way to link the narratives of oppression and repression — censorship and self-censorship — as they in- teract in the author's production of a textual series. Miller's (intertextual) adaptation of Barthes formulates a "political intertextuality" broader than Jameson's Marxist horizon, one that insists upon the significance of the author's "signature," on a historically specific configuration of gender, class, race, sexual preference, religion, and so forth. And my own (intertex- tual) grafting of Freud's grammar with the intertextual methods of all these critics frees textual criticism from the confinements of a search for the perfect text by focusing on textual process, by seeing all texts as "sur- faces" that intersect with other texts. It also provides a method for analyzing those points of surface intersection as part of a psychic and linguistic negotiation between desire and denial — both conscious and unconscious — as these are historically constructed.

Second, the case of Joyce — his textual suppression of the mother as sub- ject and her insistent return — prefigures the hidden gender narrative in the current critical discourses of intertextuality. Stephen's (and Joyce's) flight to Paris, the cultural mecca of the modern, frees him temporarily from the Irish sow who eats her farrow. Kristeva too heads for Paris, to the cen- ter of the poststructuralist revolution. There she contributes significantly, especially with her concept of intertextuality, to the "death of the author" and, related to it, the suppression of the historically specific signature and subjectivity of the writer within the discourses of critical theory. There she introduces Bakhtin's disruptive heteroglossia, only to suppress his influence by her concept of anonymous intertextuality. Both exiles share the experience of colonization, Joyce as Irish, Kristeva as Bulgarian and female. Both clear a space for themselves by suppressing their origins: Joyce, by repressing the m/other; Kristeva, by erasing the idea of origin itself. For Joyce, the woman whose subjectivity he has repressed returns repeatedly in the transferential scene of writing. Perhaps this return prefigures the return of the maternal body in Kristeva's theory of textuality. In *Revolution in Poetic Language*, as well as in her later essays, Kristeva privileges the Semiotic register of language as the sign of the avant-garde, precisely that part of language tied to the repressed memory of the maternal body that erupts into the Symbolic, that disrupts the Law of the Father associated with Western humanism. Perhaps, in turn, the return of the mother in the textual practices of Joyce and Kristeva prefigures the return of the signature and historically specific subject into the discourse of intertextuality.

Finally, my (intertextual) readings of Kristeva and Joyce suggest that intertextuality can serve not only as example, but also as the principle of the dialogic evolution/revolution of critical concepts as they are historically developed and disseminated. The cultural narrative I have proposed for the *agon* between influence and intertextuality with the death and the (re)birth of the author as its turning point is not meant to promote a synchronic dialectic in which some grand synthesis of the two is teleologically implied. Instead, I have suggested that the formation and dissemination of ideas are rooted in a historical process as an overdetermined diachronic narrative moving through different spaces and times. At its "birth," intertextuality by its self-definition denied its origins in the discourse of influence. But as the term spread intertextually, the author whose death it had proclaimed insistently returned, particularly as intertextuality was transposed into American critical discourses. We have come full circle, back to the fabric of a text, this time an intertextual web of critical discourses that are endlessly woven and re-woven. Central to this (intertextual) reweaving of the critical discourses of intertextuality is the reinsertion of the author, along with some of the biographical and historical methodologies of influence studies, back into the pattern of the fabric.

NOTES

I am indebted to Elaine Marks and to the Draft Group, especially Eric Rothstein and Thomas Schaub, for challenging criticisms to an earlier version of this essay. The section on Joyce was presented at the International Symposium on James Joyce, Venice, June 1988.

1   In *Desire in Language*, "Word, Dialogue, and Novel" is dated 1966 and "The Bounded Text" is dated 1966–67; both essays appeared in her first volume of essays *Recherches pour une sémanalyse* in 1969. Kristeva, along with Tzvetan Todorov, another expatriate from Bulgaria, are generally credited with introducing Bakhtin to the French critical scene in the mid-sixties.

2   See Bloom, *Anxiety of Influence* and *Map of Misreading*. The essays in *Desire in Language* similarly feature Barthes, Céline, Beckett, Sollers, Giotto, and Bellini. Kristeva does not put women writers in this position of authority. Only the Virgin Mary, in her abjectness and grief, occupies the place of "teacher" to Kristeva's stance as "disciple" in "Stabat Mater."

3   Quotations from Barthes's "The Death of the Author" are from Stephen Heath's 1978 translation of *Image-Music-Text*. The 1986 translation by Richard Howard in *The Rustle of Language* is different. The earlier translation is the version that has been so influential in the United States. Barthes's essay was first published in 1968, but he may well have been presenting these ideas earlier in his seminar. After her arrival in Paris in 1966 on fellowship, Kristeva was a student in Barthes's seminar, where he quickly recognized her talent, according to Elaine Marks (conversation with author). At about the same time, Michel Foucault was formulating his own version of authorial anonymity in his essay "What Is an Author?" first given as a talk at the Société Française de Philosophie and published in its bulletin in 1969, then revised before translation into English (Harari 13, 43). Until intellectual histories of Paris in the sixties are written, it will be extremely difficult to make any claims for "origin" or "influence," even accounting for the problematic nature of such a task in the first place.

4   The diachronic moment in Barthes's essay intersects with Foucault's sustained analysis in "What Is an Author?" of the cultural and ideological production of "the author" as a "role function" in discourse. Like Kristeva and Barthes, Foucault regards the text as a site of "anonymity." The "author" is a "function" played out in the text onto which readers "project" their own needs, which they identify with the author's "intention." But Foucault does not agree with Barthes's isolation of the text from history and ideology. Foucault's concept of culture as intersecting discourses represents a form of the concept of intertextuality that emphasizes the production of ideology. See Harari (40–44).

5   See also Barthes, "To Write: An Intransitive Verb?" (1966), "From Work to Text" (1971), "The Rustle of Language" (1975), and "The Discourse of History" (1967) collected in *Rustle*. *Roland Barthes by Roland Barthes*, his "autobiography," represents a culmination of Barthes's theories of language and (non)referentiality. But see also *Camera Lucida*, written after the death of his mother, where he returns to concepts of reference and origin.

6   See also Barthes, "From Work to Text" (1971), in *Rustle*.

7   The text-as-psyche is a defining characteristic of Kristeva's blend of semiotics, psychoanalysis, and Marxism.

8   I am, of course, adapting Bloom's concept of an oedipal rivalry between generations of poets to the contemporary history of the concepts influence and intertextuality.

9   Culler quotes from *Revolution in Poetic Language (Pursuit* 106). Kristeva's discussions of writers and artists often introduce information based on biography, a methodology associated with influence studies. See for example Kristeva, "Motherhood according to Bellini" (*Desire* 237–70).

10 See for example Bloom's dialogic theory of influence in *The Anxiety of Influence.* See also my *Psyche Reborn: The Emergence of H.D.*, which was conceived in the mid-seventies as (in part) an influence study before I had heard of the term intertextuality. It illustrates how the discourse of intertextuality was already present within the discourse of influence; its central thesis is that the "process of influence" was "dialectical" and "revisionist": "Freud's enormous influence as a catalyst to H.D.'s artistic self-definition was paradoxically dependent on her capacity to disagree with his most fundamental presuppositions" (87).

11 It is beyond the scope of this essay to test this speculation, but Hugh Kenner's *The Pound Era* and my *Psyche Reborn* fit this pattern as different histories of modernism.

12 See Kristeva's "Women's Time" for a discussion of this cultural moment in Europe.

13 I am indebted to Thomas Schaub and Gordon Hutner for pointing out to me the relevance of this cultural and political history to my argument.

14 See for example Fox-Genovese and Friedman, "Autobiographical Selves."

15 See also Yaeger. There is considerable variation in these positions. Baym argues against any theorizing, including poststructuralist model building. Christian and Fox-Genovese address the politics in the profession and the new hegemony of white male theorists who have set up an elitist preserve based in European thought that keeps out most women and people of color.

16 See also Homans, Poovey, Yaeger, and Alcoff. Although Jardine writes in the "Preliminaries" to *Gynesis* that she wants to combine American feminism and poststructuralism on the issue of woman as subject, the book examines how "woman" functions as necessary sign in male discourse, not how women themselves speak.

17 Miller's "political intertextuality" itself constellates a body of feminist criticism that has assumed the agency of the woman writer in intertextual dialogue with precursors and peers. In addition to Sandra M. Gilbert and Susan Gubar's feminist/Bloomian literary histories, Rachel Blau DuPlessis writes of women's intertextual practice in her influential "For the Etruscans": "Artistic production. The making, the materials the artist faced, collected, resolved. A process of makings, human choice and necessity. . . . Any work is a strategy to resolve, transpose, reweight, dilute, arrange, substitute contradictory material from culture, from society, from personal life. And (the) female aesthetic? Various and possibly contradictory strategies of response and invention shared by women in response to gender experiences" (280). See also Yaeger, *Honey-Mad Women,* in which she states: "My thesis in chapter 5 is that we need . . . to say women writers have incorporated men's texts in their own and entered into dialogues with these texts that these male writers have refused to initiate" (30); Susan Howe's description of Emily Dickinson's in-

tertextual response to European precursors: "Forcing, abbreviating, pushing, padding, subtracting, riddling, interrogating, re-writing, she pulled text from text" (29); and my own essays conceived as intertextual studies in the early eighties, "'I go where I love,'" "Gender and Genre Anxiety," and "Palimpsest of Origin."

18   I am focusing on the operation of "influence" in the importation of French poststructuralism into the United States. But there may be a similar resistance in French criticism to the "(new) monolith." See for example Wittig's reference to an intertextuality in which the author is still clearly present in "The Mark of Gender"; and a British volume entitled *A Dictionary of Modern Critical Terms*, edited by Roger Fowler, in which intertextuality is defined under the general category "Creation" in the context of Marxist criticism: "there are previous writings, equally ideologically informed, which the writer, in that practice known as *intertextuality*, may also transform" (45). For Fowler and Wittig, the author's agency is assumed in the "practice" of intertextuality.

19   Of course, French was not always the language of the conqueror. Some five centuries before the French conquest changed the formation of English, French developed out of the Romans' conquest of the Celts and Germanic peoples. No language is "pure."

20   Eric Rothstein suggests provocatively that "the homogeneity of French is itself challenged by . . . the heteroglossia brought to it by the Bulgarian émigrée with her notoriously difficult texts in French . . . and her insistence on bypassing all language, those of her mother-tongue and of her new *patrie* alike, with the maternal paralinguistic of the universal *chora*" (comment to author).

21   For a discussion of women's writing in the modernist period as a return of the repressed in relation to male modernism, see my "Return of the Repressed in Women's Narrative."

22   See my "Return of the Repressed in Women's Narrative" for further discussion of this psychoanalytic method of textual criticism. For a related critique of the assumption of the intended text in textual criticism, see McGann. He advocates a historically grounded analysis of multiple drafts and editions, in effect an intertextual criticism, but not one that uses psychoanalysis.

23   For Freud's clinical papers defining transference, repetition, and remembering, see especially "The Dynamics of the Transference" (1912) and "Further Recommendations in the Technique of Psychoanalysis: Recollection, Repetition and Working Through" (1914) in *Therapy and Technique*.

24   For the history of *Stephen Hero*, see Spencer's Introduction. For comparison's of *Stephen Hero* and *Portrait*, see for example Ellmann (296–99) and MacCabe.

25   In *Return of the Repressed in Modernist Narratives*, a work-in-progress, I show in detail how the four components of the dream-work govern the textual transformation of *Stephen Hero* into *Portrait*.

26   The reduction of *Stephen Hero*'s Emma Cleary (a fully drawn character as the "new woman" whom Stephen loves) into *Portrait*'s enigmatic E.C. (a figment of Stephen's desire) is another version of the maternal narrative. See Scott for a comparison of Emma and E.C., as well as the changes Joyce makes in other strong female characters.

27 The point Joyce makes here is similar to the one Virginia Woolf makes in *A Room of One's Own*, where she thought after she was locked out of the library at Oxbridge: "And I thought how it is worse perhaps to be locked out; and I thought how it is worse perhaps to be locked in" (24).

28 See for example Lacan, "The Purloined Letter" and "The Signification of the Phallus."

29 For other discussions of the importance of woman-as-signifier in the development of (male) modernism and postmodernism, see Jardine, Gilbert and Gubar, and Van Boheemen.

30 See Homans' treatment of the Lacanian "myth" of language, in which she argues that his theory, which reflects the dominant "myth" of language in Western culture, requires the murder of the mother, synonymous with the repression of the "literal" (1–39).

31 See also Van Boheemen and Ferrer for discussion of Stephen's repressed guilt about his mother in *Ulysses*.

WORKS CITED

Alcoff, Linda. "Cultural Feminism versus Post-Structuralism: The Identity Crisis in Feminist Theory." *Signs* 13 (Spring 1988): 405–36.

Baym, Nina. "The Madwoman and Her Languages: Why I Don't Do Feminist Literary Theory." In Benstock 45–61.

Barthes, Roland. *Camera Lucida: Reflections on Photography.* 1980. Trans. Richard Howard. New York: Hill and Wang, 1981.

Barthes, Roland. "The Death of the Author." In *Image-Music-Text*, trans. Stephen Heath, 142–48. New York: Hill and Wang, 1977.

Barthes, Roland. *Roland Barthes by Roland Barthes.* 1975. Trans. Richard Howard. New York: Hill and Wang, 1977.

Barthes, Roland. *The Rustle of Language.* 1984. Trans. Richard Howard. New York: Hill and Wang, 1986.

Benstock, Shari, ed. *Feminist Issues in Literary Scholarship.* Bloomington: Indiana UP, 1987.

Bloom, Harold. *The Anxiety of Influence.* New York: Oxford UP, 1973.

Bloom, Harold. *A Map of Misreading.* New York: Oxford UP, 1975.

Christian, Barbara. "The Race for Theory." *Feminist Studies* 14 (Spring 1988): 67–80.

Cixous, Hélène. "Reaching the Point of Wheat, or A Portrait of the Artist as a Maturing Woman." *New Literary History* 19 (Autumn 1987): 1–23.

Culler, Jonathan. *The Pursuit of Signs: Semiotics, Literature, Deconstruction.* Ithaca: Cornell UP, 1981.

Culler, Jonathan. *Structuralist Poetics: Structuralism, Linguistics, and the Study of Literature.* Ithaca: Cornell UP, 1975.

Culler, Jonathan. "Textual Self-Consciousness and the Textual Unconscious." *Style* 18 (Summer 1984): 369–76.

Derrida, Jacques. *Writing and Difference*. 1967. Chicago: U of Chicago P, 1978.

DuPlessis, Rachel Blau. "For the Etruscans." 1979. In *The New Feminist Criticism*, ed. Elaine Showalter, 271–91. New York: Pantheon, 1985.

Ellmann, Richard. *James Joyce*. Rev. ed. New York: Oxford UP, 1982.

Felman, Shoshana. *Lacan and the Adventure of Insight: Psychoanalysis in Contemporary Culture*. Cambridge: Harvard UP, 1987.

Felman, Shoshana. "Turning the Screw of Interpretation." *Yale French Studies* 55/56 (1977): 94–207.

Ferrer, Daniel. "Circe, Regret and Regression." In *Post-Structuralist Joyce: Essays from the French*, ed. Derek Attridge and Daniel Ferrer, 12–44. Cambridge: Cambridge UP, 1984.

Foucault, Michel. "What Is an Author?" In *Textual Strategies: Perspectives in Post-Structuralist Criticism*, ed. Josué V. Harari, 141–60. Ithaca: Cornell UP, 1979.

Fowler, Roger. *A Dictionary of Modern Critical Terms*. Rev. ed. London: Routledge & Kegan Paul, 1987.

Fox-Genovese, Elizabeth. "To Write My Self: The Autobiographies of Afro-American Women." In Benstock 161–80.

Freud, Sigmund. *Beyond the Pleasure Principle*. Trans. James Strachey. New York: Norton, 1961.

Freud, Sigmund. *Civilization and Its Discontents*. 1930. Trans. James Strachey. New York: Norton, 1961.

Freud, Sigmund. *General Psychological Theory*. Ed. Philip Rieff. New York: Collier, 1963.

Freud, Sigmund. *The Interpretation of Dreams*. 1900. Trans. James Strachey. New York: Avon, 1965.

Freud, Sigmund. *Therapy and Technique*. Ed. Philip Rieff. New York: Collier Books, 1963.

Freud, Sigmund. *Totem and Taboo*. 1913. Trans. James Strachey. New York: Norton, 1950.

Friedman, Susan Stanford. "Gender and Genre Anxiety: Elizabeth Barrett Browning and H.D. as Epic Poets." *Tulsa Studies in Women's Literature* 5 (Fall 1986): 203–28.

Friedman, Susan Stanford. "'I go where I love': An Intertextual Study of H.D. and Adrienne Rich." *Signs* 9 (Winter 1983): 228–46.

Friedman, Susan Stanford. "Palimpsest of Origins in H.D.'s Career." *Poesis* 6 (1986): 56–73.

Friedman, Susan Stanford. *Psyche Reborn: The Emergence of H.D.* Bloomington: Indiana UP, 1981.

Friedman, Susan Stanford. "The Return of the Repressed in Joyce: (Self)Censorship and the Making of a Modernist." Paper presented at International Symposium on Joyce. Venice, June 1988.

Friedman, Susan Stanford. "Return of the Repressed in Women's Narrative." *Journal of Narrative Technique* 19 (Winter 1989): 141–56.

Friedman, Susan Stanford. "Women's Autobiographical Selves: Theory and Practice." In Benstock 34–62.

Gallop, Jane. "Lacan and Literature: A Case for Transference." *Poetics* 13 (1984).

Gilbert, Sandra M., and Susan Gubar. *No Man's Land: The War of the Words.* New Haven: Yale UP, 1987.

Harari, Josué V., ed. *Textual Strategies: Perspectives in Post-Structuralist Criticism.* Ithaca: Cornell UP, 1979.

Henke, Suzette. "Stephen Dedalus and Women: A Portrait of the Artist as Young Misogynist." In Henke and Unkeless 82–107.

Henke, Suzette, and Elaine Unkeless, eds. *Women in Joyce.* Urbana: U of Illinois P, 1982.

Homans, Margaret. *Bearing the Word: Language and Female Experience in Nineteenth-Century Women Writers.* New Haven: Yale UP, 1986.

Howe, Susan. *My Emily Dickinson.* Berkeley: North Atlantic Books, 1985.

Jameson, Fredric. *The Political Unconscious: Narrative as a Socially Symbolic Act.* Ithaca: Cornell UP, 1981.

Jardine, Alice. *Gynesis: Configurations of Woman and Modernity.* Ithaca: Cornell UP, 1985.

Joyce, James. *A Portrait of the Artist as a Young Man: Text, Criticism, and Notes.* Ed. Chester G. Anderson. New York: Viking, 1968.

Joyce, James. *Stephen Hero.* Ed. John J. Slocum and Herbert Cahoon. New York: New Directions, 1963.

Joyce, James. *Ulysses: The Corrected Text.* Ed. Hans Walter Gabler et al. New York: Vintage Books, 1986.

Kamuf, Peggy. "Replacing Feminist Criticism." *Diacritics* 12 (Summer 1982): 42–47.

Kamuf, Peggy. *Signature Pieces: On the Institution of Authorship.* Ithaca: Cornell UP, 1988.

Kennedy, Gerald. "Roland Barthes, Autobiography and the End of Writing." *Georgia Review* 35 (Summer 1981): 381–400.

Kenner, Hugh. *The Pound Era.* Berkeley: U of California P, 1971.

Kristeva, Julia. *Desire in Language: A Semiotic Approach to Literature and Art.* Ed. Leon Roudiez. Trans. Thomas Gora et al. New York: Columbia UP, 1980.

Kristeva, Julia. *Revolution in Poetic Language.* Trans. Margaret Walker. New York: Columbia UP, 1984.

Kristeva, Julia. "Stabat Mater." In *The Female Body in Western Culture: Contemporary Perspectives*, ed. Susan Rubin Suleiman. Cambridge: Harvard UP, 1986.

Kristeva, Julia. "Women's Time." 1979. Trans. Alice Jardine and Harry Blake. *Signs* 7 (Autumn 1981): 13–35.

Lacan, Jacques. "Seminar on 'The Purloined Letter.'" In *The Purloined Poe: Lacan, Derrida, and Psychoanalytic Reading*, ed. John P. Muller and William J. Richardson, 55–76. Baltimore: Johns Hopkins UP, 1988.

Lacan, Jacques. "The Signification of the Phallus." In *Ecrits: A Selection*, trans. Alan Sheridan, 281–90. New York: W. W. Norton, 1977.

MacCabe, Colin. *James Joyce and the Revolution of the Word.* London: Macmillan, 1978.

McGann, Jerome J. *A Critique of Modern Textual Criticism.* Chicago: U of Chicago P, 1983.

Miller, Nancy K. "Arachnologies: The Woman, the Text, and the Critic." In *The Poetics of Gender*, ed. Miller, 270–96. New York: Columbia UP, 1986.

Miller, Nancy K. "Changing the Subject: Authorship, Writing, and the Reader." In *Feminist Studies — Critical Studies*, ed. Teresa de Lauretis, 102–20. Bloomington: Indiana UP, 1986.

Miller, Nancy K. *Subject to Change: Reading Feminist Writing*. New York: Columbia UP, 1986.

Miller, Nancy K. "The Text's Heroine: A Feminist Critic and Her Fictions." *Diacritics* 12 (Summer 1982): 48–53.

Plottel, Jeanine Parisier, and Hanna Charney, eds. *Intertextuality: New Perspectives in Criticism. New York Literary Forum* 2 (1978).

Poovey, Mary. "Feminism and Deconstruction." *Feminist Studies* 14 (Spring 1988): 51–66.

Riffaterre, Michael. "The Intertextual Unconscious." *Critical Inquiry* 13 (Winter 1987): 371–85.

Scholes, Robert, and Richard M. Kain. *The Workshop of Daedalus: James Joyce and the Raw Materials for A Portrait of the Artist as a Young Man*. Evanston: Northwestern UP, 1965.

Scott, Bonnie Kime. *Joyce and Feminism*. Bloomington: Indiana UP, 1984.

Ulmer, Gregory. "The Discourse of the Imaginary." *Diacritics* 10 (March 1980): 61–75.

Van Boheemen, Christine. *The Novel as Family Romance: Language, Gender, and Authority from Fielding to Joyce*. Ithaca: Cornell UP, 1987.

Wittig, Monique. "The Mark of Gender." In Miller, *Poetics of Gender* 63–73.

Woolf, Virginia. *A Room of One's Own*. 1929. Rpt. New York: Harcourt Brace Jovanovich, 1957.

Yaeger, Patricia. *Honey-Mad Women: Emancipatory Strategies in Women's Writing*. New York: Columbia UP, 1988.

CHAPTER 7

Allusion and Intertext:
History in The End of the Road

THOMAS SCHAUB

Readers of John Barth's early novel, *The End of the Road*, regularly inter-pret the novel without reference to its contemporary history, as though it were primarily a narrative about the inherent shortcomings of representa-tion. A number of steering mechanisms have helped keep readers on this line: not only does the novel's speaker, its autobiographical confessor, deflect our inquiry in self-serving ways, Barth himself has consistently described the novel ahistorically, as the second half of a philosophical farce which carries "all non-mystical value-thinking to the end of the road."[1] David Morrell, author of the single critical biography on Barth, calls the fiction Barth's only "novel of ideas."[2] For the most part, subsequent crit-icism has followed these suggested leads, with the result that most com-mentary upon the novel revolves around this frequently cited passage: "To turn experience into speech — that is, to classify, to categorize, to concep-tualize, to grammarize, to syntactify it — is always a betrayal of experience, a falsification of it; but only so betrayed can it be dealt with at all."[3]

From an intertextual point of view, this exclusion of history can only re-sult from a critical myopia, since any text is necessarily historically pro-duced and can be nothing more (or less) than a concatenation of prior writings. Though some theorists restrict such writings to other literary texts, others, like Bakhtin, specifically describe the novelistic text as a heteroglossia of social voices exerting pressure upon the form of the novel.[4] How then reveal, in Barth's stubborn novel, the historical contingency of his/its private intention? Can we show a multitude of cultural discourses traversing the text? And if we can, are they trespassing or are they there with the author's permission? Can we achieve this demonstration through the lexicon of influence and allusion, or do we need intertextuality?

The concept of intertextuality seems critical to the reader interested in historicizing particular texts. Indeed, the popularity of intertextuality issues from a pervasive desire to resituate texts within a history construed "textually" — as "always already" textualized or mediated by sign systems of one sort or another. By deploying the metaphors of "mosaic," "network," and "social text," as Kristeva and Barthes do, theorists of intertextuality encourage us to think of a text as part of, and invaded by, a larger "social text" — rather than as a diamond in a "setting" or "context."[5] Similarly, for Bakhtin a multivoiced social history exists inside the text: "the internal social dialogism of novelistic discourse requires the concrete social context of discourse to be exposed, to be revealed as the force that determines its entire structure . . . from within" (*Dialogic Imagination* 300). Because intertextuality permeates the text from within, not unlike Jameson's idea of "narrative unconscious," the concept invites historical interpretation.[6] Most theorists of intertextuality try to dialogize texts, looking for "dynamic exchanges" or, in Stephen Greenblatt's words, "expressions of ongoing social dialogue" which succeed in identifying the text as a "blend" of discourses: "in short, a sustained collective enterprise."[7] Thus the concept of intertextuality helps satisfy the critical desire to situate texts within history defined as a system of representation, a vast intertextual space.

For those unfamiliar with the novel, *The End of the Road* is the story — an autobiographical confession — Jacob Horner tells of his psychologically induced physical paralysis, the efforts of an uncertified black doctor to cure him, his ménage à trois with Rennie and Joe Morgan, and the death of Rennie Morgan during an attempted abortion by Horner's doctor. Much of the dialogue in the book sets forth Joe Morgan's "non-mystical value thinking" — his belief that one may be committed to particular values even though they have no absolute or transcendent origin, so long as one holds to them rationally, consistently, and seriously. Joe's wife Rennie has tried to adopt her husband's views and habits of rational thought, but Jake Horner, as his name suggests, plays devil's advocate and succeeds in exposing the weaknesses of her husband's convictions. Hence the adultery, the uncertain paternity, and the botched abortion which follow. Though written in the fall of 1955 (and not published until 1958), the novel is set in the three years prior to the court ruling against segregation in the schools, and of course before dramatic advances in contraception technology and both public and legal acceptance of abortion.

The ahistorical effect of the narrative may be ascribed to the guilty speaker who has an interest in evading responsibility for his unethical behavior (sleeping with Rennie). Throughout he argues for a "special kind of integrity" — a kind of loyalty to his "plurality of selves" (136) and his "inability to play the same role long enough" to accept responsibility for the actions any one of them might commit (176). Having gotten this far, some readers might already feel an uneasiness not only with Horner but also with the novel's conceptual integrity: because Jake Horner is clearly the agent of Joe Morgan's destruction, his nihilism is supposed to show the inadequacy of Joe Morgan's nonmystical value thinking. But just as clearly, Horner is also a Little Jack Horner, who, finding himself in a corner, concocts an intricate philosophical defense of his behavior, so that the entire novel, or narrative confession, is nothing more than an extended rationalization (what a good boy am I).[8]

This prospect has disturbed most commentators on the novel. Both Campbell Tatham and Tony Tanner, for example, reject the ethical implications of Horner's conclusions. "Those things which usually circumscribe consciousness and . . . help to condition thought have receded or been excluded and in the resultant cleared ground the mind runs free."[9] For the most part, the novel itself produces this ethical reaction, because the graphic description of Rennie's death stays with the reader as a rebuke to the inhuman theorizing of the two men who compel her divided loyalty. But this rebuke predicates the existence within the novel of something with constant value — animal life, vitality — and reinstates the necessity for conventions of social behavior to protect that value. Further, this value isn't "mystical" but firmly anchored in the absolute of "experience" or "feeling" — an animal sympathy that Jake feels for Rennie during their drive to the scene of the abortion. Implicitly, the narrative ends up arguing for ideology, for plans and ideas, for material changes in human law — for the right of black people to practice medicine or a woman's right to an abortion, either of which would have saved Rennie's life. In a book whose subject is the arbitrariness of convention — underlying all social formations, including personal identity and communicability — the inescapably social nature of the sign is curiously overlooked.

Another way of fixing the novel's discomfort with itself might be to say that the novel seems unable to extricate itself from Horner's point of view. Despite the fact that Horner is entirely discredited, his theorizing remains the aesthetic foundation of Barth's novel, and in fact many of Horner's speeches reappear in Barth's interviews as straight assessments of the artist's problems and compromises. Thus, for example, Horner's assertion that turning experience into speech is "always a betrayal" reappears regularly in Barth's essays and interviews. In one of these, with Alan Prince, Barth argues that one way to come to terms with the difference between art and life "is to define fiction as a kind of true representation of the distortion we all make of life . . . a representation of a representation." Once we accept this fact, he says in another interview, we can enjoy the tricks of art as "good clean fun."[10] Presumably we may appreciate in art what we do not permit in life, though both are distorted representations.

To understand this contradiction—that Barth's novel repudiates the character who voices its aesthetic foundation—we might look for historical intertexts of *The End of the Road* which allow us to read the novel dialogically, as a book produced in relation to social themes and pressures of its time. If this is possible it must mean that the steering mechanisms of narrative voice, authorial comment, and textual allusion exist together with intertextual voices in the same "sign," to use Volosinov's terminology: on the one hand the novel carries the mark of private intention; on the other it bears the furtive mark of its cultural present, the ready-to-hand, the apparently natural.

This intersection of voices comes forcibly to our attention during those moments when Horner experiences a near-empty consciousness and he is paralyzed by the absence of any reason to act. Describing the onset of the disease, Horner tells his reader: "I simply ran out of motives, as a car runs out of gas." During these periods of immobility, the contents of Horner's mind are replaced "by that test pattern of my consciousness, *Pepsi-Cola hits the spot*, intoned with silent oracularity" (69). This mental event is described four times in the novel, the first appearing after Jake has accepted a dinner invitation from Rennie and Joe Morgan:

> I went back to my rocker and rocked for another forty-five minutes. From time to time I smiled inscrutably, but I cannot say that this honestly reflected any sincere feeling on my part. It was just a thing I found myself doing, as frequently when walking alone I would find myself repeating over and over in a judicious, unmetrical voice, *Pepsi-Cola hits the spot; twelve full ounces: that's a lot*—accompanying the movement of my lips with a wrinkled brow, distracted twitches of the corner of my mouth, and an occasional quick gesture of my right hand. Passersby often took me for a man lost in serious problems, and sometimes when I looked behind me after passing one I'd see him, too, make a furtive movement with his right hand, trying it out. (36)

Almost any reader with a smattering of literary-intellectual history will hear a multitude of textual voices in this passage, from advertising and popular idiom to philosophy and literature. The paragraph is a convenient example of what Kristeva means by a "mosaic of quotations,"[11] but the kind of conclusions we may draw from them depends upon whether we read them as allusions reinforcing an authorial intention or as linkages which betray the presence of intertexts modulating the novelistic process from within.

In the view of many intertextual theorists, even the attempt to identify a quotation's source is beside the point, but doing so may help us clarify the implications of the way we read a mosaic of quotations. The very phrase invites the question "quoting whom?" and reading the quotation above, American readers may answer that *Moby-Dick* is being cited, for the words "inscrutably" and "wrinkled brow" figure prominently (and jointly) in Melville's novel, repeatedly attached not only to Ahab and Moby-Dick, but to the world and its representation as well.[12] Perhaps more important, whether we view the Melville resonance as one implanted by Barth (*his* allusion) or one the reader hears, the choice appears to be in the hands of the reader—a fact which in itself seems to reinforce the view of intertextuality set forth by Barthes in "Work to Text." Allusion begins to look like a kind of critical ideology which narrows the reader's freedom in behalf of an empiricist boundary or limit designated the "author." The result of the ideology of allusion is that the reader remains confined within the steering mechanisms of the text—we need not assign an authorial intention—which are themselves ideologically driven. We see how this (what Althusser calls the "speculary" structure of ideology) produces an ahistorical criticism: although I know of no reading of *The End of the Road* which takes Melville's voice into account, one may easily incorporate the Melville resonance as an allusion reinforcing the kinds of arguments that have already been made about the novel.

For example, it is an unexplored assumption of Barth scholarship that the novel owes something to an existentialist context.[13] The truth of this may be observed in the passage quoted above, especially in the sentence "I cannot say that this honestly reflected any sincere feeling on my part." Though composed from everyday idiom, this sentence will be recognized by many readers as a formulation generated by Sartrean discourse, and they will be rewarded later when Horner's black therapist orders him to read Sartre, and snorts at the idea of sincerity: "If you sometimes have the feeling that your mask is *insincere*—impossible word!—it's only because one of your masks is incompatible with another" (85).

To treat this as an allusion planted by Barth would mean turning to Sartre's conception of the self and ideas of sincerity, freedom, and bad faith. Treating Sartre's presence as an intentional gesture by Barth to reinforce and enrich his vision, a reader would discover that the discourse of "sincerity" is borrowed directly from Sartre's writings, in which the impossibility of sincerity follows logically from his conception of the "pre-reflective cogito," set forth in "La transcendance de l'égo: Esquisse d'une description phénoménologique" (1936–37) and *L'être et le néant* (1943).[14] The black doctor's expostulation neatly reproduces the conflict in Sartre's thought between the structure of consciousness and the idea of sincerity: "the original structure of 'not being what one is' renders impossible in advance all movement toward being in itself or 'being what one is.' . . . How then can we blame another for not being sincere or rejoice in our own sincerity since this sincerity appears to us at the same time to be impossible?" This is also, for Sartre, the source of "ethical anguish" — for the self founded in the freedom of nothingness can never have any foundation which doesn't at once call into question both itself and any values the self might seek to establish upon it.[15]

Horner enacts, to a farcical extreme, the dialectical contradictions of Sartre's thought. We should note, for example, that Horner, by admitting the absence of sincere feeling, implicitly claims the virtue of candor — of being sincere. With a special kind of existential integrity, Horner loyally adheres to the processes and conditions of consciousness, as he does in the opening words of his confession: "In a sense, I am Jacob Horner." Faithfully Sartrean, the statement of identity presupposes an "I" prior to and other than the one predicated. The very act of self-identification objectifies the self (the "I" or "transcendental ego") as distinct from consciousness. No degree of exactitude or phraseological qualification ("in a sense") can ever succeed in closing this gap between the "I" and the consciousness of the "I." The empty consciousness constantly recedes, backpeddling from the objects of its attention, from every effort to fill itself or become. The "self," Sartre asserts in *The Transcendence of the Ego*, is "sheer performance" (94).

Treated as an allusion, this Sartreanism easily coincides with (and helps explain) the echoes of Melville, for one might argue that Barth is translating the contrasts between Ahab's assumptions of "depth" or "cause" (Ahab's maniacal determination to "strike through the mask") and Ishmael's persistent reminder that "surface" only gives way to more surface into the contemporary idiom of existentialism, which repudiates essence. In this scenario, the popular idioms of the passage ("a thing I found myself doing" and "when walking alone I would find myself repeating") reproduce the conflict between Ahab's obsession and Ishmael's mild-mannered nihilism, for the popular idiom is at once the speech pattern of the everyday (Cartesian) assumption that consciousness is a reflective interiority (as the passerby here assumes) and Sartre's refutation of that concept. This internal dissonance reinforces the oscillation in the passage between an Ahab figure ("inscrutable" with "wrinkled brow") and an Ishmael figure (who comes upon Ahab, "finds himself") who survives to tell the story, the alienated outcast who begins the tale as Ishmael does through an act of self-naming ("In a sense, I am Jacob Horner": "Call me Ishmael"). Melville's two characters are here reproduced in postwar America as the schizophrenic dialectic of Sartrean consciousness.

All of this helps reinforce the reading which the book itself promotes: Jake is the man without qualities set loose upon the well-intentioned but naive pragmatist Joe Morgan. Like Ishmael, Horner is alienated, an out-sider, one who signs on to a microsociety—in this case the world of the Morgans—and like Ishmael survives to tell the story.

The works of Sartre and Melville far from exhaust the texts positioned in this novel. Readers familiar with Restoration drama may spot "Jacob Horner" as an allusion to the rake (named "Harry Horner") in Wycherley's *The Country Wife* (1675) and thus anticipate that Barth's character will also be the undoing of the society he enters. ("Jacob" means "supplanter"—from Jacob's theft of Esau's inheritance.) As in Wycherley's play, *The End of the Road* begins with a scene between Horner and a quack doctor; the entire plotting of both texts relies upon the "alliance" (the word is Barth's) between them; and in both "Horner" cuckolds the resident male. In *"The Country Wife* Comes to *The End of the Road,"* Daniel Fraustino has out-lined many of these parallels but doesn't answer why such an allusive resonance would suit Barth's purposes.[16] Here again one may remain with-in the parameters of the novel's bias by suggesting that cuckoldry serves as a sexual metaphor for the nothingness which, Sartre wrote, "lies coiled at the heart of being." Nothingness is modeled in Barth's novel as a rake, undoing the ties that bind—of self, marriage, society, and language.

So long as we remain within the ideology of allusion, reading goes smoothly, for the collapsible binary we have been noting—being and nothingness, interiority and surface—continues to proliferate with self-confirming naturalness in the major dramatic opposition of the novel. Contrary to the exhausted Horner, who has a "vacuum" for a self (80), Joe is "terribly energetic" (14) and self-consistent. Rennie contrasts the two men: "You're not *real* like Joe is! He's the same man today he was yesterday, all the way through. He's genuine!" (64). The ghosts of Sartrean and Melvillean speculation lurk in these characterizations: in the enforced, rational adherence to his chosen values, Joe embodies Sartre's *"spirit of seriousness"* (*Being and Nothingness* 626) and is a caricature of "being-in-itself." Though "nothing is ultimately defensible," Joe tells Jake, "a man can act coherently; he can act in ways that he can explain, if he wants to" (43). The impossibility of sincerity is presented as the canker of this in-genuous position, and the source of all the violence and destruction within the novel. Horner is the agent of that destruction because his identity is pure process, indifferent to the "bad faith" of the accumulated self; the inescapable nothingness or freedom of the for-itself erodes the stability of the Morgan marriage.

This marriage, moreover, is given a utopian resonance which eventually reminds us of Gulliver's journey to the land of the Houyhnhnms. The mar-riage of Rennie and Joe Morgan is a kind of Brook Farm experiment in husband-wife, male-female relations. "We'd stay together as long as each of us could respect everything about the other," Rennie tells Jake. Because Joe's idea of a marriage requires "the parties involved be able to take each other seriously," he likes Jake's needling Rennie: "in spite of your making fun of Rennie you seem willing to take her seriously. Almost no man is willing to take any woman's thinking seriously" (56, 42, 41). Joe's consistency, his sureness and lack of indecision, his rationality and absence of "craft or guile" (30) are enough to suggest that the Morgan world is an echo of Swift's Houyhnhnms, but the intentionality and coherence of that suggestion increase when we discover that a "Morgan" designates a specifically American breed of light horses, progeny of one prepotent Vermont stallion. As is true for the Houyhnhnms, the land of the Morgans is one in which all behavior is governed (or tries to be) by placid and self-assured reason. If in Swift's tale "houyhnhnm" means "perfection of nature," then in this one "Morgan" — by meaning "horse" — subsumes all the smug confidence with which Swift's horses beg the question of their own reasoning's foundations and banish from existence all they do not understand as "the thing that was not." References to horses saturate the novel, not only because Rennie is an accomplished horsewoman, but because Joe consistently distinguishes between "horseshit" or "nonsense" on the one hand, and rational (horse) "sense" on the other. Like horses, both Rennie and Jake have the habit of "whipping" their heads from side to side, and "Rennie" sounds a bit like "whinny." Additionally, the text underscores the Swiftean parallels by pointing to itself in ways that expose the fiction itself as a mask: "Whoa, now!" Jake says to Rennie; listening to Joe, Jake "gave the horse his head"; and driving to the abortion, Rennie speaks "hoarsely."[17] The complex referentiality of the word *horse* achieves an admirable coherence in the novel's final example, when Horner compares man's reason to the Trojan horse by invoking the story of Laocoön: "It was no use: I could not remain simple-minded long enough to lay blame — on the Doctor, myself, or anyone. . . . [My] limbs were bound like Laocoön's — by the twin serpents of Knowledge and Imagination, which, grown great in the fullness of time, no longer tempt but annihilate" (187).

We may bring our allusive readings to a close by noting that all of the above references can be brought into alignment with the novel's (unacknowledged) quotation of the first proposition in Wittgenstein's *Tractatus Logico-Philosophicus*: "The world is all that is the case" — a view espoused by Horner's doctor as being eminently pragmatic. The reader abiding by the methodology of allusion might turn to Wittgenstein's treatise, and find there the view that values and ethics resist formulation in language: "It is clear that ethics cannot be put into words" (6.421); "The sense of the world must lie outside the world. In the world everything is as it is, and everything happens as it does happen; *in* it no value exists — and if it did exist, it would have no value" (6.41).[18]

Using this complex set of texts as allusions, one could argue that Barth *intended* to set Jake "loose" on Joe in order to show the unworkability of a value system based upon an arbitrary act of reason. Barth constructed the narrative to show that experience — what happens — is too multiform and overwhelming to be apprehended or controlled by either reason or representation. Sartre's rationalism undoes itself in the struggle between Jake and Joe, and the body of the text, Rennie, is the morbid consequence.

Such, we might say, is the allusive ideology of *The End of the Road*. What it produces are readings that reproduce not only the ahistorical evasion of its narrator but more generally the ahistoricism of the novel and of cold war fiction generally. This was noted of fifties fiction by Irving Howe in different terms, when, at the end of the decade, he described recent output as "moral" but not "social."[19] More recently, Carolyn Porter and Russell Reising have summarized the literary criticism of the period as being similarly indifferent to the historical or social constitution of the imagination.[20] But that ahistoricism is itself historically produced and for the rest of the essay I'd like to focus on the intertextual presence of that history in *The End of the Road*, for it will help us, I think, to see what produces that dissonance within an art conceived as "good clean fun."

The ideology of allusion prevents the reader from noting ways in which the novel evades the coherence which seems to inhere within it. To say this isn't to imagine the act of authorship as a form of subterfuge, but to remind ourselves that the very idea of the author predetermines kinds of readings and ignores others. Specifically, the author-intention-coherence complex that the ideology of allusion reinforces automatically sets aside the true historicity of the novel, for the reader seeking only a subject overlooks, like a purloined letter, the presence of historical discourse constituting the subject. The substantial contribution of intertextual thinking lies in its ability to induce a kind of Rorschach oscillation in the readers' perceptions, alerting them to the simultaneous function of signs as allusions and as linkages to intertexts of the social space. The "natural reader" of *The End of the Road* wouldn't have to spot these intertextual links; they would function automatically, with the same effortlessness as they did in helping to generate the text in the first place. Which is to say that intertextuality works to confirm an ideology — to make a work's ideology appear unquestionable, to go without saying, since the contemporary reader is soaked in the same complex of social voices which constitute the text. This intertextual voicing, then, becomes audible only for the historicizing critic; one may hypothesize, in fact, that it can become conscious *only* in retrospect.

Thus the intertextual reader is less interested in noting how Barth uses Melville and Sartre to help establish the novel's coherence than in explaining why Melville, Sartre, Wycherley, and Swift would seem so apt for his purposes — or why Barth's approach to dramatizing the inadequacy of "non-mystical value thinking" is carried out in terms drawn from a characteristic complex of preoccupations and narratives produced by postwar literary-liberal culture: The book isn't about those subjects, but those subjects are sedimented within the rhetoric of the fiction, are mediating and tuning the novel at every point.

It follows from the suppositions of intertextuality that some kind of circulation within the sign between allusion and intertext is inescapable. A criticism which acknowledges such mediation "develops" the cultural text like a photographic negative, thus historicizing it. For example, we noted earlier that the name "Morgan" alludes to part IV of *Gulliver's Travels*, but mere allusiveness didn't reveal the mediating nudge of contemporary social history generating the aptness of Swift's satire to the story Barth set out to tell. Once we begin to historicize this reference, to see it as generated by the social and political discourses of the fifties, it isn't too hard to see Barth's "allusion" as a link to the "end of ideology" intertext, in which the "goodness" of human nature and the likelihood of social rationality are reappraised. Within that narrative, Swift's satiric portrait of human irrationality served to confirm and reinforce contemporary assessments of recent history and politics. Further constituting that social text are the discourses of totalitarianism, the anxiety of freedom, rebellion and conformity, mass society, irrational man, and others familiar to students of cold war culture. The discourse of "realism" that arose in response and which one finds informing foreign policy as well as theology and literary criticism is a fifties Toryism in which the Augustan reminders of human limitation gain renewed force.

Hundreds of articles and books might be cited in support of this effort to identify a cultural intertext. The most important appeared during and immediately after World War II: Fromm's *Escape from Freedom* (1941), Niebuhr's *The Children of Light and the Children of Darkness* (1944), Schlesinger's *The Vital Center* (1949), Trilling's *The Liberal Imagination* (1950), and Niebuhr's *The Irony of American History* (1952). Recently, literary scholarship has been giving increased attention to the New Criticism as an expression of this social and political shift in attitudes, but historians have long ago documented it. See for example Mary Sperling McAuliffe's *Crisis on the Left: Cold War Politics and American Liberals, 1947–1954*, especially the chapter titled "A New Liberalism." As early as 1959, historian John Higham noted "The Cult of the 'American Consensus'" in postwar reappraisals of American history, which he describes as "a massive grading operation to smooth over America's social convulsions."[21]

Once we see Barth's intention to put an end to "all non-mystical value-thinking" mediated by the social text of this postwar conservatism, our understanding of the novel's major characters is transformed. We give new emphasis to the specifically American character of the "Morgan" as a Vermont horse, and Joe appears now clearly as a vestigial offspring of Emersonian self-reliance. Furthermore, that Joe has degrees in literature, philosophy, and history, and is writing a dissertation on "the saving roles of innocence and energy in American political and economic history" (61), marks him as a radical humanist, the upbeat American version of the European Enlightenment and a typical target of cold war admonitions from Schlesinger, Hartz, Van Woodward, Niebuhr, and Kennan. Finally, within the anti-ideology discourse of the fifties, Morgan emerges as the scapegoat of contemporary politics, a figure of naive radicalism and liberal reason, attacked from the right and the "vital center" alike. Jacob Horner, on the other hand, now reappears as the Europeanization of American literature, a figure of weary sophistication and neurasthenia, introduced into Morgan's "ingenuous" (the word is Horner's) realm much as Humbert Humbert is inserted by Nabokov into the American household of Dolores Haze. This typical cold war scenario or conflict is reproduced in the contrast between Jake and Joe, and subsumed (as narrative) beneath the mask of Satire, rewritten in contemporary idiom as the smirk of nothingness.

If this transformation seems too abrupt to compel assent, let me return to the passage with which we began and the Pepsi jingle occupying Horner's consciousness: "*Pepsi-Cola hits the spot; twelve full ounces: that's a lot.*" Certainly the Pepsi couplet in the novel, tucked between the two Ahab markers, alludes to the advertising jingle of the social text, but its allusive function doesn't take us very far, merely eliciting a comic disparity between manner and meaning. On the other hand, if we take this ad slogan to be the presence within the novel of a strand of heteroglot discourse — the idiom of mass advertising — then we are suddenly pondering a cultural voice which seems incidental to the narrative Barth has concocted. Intertextuality allows this prerogative: it assumes that writers cannot remain in total control of the systems of reference their words bring into play, expecially once the reader has been released from any obligation to look for a text's meaning within the system of coherence he has been told may be found there.[22] The Pepsi slogan seems to cross the single-minded highway of intentionality like an inviting side road, and the intertextual reader may, if he wishes, detour and have a look around.

The Pepsi jingle was one of the very first commercials to operate on the principle of repetition ("product recognition") so familiar to us now. In *No Time Lost*, former president of Pepsi-Cola Walter Mack tells the story of the moment when two unknown free-lance writers approached him with lyrics they had set to the melody of "John Peel," a traditional English hunting song:

> Pepsi-Cola hits the spot,
> Twelve full ounces, that's a lot,
> Twice as much for a nickel, too,
> Pepsi-Cola is the drink for you.

According to Mack, he bought the song for two thousand dollars, but none of the national radio stations would sell him time for the jingle because "nobody at any of the big networks would consider anything less than five minutes. . . . Even my own advertising agency argued against it, maintaining the public wouldn't pay any attention to a little ditty unsupported by hard sell."[23] Mack then turned to small radio stations in New Jersey, and the success of this new technique was quickly established.

In *The Cola Wars*, J. C. Louis and Harvey Z. Yazijian confirm Mack's account that Pepsi's fifteen-second jingle, without accompanying pitch, was the first of its kind. They point out that the advertising novelty was "phenomenally successful" and came to be called "'the most famous oral trademark of all time.'" This commercial, they conclude,

was played an estimated six million times. In 1941 alone, the ad was broadcast in one form or another over 469 radio stations in all variations and tempos and for all occasions from concerts and theatre to the World Series. By popular demand, copies were sent to the owners of fifty thousand juke boxes. A survey conducted in 1942 revealed that the jingle was the best-known tune in America.[24]

Strictly speaking, the intertext for this jingle, the background or "common opinion" upon which the entire ad campaign depended, was the marketing of Pepsi's competitor, Coca-Cola, which sold six ounces of its elixir for the same nickel that bought "twelve full ounces" of Pepsi. The jingle calls attention to how full and large the bottle is, but within novelistic discourse this advertisement is transformed by irony and becomes the sign of Horner's empty consciousness. At the same time, Horner's mannerisms give him the appearance of depth, of being — like Ahab at his chart — in deep thought ("a man lost in serious problems"), though he is thinking nothing.

By signifying emptiness while advertising fullness, the jingle thus reproduces the empty/full binary of the novel, most evident in the dramatic pairing of Jake (who has "run out of gas") and Joe (who is "terribly energetic"), and seems at home with the ideologically motivated allusiveness we have already noted. But in fact this particular version of that binary exposes its specifically historical basis in the American conflict between commercial promise and culture product.

Because the Pepsi jingle appears in Barth's novel at just those times when Jake Horner's consciousness is empty — but for the jingle — the jingle of fullness and value ("more bounce to the ounce" — Mack soon added more sugar to his drink than Coke had in its bottle) signifies the ability of mass market advertising to influence consumption by means other than direct appeals to reason or consciousness. An executive at the ad agency handling the Pepsi account remembered, "What made the jingle great . . . and what saved it from dying long ago, was Mack's decision to play the song alone."[25] The jingle's success in saturating the culture is demonstrated not only by its automatic appearance within Horner's consciousness, but also by Barth's use of it. The intrusion of the jingle seems like a perfect instance of Adorno and Horkheimer's assertion that "the might of industrial society is lodged in men's minds,"[26] because the passerby's imitation of Horner's meaningless gestures reproduces modern advertising's indifference to reason or the hard sell. The mannerisms which signify deep thought propagate themselves, just as the jingle itself was propagated, surfacing unbidden in the mind of the consumer. With the Pepsi jingle, the correspondence between appearance and depth, the name and the thing, is translated into that between an advertisement and product.

Through the Pepsi jingle this endlessly variable binary is connected with capitalism, and the culture of quantity, which, though there is no mention of this anywhere in the novel, seems to be equated with its reverse: that quantity carries within itself "emptiness." Capital excavates the private consciousness and puts there in its place the public discourse, the robot-like directives and reflexes of consumerism — what Adorno and Horkheimer in 1944 called "cultural totality," or C. Wright Mills, addressing the same threat, called the "cultural apparatus."[27]

We should note that early-twentieth-century writing often focused upon the decline of culture resulting from middle-class commercial values, but this characteristic stance is surprisingly obscured in Barth's work, appearing here only as a subliminal fear of mass culture rather than constituting the dramatic engagements of characters in setting and plot. This threat of cultural totality is reinforced when Horner later describes the Pepsi ditty as "that test pattern of my consciousness" (69). Thus one mass medium's emptiness (the test pattern of the relatively new television) "reads" another's (the Pepsi commercial), both indicating a minimal consciousness that is plugged in, but on or in which nothing is playing save nothingness itself. By exposing this cultural intertext we displace metaphysical discourse (Sartrean "nothingness") and reveal its material basis, here signaled to us openly as the enervation of mass culture: the thoughtless, the sold, the consumer, that on or through which capitalism plays its self-sustaining message. And this typical cold war attitude, which we see everywhere in the contempt for "mass culture" and in the fear of "populism" as the source of right-wing reaction, is revealed as part of the submerged intertext producing and fissuring the novel.

Mass consciousness is thus equated with passivity, with the role of receiver, and with any thing or person that performs the signals broadcast by others. Not surprisingly, through such characters as Peggy Rankin and Rennie Morgan, this consciousness is sexually coded as a characteristic feminine susceptibility, but the gender marking isn't rigidly applied to particular characters by sex. Instead sexual relations are part of a struggle for power reproduced throughout the novel as a shifting relation between characters, as they occupy the position of master or slave. That is, we don't really have a simple struggle between Joe and Jake, but instead a power dynamic that plays itself out in every meeting of any two characters, in which one attempts to make the other awkward, emptying him or her of self through strength of personality. Thus Horner reports it "is impossible to be at ease in the Progress and Advice Room" of the doctor, who makes one feel "as if you hadn't a personality of your own" (2). Rennie willingly accedes to her colonization by Joe: "I think I completely erased myself, Jake, right down to nothing, so I could start over" (57). The extremity of Rennie's rebirth lies coded within her name, for Rennie was christened "Renee" meaning "reborn" and underscores the conventional gender coding of the master-slave relation throughout the novel.[28] The two women, Peggy Rankin (piggy rank 'n file?) and Rennie MacMahon ("reborn son of man"), are bred in the small town of Wicomico (what's so funny?), while the men are cerebral gods that descend upon them from the urban worlds of New York and Baltimore with all the force of modern advertising.

Horner's sexual status varies: when he is merely a TV screen, the passive receptor of another's ideology, he is filled or impregnated by culture, though at those moments he is not so much "female" as he is gelded, made impotent. On the other hand, Jake maintains a virulent machismo in his relations with Peggy Rankin, a local schoolteacher he picks up at the beach (a "bird who perches on the muzzle of [his] gun" [22]). With Rennie, he is less stable, keeping the upper hand so long as they debate abstractly, but occupying a more passive role when she teaches him to ride horses. In their first adultery, in fact, Rennie is "on top." Rennie, though unsure with the men in her life, shows no restraint in dictating to her horse, when she topples him over backwards to teach him a lesson: "'That'll fix him,' she grinned" (49). Because this episode follows only a few pages after Joe's account of knocking Rennie out with a blow to her head: "I suppose it was rough, slugging Rennie," he tells Jake, "but I saw the moment as a kind of crisis. Anyhow, she stopped apologizing after that" (44).

In scenes such as these the cold war association of ideology with violence reappears. These power relations are maintained through violence, even though the characters think they are winning or acceding because of the strength of logic, articulation, or representation. When Jake is paralyzed again by the doctor's bullying "therapy," and is unable to respond, the doctor leaps on him, pounding him roughly. Rennie, too, labors under an illusion: "He'll always be able to explain his positions better than I can" (57), she says of her husband. This isn't to say that articulation itself is negligible, but to reveal (on the contrary) this novel's insistence that articulation — to unite, or join — is a form of violence within civilization, masking what is at root a struggle for power, for being itself at the expense of the other's self-possession.

In dramatizing such a belief, Barth's novel was only reproducing a contemporary view of liberalism, for which Sartre supplied the philosophical rationale: "Thus I am brought to that paradox," he writes in his discussion of relations with others, "which is the perilous reef of all liberal politics and which Rousseau has defined in a single word: I must 'force' the Other to be free."[29] This is precisely the paradox illustrated by Joe's slugging Rennie, but one which comes into plausible relief only when read in Niebuhrian rhetoric as the "irony of American innocence." According to this view, the naive liberal is a latent totalitarian, a point made over and over by numerous writers, but Trilling's admonitions are representative: "Some paradox of our natures leads us, when once we have made our fellow men the objects of our enlightened interest, to go on to make them the objects of our pity, then of our wisdom, ultimately of our coercion."[30] Representation in this book always involves violence imposed upon another, because any coherent position, identity, or narrative exercises an imperialism of form — the aesthetic version of what Daniel Bell coined as "the end of ideology." This is the underlying social and sexual politics of the novel's most quoted passage: "To turn experience into speech . . . is always a betrayal of experience, a falsification of it; but only so betrayed can it be dealt with at all, and only in so dealing with it did I ever *feel a man*, alive and kicking." Later, he adds, "and to the connoisseur it's good clean fun" (119, emphasis mine, 135).

Of course with this development we begin to see how operations within the narrative raise issues about the ideological form of the narrative itself. Set against Pepsi consciousness (passive, without reason, pure receptivity, emptiness open to the rhetoric of fullness) is articulation, authorship, fiction-making. Here the storyteller is a free-floating masculine god, his articulation a form of divine violation or rape. When Horner's mind is active, inventive, combative, full of wit, he is lifted out of the realm of the passive consumer, the inarticulate masses who are prey to the thought control of cultural totality.

Representation is thus shown by this novel to be caught in a double bind: on the one hand, all representation implicates the artist in betrayal and violence; on the other, failure to exercise the power of representation condemns one to colonization by the Other, specifically coded in this novel as mass culture (Pepsi commercials) and feminine passivity (Rennie's self-erasure). Buried within the Pepsi reference is the fifties discourse of those who thought the most radical act of the artist lay in remaining aloof from the incursions of mass culture.[31] Barth's novel represents that historically produced conclusion as an ahistorical consequence of representation, but the novel itself is equally a creation and part of that social text, insofar as it presents itself as the active counter to the passivity of advertising consciousness. The novel exists as wit and invention, the entire narrative testifying to the private consciousness as a source of cleverness rising above the enervations of mass culture. The two terms — Pepsi/novel — comprise a single contestatory unity, through which the conflict within liberal culture between a desire for action and a new suspicion of the masses is played out in literary culture as a battle between High Art and Mass Culture. Art, as self-negation, arises as an alternative to both the passivity of the masses (Rennie) and the naiveté of radical action (Joe).

This divorce of art and politics remains a motive buried within the novel and comes to the fore only indirectly, in an argument between Horner and one of his students, a boy named Blakesley. Here, too, the circulation of allusion and intertext generates divergent but related readings. Horner is in the midst of giving a lesson in Prescriptive Grammar, when Blakesley interrupts to ask why the rules of grammar need be slavishly memorized if no one follows them. "English was invented before grammar books," he argues.

This is the ideological center of the novel, the passage through which emerge the most obvious social concerns (and consequences) of the narrative. For the student has based his objections to prescriptive law upon democratic cliché: "this is supposed to be a democracy, so if nobody but a few profs ever say, 'To whom were you just now speaking?' why go on pretending we're all out of step but you?" (128). The exchange between Horner and Blakesley is a set piece of classroom discourse, in which the brash populist sneers at the custodian of tradition and convention, and it brings to the fore the political importance of the sign as a battleground of class conflict.

Blakesley, it's clear at this point, is a substitute for Joe Morgan — a man of independence and ideas questioning the forms and conventions which maintain social stability. "A Joe Morgan type, this lad: paths should be laid where people walk," Horner thinks. "I hated his guts" (128). The figure of Blakesley reinforces our view of Morgan as an ingenuous liberal, and establishes the underlying motive for the novel's extraordinary and gratuitous hostility to the Morgan world. Through "Blakesley," Joe Morgan's energetic innocence is associated with the dead end of Romantic rebellion and liberal hopes for the masses. Although Morgan is portrayed throughout — as Blakesley is here — as an American nonconformist, through Blakesley his individualism is conflated with democracy (the way people really speak), further situating Morgan within the contradictions of liberalism and the postwar discourse of "mass society."

Horner's defense deftly sidesteps the problems of majority power by an appeal to the arbitrary, contractual character of language. While Horner drives his point home, however, the textuality of the passage betrays the somewhat different set of concerns we have been developing. "Mr. Blakesley," Horner asks, "what does the word *horse* refer to?" (128). Horner's question suddenly invokes that moment in the second chapter of *Hard Times* (titled "Murdering the Innocents") when Gradgrind asks the circus girl Sissy Jupe, "Give me your definition of a horse." Dickens invented the dialogue between Gradgrind and Sissy Jupe as a confrontation between Utility and Imagination, in order to expose the inhuman, mechanical forces of laissez-faire capitalism. In part, Dickens was moved to write *Hard Times* as a result of having witnessed the labor conditions and unrest in the manufacturing town of Preston.

Thus we have at least three levels of meaning operating simultaneously in Horner's dialogue with Blakesley: (1) the discourse on language, Horner's ostensible subject; (2) the allusion to *Hard Times* invoking Dickens' critique of utilitarianism; and (3) the postwar relations of art and politics which serve as the intertext to the Dickens allusion. That is, Barth's allusive "intertext" conjures up not only a prior text that reinforces the overt rhetoric of his fiction, but also a prior relation of artist and society that contradicts the elitist aesthetic of *The End of the Road*.

This intertextual link exposes the novel's subliminal meditation upon the relations of representation to the social and political conflicts of society, despite the novel's insistence that these conflicts have their source not in social and political history, but within the character of language itself. The word *horse*, Horner reminds Blakesley, "is just a symbol . . . a noise that we make in our throats or some scratches on the blackboard. . . . the significances of words are arbitrary conventions, mostly; historical accidents." Horner concludes with the inherent conservatism of the intertextual point of view: "You're free to break the rules, but not if you're after intelligibility. If you *do* want intelligibility, then the only way to get 'free' of the rules is to master them so thoroughly that they're second nature to you" (129).

Barth's allusion to the ideological battle of Dickens' *Hard Times* transforms the issues of Dickens' dialogue into those of the "affluent society" and its discourses, in which the hard times of the depression decade have been left behind, replaced by the threat of totalitarianism lurking within the manifestations of mass society. Barth's allusion stands bracketed as a nostalgic reference to a time when the artist felt the urgencies of political involvement. Now, the novel seems to say, the long effort to unite the artist with progressive politics has come to an end of the road.

Typically, readers have ignored the political struggle which lies beneath Horner's rationalizations about the problematics of representation, and have pretty much taken Barth/Horner at their word: some kind of syntax — inherently reductive and distorting — is necessary to the intelligibility of one's self, others, history, and the stories or fictions one tells if these are to be "social" phenomena. But the theoretical or abstract nature of the debate, which has been the primary focus of Barth criticism, is inseparable from the social practice which the novel enacts. Horner's position actually removes the possibility of change from the world of social history or politics and isolates it within the world of "articulation" — narrative art. Other glaring instances of this displacement are embedded within the givens of the novel's plot. The apparent blind alley into which this ménage à trois has taken them is a historical illusion, after all, dependent upon the imperfect development of prophylaxis and laws prohibiting abortion. Further, legalized segregation prevents the black doctor from writing Rennie a prescription or administering the abortion in the comparative safety of a hospital. And these legal conventions, of course, are sustained by the social conventions of the culture.

Set in the period from 1951 to 1953, and written in the fall of 1955, a year after desegregation of the schools (May 1954), the novel might be read as calling attention to the arbitrary, historical nature of these conventions. After all, such is Horner's argument to Blakesley; but Horner uses it to defend the status quo rather than advocate reform. One imagines that for many readers in 1958 (when the novel was eventually published), the black doctor's inability to buy himself a cup of coffee in the bus station where he finds the immobilized Horner would have been a pointed anachronism, for which not only *Brown v. Board of Education*, but also the Montgomery boycott and the growing civil rights unrest would serve as intertexts.

In fact, however, the social dimension of *The End of the Road* is never mentioned, either in reviews or in the criticism.[32] Surely this is the result of readers following the markers of allusion and intentionality, all of which point to the inherent problematics of representation as the source of social conflict rather than the other way around. The aesthetics of the novel reinforce this repression of the plot's historicity because, despite the graphic description of Rennie's botched abortion which seems to remind readers of a world of feeling and value beyond language, that world exists only in and through the textual surface of the fiction. Although readers have generally grown impatient with Horner's self-interested rationalizing well before the abortion scene, the novel cannot disentangle itself from his love of articulation and the art of betrayal upon which its narrative intelligibility depends. After all, Horner notes the time he begins to write his story as October, 4, 1955, a year and five months after Chief Justice Earl Warren read the opinion overturning *Plessy v. Ferguson,* and coinciding with the period in which Barth wrote the story Horner tells.

Jake's discontent with himself, then, is the shadow of Barth's discomfort, as both withdraw into an ahistorical aestheticism, founded upon the ineradicable limits of representation: "given my own special kind of integrity, if I was to have [friends] at all I must remain uninvolved — I must leave them alone" (176). In his room after Rennie's death, Horner reads the bust of Laocoön as an allegory of the times: "my limbs were bound like Laocoön's — by the serpents Knowledge and Imagination, which, grown great in the fullness of time, no longer tempt but annihilate" (187). Knowing too much and imagining too well, human society is breached from within, by the Trojan horse of reason itself.

Georg Lukács has called such conclusions the "contemplative" rendering of an essentially political view, but they were common enough within the literary-intellectual community of the postwar years. When R. W. B. Lewis published *The American Adam* in 1955, he concluded his study with a comment upon "The Contemporary Situation":

The picture of man sketched by the dominant contemporary philosophies and ologies shows us a figure struggling to stand upright amid the most violent crosscurrents: the American as Adam has been replaced by the American as Laocoön; the Emersonian figure — "the plain old Adam, the simple genuine self" — has been frowned quite out of existence.

This picture, he adds, is "clearly warranted."[33] Barth's novel describes the end of an idea held by Schiller and Lessing, in which art is the embodiment of freedom in beauty — Horner refers to Lessing's treatise once, noting of his "friend Laocoön" that his "grimace was his beauty" — for the form of freedom in postwar discourse, as Sartre argued, is not beauty but "anguish."[34] We may think of *The End of the Road* as the effort to overcome Lessing's distinction between stone and poetry: as narrative sculpture, the novel exposes the statue's latent pain and torment, which Lessing thought the sculpture could not afford to acknowledge.

As this sculptural, plastic aspiration came to dominate Barth's experiments with narrative, from *Lost in the Funhouse* (1968) through *Letters* (1979), critics have seen in it the persistence of modernism, but intertextual scrutiny shows that persistence mediated throughout by the more lateral discourses of the cold war. Thus the social text of *The End of the Road* begins to emerge like a photograph coming up beneath the developer. Barth's *The End of the Road* records a circulation between private intention and its intertextual saturation: the novel *is* that circulation.

We should note that the "end of ideology" discourse inscribed within Barth's novel was itself an object of critique as those who deployed it were accused of obscuring their own ideology. The "definition of myth in a bourgeois society," Roland Barthes wrote in *Mythologies* (1957), "is depoliticized speech." In his view at that time, "myth has the task of giving an historical intention a natural justification, and making contingency appear eternal. Now this process is exactly that of bourgeois ideology." The relevance of this view to Barth's novel is probably already too evident by now to require further remark. By representing the immobilization of the radical thinker as the natural consequence of thought itself, the novel represses the historicality of the plot's circumstances, and mystifies such politically malleable factors as segregation and anti-abortion laws. The "very end of myths," Barthes continues, "is to immobilize the world" and discourage "man against inventing himself."[35]

In an essay on existentialism (1949), Lukács attacked Heidegger and Sartre, dismissing "the myth of nothingness" as so much bourgeois "sophistry": "The nothingness which fascinates recent philosophers is a myth of declining capitalist society."[36] One can think of few postwar novels that demonstrate Lukács's point as well as Barth's, for the novel appeals to the story of Laocoön and to the literary authority of epic itself as a timeless warning, admonishing the artist of the futility of prophecy and political commitment; in fact, Jacob Horner leaves the statue behind him when he joins the black doctor at his Remobilization Farm. Horner's confession, one gathers, is a form of therapy through which the difficulties of historical engagement are circumvented by the power of black ink, the printed word giving order to the blank whiteness of the page. But this evasion is unsuccessful: though the novel pretends that it comes to us from some place outside of town, beyond the human community, its textual constitution is a social mosaic of the very discourses it seeks to escape.

NOTES

1 In an interview with George Bluestone, "John Wain and John Barth: The Angry and the Accurate," *Massachusetts Review* 1. 3 (May 1960):586.

2 David Morrell, *John Barth: An Introduction* (University Park: Pennsylvania State UP, 1976), 16.

3 John Barth, *The End of the Road* (New York: Doubleday, 1988), 112.

4 See M. M. Bakhtin, *The Dialogic Imagination*, ed. Michael Holquist, trans. Caryl Emerson and Michael Holquist (Austin: U of Texas P, 1981), especially "Discourse in the Novel."

5 For Kristeva and Barthes, see Kristeva, *Desire in Language*, ed. Leon S. Roudiez, trans. Thomas Gora et al. (New York: Columbia UP, 1980), 66, and Barthes, *Image-Music-Text*, trans. Stephen Heath (New York: Hill and Wang, 1977), 161, 164.

6 See Fredric Jameson, *The Political Unconscious* (Ithaca: Cornell UP, 1981), "On Interpretation."

7 These quotations come from Frank Kermode's review of Greenblatt's *Shakespearean Negotiations*, "The New Historicism," *New Republic*, February 29, 1988, 31–34, and Greenblatt's essay "Exorcism into Art," *Representations* 12 (Fall 1985): 20, 21.

8 Many commentators on the novel have noted the reference to the children's rhyme. Barth himself calls it to our attention in an interview with John Enck, "John Barth: An Interview," *Wisconsin Studies in Contemporary Literature* 6 (1965): 12.

9 See Charles Harris, *Passionate Virtuosity* (Urbana: U of Illinois, 1983), 44–49, and Tony Tanner, *City of Words* (New York: Harper & Row, 1971), 240.

10 Alan Prince, "An Interview with John Barth," *Prism* (Spring 1968):54, and Enck, "John Barth: An Interview" 6.

11 Kristeva, *Desire* 66.

12 In "The Chart," for example, we read, "While thus employed, the heavy pewter lamp suspended in chains over his head, continually rocked with the motion of the ship, and for ever threw shifting gleams and shadows of lines upon his wrinkled brow, till it almost seemed that while he himself was marking out lines and courses on the wrinkled charts, some invisible pencil was also tracing lines and courses upon the deeply marked chart of his forehead" (298). Moby-Dick, too, is "distinguished" by "a peculiar snow-white wrinkled forehead" (281), in which Ahab sees an "an inscrutable malice." It is "that inscrutable thing" Ahab hates, but he himself is branded "that inscrutable Ahab" (325), and the rocking motion imparted to the lamp above his head is "borrowed from the sea; by the sea, from the inscrutable tides of God" (257). Citations from Penguin Edition, editor Harold Beaver.

13 Harris, for example, mentions existentialism only in passing. The only essay I know of which explores the philosophical positions of the novel with any adequacy is Jacquelyn Kegley's "*The End of the Road*: The Death of Individualism," in *Philosophy and Literature*, ed. A. Phillips Griffiths (Cambridge: Cambridge UP, 1984), 115–34.

14   In English translation, *The Transcendence of the Ego*, trans. Forrest Williams
     and Robert Kirkpatrick (New York: Farrar, Straus and Giroux, 1957); *Being
     and Nothingness*, trans. Hazel Barnes. (New York: Philosophical Library, 1956).
     The translation dates of these works raises the relevant question of whether
     or not Barth, if not fluent in French, could have read them before writing
     The End of the Road. This helps identify a nice distinction between "source"
     and anonymous "intertext," for Sartrean ideas infiltrated American thought
     long before these translations appeared. Another possibility is that Barth
     read the chapters of *Being and Nothingness* collected by Hazel Barnes in *Ex-
     istential Psychoanalysis* (New York: Philosophical Library, 1953). This volume
     contains Sartre's discussion of "bad faith."

15   *Being and Nothingness* 62, 37–39.

16   Daniel Fraustino, "*The Country Wife* comes to *The End of the Road*," *Ari-
     zona Quarterly* 33.1 (Spring 1977):76–86.

17   Two essays have been written about the "horse" motif: the first, by Jack David,
     "The Trojan Horse at The End of the Road," *College Literature* 4 (Spring 1977):
     159–64, notes the presence of horse imagery, which he sees culminate in the
     reference, through Laocoön, to the Trojan horse; the second, by Robert V.
     Hoskins III, "Swift, Dickens, and the Horses in *The End of the Road*," *James
     Madison Journal* 37 (1979): 18–32, traces the sources of the horse imagery
     and is far more interpretive, suggesting, for example, that Gradgrind's insis-
     tence upon "facts" is "essentially what Jake Horner's Doctor offers as 'Infor-
     mational Therapy'" (26). This seems right to me and should be placed, as
     Barth does, within Wittgenstein's proviso that everything that is the case, the
     facts of the world, cannot include values and ethics. See above, p. 188. Hoskins
     does not notice that the conversation between Sissy Jupe and Gradgrind is
     reproduced in the debate between Blakesley and Jacob Horner. See pp. 127–
     30 of the novel, and above, pp. 196–98.

18   Ludwig Wittgenstein, *Tractatus Logico-Philosophicvs*, First German edition,
     1921. I have used the translation by D. F. Pears and B. F. McGuinness (Lon-
     don: Routledge & Kegan Paul, 1961).

19   Irving Howe, "Mass Society and Postmodern Fiction," *A World More Attrac-
     tive: A View of Modern Literature and Politics* (New York: Horizon, 1963), 93.

20   Carolyn Porter, *Seeing and Being* (Middletown, Ct.: Wesleyan UP 1981),
     3–22; Russell Reising, *The Unusable Past* (New York: Methuen, 1986), esp.
     31–37.

21   Mary Sperling McAuliffe, *Crisis on the Left: Cold War Politics and American
     Liberals, 1947–1954* (Amherst: U of Massachusetts, 1978), 63–74; John Higham,
     "The Cult of the 'American Consensus,'" *Commentary* 27.2 (February 1959):94.

22   To be fair, Bakhtin seems to retain the concept of authorial intention and con-
     trol: "When heteroglossia enters the novel it becomes subject to an artistic
     reworking" (*Dialogic Imagination* 300).

23   Walter Mack, *No time Lost* (New York: Atheneum, 1982), 134–36.

24   J. C. Louis and Harvey Z. Yazijian, *The Cola Wars* (New York: Everest House,
     1980), 68–69.

25   Ibid. 68.

26 Max Horkheimer and Theodor Adorno, "The Culture Industry: Enlightenment as Mass Deception," *Dialectic of Enlightenment*, trans. John Cumming (New York: Continuum, 1987), 127.

27 Ibid. 126; C. Wright Mills, "The Cultural Apparatus," collected in *Power, Politics and People* (New York: Ballantine, 1963), 405–22.

28 Jack David notes the significance of this etymology, though he does not similarly analyze Rennie's maiden name (MacMahon). Incidentally, Hoskins notes that "Morgan" is "a type of horse," but not specifically an American breed descending from a prepotent Vermont stallion.

29 *Being and Nothingness* 409.

30 Again, it is difficult to set forth the extent of this view, but its penetration throughout the culture of thought may be suggested on the one hand by Trilling's remark (made in a lecture he gave in 1947 at Kenyon), and on the other by George Kennan's assertion a few years later, "It is a curious thing, but it is true, that the legalistic approach to world affairs, rooted as it unquestionably is in a desire to do away with war and violence, makes violence more enduring, more terrible, and more destructive to political stability" (*American Diplomacy 1900–1950* [New York: NAL, 1951], 87).

31 This Mass-Cult discourse will be familiar to many readers, but again a few examples may help establish its existence. Clement Greenberg's "Avant-Garde and Kitsch" published in *Partisan Review* in 1939 is a good start; Dwight Macdonald is probably the most well-known postwar "theorist" of mass culture in (among other places) "Masscult & Midcult" (*Against the American Grain*); Philip Rahv's concluding remark in his response to the "Our Country and Our Culture" symposium in *Partisan Review* (May–June 1952) is representative: "if under present conditions we cannot stop the ruthless expansion of mass-culture, the least we can do is to keep apart and refuse its favors" (310).

32 As I noted at the beginning of the essay, several readers have been disturbed by what seems to be the callous results of the novel's aesthetic. See Campbell Tatham, "Message [Concerning the *Felt* Ultimacies of One John Barth]," *Boundary 2* 3.2 (1975): 259–87, and Tony Tanner, *City of Words*. Charles Harris defends the novel's ethics in *Passionate Virtuosity*. In none of these discussions does any social dimension, textual or otherwise, appear.

33 R. W. B. Lewis, *The American Adam* (Chicago: U of Chicago P, 1971), 195.

34 The word in this instance is Sartre's, describing freedom. See *Being and Nothingness* 62.

35 Roland Barthes, *Mythologies*, trans. Annette Lavers (New York: Hill and Wang, 1972), 142, 155.

36 Georg Lukács, "Existentialism," collected in *Marxism and Human Liberation* (New York: Dell, 1973), 251, 254.

CHAPTER 8

Influence? or Intertextuality?
The Complicated Connection
of Edith Sitwell with Gertrude Stein

CYRENA N. PONDROM

In the early twenties Edith Sitwell, already the most notorious and discursively most radical avant-garde poet on the British scene, became fascinated with the work of Gertrude Stein. Not only did she persuade Stein to agree to read her important theoretical statement "Composition as Explanation" at Cambridge and Oxford, Sitwell declared the presence of one of Stein's prose poems in a poem of her own. "Jodelling Song," she announced in a note to the poem, "is founded on Gertrude Stein's 'Accents in Alsace' . . . contained in her book, *Geography and Plays*" (*CP* 142, 425; *RE* 62, 95). That open assertion of similitude has not always been accepted by subsequent scholars, and one has called the Sitwell poem as unlike Stein's as "a text that limits its mobility by following a fixed set of rules" differs from "one that allows for free play."[1]

Both Sitwell's claims to relationship with Stein and subsequent revaluations give rise to some illuminating questions about the purposes and presuppositions of claims (and disclaimers) of influence. What goals are served by Sitwell's apparent attribution of influence to Stein? by later refutations? What do assertions or refutations of influence leave out? These questions are greatly complicated by the inseparable issue[2] of both Stein's and Sitwell's relationships to the French symbolists' literary successors, Apollinaire, Cocteau, and the surrealists. Sitwell was an unremitting and enthusiastic reader of Rimbaud, who was translated by her tutor and long-time companion, Helen Rootham; she was well aware of the parallels between the earlier Picasso-Satie-Cocteau presentation of *Parade* and her own *Façade*; she was an enthusiastic reader of Apollinaire's *Alcools,* albeit possibly a belated one,[3] and she articulately denounced the surrealists, with whom she was sometimes compared. Stein, in turn, never acknowledged an acquaintance with the French symbolists, but had considerable opportunity to provide her own work as an influence — or intertext — for the early experiments of both Cocteau and Apollinaire. Cocteau, for one, acknowledged her priority and inspiration for his first experimental prose work, *Le Potomak* (written 1913–14, published 1919):

> Un soir j'entendis rire des camarades autour d'un poème d'une Américaine. Or ce radiotélégramme atteignait vite mon coeur.
> "Dîner, c'est ouest," décide simplement Mlle. S. au milieu d'une page blanche.
> . . . Ce qui offusquait ce groupe, la farce américaine, me parut au contraire une preuve de confiance délicate. (*Le Potomak* 12–13)[4]

The introduction of these figures — who may be seen in varied roles as alternative "sources," rivals from whose work Sitwell sought to distinguish herself, mere parallels, or reinforcers of an inspiration derived from elsewhere — highlights a major deficiency of the traditional study of influence. Usually focused on linear, single-source, and unidirectional relationships, traditional influence study has not possessed the vocabulary necessary to describe the interaction of polymorphous "sources" that overdetermine the characteristics manifested by a given literary work. Here it becomes useful to invoke Roland Barthes's description of a text as "a multi-dimensional space in which a variety of writings, none of them original, blend and clash" (146) and Julia Kristeva's assertion that "every signifying practice is a field of transpositions of various signifying systems (an inter-textuality)" (*Revolution* 60). In the space of a Sitwell poem of this period, thus, Sitwell's understanding of Stein's practice, of Rimbaud's, of Cocteau's and perhaps Apollinaire's, and of the latter two poets' readings of Stein herself would confront each other, in the presence of the writer's clear desire to differentiate herself from surrealist dogma. And the textual metaphor reminds the critic that even these multiplicities are not exhaustive, but a set delimited with inescapable arbitrariness on the field upon which Sitwell's texts are in play.

More useful than asking how Sitwell imitated Stein, then, is asking how she *transformed* Stein's representational practice, particularly when she brought it together with parallel but divergent practices. Kristeva has called "the intersections of a given textual arrangement (a semiotic practice) with the utterances (sequences) that it either assimilates into its own space or to which it refers in the space of exterior texts (semiotic practices)" an "ideologeme" (*Desire* 36). To use her language, the question of the Stein-

Sitwell relationship is not so much a study in influence as an effort to describe selected aspects of the ideologeme of several Sitwell texts of the early twenties. I will here examine Sitwell's transformation of Stein. But one can conclude from this examination neither a single nor a simply linear interaction. The adaptation of Stein's practice by Sitwell is both modified and reinforced by her admiration of Rimbaud and her dislike for aspects of surrealist practice. And there exists the clear possibility that practices of Apollinaire or Cocteau are also intertexts which would also reinforce some Steinian practices.

At the same time one need not abandon some of the strategies of more traditional influence study. The extent to which texts by Stein contribute to determining the direction of experiments by Sitwell can be estimated by examining Sitwell's work before and after her first major encounter with Stein's texts. Unpublished correspondence between Stein and Sitwell corroborates that particular writings were available to Sitwell and could function directly as intertexts. That these two women interacted and that their interaction has consequences in the development of modernist literature are facts which have political, social, and ideological as well as literary meaning. The literary subject, the fact of agency and intention, and the historical situation of the two writers are significant. Although Kristeva has been at pains to dissociate intertextuality from source studies (*Revolution* 60), one effect of the examination of the Sitwell-Stein interaction is to show that both influence and intertextuality are concepts enriched by attention to the implications of the other.

I

First, let us consider *why* Sitwell made such a nearly unprecedented attribution of influence to one of her contemporaries. (Such an inquiry, of course, has access only to implications and ends served — not to the mind or subconscious of the subject.) It is remarkable that Sitwell's source annotation has inspired so little curiosity; such explicit assertions of imitation are hardly conventional. After all, only a few years before, Pound had so heavily edited Eliot's *The Waste Land* that its final form owed its distinguishing characteristics to that intervention, but neither man explicitly acknowledged the collaboration. And Sitwell herself, despite plentiful manuscript evidence to the contrary, has been habitually stereotyped in terms of traditional female rivalry.[5]

Sitwell encountered "Accents in Alsace" in Stein's *Geography and Plays* (1922); she published her own transformation of it in *Rustic Elegies* in 1927, writing Stein on April 25, 1927, "By the way, I'm having my own new book sent to you from the publisher. It contains a variation on a theme from 'Accents in Alsace.' I do *hope* you will like it" (UL). During the years between 1922 and 1927 Sitwell's reputation at least equaled and probably exceeded Stein's. Stein was well known in avant-garde art circles and was a mecca sought out by expatriate Americans, but her work had found only a limited public audience. She had published three books by 1922, the first at her own expense, and issued a fourth, *The Making of Americans,* in 1925, through Contact Editions, a press funded by Bryher and directed by expatriate Robert McAlmon. A fifth, the monograph of her English lecture "Composition as Explanation," was issued by Hogarth Press at least in part as a result of the intervention of Sitwell. She had enjoyed only limited success in securing periodical publication. Sitwell, on the other hand, was the author of fourteen volumes by 1927, including four issued by Duckworth, a major commercial press, and was widely known both as the editor of the annual experimental anthology *Wheels* (1916–21) and as the author of *Façade,* which had elicited a critical furor on its first public performance.

Sitwell's acknowledgment of Stein, then, is not likely to be a claim to fame by association, except as a subsidiary effect. Instead it has the character of publicly acknowledging a political alliance. As when a professor testifies to the excellence of the student by saying she herself has learned from her, Sitwell sought to enhance Stein's reputation by demonstrating that she was willing to be an imitator. Sitwell actively sought to spearhead a movement of literary experiment, and she was tireless in trying to secure for Stein the recognition and exposure Sitwell felt were her due. This motivation seems explicit in her letter a few months before Stein's scheduled lecture at Oxford and Cambridge: "If it were possible to work harder at missionary work than I am working now, I would, as your presence will make the work far easier. I have discovered that the average semi-intelligent person judges pioneer work largely by the personality and appearance of the writer. An important and magnetic personality wins half the battle" (UL, January? 1926).

Sitwell's feminist consciousness, her self-awareness of a commitment to further the work of another woman writer, and her perception of gifted women writers as a marginalized (even besieged) group, are also clear in other letters to Stein:

A great writer like yourself is absolutely bound to win through. There can't be any question about it. Meanwhile, of course one does hate the insults. People have now taken to insulting me publicly. A gentleman who writes bad novels, at a public dinner at which I was a guest, said in his speech "modern literature suffers from sexual unrest,—and Miss Edith Sitwell is a notable example of this!" So courteous! But it shows what one has to put up with. (UL, January 1, 1926)

Clearly Sitwell has a political intent in documenting that powerful ideas are not the province of men alone, as much as critical and theoretical intent in seeking to illustrate that her own decentered, illogical, and subversive texts operate in an emerging tradition that encompasses Stein as well. Whereas her own claim to have initiated new ideas in literature would always be exposed to the disclaimer of the one allegedly influenced, there is no easily persuasive rebuttal to her declaration that another woman has influenced *her*. Her attribution of influence, thus, is as much about power (and the formation of alternative hegemonies) as about originality.

That probably is always true. It is not at all necessary that a literary form or practice *originate* with the writer identified as influential, despite the rhetoric of originality which has in the last two centuries accompanied discussions of influence. Instead the "great writer" is one who implements the practices in question in a framework which makes them seem coercive to those who follow.[6] He is also one whose work meets the ideological purposes of the evaluator. In romantic and postromantic discourse, attribution of originality helped to satisfy those purposes, though it need not always be so. But it is always true that an assertion of influence is an assertion of power.

Here again traditional influence discussions have often lacked the vocabulary to articulate the way in which power makes itself felt in the transmission of influence. As Baxandall, and Rothstein and Clayton, have persuasively argued, the simple interpretation of the source as agent, acting directly on the recipient, is insufficient to explain the phenomenon. Instead, one is again profited by invoking a blend of the theories of influence and intertextuality, for to understand influence is to understand that one has a dialectic between the agency of human subjects and the agency of texts. In the case of literary influence, we are talking about the agency of a text—but of a text given its specific form by the skill and reflexive insight (and the fortuitous historical position) of a writer. She or he creates structures of words capable of eliciting and supporting some organization(s) of experience, and these structures then exert a (coercive) power, eliciting a response in the recipient that transposes some of the features of the agent text. Or, to use a different vocabulary, the text produces a certain use of itself. This use is in turn qualified by the human agency of the recipient, by what Gertrude Stein would have seen as the writer's capacity (or lack of capacity) to be authentic.

Stein described this reciprocal relationship as follows:

Each period of living differs from any other period of living not in the way life is but in the way life is conducted and that authentically speaking is composition.

After life has been conducted in a certain way everybody knows it but nobody knows it. Any one creating the composition in the arts does not know it either, they are conducting life and that makes their composition what it is, it makes their work compose as it does.

Their influence and their influences are the same as that of all of their contemporaries only it must always be remembered that the analogy is not obvious until as I say the composition of a time has become so pronounced that it is past and the artistic composition of it is a classic. (CE 517)[7]

Power is the real normative issue in influence discussions. And that is why the idea of influential women has been so foreign to our literary-critical discourse. Long before Moers' *Literary Women* or Showalter's *A Literature of Their Own,* or Harold Bloom's explicit argument that influence is the epic of inheritance between fathers and sons, Edith Sitwell implicitly recognized the importance of establishing a chain of practices shared from woman to woman. She seeks to establish an alternative canon in which both she and Stein — as well as selected male writers — have a place.

And conversely, I suspect, similar concerns to establish or maintain the power of a restricted canon — one that may embrace Stein in the company of Rimbaud, Williams, Pound, Beckett, and Ashbery, but which does not "stretch" to Sitwell — inform later evaluation of Sitwell's claims to have been the recipient of influence. As I have argued elsewhere, neither feminist critics nor others in recent discussions of value have offered persuasive alternatives to politics (and the power relationships which are intrinsic to politics) as a foundation for canon formation.

II

If both Sitwell's and Perloff's statements about the "influence" of Stein on Sitwell have an end at least as political as literary, are they less "factual" as a result? Is it possible to make any assessment of the significance of Stein to Sitwell, and Sitwell to that broader stream of poetry Perloff has called "indeterminant"? To begin to answer that question we should turn to some of the history of Sitwell's response to Stein.

Over a period of two years, Sitwell wrote reviews of Stein's *Geography and Plays* (1922) for several journals, and incorporated comments about Stein in essays of her own. One can chart, then, Sitwell's evolving attitude toward Stein with some precision. In one of the earliest of these reviews (July 14, 1923), Sitwell candidly confessed her own ambivalence:

It has taken me several weeks to clarify my own feelings about Miss Stein's writings. Her work appears to have a certain amount of real virtue, but to understand or apprehend that virtue a reader would have to study Miss Stein's methods for years, and intimately; whereas this is the first book of hers that I have read. . . . I think it is indisputable that Miss Stein has a definite aim in her work, and that she is perfectly, relentlessly, and bravely sincere. She is trying to pull language out of the meaningless state into which it has fallen, and to give it fresh life and new significance. . . . I hope I shall not be regarded as a reactionary, but I am bound to say that I prefer words, when collected into a sentence, to convey some sense. And Miss Stein's sentences do not always convey any sense — not even a new one. (*Nation*)

Sitwell concluded the assessment by praising Stein's "valuable pioneer work" but urging young writers not to imitate her. By April 1926, in a review of *The Making of Americans,* Sitwell had so far revised her judgment as to call *Geography and Plays* "one of the most exciting books of our time" (*New Criterion* 391), and shrewdly assessed *The Making of Americans* as a less radical attack on the conventions of language. In the interim, in *Poetry and Criticism,* Sitwell had explicitly linked the new and radical enterprise of the modernist poet to the abstract movement in art, and had cited Stein as a primary example:

. . . the modern poet . . . stylises his works in the same manner as that in which (varying according to the personality of their genius) the douanier Rousseau, Picasso, Matisse, Derain, Modigliani, Stravinsky, Debussy, stylise, or have stylised, theirs. That is all; if we grasp that fact the whole matter becomes easy. What may appear difficult is the habit of forming abstract patterns in words. We have long been accustomed to abstract patterns in the pictorial art, but nobody to my knowledge has ever gone so far in making abstract patterns in words as the modernist poet has. . . . There is, of necessity, a connecting thread running through each pattern, otherwise it would not be a pattern. But I can understand that the person who does not realise the necessity of cultivating all the possibilities of words as a medium — of understanding that medium — may be puzzled. . . . Miss Gertrude Stein . . . is an admirable example of the case in point. (30–31)

Sitwell goes on to cite the example of "The Portrait of Constance Fletcher." It is the very text which Marianne DeKoven has shown is the moment of transition for Stein from her repetitive style to a style in which selection is unfettered, and combination or grammar is suppressed to permit words movement in a more nearly indeterminant relationship to each other (64).

Is there any comparable difference between the poems which Sitwell wrote after she began her really experimental work but before reading *Geography and Plays* and those which she wrote during her most intense contacts with Stein? We may examine this question by considering the common characteristics of three poems published in 1920 or 1921 and conting them with the practices observable in "Jodelling Song" (and some other poems written after Sitwell's reading of *Geography and Plays*). The first three are "En Famille," which appeared in *The Chapbook* in July 1920 (CP 128–29); "Aubade," one of Sitwell's favorite illustrations of her own work, which appeared in the *Saturday Westminster Gazette*, October 2, 1920 (CP 16); and "Trio for Two Cats and a Trombone," which also appeared in the *Westminster Gazette,* September 3, 1921 (*CP* 120–21). All three poems demonstrate the synaesthetic metaphor which Rimbaud proclaimed in his letter to Paul Demeny of May 15, 1871, and made famous in the poetic manifesto "Voyelles":

> A noir, E blanc, I rouge, U vert, O bleu : voyelles,
> Je dirai quelque jour vos naissances latentes :
> A, noir corset velu des mouches éclantes
> Qui bombinent autour des puanteurs cruelles,
>
> Golfes d'ombre; E, candeurs des vapeurs et des tentes,
> Lances des glaciers fiers, rois blancs, frissons d'ombelles . . .
> (103)

The poet, Rimbaud said, must be a seer, and must start by seeing into himself: "La première étude de l'homme qui veut être poëte est sa propre connaissance, entière; il cherche son âme, il l'inspecte, il la tente, l'apprend (254). The next step is a long and deliberate derangement of the senses: "Le Poëte se fait *voyant* par un long, immense et raisonné *dérèglement de tous les sens* (254). Such a derangement of the senses is visible in "Aubade," in which the "morning light creaks down again," rain is "hardened by the light," and "dawn light lies whining." In "Trio for Two Cats and a Trombone," "the light is braying like an ass" and the sea is "castanetted." Such images are more muted in "En Famille," but their trace is present: shutters are imagined to fall "with a noise like amber softly gliding," and the sea is "peruked." One of the poems ("En Famille") manifests a motif which dominates Rimbaud's *Une Saison en Enfer*, the imaginative journey to hell (a setting which also appears in such early Sitwell poems as "Mandoline," "Barber's Shop," and "Singerie"). Both of the other two poems have a hallucinatory quality — "Aubade" in the surreal setting of dawn's transition from dark to light and "Trio" in the Alice-in-Wonderland world of courting dolls — that is reinforced by incantatory rhythms.

All three of these poems show the distinctive hallmarks of Sitwell's early experimental work:

exploration of an interior, subconscious, or dream world;

implicit contrast of that inner world — which is sometimes threatening — with the artificiality, hierarchy, and mendacity of the public, social realm;

symbolic treatment of the power of sexual meanings; and
explicit experiment with the communication of moods through sound and
rhythm, without regard to the semantic content of words.

In "En Famille" the submerged psychic world, with its hints of incest, its oedipal struggles, is imaged as the world of Myrrhina in hell, preening behind "siesta shutters." It is a world of frank acknowledgment of feeling, from which the family is shut off by the Admiral/father's ceaseless invocation of the hierarchical rules of military and social rank, religion, and manners. In the eyes of Sir Joshua Jebb, there is no escape from the realm of the "properly proper," which places the real hell on earth.

The inner world of "Aubade" is a world of loss—loss so profound one is tempted to call it absolute. Sitwell has acknowledged that this is a poem about a state of consciousness, about a young girl so shut off from the sensory experience of sight and sound that "she scarcely knows even that she is suffering" ("Modernist Poets" 82). In another place Sitwell acknowledged that the model for the Jane of the poem is herself (*TCO* 86). But her explication of the moods created by the rhythms of the lines stops with a stress on the psychic experience of intense observation of the dawn kitchen scene in rain. Understandably, she does not offer a reader's guide to the experience that led this Jane—clearly a plain Jane, "Tall as a crane" with "cockscomb-ragged hair" (like Sitwell herself)—to perceive the morning that finally comes as a light that "creaks down again." She does not interpret the stairs Jane is invited to descend, or the "dull blunt wooden stalactite of rain," nor does she explain why the "creaking empty light" which "Will never harden into sight, / [and] Will never penetrate your brain" produces such sorrow. She simply leaves the girl's "Cockscomb flowers that none will pluck" to speak for themselves in these "eternities of kitchen garden." Despite the insistent appearance of clearly phallic imagery, critics early and late have taken Sitwell's explanation of this poem at face value (Cevasco 17–18).

In "Trio for Two Cats and a Trombone" the inner dimensions of the courtship ritual are suggested by the "public" behavior of the courting dolls; the effect is very like puppet theater or the dramatization of dream. This effect is heightened by the sense of indefinite time, accomplished by references to light which resist interpretation in clock terms. The drama is carried out with all the social stereotypes of seduction and mastery, and breaks off with voices "shrill / as the steely grasses' thrill" as the language gallops in a frenzy of explosive consonants, in trochaic rhythm with heavy ictus and a final spondee. The semantic slip away from sense in these final lines is part of the "meaning":

To the jade "Come kiss me harder"
He called across the battlements as she
Heard our voices thin and shrill
As the steely grasses' thrill,
Or the sound of the onycha
When the phoca has the pica
In the palace of the Queen Chinee!

These poems rely in a significant way on the nonlexical — and in that sense, abstract — patterns of sound and rhythm for their meaning. For these rhymes and rhythms Sitwell espoused a system of correspondences. Quoting Poincaré, she asserted "the accident of a rhyme calls forth a system from the shadow" ("Modernist Poets" 79). She could have been quoting Pound: "I believe in an absolute rhythm. I believe that every emotion and every phase of emotion has some toneless phrase, some rhythm-phrase to express it" (84). These poems rely heavily on the power of successive images or scenes to invoke the appropriate mood, a method that could be described by Eliot's doctrine of the objective correlative. But a narrative line persists at a clear surface level, in addition to a submerged narration that is psychological. Moreover, none of these poems disrupts the normal functioning of the process of semantic selection, unless the "nonsense language" of the end of "Trio" is taken to be an example of that practice. It is here, I think, that we can see the challenge that Stein presented to Sitwell.

Sitwell's notes to "Jodelling Song" say, "This is founded on Gertrude Stein's 'Accents in Alsace' (The Watch on the Rhine) contained in her book, *Geography and Plays*" (*CP* 425); she then quotes the twelve-line section named "The Watch on the Rhine":

Sweeter than water or cream or ice. Sweeter than bells of roses. Sweeter than winter or summer or spring. Sweeter than pretty posies. Sweeter than anything is my queen and loving is her nature.

Loving and good and delighted and best is her little King and Sire whose devotion is entire[,] who has but one desire to express the love which is hers to inspire.

In the photograph the Rhine hardly showed[.]

In what way do chimes remind you of singing.[?] In what way[s] do birds sing.[?] In what way are forests black or white.[?]

We saw them blue.

With for get me nots. [forget-me-nots]

In the midst of our happiness we were very pleased.[8]

(*GP* 415)

The larger piece from which the lines are drawn, a seven-page text next
to the end of *Geography and Plays,* composed in 1918, is one of Stein's
exercises in mixed genre. It is subtitled "A Reasonable Tragedy" and contains brief (nonconsecutive) acts, scenes, and subtitled sections which
variously resemble prose fiction, prose poems, free verse, and doggerel.

One of the dominant attributes of this text is the defeat or displacement
of expectations — linguistic, idiomatic, and generic. An examination of
Sitwell's poem in the context of Stein's shows that it shares this attribute.
To begin with, Sitwell's citation implies that she has quoted the relevant
lines. A cursory inspection of the whole shows this is not true, for "Jodelling Song" begins with two lines drawn from a section of "Accents in Alsace" immediately preceding the quoted lines:

> All the leaves are green and babyish.
> How many children make a family.
>
> (*GP* 415)

Sitwell's poem begins:

> "We bear velvet cream,
> Green and babyish
> Small leaves seem; each stream
> Horses' tails that swish,
>
> And the chimes remind
> Us of sweet birds singing,
> Like the jangling bells
> On rose-trees ringing. . . . "

Furthermore, it becomes immediately evident that Sitwell's assertion that
her poem is "founded on" the other one implies a looser connection than
simple similitude. The Stein text foregrounds some poetic elements; it begins in dactylic rhythm with trochaic substitution at the end of a line (i.e.,
at the end of each sentence), and uses both end and internal rhyme; however, the second half of the poem reverts to prose rhythms. Sitwell's verses,
on the other hand, are clearly poetry; she uses a regular *abab* or *abcb*
rhyme scheme and a rhythm adapted from the jodelling call to establish
one of the important disjunctions of the poem — the contrast between the
freedom and exultation of the jodelling call and the confinement of human beings in the chains of mortality.

The poem is not in any conventional sense an imitation, then. It can
be fairly understood as a transposition of the linguistic practices of Stein,
however, in some ways which are not apparent in Sitwell's earlier poems.
One of the most important disruptions of conventional linguistic practice
in Stein's style derives from a conflict between the propositional form of

the sentence and its semantic content. For example, even where the conventional subject-verb-object structure is preserved, and the appropriate part of speech is selected in each position, the lexical content of some of the words is such that the proposition is nonsense. The reader is forced to displace the proposition in ways that enable its lexical meanings to make sense. Because these displacements result in incomplete verbal structures, possible meanings proliferate and a single meaning never emerges as final and complete.

An analogous practice is clearly evident in Sitwell's "Jodelling Song." For example, in the line "We bear velvet cream" the verb "bear" can have at least three meanings: carry, endure, and give birth to. None of the three is perfectly completed by the objective phrase "velvet cream," although the sense *to carry* comes closest. The indeterminacy is intensified by the fact that the phrase may be either adjective/noun or noun/adjective; do we bear cream with a velvety texture or velvet with a creamy color? The strategy is one of unexpected modification, with undetermined reference. The context does nothing to resolve the ambiguity; the relationship of the assertion "Green and babyish / Small leaves seem" to "We bear velvet cream" is completely paratactic.

The images and incidents which succeed each other seem to have symbolic psychic significance. But coherent meaning may be achieved only if we presume a hidden story, of which we see only interrupted surfaces, deformed and displaced as in the dream-work. In an act of interpretation, the reader cannot evade her role as writer of the text, supplying the connectives which specify a relationship among the poem's paratactic elements, and thus constructing a narrative. To call this text one that does not "[allow] for free play" but "follow[s] a fixed set of rules" (Perloff 85) seems to me an unwarranted narrowing of the poem's possibilities.

Both Stein's and Sitwell's texts deal with the possibility of love within an environment in which human beings do not control human destiny. Both texts juxtapose the symbolically benign — even beneficent — landscape of Western Europe (Alsace or Switzerland) in the spring and images of threat and violence. Both use similar images to suggest these antithetical messages — forget-me-nots, forests white and black (either with snow or in a photograph), chimes, and singing birds. But the commonalities stop with materials and method — they do not extend to message. The threat in Stein's poem is explicitly historical; the occasion of the poem is her visit to Alsace immediately after the Armistice in World War I, and the threat is chillingly historically specific; the first section of "Accents in Alsace" asks about a jeopardized family: "And how did they escape by paying somebody money. That is what you did with the Boche" (*GP* 409). The love story is a triumph of perception over context. Despite the intrusion of history ("In the photograph the Rhine hardly showed"), the "queen" and "little King" put aside everything except expressing the love which they mutually inspire. It is a triumph of imposing one's own values on the world: "In the midst of our happiness we were very pleased" (*GP* 415).

Sitwell's view is much bleaker — and less contingent. The ominous backdrop for the revivified spring is the life cycle that moves inexorably from birth to death. Even though "The chimes remind / Us of sweet birds singing" (*CP* 142), no period of human ecstacy is more than a brief moment: "Man must say farewell / To parents now" and to the legends and stories of childhood — "William Tell, / and Mrs. Cow"; he must also bid good-bye to the other self-deceiving stories about experience — "stork and Bettes, / And to roses' bells, / And statuettes." Even the lovers' forget-me-nots, the achievements of imagination ("clouds like inns"), and the rituals of mythic celebration (the nectar in Ganymede's cup) are transitory deceptions which conceal the reality of experience. Ganymede's friends (his "true and fond / Ones") "seek their graves" (*CP* 143). The content is vastly different, although significant elements of method are much the same.

But the conflict between the conventions of combination and those of selection which Sitwell transposes from Stein takes its place in a text in which Sitwell also maintains some highly visible attributes of metric order and control. In Sitwell's poetic theory, pattern might be abstract or illogical, but the very fact of its appearance as pattern bespoke human agency. Just as Rimbaud called for a deliberate, even a reasoned, derangement of the senses, Sitwell would not acquiesce in an aesthetic which valorized the relinquishing of aesthetic control. Like the surrealists, she called for literary exploration of the "subconscious soul" ("Modernist Poets" 79), and both Freudian symbolism and free association seem ordering principles in some of her poetry. But unlike the surrealists, she denounced an aesthetics of chance as both unethical and deceptive. Consequently, the alterations of conventional linguistic and narrative practices which Sitwell admired in Stein take their place in her own poetry in a field in which they are modified by her adaptation of Rimbaldian principles of *deliberate* "derangement of the senses" and by her clearly stated hostility to the surrealists' aesthetics of chance. The result is not slavish imitation or a rigid hierarchy of influencer and influencee. But neither is it an anonymous text in which the situation of the writer as woman and agent, colleague of Stein and initiator of poetic practices which reflect her experience, is irrelevant. The result instead is a distinctive voice which can be appreciated as one thread in the polymorphous fabric of female modernism.

NOTES

1 Perloff (85). Perloff in this volume is committed to demonstrating the significance of Rimbaud as a literary source for one of the powerful strains of modernism — a strain often unjustly minimized in Anglo-American criticism. In keeping with the customary practice of influence scholars, Perloff accords substantial weight to Sitwell's own statements about what she is doing and how she reads both her poems and Stein's. She concludes that Sitwell substitutes the arbitrary rules of the board game for the undecidability of free play manifested in both Rimbaud and Stein, and hence does not belong to Perloff's canon of the modernist "great tradition."

2 By asserting that the question of Stein's and Sitwell's relationships to both recently dead and contempory French poets is inseparable from an understanding of their own relationship, I am implying a call to revise our understanding of influence by incorporation of some of the concepts of intertextuality. As shall later be clear, however, I am nonetheless unwilling to relinquish the concept of influence in favor of a radical definition of the intertextual.

3 Her hyperbolically laudatory letter to Maurice Bowra of March 17, 1945, implies that *Alcools* is new to her (*Selected Letters* 127–28), but the volume was importantly discussed in avant-garde journals in England in the very years in which Sitwell began writing her own poetry and editing *Wheels*.

4 The reference is to a poem in Stein's *Tender Buttons*, 1914. The line Cocteau translates into French is the complete text of the poem.

5 Glendinning's comment is typical: "Edith, in the 1920's or at any other time, did not care for professional competition from her own sex. She did not want to believe that there was any worth speaking of" (104). See also Elborn (30).

6 John Skelton, for example, is a writer of remarkable originality in terms of departure from the traditions he inherited, but his historical position did not situate him to greatly "influence" his successors. Or one may think of Sir Thomas Wyatt, who unarguably imported the Petrarchan sonnet into England, but whose "influence" and stature have been deemed significantly less than those of some of his successors who used it.

7 Consider also: "Those who are creating the modern composition authentically are naturally only of importance when they are dead because by that time the modern composition having become past is classified and the description of it is classical. That is the reason why the creator of the new composition in the arts is an outlaw until he is a classic, there is hardly a moment in between. . . .There is almost not an interval. For a very long time everybody refuses and then almost without a pause almost everybody accepts. . . . Now the only difficulty with the volte-face concerning the arts is this. When the acceptance comes, by that acceptance the thing created becomes a classic." Stein (CE 514–15).

8 Sitwell's quoted version is punctuated differently from Stein's. Sitwell variants are shown in square brackets.

WORKS CITED

Barthes, Roland. "The Death of the Author." In *Image-Music-Text,* trans. Stephen Heath. New York: Hill & Wang, 1977.

Cevasco, G. A. *The Sitwells: Edith, Osbert, and Sacheverell.* Boston: G. K. Hall, 1987.

DeKoven, Marianne. *A Different Language: Gertrude Stein's Experimental Writing.* Madison: U of Wisconsin P, 1983.

Elborn, Geoffrey. *Edith Sitwell: A Biography.* Garden City, NY: Doubleday, 1981.

Glendinning, Victoria. *Edith Sitwell: A Unicorn among Lions.* London: Weidenfeld, 1981.

Kristeva, Julia. *Desire in Language: A Semiotic Approach to Literature and Art.* Trans. Thomas Gora, Alice Jardine, and Leon S. Roudiez. New York: Columbia UP, 1980.

Kristeva, Julia. *Revolution in Poetic Language.* Trans. Margaret Waller. New York: Columbia UP, 1984.

Perloff, Marjorie. "Poetry as Word-System: The Art of Gertrude Stein." In *The Poetics of Indeterminacy.* Princeton: Princeton UP. 1981.

Pondrom, Cyrena N. "Gender and the (Re)formation of the Canon—Is Politics All?" *ADE Bulletin* 91(1988):21–28.

Pound, Ezra. *Gaudier-Brzeska.* New York: New Directions, 1970.

Rimbaud, Arthur. *Oeuvres complètes.* Paris: Gallimard, 1946.

Sitwell, Edith. *Collected Poems.* London: Macmillan, 1957. (Cited as *CP.*)

Sitwell, Edith. *"The Making of Americans.* By Gertrude Stein." *New Criterion* 4 (April 1926):390–92.

Sitwell, Edith. "Miss Stein's Stories." *The Nation & The Athenaeum* 33 (July 14, 1923):492. (Cited as *Nation.*)

Sitwell, Edith. "Modernist Poets." *Echanges* 3 (June 1930):77–91.

Sitwell, Edith. *Poetry and Criticism.* London: Hogarth, 1925; New York: Henry Holt, 1926.

Sitwell, Edith. *Rustic Elegies.* London: Duckworth, 1927. (Cited as *RE.*)

Sitwell, Edith. *Selected Letters, 1919–1964.* Ed. John Lehmann and Derek Parker. New York: Vanguard, 1970.

Sitwell, Edith. *Taken Care Of: The Autobiography of Edith Sitwell.* New York: Atheneum, 1965. (Cited as TCO.)

Sitwell, Edith. Unpublished letters from Edith Sitwell to Gertrude Stein, held in the Beinecke Rare Book and Manuscript Library, Yale University. Letters in the text are cited by date wherever possible. (Cited as UL.)

Stein, Gertrude. "Composition as Explanation." In *Selected Writings of Gertrude Stein,* ed. Carl Van Vechten. New York: Vintage, 1972. (Cited as CE.)

Stein, Gertrude. *Geography and Plays.* Boston: Four Seas, 1922. (Cited as *GP.*)

CHAPTER 9

"For inferior who is free?" Liberating the Woman Writer in Marianne Moore's "Marriage"

LYNN KELLER

Marianne Moore's poem "Marriage" is, among other things, a personally motivated debate about the potential benefits and the dangers of entering into marriage, a meditation on relations between the sexes more generally, and an exploration of the nature of paradise and of the fall.[1] One of the longest and most complex of Moore's works, the 1923 poem also provides a multifaceted examination of the dynamics of influence and intertextuality as they affect the woman poet, particularly one writing when few respected female poets could be identified among her predecessors. Although "Marriage" expresses merely the perspectives of one modernist individual, it also suggests ways in which current critical understandings of influence and intertextuality might be modified to account better for the relations to other texts of works by women and by members of minorities marginal to the dominant literary tradition.

While Moore's poem concerns and contains multiple debates, issues surrounding intertextuality and influence are not its apparent subject. The poem seems to focus on the topic announced by its title, and much interpretive activity has concentrated on discerning just what Moore is saying about marriage. From its opening lines "Marriage" takes a boldly argumentative stance about matrimony, daring to challenge the revered institution and to admit how much "we are still in doubt" about it. Trying to imagine "what Adam and Eve think of it by this time," the speaker depicts those archetypal figures as simultaneously members of modern society and inhabitants of Eden whose breathtaking beauty and deep flaws she considers. According to the revisionary narrative threaded through the poem, Adam

219

"stumbles over" marriage, as if it were a "trivial" obstruction on which an inattentive pedestrian might trip, while seeking a way to extinguish the powerful fires of his sexual desire. Marriage proves "unhelpful," as is demonstrated in the later sections of the poem depicting the interactions of a generic married pair, presumably east of Eden. "He" and "She" quarrel nastily and insult each other among interspersed, often cynical, remarks not attributed to the gendered characters concerning Hymen, friction between the sexes, men's and women's unequal access to power, and other marriage-related issues. All of this postlapsarian material leads to what seems a general dismissal of the married as "savages / condemned to disaffect / all those who are not visionaries / alert to undertake the silly task / of making people noble," though that is followed — somewhat contradictorily — by riddling generalizations about the mysteriousness of love and the value of certain kinds of opposition in interpersonal relations. Critics differ widely in their interpretations of the poem's ending: some find there elements of a "visionary"'s faith in a rare but valuable relation of "opposites / opposed each to the other, not to unity"; others see only a strong warning against imagining that one can have both personal liberty and matrimonial union.

The difficulties critics have evaluating the poem's stance and determining what weight or tone to attach to particular statements within it derive in large part from the mosaiclike character of the poem's construction: phrases or brief lines borrowed from a variety of sources and frequently set off by quotation marks make up a significant portion of the poem. Mosaic provides a better analogy than collage, a term frequently applied to modernist writing, because "collage" suggests pasting together fragments of different materials with only a paratactic relation to each other. The bits and pieces in various voices and shifting tones taken from diverse contexts that Moore incorporates into "Marriage" are worked into an apparently cohesive whole, cemented into close relation through her elaborately extended syntax.[2] The poem is composed of many voices ranging in tone from ecstatically lyrical to matter of fact to caustic and cynical, and the text invokes a bewildering range of reference, yet its syntactic order directs the reader toward some unifying perspective. The use of quotation marks particularly complicates the critic's task of discerning Moore's (or her speaker's) relation to the poem's contents since the marks raise questions about the implied author's attitude toward the quoted material; none of her sources need express her own views, though many of them might do so.

In addition, Moore's inclusion of quotations and accompanying notes at the end of the volume considerably expands her subject matter and the intellectual context for her arguments about marriage.[3] With the breadth of reference that her notes and quotations supply, Moore implicitly locates marriage within sociocultural and historical contexts as well as mythic ones and raises issues of gender that extend well beyond that institution. Further, the large number of lines attributed to other writers suggests that Moore was, with typically modernist reflexivity, consciously writing not only about marriage or intersexual relations before and after the fall but also about *writing about* those subjects. She is aware that her own thinking about marriage echoes and answers the thoughts others have recorded over the centuries in masques and epithalamions, in theological treatises on spousal duties, in essays on woman's nature or on relations between the sexes, and in fictional depictions of romance and of marital relations. Her citation of others' words marks this awareness of her poem as, in Barthes's words, "a multi-dimensional space in which a variety of writings, none of them original, blend and clash" (146). But rather than passively recording this nonoriginary situation, her usage of quotations and notes embodies her analysis of how issues of gender relations affect literary traditions and conventions, and it displays her conscious concern with the place of her poem and of women's writing more generally in an expansive cultural and literary intertext. It is, then, through the quotations and allusions and through the notes — together comprising what I shall call the documentation — that influence and intertextuality enter into the poem's subject.[4]

Like so many aspects of Moore's work, her documentation is distinctive and, even given that the concurrent practices of Eliot and Pound provided examples against which Moore could define her own practices, remarkably inventive.[5] Selected to stress Moore's active role — her making visible several kinds of relations her poem has with other texts — the term documentation will suggest the following: First, Moore thoroughly appropriates the preexisting material so that it is unapologetically shaped by her and put to her own uses. Second, the preexistent material relates to Moore's (admittedly broad) topic and is included partly so that she may exhibit different points of view by citing others addressing that topic. Third, the provenance of the references is unimportant except as it aids documentation — that is, as it bulwarks the poem's contents, whether by being authoritative, by establishing that certain views are shared by others, by invoking contexts, justifying assertions, and/or by sharpening the expression of points Moore wishes to make. Consequently, the value of the references lies solely in the way they can be appropriated for use in the poem — not, as for Eliot and Pound, in the culture they didactically represent. Finally, Moore's documentation establishes her poem as social text, in dialogue with its society's values, participating in current and longstanding debates on social issues.

Moore does not employ a consistent format in the documentation for "Marriage": sometimes her notes provide full citations that a reader could use to locate the quotation in its source; sometimes they provide only an author's name, even a virtually unknown one; sometimes Moore includes discursive comment and expanded quotation, frequently not. Such variations are one indication that Moore is using documentation for diverse functions. In what follows I shall propose that Moore's various strategies emphasize two kinds of relationships her poem has with other texts. One, associated with tradition, is closely related to conventional understandings of influence. The other brings into focus relations that since Moore's time have come to be associated with intertextuality: a weaving together of anonymous or of not necessarily literary or "high cultural" texts that create the conditions for one's own utterance and situate it in broadly cultural terms. It is my contention that Moore is entertaining versions of both influence and intertextuality and playing them against one another so as to create and legitimize a place for herself as a woman writer. That place lies both within and outside the recognized literary tradition and the current practices of her male modernist peers. Associating an influence-based understanding of literary history with the perpetuation of patriarchal power and of woman's silence, she employs an essentially intertextual model and method as a subversive tool that permits a better understanding of the woman artist's position and opens for her some less restricted avenues of creative expression.

When Marianne Moore was composing "Marriage," T. S. Eliot had recently put a new spin on the term "influence."[6] In his 1918 essay "In Memory of Henry James," he presented influence as a casual matter with little bearing on an artist's real stature (whether the artist be influenced or influential) :

The "influence" of James hardly matters: to be influenced by a writer is to have a chance inspiration from him; or to take what one wants; or to see things one has overlooked; there will always be a few intelligent people to understand James, and to be understood by a few intelligent people is all the influence a man requires. (1)

According to this formulation, the influenced writer is in an active position of taking what suits his or her fancy and is in no way overwhelmed by the predecessor. In "Tradition and the Individual Talent," written the next year, Eliot further counters the tendency to regard evidence of one's having been influenced as proof of one's inferior artistic standing; he proposes a correction to the tendency to insist, when we praise a poet, upon those aspects of his work in which he least resembles anyone else. In these aspects or parts of his work we pretend to find what is individual, what is the peculiar essence of the man. . . . Whereas if we approach a poet without this prejudice we shall often find that not only the best, but the most individual parts of his work may be those in which the dead poets, his ancestors, assert their immortality most vigorously. (4)

The desirable presence of the "dead poets" in an artist's work — what would commonly be designated their influence, with some derogatory suggestion of the work's derivative character — is what Eliot labels "tradition." This influence-based tradition is something his ideal artist actively desires and labors to acquire.

Moore's thinking about influence and tradition bears strong affinities with Eliot's and may be, as John Slatin has argued, indebted to his essays. She seems to have shared or adopted some of Eliot's sense of influence as a matter of graceful and grateful borrowing that need not reduce the borrower's individuality. As we shall see from the example of "Marriage," she used the frequent quotations in and notes to her poems of the early 1920s partly to acknowledge such debts. Furthermore, for Moore as for Eliot, the concept of influence was inextricably bound with perpetuation of the tradition of "the whole of the literature of Europe from Homer"; from the example of individual works and authors the later writer may gain access to entire systems of conventions. But she did not share Eliot's sense that one must actively labor to acquire a tradition or that this tradition is completely valuable. Certainly, she appreciated a broadly educated mind and scorned those "self-wrought Midases of brains / whose fourteen-carat ignorance aspires to rise in value" ("The Labors of Hercules," *Poems* 53). Yet Moore's procedure in "Marriage" suggests that as a woman artist she felt the tradition very much imposed upon her and regarded it as a force to be resisted with the same "criminal ingenuity" that enabled her to evade entrapment in marriage. The tradition, like so many deep-seated assumptions of patriarchy, seemed in some ways inescapable; advertising her connections with the tradition could serve certain limited functions, but in the early 1920s Moore's creative energies were devoted primarily to minimizing the tradition's hold on her and maximizing her control over its presence in her own writing.

While many of Moore's critics have, as John Slatin has noted, denied her a tradition and denied the allusive function of her quotations ("Natural Historian" 274–75), in "Marriage" (as elsewhere) Moore displays the considerable impact the established tradition has had on her work. Despite Hugh Kenner's claim that Moore's quotations are "seldom (never?) familiar quotations," that they are "not allusions . . . but found objects, slivers of excellence incorporated into the *assemblage*," and that her "notes are not,

like the notes to *The Waste Land*, part of our education; we are not meant
to look up the sources" (102), in fact the "excellence" of Moore's quotations
is often not inherent but conferred upon them by her felicitous use, while,
as I hope to demonstrate, looking up their sources can prove educative.
Moreover, "Marriage" contains a number of unacknowledged allusions as
well as noted references to works by authors as canonical or as associated
with high culture as those Eliot drew upon. Moore alludes to Milton,
Shakespeare, Burke, Hazlitt, Bacon, and with the first two even uses familiar phrases from their works. These borrowed bits she employs in what
I will refer to as tradition-documentation: she is establishing her familiarity with the recognized tradition and acknowledging the impact of individual masters' words upon her own. The concept of influence is strongly
invoked by such tradition-documentation because Moore, like Eliot, sees influence in the context of perpetuating the tradition, as the mechanism for
its transmission, characteristically from male progenitor to male descendent.

For the woman writer (as for any writer marginal to the tradition because of class, race, or ethnic background), tradition-documentation demonstrates a kind of anxiety of noninfluence. That is, even if she is ambivalent about the patriarchal tradition — as I shall argue Moore most certainly
is — she nonetheless desires to claim her own place in its economy. Whereas
the well-educated white male writer may, as Harold Bloom claims, struggle
to prove his difference from his fathers,[7] the marginal writer has something
to gain by establishing her/himself as securely enough within the tradition
to be influenced by it. In order to prove that she/he is not inferior, the
marginal writer may aspire to belong to that exclusive boys' club whose
members can casually drop names and lines from the classics; thus, Moore's
allusions in "Marriage" to Shakespeare, Milton, and the like constitute
her membership credentials. The unmarked allusions particularly (Milton's name, for instance, does not appear in the notes, and Shakespeare
is alluded to more often than the single note to him indicates), by suggesting that Moore knows the work of her great predecessors so well that
she quotes them almost collegially, establish her immersion in the respected
tradition. Through these apparently casual (though probably quite deliberate) allusions and their evocation of the familiar dynamics of patrilineal
influence, she claims an authority which her gender might otherwise leave
open to question.

We need not see all of Moore's investment in the idea of influence as
deriving defensively from a need to establish authority. No doubt there
is considerable truth in her claim in "A Note on the Notes" to the *Collected Poems* that she includes notes to establish her probity by acknowledging her borrowings. Many of her references to established figures pay
tribute to artists and thinkers whose work she respects. In a 1948 essay,

she speaks of "direct quoting" as "that difficult but . . . best method of exhibiting a personality" (referring to the personality of the one quoted) (*Prose* 419). We may probably assume that the poet who quotes from and cites in "Marriage" both Edmund Burke and Hazlitt's "Essay on Burke's Style" is genuinely interested in that political theorist and his works. We may assume, more generally, that as she values integrity and distinction in particular individuals' writing, she believes in individual authorship, delights in earlier writers' felicitous phrases, and sincerely respects their chronological precedent: "if a thing has been said in the very best way, how can you say it better? If I wanted to say something and somebody had said it ideally, then I'd take it but give the person credit for it. . . . If you are charmed by an author, I think it's a very strange and invalid imagination that doesn't love to share it" (Tomlinson 30). Yet even as she presents this conventional reasoning, the contrast between Moore's figure of sharing, conveying a pleasure in the dispersal of literary treasures and in the generation of community, and Eliot's language of private possession and appropriation, "tak[ing] what one wants," suggests a divergence of her perspective from his.

Once she has used quotations and allusions to demonstrate her right to a place within the established tradition, and once she has singled out a few figures she wishes respectfully to recognize as her forebears or particular uses of language she wishes to establish as exemplary, the modernist woman writer finds herself in a problematic position. The club to which she has earned admission remains a hostile environment in which women artists — especially poets — are at best granted the status of oddball genius like Dickinson, but more often patronized as trivial, sentimental "poetesses." Since it is not in the interests of patriarchy to allow women full voice, even those token women allowed into the male intellectual world who attempt to use their full verbal powers risk encountering (to use phrases from "Marriage") the "spiked hand / that has an affection for one / and proves it to the bone"; they are "constrained in speaking" in myriad ways. Even in the supposedly liberated 1920s the woman writer who gained recognition within male-dominated literary circles remained partially disenfranchised. Judging from the remarks of W. C. Williams in his *Autobiography*, Moore was not regarded as equal to the male members of the avantgarde *Others* group with which she was associated; Williams recalls her as the group's "caryatid" and "saint," suggesting traditionally feminine roles of providing support and moral inspiration for the male creators (146).[8] Having read *Feminine Influence on the Poets*, a book she calls to her readers' attention by citing it in her notes to "Marriage," Moore would be particularly aware that while women have been the subject and inspiration of many poems by men, "it would not be easy to show that women have had any great influence upon English poetry by their own practice of the art" (Thomas 49). The contents of "Marriage" suggest that she shared the desire of Milton's Eve (when she contemplated keeping to herself the wonders of the apple of knowledge) to make woman "more equal" — "for inferior who is free?" (*Paradise Lost*, 9.823, 825).

How to make women "more equal" was a subject of considerable debate among feminists in the 1920s, as it has been since: should women aspire to prove female equality by succeeding as men do, or should they establish an alternative female standard? Moore signals an ambivalent stance in "Marriage" in her deployment of remarks by the outspoken feminist educator M. Carey Thomas, who, as president of Bryn Mawr College when Moore was a student there, had considerable impact on her thinking.[9] As presented in the body of the poem, Thomas' abbreviated lines seem to dismiss scornfully the male "monopolist's" quest for badges of glory and conquest, "stars, garters, buttons / and other shining baubles." Yet Moore includes in her notes a fuller quotation in which the derogatory "baubles" receives diminished emphasis, while men's desire for recognition and the difficulty of their labors gain considerable sympathy:

men practically reserve for themselves stately funerals, splendid monuments, memorial statues, memberships in academies, medals, titles, honorary degrees, stars, garters, ribbons, buttons and other shining baubles, so valueless in themselves and yet so infinitely desirable because they are symbols of recognition by their fellow-craftsmen of difficult work well done.

Reading the note (which accurately reflects Thomas' lifelong pursuit of women's equal access to opportunities and privileges usually reserved for men), one understands that a woman might well prize such recognition, all the more because her gender would make it even harder to attain; the male standards are not simply to be derided.

The patriarchal notion of influence would seem to inspire in Moore a comparable ambivalence: she needs to establish her right to be influenced within the dominant tradition, yet remaining within that male tradition would stifle her. She feels some allegiance to and identification with that tradition, yet she remains enough of an outsider to contribute to the discovery or construction of alternative ways of understanding the generation and transmission of texts. Freeing herself as writer — and thereby contributing to the liberation of women writers generally — demanded subverting the importance of influence in part, I shall argue, by showing herself to be influenced by materials that would ordinarily be snubbed by those who believe in influence and an elevated tradition, and more generally by playing an intertextual model of the generation of texts against the influence-based one.

From the opening lines of "Marriage" the speaker establishes herself as in some sense already a freed individual. Adopting the dichotomy Moore employs in her essay on H.D.'s *Hymen* that appeared in January of 1923, the presumably female speaker of "Marriage" would fit the category of "intellectual freelance" rather than that of "eternally sleeping beauty, effortless yet effective in the indestructible limestone keep of domesticity" (*Prose* 82).[10] Instead of paying tribute to matrimony in conventional terms of sacred Christian bond or romantic ideal, the "freelance" narrator begins with the mocking critique of an outsider:

> This institution
> perhaps one should say enterprise
> out of respect for which
> one says one need not change one's mind
> about a thing one has believed in,
> requiring public promises
> of one's intention
> to fulfill a private obligation:
> I wonder what Adam and Eve
> think of it by this time,
> this fire-gilt steel
> alive with goldenness;
> how bright it shows —
> "of circular traditions and impostures,
> committing many spoils,"
> requiring all one's criminal ingenuity
> to avoid!

She is alert to inconsistencies and ironies (the confusion of public and private, of intention and performance), and as a kind of "criminal" marriage evader she is keenly aware of the many ways in which marriage is woven into the social fabric. The speaker, then, immediately establishes the authority of her vision as that of one free to survey farther than could a person imprisoned within the "limestone keep" of domesticity, for which marriage is a cornerstone. Paralleling her creation of a self-possessed speaker whose view of marriage, however enmeshed in tradition, is significantly liberated from it, Moore's very process of writing enacts a liberating alternative to Eve's entrapment.

Interestingly, the most damning words in her opening passage are in quotes (taken from Francis Bacon, the notes inform us, though without indicating where), so that the speaker need not take responsibility for them — while she also need not let on that Bacon in fact was addressing a different topic.[11] This first quotation, therefore, does far more than establish Moore's familiarity with the work of a great master or suggest his

influence on her thought: it releases her from conventional feminine do-
cility and decorum, enabling her to criticize the institution that many regard as women's sole purpose, without discrediting herself. Throughout
the poem Moore deploys quotations like Bacon's to maintain the authority of her speaker not merely by suggesting through tradition-documentation
a perspective that has considerable learning behind it, but also by demonstrating (or appearing to demonstrate if actually only playing at it) that
the views presented are shared or well-founded, not merely idiosyncratic
fancies. Further, she is pointing to the interaction between her poem and
the extraliterary world where men and women struggle and debate. This
is one sense in which her quotations serve an intertextual function.

   Discussions of intertextuality usually assume that authorial intention
(if the concept of author is admitted at all) is irrelevant to the ways in
which texts are inevitably webs of other texts, their signifying practices
made possible by "anonymous discursive practices, codes whose origins
are lost" (Culler 103).[12] Moore's writing is indeed dependent on multiple
anonymous and untraceable texts. Here, however, I am dealing only with
particular manifestations of the poem's intertextuality to which authorial
strategy is central.[13] In fact, in calling attention to strands of an intertextual web that usually escapes sight, Moore extends her authority for she
subsumes within her argument the very sorts of voices that a resisting intertextual reader might otherwise introduce to undermine it. I will use the
term system-documentation (chosen to emphasize that Moore points to
larger social, cultural, and verbal systems within which and out of which
literary texts arise) to designate the various strategies by which Moore displays and manipulates intertextuality in the documentation of "Marriage."

   System-documentation supports and extends the poem's explicit assertions of how consistently throughout history men shaping the development of Western civilization — from Adam to Saint Paul to Daniel Webster
to Ezra Pound — have suppressed and silenced women. In the poem Adam,
far more than Eve, uses language to maintain power: "alive with words,"
he "has prophesied correctly — / the industrious waterfall, / 'the speedy
stream / which violently bears all before it . . . '" (ellipsis added); that is,
in self-fulfilling prophecy, he proclaims his own power to direct civilization and destroy what stands in his way. He pompously declaims about
"past states, the present state, seals, promises [including, we presume,
"public promises" like marriage vows] / the evil one suffered, / the good
one enjoys, / hell, heaven, / everything convenient / to promote one's
joy" — pronouncing on how we are to perceive our world while invoking
the dichotomies upon which patriarchal society rests. In doing so, however, he "forget[s] that there is in woman / a quality of mind / which as

an instinctive manifestation / is unsafe" to his way of being—more on that in a moment. Even during their courtship the man is deaf to the meaning of woman's words so that his words erase her self-expression; he responds to her request "*I* should like to be alone" by imposing his own desires: "I should like to be alone; / why not be alone together?" Later, when marriage has proved a disappointment, the man—now designated "He" and speaking in part words of Ezra Pound—uses his verbal skills brutally to link women and women's bodies with horrible death and decay.

Moore's method emphasizes that it is not merely *personal* "experience" which "attests / that men have power / and sometimes one is made to feel it." In quoting from a range of sources, including some which themselves examine multiple texts, Moore engages a broad cultural intertext to document the ubiquity of misogyny—and ironically mimicking women's silence, she allows men to speak it for themselves. Her documentation suggests the pervasiveness of the misogynist notion that—this time from *The Syrian Christ* though the words seem presented as if "He" speaks them—"the fact of woman is 'not the sound of the flute / but very poison.'" As with the M. Carey Thomas passage mentioned above, the additional material Moore provides in the note enables the reader to perceive a social context to which the poet is reacting, this time through phrases with forceful implications for female writers: "Silence of women—'to an Oriental, this is as poetry set to music.'"[14] The statement, besides indicating male appreciation of women's silence as something of great beauty, suggests that a woman may be a poet only to the extent that she remains mute; the logic is all too familiar, comparable to the colonialists' saying, "the only good Indian is a dead Indian." System-documentation, by demonstrating the pervasiveness of the constraints on women's expression, makes it clear why Eve is "constrained in speaking of the serpent." It provides an explanation—other than female inferiority and ineptitude—why, as Edward Thomas notes in *Feminine Influence on the Poets,* "far too often [women] have written as if they were only an inferior kind of man" (49) and why only limited material can be found "expressing a woman's point of view and addressed to women" (54).

What resources have women against such male power, verbal and otherwise? The poem suggests several answers: Most obviously, women may attempt to fight back essentially on men's terms by repaying insult with insult: "this butterfly, this waterfly, this nomad," etc. But "She" is no more admirable than "He" in doing so and no less locked in self-love. Women are better off not aspiring to exact equality when it comes to such demeaning behavior. Alternatively, women may resort to "imperious humility," using the appearance of deference and modesty to usurp male control and command; but, like Carey Thomas, Moore is offended by the convention that "secrecy and guile are the only refuge of a down-trodden sex" (*Prose* 417). More promising is a third strategy that is enacted by the poem's speaker and suggested in Moore's first description of Eve: a reaching beyond the monolithic force of phallic power and of its linear transmission via influence to a multiplicity associated in the poem, as it is in the theories of today's French feminists, with the feminine. This strategy is both presented and performed in Moore's documentation.

Eve, we are told, is "able to write simultaneously / in three languages — / English, German and French — / and talk in the meantime." Once again Moore's notes provide significant additional information:

[She] takes advantage of her abilities in everyday life, writing her letters simultaneously with both hands; namely, the first, third, and fifth words with her left and the second, fourth, and sixth with her right hand. While generally writing outward, she is able as well to write inward with both hands. "Multiple Consciousness or Reflex Action of Unaccustomed Range," *Scientific American*, January 1922.[15]

Surely Moore is as much amused by such pretentiousness in "everyday life" as she is intrigued by the woman's powers; yet in the fluid dynamics of her text, ironic play does not preclude simultaneous serious invocation. Read seriously in the context of the poem, this passage exphasizes not only that Eve's extraordinary powers are manifest in written letters rather than in speech like Adam's — suggesting that women are in fact well suited to authorship — but also that woman's consciousness is "multiple" in contrast to the "monopolist[ic]" male mind. (A parallel distinction seems to be made through Moore's handling of water imagery in relation to the two genders. Adam is associated with unidirectional aquatic motion, "the industrious waterfall, 'the speedy stream / which violently bears all before it. . . .'" Eve is linked with a gentler, more encompassing motion generated not from one channel but from all sides; her vision of paradise is of "the heart rising / in its estate of peace / as a boat rises / with the rising of the water.") The quotation-studded construction of "Marriage," drawing upon an "unaccustomed range" of allusions and syntactically weaving many dissonant voices into one, enacts a comparable multiplicity. Moore takes pains in this poem to keep the voices, the dictions, the tones and perspectives various, in large part through quotation and quotation marks. Yet she binds together the multiple voices and lexicons so that they represent not Eliot's disjunct fragments of a blasted culture but the various impulses within a single, flexibly inclusive mind.[16] The poem's consequent freedom to explore perspectives on marriage and gender counter to the dominant patriarchal ideology suggests that cultivating a "multiple consciousness" enables the woman writer to assert herself against patriarchal power. Multiple consciousness, then, would seem to be the "quality of mind" "in woman" that is "unsafe" to the conceptual orders maintaining patriarchy.

As part of the system of patriarchal power, conventional perspectives on literary production and literary tradition that have muted so many women are challenged in Moore's multivocal system-documentation. With quotations within quotations, and multiple sources quoted in a single passage already within quotes, with indeterminate referents and shifting names, Moore purposefully muddies the waters of attribution. In so doing, she undermines the notion of discrete, authored works and the idea of (patrilineal) influence according to which the work of one writer stands as a monumental presence, rather like the statue of Webster in Central Park cited in the poem's closing lines, ready to impose its neatly quotable words upon subsequent writers. She denies any single direction of literary transmission, any single tradition on whose course contemporary authors must be borne, invoking instead an intertextual ocean of signifiers on which authors sail, selecting for display or use now one piece of verbal flotsam, now another.

To mobilize her critique/destabilization of the influence-based tradition in which conventions have been formed, reinforced, and transmitted through a series of author-to-author encounters, Moore draws on sources that reflect an intertextually multiple and nonhierarchical consciousness. Calling attention to the fact that many of her quotations derive from sources most authors and readers would regard as trivial, Moore in *The Complete Poems* introduces the notes to "Marriage" with what might seem a coy disclaimer: "Statements that took my fancy which I tried to arrange plausibly."[17] Rather than interpreting this as posed modesty, a quaint costume comparable to Moore's tricornered hat of later years, we should appreciate the radical revaluation of the canon announced here. For the line suggests that quoted sources are legitimately selected not on the grounds of their importance to Western intellectual tradition, but simply because they are at hand and accord with whimsical personal preference. Anticipating the epistemological stance of more recent feminists, Moore allows her individual predilections to take precedence over received authority. (Perhaps Moore also takes a gibe at the didactic and prescriptive aspect of Eliot's and Pound's allusions; *she* claims no particular importance for the texts *she* cites.) In the case of this poem, Moore's "fancy" led her to once-popular novels like *Christie Johnstone*, poems by amateurs such as her friend Mary Frances Nearing or Hagop Boghossian (identified in the notes to *Observations* as a member of the Department of Philosophy at Worcester College, Massachusetts [103]), advertisements, and book reviews, as well as works of "high culture" like *The Tempest* or "Ecclesiasticus."

Even "Ecclesiasticus," however, Moore actually approaches through a demotic — and gender conscious — source: the original citation in *Observations* reads "Ecclesiasticus; Women Bad and Good — An Essay; Modern
Reader's Bible; Macmillan" (103–4).

Just as all the quotations are equally statements that took her fancy,
all serve equally well as the stuff from which to construct poems. Moore's
mosaic technique of "plausible arrangement" is boldly democratizing in
that fragments of canonical works are treated the same as, and largely
indistinguishable from, bits of popular culture. The canonical works are
thereby rendered dispensible and their absolute authority denied; their
inclusion emerges as a chance event. (Indeed, in "An Octopus," composed
at the same period, canonical authors provide sources for almost no quoted
material.) Quoting from a multitude of kinds of sources, Moore deflates
the status of allusion and the related concept of influence: anyone's words
encountered in any aspect of daily living may catch in the poet's mind and
provide material for her composition.

Moore is responding to innumerable stimuli of a rich cultural intertext,
her system-documentation implies, of which the literary canon is only a
small part. In citing an advertisement in *English Review* (one, by the way,
not to be found in the issue she names) or an article in *Scientific American*, Moore impresses on her reader the multiplicity of materials upon
which the artist inevitably draws. By conscious effort she makes visible
part of her own intertext — the corpus of texts brought to her mind by
what she is writing, most of which usually remain invisible — in order to
heighten the reader's consciousness of all the nonhierarchical, often indeterminate connections constantly operating in both artistic creation and
interpretation.

Moore' announcement about "statements that took [her] fancy," by
suggesting a plenitude of potential choices, also suggests the pervasiveness of the kind of passage that could serve her purpose in this particular
poem. Contrary to critical assumptions that her sources bear no relation
to her subject — Bonnie Costello, for example, asserts that "her borrowings do not extend the meaning of her poem into the worlds they allude
to" (185) — many of the documented quotations derive from works considering marriage or the relations among the sexes, nearly all from a male
point of view, and recognizing this enriches one's understanding of the
poem. Titles like *Filles et Garçons* and *Femina*, for instance, announce
society's preoccupation with issues of gender. Moore's prefatory explanation indicates that one could easily find other equally serviceable examples
of men like Godwin or Hartmann making pronouncements about marriage; novelists like Trollope and Charles Reade depicting love, courtship,
and marriage; poets like Pound insulting wives; biblical tales like Esther's

("the Ahasuerus *tête-à-tête* banquet'") relating wives' attempts to control political events through their husbands; and even a few women's voices like Carey Thomas' exposing or refuting the patriarchal and misogynist orientation of our culture. If one opens, say, *Christie Johnstone*, one finds in its closing pages lavish praise of marriage as a "divine institution" affording "glimpses of Heaven's design": "In that blessed relation alone two interests are really one, and two hearts lie safe at anchor side by side" (305–7). Neither this view nor any other presented within Moore's sources need represent Moore's, but such passages are significant background to her argument. Moore's prefatory remark, then, establishes her quotations as almost randomly chosen exempla of social realities; again, Moore is using her documentation not primarily to place her work within a literary context, but to place the argument of her poem in the extraliterary world. The notes document causes, representative of pervasive biases, that logically determine the feminist attitudes and the wariness of marriage expressed in the poem.

Moore's casual handling of both the quotations themselves and their documentation further erodes the value conventionally attached to authorship and originality, serving further to reinforce awareness of intertextuality rather than influence. She does not treat these quotations as treasured evidence of past cultural achievements; they are simply, as she says in "Poetry," the "raw materials" of her art. Consequently, Moore takes no particular care to be accurate about sources: she misspells Christie Johnstone as Johnston; she wrongly identifies a line as a translation from Amos that is in fact part of an explication;[18] she mistakes the date and title of the *Scientific American* article; she provides no information about where in Godwin's or Bacon's oeuvre we might find their phrases. She leaves many borrowings unacknowledged; for instance, while she cites several passages from Baxter, she does not acknowledge that the first two of four lines within quotations — "the speedy stream / which violently bears all before it" — derive also, with slight modification, from *The Saints' Everlasting Rest* (432). She makes nothing of changing the words of her sources (e.g., the original of "as high as deep / as bright as broad / as long as life itself" reads "as high, as deep, as broad, as long as Love itself" [Baxter 509]).[19]

Such policies are particularly noteworthy in a woman renowned for valuing "relentless accuracy" and painstaking precision, one who appreciated punctuation as contributing to moral/social order, as "a form of punctuality" (Kenneth Burke in Tomlinson 125). Her disregard for what scholars would consider accuracy in documentation suggests that she does not share the academy's belief that this is an area in which "accuracy" applies. Either her casualness is a manifestation of her belief that preexisting arrangements of words are raw materials to be guiltlessly modified and recycled, or it is a deliberately subversive gesture, flaunting her refusal mechanically to curtsy before her fathers; quite probably there are elements of both stances in her procedure.

Among the more notable oversights in Moore's documentation is her failure to acknowledge the presence of lines from Milton in her poem or the importance of Milton's epic in shaping its content. Obviously, Milton's depiction of paradise and the fall in *Paradise Lost* — a work Moore had known since early childhood when her mother read it aloud to her and Warner (Holley 2) — stands behind much of "Marriage" as a powerful precedent Moore struggles against, critiques, and revises.[20] Earlier I suggested that Moore's failure to identify all the quotations from canonical authors served as tradition-documentation establishing her authoritative familiarity with the canon. Let me suggest now that particularly Moore's omission of quotes or notes to designate phrases from Milton serves at the same time a very different system-documentation function: it diffuses the authority of Milton, and that of all the great masters with him. Milton becomes simply the voice of patriarchy, the speech of its intertext, not a great creator but merely the automatic perpetuator of stereotypes that have supported patriarchy for at least two thousand years. Her handling of Milton — by which she attempts to diminish his stature and the monumentality of works within the orthodox tradition — provides the poem's fullest demonstration of her attempts at women's liberation via intertextuality.

Milton seems to have regarded his own work as the culminating achievement in the tradition of heroic epic. For instance, in *Paradise Lost* he explicitly vies for stature with the major poet-prophets who preceded him, including "blind *Maeonides*" (Homer) (3.35). He ironically paraphrases Ariosto in order to boast of his own superior inspiration in pursuing "Things unattempted yet in Prose or Rhyme" (1.16). Deflating such narcissism, Moore's allusion to *The Syrian Christ* helps place Milton, as biblical interpreter, within an elaborate intertextual network. Rihbany, its author, argues that since Jesus was a Syrian, many scriptural passages can be properly understood only in terms of Syrian culture and customs: "correct understanding depends on accurate knowledge of their original environment" (5). A large section of the book entitled "Sisters of Mary and Martha" — the section from which Moore's quotation comes — examines Syrian attitudes toward women, and the context for the quoted lines is a discussion of why Paul says in the First Epistle to the Corinthians, "Let your women keep silence in the Churches: for it is not permitted unto them to speak; but they are commanded to be under obedience" (333). Rihbany's essentially intertextual approach to the Bible would suggest that Milton, like Saint Paul before him, is merely the voice of his misogynist, woman-silencing culture.

By not mentioning Milton's name or the title of his work, Moore attempts to erase his authorship. At the same time, her poem is implicitly in dialogue with his as she revises his representation of the fall by placing far greater responsibility on Adam and mocking the story that so easily "exonerates" him. Moore's most notable borrowing from Milton occurs in her first description of Adam:

> And he has beauty also;
> it's distressing—the O thou
> to whom from whom,
> without whom nothing—Adam;
> "something feline,
> something colubrine"—how true!
> a crouching mythological monster
> in that Persian miniature of emerald mines,
> raw silk—ivory white, snow white,
> oyster white and six others—
> that paddock full of leopards and giraffes—
> long lemon-yellow bodies
> sown with trapezoids of blue.

As "something colubrine" Adam is explicitly identified with the serpent; visually too, he, rather than Eve, appears "the central flaw" in an ornate scene of white purity and ordered beauty. The phrases drawn (without acknowledgment) from Milton are part of Eve's reply to Adam's urging that they "not think hard one easy prohibition":

> O thou for whom
> And from whom I was form'd flesh of thy flesh,
> And without whom am to no end, my Guide
> And Head, what thou hast said is just and right.
>   (4.440–43)

By raising the possibility that Adam was the satanic seducer, Moore's presentation of Adam as monster makes Eve's deference not merely ludicrous but self-destructive. At the same time, Moore's offhanded abbreviation of Milton's lines treats them more as cultural signpost than as an individual's artistic achievement.

"Marriage" suggests that Milton's version of the fall—derived, of course, from Genesis—is transparently male self-justification and self-glorification, an "invaluable accident / exonerating Adam." There Adam is the helpless victim of passion—mockingly underscored by Moore in her verbs: "*unnerved* by the nightingale / and *dazzled* by the apple, / *impelled* by 'the illusion of a fire / effectual to extinguish fire,' / . . . he *stumbles* over marriage" (emphasis added). Yet Moore's repeated mention of the nightingale brings to mind not only *Paradise Lost* but also the well-known myth of Philomela (also recently evoked in Eliot's *The Waste Land*); in that tale, Moore would have us remember, the violated woman/nightingale is man's victim, not the other way round. And whereas Milton frequently reminds his readers that Eve is Adam's inferior in everything except beauty, Moore presents an Eve who is in significant ways superior to her spouse. Although just as narcissistic as Adam (that, too, is revisionary in that Milton stressed only Eve's narcissism), because she is less vicious and wittier than he she seems more deserving of the reader's sympathy.

Even if Moore's Adam is not to blame for the fall as a satanic seducer, he certainly must share responsibility for it with Eve, since in "Marriage" the fall seems to occur with the initiation of self-consciousness. Perhaps because he is entranced with his own oratorial display (the sequence of Moore's presentation invites a causal interpretation), Adam "perceives what it was not / intended that he should; 'he experiences a solemn joy / in seeing that he has become an idol.'" "He loves himself so much, / he can permit himself / no rival in that love." Eve is equally idolatrous in self-love (though the presentation of Adam's corruption before mention of hers might suggest that his was the first fall): "She loves herself so much / she cannot see herself enough." In this sense, Moore's two genders are both to blame for the failure of the first marriage, "that first crystal-fine experiment."

Moore's quarrel is less with Milton, however, than with the cultural intertext which created *Paradise Lost* through him, and therefore she avoids letting her poem become simply a revision of his epic. To make it that would reinstate him as determinately influential forefather. Instead, she tries to free herself from his authority and that of the patriarchal tradition he represents enough to present a woman's perspective. That doubly conscious perspective includes the patriarchal view, since woman is unavoidably complicit in perpetuating the patriarchal culture that envelops her — just as she cannot entirely escape notions of individual authorship and individual influence, or idealizing visions of marriage — but the feminine perspective is also distinct from it.

The other name notably absent from Moore's notes is T. S. Eliot. In this case, too, Moore treads a kind of tightrope. She wishes to acknowledge certain affinities with the man and his thought (just as the multiple citations of theological studies like Baxter's and Smith's align her with Milton as a Christian writer), even to point to the influence of his work. Yet she also needs to expose the problematic aspects of Eliot's work for women, particularly for the woman writer. As a further complication, she needs in addition to diminish the man's stature, virtually to deny his authorial existence, by revealing what one might consider his influence to be merely a transmission of restrictive cultural codes and conventions, a process of cultural and linguistic systems to which individual authors are irrelevant.

The very presence of the notes to "Marriage" suggests that Moore is in dialogue with Eliot, whose annotated *Waste Land* had bowled over the literary avant-garde just prior to Moore's beginning work on her poem.[21] She may even have had Eliot's precedent in mind when she added notes to a poem that first appeared without them. But while her inclusion of notes may mark her debt to Eliot, Moore's documentation serves contrary functions to his, just as her poem presents a contrasting perspective. The extent to which Moore composed "Marriage" or its notes as a direct response to *The Waste Land* remains unclear, but that obscurity may itself be part of Moore's strategy. If my overall thesis is correct, she may indeed have intended to challenge Eliot while intending too to create an aura of independence that would appear to place her outside his sway. For Eliot's work and the power Eliot wielded in literary circles represented exactly the kind of problem her own poem attempts to solve, partly through critical (often ironic) attack but largely through the creation of alternatives.

Compared with the documentation of "Marriage," Eliot's notes are self-centered and patronizing — traits associated also with Moore's Adam (and, as suggested above, demonstrated by Milton). They are egotistical in that they serve explicitly to "elucidate the difficulties of the poem," referring back to the author and his intentions, not out into the world. Note, for instance, the predominance of "I" in the following note to line 46 of "The Burial of the Dead":

I am not familiar with the exact constitution of the Tarot pack of cards, from which I have obviously departed to suit my own convenience. The Hanged Man, a member of the traditional pack, fits my purpose in two ways: because he is associated in my mind with the Hanged God of Frazer, and because I associate him with the hooded figure in the passage of the disciples to Emmaus in Part V. The Phoenician Sailor and the Merchant appear later; also the "crowds of people," and Death by Water is executed in Part IV. The Man with Three Staves (an authentic member of the Tarot Pack) I associate, quite arbitrarily, with the Fisher King himself.

While Moore's work is arguably more difficult than Eliot's, she does not patronize her audience by explaining the significance of her lines or by calling attention to recurring motifs. There is, too, an elitist element in Eliot's notes absent from Moore's documentation. One does not need Eliot's explanation to sense what he admitted in 1950 when discussing his poem's allusions to Dante: "I gave the references in my notes, in order to make the reader who recognized the allusion, know that I meant him to recognize it, and to know that he would have missed the point if he did not recognize it" ("What Dante Means to Me" 128). For none of Moore's quotations is recognition "the point" since she is not glorifying the past or the tradition.

As Milton was in his day, Eliot was in Moore's time a prime example of a man transmitting his culture's misogyny, and because he was Moore's contemporary his work would represent a more urgent threat than Milton's to her feminist orientation. *The Waste Land*'s "sweet ladies" are in myriad ways terrifying, distasteful, or despicable. From germ-infested Madame Sosostris to her Tarot pack's dangerous "Belladonna, the Lady of the Rocks," from the near-hysterical neurasthenic of "The Game of Chess" to unfaithful, rotten-toothed Lil and her husband-stealing acquaintance, from the degraded Thames nymphs to the dehumanized typist in her underwear-bedecked apartment, the poem's women are associated with sordidness, subterfuge, and corruption.

In "Marriage" Moore is ready to admit woman's human failings, even to acknowledge that certain defects may be characteristically female, but she avoids degrading stereotypes and she would never use women, as Eliot does, as the primary symbols of society's ills. No less aware than he of the battle and the babble between the sexes, Moore is determined to counter the imbalances of her culture's prejudices. Thus, her Eve is a far more compelling figure than Adam, presented as a real person to whom Moore's speaker has responded with passion and deep appreciation:

> Eve: beautiful woman —
> I have seen her
> when she was so handsome
> she gave me a start,
> able to write simultaneously
> in three languages —
> English, German and French —
> and talk in the meantime;
> equally positive in demanding a commotion
> and in stipulating quiet.

The subsequent lines announcing that "Below the incandescent stars / below the incandescent fruit, / the strange experience of beauty; / its existence is too much; / it tears one to pieces" — which may bring to mind the agony of Milton's Satan as he observes the happy couple in Eden — seem particularly tied to "one's" experience of woman. Despite the speaker's appreciation of womanly beauty, Moore's poem deemphasizes female sexuality — which so preoccupied Eliot, and Milton before him — in order to claim for women more intellectual powers and to place female sexual abuse (like that of Philomela, who had to become a nightingale in order to obtain what Eliot calls "inviolable voice") and the sexual possession of marriage within a larger context of female oppression.

A desire to disempower the tradition maintained through generations of egotistically individual talents and the patriarchal perspective their texts sustained led Moore to cultivate a mode of textual construction and documentation reflecting a multiplicity of mind and a multifaceted intertextuality that challenged inherited structures of authority. (Male modernists were engaged in inventions that were in some ways similar, but which did not originate in rebellion against patriarchy.) Moore's conscious attention to intertextuality expressed via system-documentation enabled her to demonstrate how patriarchy is perpetuated through literary works, revealing them to be tissues of preexistent texts, sign systems, and cultural codes. More constructively, Moore's focus on intertextuality enabled her to discern ways women writers might capitalize on its nonhierarchical character to gain greater freedom from the controlling fathers whose works, when seen in an intertextual context, comprise only a portion of the ambient texts.

In addition to illuminating the situation and resources of the modernist woman writer, Moore's strategies of documentation may prove instructive for theorists of influence and intertextuality. As the documentation of "Marriage" reveals, practices of writers from nonhegemonic groups demonstrate that influence can productively be seen in more ideologically charged and less author-centered terms, not as an encounter between two individuals involving the handling of specific literary conventions but as an essentially impersonal, culturally conservative process of transmitting values and ideology. Similarly, Moore's practices in "Marriage" demonstrate that intertextuality may productively be seen in less autonomously logocentric terms than has usually been the case. The author (understood as a gendered and historically specific subject position) as well as his/her seemingly deliberate strategies may usefully be invoked in connection with intertextuality, particularly when dealing with works by those whose inferior social status partially alienates them from the codes and conventions of the dominant culture. Such writers are in a position to apply self-conscious selection to more of the texts and systems that speak in their writings than is a middle-class white male whose comfortable integration into the culture, its literary tradition, and its dominant ideology renders him less aware of the codes that transmit its biases.

NOTES

1 For information about the biographical relevance of marriage to Moore at
   the time of the poem's composition, see Laurence Stapleton (40–41); Margaret
   Newlin; and Lynn Keller and Cristanne Miller.
     My reading of the poem in the present essay is everywhere indebted to Crist-
   anne Miller because of our extended discussions during our collaboration on
   "The Tooth of Disputation: Marianne Moore's 'Marriage.'" I would also like
   to thank both Jeanne Heuving and John Slatin for allowing me to read their
   excellent unpublished work on "Marriage," and John Slatin and Eric Rothstein for providing particularly helpful comments on drafts of this essay.

2 Focusing on the poem "Novices," John Slatin in *The Savage's Romance* (136–
   40) explores the significance of the difference between Eliot's discontinuous
   procedures in *The Waste Land* and Moore's drawing together diverse materials into "grammatically continuous sequence." Slatin views Moore as asserting an identity between past and present and requiring the present's conform-
   ing to the past; I see her practices as far less conservative.

3 The notes did not appear in the poem's first publication as *Manikin* 3. They
   first appeared in *Observations* and were subsequently revised, usually to shorten
   them. Among the changes Moore made in the poem for later versions were
   a few that affected the quotations and notes: She added the quotation marks
   around the line "Married people often look that way," which she then attributed to C. Bertram Hartmann. She changed the phrase "one's self love's
   labor lost" first to "one's self quite lost" and then to "self-lost," thereby elimi-
   nating the echo of Shakespeare. After *Observations* she moved the quotation
   marks so that the lines "The fact of woman / is 'not the sound of the flute /
   but very poison'" were no longer attributed to "He."

4 Critical attention to Moore's use of quotations is increasing. Among the best
   extended treatments (with quite different perspectives) are Slatin's in *The
   Savage's Romance* and Margaret Holley's in *The Poetry of Marianne Moore*.
   Slatin stresses the allusive function of Moore's quotes, analyzing them as a
   means of triangulated engagement with her male modernist contemporaries.
   Holley attends to the ways in which Moore's handling of quotations changes
   over her career, but she emphasizes (as I do) the ways in which Moore's quotes
   highlight intertextuality and mark the poet's "dependence on the discourse
   and textual possibilites of the larger cultural milieu" (42).

5 Of course, Moore's practices may equally have affected Pound's and Eliot's.
   Thirty years ago R. P. Blackmur suggested that "Pound may have partly derived his method [in the *Cantos*] from Moore" (Tomlinson 83), and Slatin attributes the discoveries of William Carlos Williams' *Spring and All* and *In
   the American Grain* in large part to Moore's example (*Savage's Romance* 11).
   Bonnie Costello notes that "when Pound read Eliot's draft of *The Waste Land*
   he marked 'Marianne' in the margin. Mrs. Eliot has asserted this is not Moore,
   but Pound could have been warning his friend against borrowing another
   poet's trademark" (184–85).

6   Both in his article "Advancing Backward in a Circle: Marianne Moore as (Natural) Historian" (320) and in *The Savage's Romance* (136–37), Slatin suggests that Moore relies on the definition of influence Eliot advances in his essay on James.

7   In his "meditation on the melancholy of the creative mind's desperate insistence on priority," *The Anxiety of Influence*, Bloom presents various forms of the "battle between strong equals, [poetic] father and son as mighty opposites, Laius and Oedipus at the crossroads" (13, 11).

8   Admittedly, Williams treats Moore less condescendingly in contemporary (rather than retrospective) documents; one senses from his reviews that analyzing her work enabled him to formulate, and probably influenced, his own understanding of modernist poetics.

9   For a discussion of Moore's feminism and that of M. Carey Thomas, see David Bergman, "Marianne Moore and the Problem of 'Marriage.'"

10 By presenting H.D. as transcending this dichotomy, Moore implies, however, that it is reductive, so we should be wary of seeing the poem's multivoiced narrator entirely in terms of one category. Despite the speaker's sharp mockery of "Marriage," she also values and perhaps longs for that domestic institution at its finest. The ultimate intellectual freedom may lie in accepting ambivalence, exploring multiple roles, and allowing internal debate. For a reading of "Marriage" that focuses on the centrality of internal disputation, see Keller and Miller, "'The Tooth of Disputation.'"

11 John Slatin was kind enough to identify for me the source of this quote: a letter to Bacon's uncle Burghley, the lord treasurer, quoted in a note to the article "Bacon, Francis," in the *Encyclopaedia Britannica*, Eleventh Edition. According to Slatin, Moore copied into her reading notebook the passage in which Bacon had written, "I have taken all knowledge to be my province," and explained that he hoped to purge science of "two sorts of rovers, whereof the one with frivolous disputations, confutations and verbosities, the other with blind experiments and auricular traditions and impostures, hath committed so many spoils . . . " (n. 136). Because I have not seen the notebook, I am unsure whether Moore's misquotation of auricular as circular occurred at the time of her original transcription; in the poem "circular" in association with "goldenness" effectively evokes the wedding band.

12 On the irrelevance of the author: Roland Barthes, for instance, proclaims in "The Death of the Author": "a text is made of multiple writings, drawn from many cultures and entering into mutual relations of dialogue, parody, contestation, but there is one place where this multiplicity is focused and that place is the reader, not, as was hitherto said, the author. The reader is the space on which all the quotations that make up a writing are inscribed without any of them being lost; a text's unity lies not in its origin but in its destination." He concludes the essay asserting that "the birth of the reader must be at the cost of the death of the Author" (148). Michael Riffaterre places similar emphasis on the reader, regarding intertextuality as "a modality of perception, the deciphering of the text by the reader in such a way that he identifies the structures to which the text owes its quality of work of art" ("Syllepsis" 625).

On intentionality: Readers troubled by my use of this term, or of "strategy" which inevitably implies intention, may regard it as a practical fiction by which the essay's argument is directed and facilitated. I am not pretending to make claims of a biographically documentable nature.

13   Culler sensibly raises the question of whether any restriction of the concept of intertextuality for practical reasons—something of which even Kristeva, who developed the notion of intertextuality, is guilty—doesn't jeopardize the general theory. Because my subject-centered focus precludes consideration of much that is usually designated as intertextual, I will introduce the term "system" to mark the specific traits of intertextuality that are of interest here, just as the term "tradition" has marked the specific traits of influence of interest in this essay.

14   In *Observations*—but not in later editions—the note continues, "although 'in the Orient as here, husbands have difficulty in enforcing their authority'; 'it is a common saying that not all the angels in heaven could subdue a woman'" (104).

15   The article actually appeared in 1923 and was in fact titled "Doing Two Things at Once." Moore's title, with a comma after "consciousness" and a question mark after "range," appears as the subtitle. The brief piece describes the "case" of one Thea Alba, whose extraordinary "ability simultaneously to control several apparently conscious acts" is documented in two photographs accompanying the text (Gradenwitz 17). Alba's "abnormal faculty" provides an apt analog for Moore's performance in the poem in simultaneously dramatizing textual relations of influence and intertextuality. Moore's "doing two things at once" might further be understood as a double voicing deriving from a double consciousness, to invoke concepts initially applied to African-American existence but now often applied to other oppressed groups as well.

16   Even if Tiresias does, as Eliot asserts in his notes, "unite" all the "personage[s]" in *The Waste Land*, that "mere spectator" does not bind the poem's linguistic fragments as does the syntax in Moore's "Marriage." In speaking with a single, inclusive mind, Moore generates a kind of personalism that contrasts with the famed impersonalism Eliot sought in his work.

17   No explanatory comment precedes the notes to "Marriage" in the earlier volumes containing the poem.

18   Smith's translation, in *The Book of the Twelve Prophets*, is: "As the shepherd saveth from the mouth of the lion a pair of shin-bones or a bit of an ear, so shall the children of Israel be saved—they who sit in Samaria in the corner of the diwan and . . . on a couch." He then explains, "To this desert shepherd, with only the hard ground to rest on, the couches and ivory-mounted diwans of the rich must have seemed the very symbols of extravagance. But the pampered bodies that loll their lazy lengths upon them shall be left like the crumbs of a lion's meal—*two shin-bones and the bit of an ear!* Their whole civilization shall perish with them" (146–47).

19   For a revealing examination of how Moore handles her sources in another poem composed at the same time as "Marriage" and of how much of her borrowed material in that poem is in fact unacknowledged, see Patricia Willis, "The Road to Paradise."

20 Willis' essay, in discussing the relation between the paradise of "An Octopus" and that of *Paradise Lost*, provides further evidence of the presence of Milton's text in Moore's thinking at this time (260–63).

21 *The Waste Land* was first published in *The Criterion* in October 1922; it first appeared in America in *The Dial* in November 1922. Boni and Liveright published the book with the notes added in mid-December. According to Patricia Willis (247, 248), Moore began working on "Marriage" early in 1923, finishing it about July; the poem was first published in 1923 in *Manikin* 3.

WORKS CITED

Barthes, Roland. "The Death of the Author." In *Image-Music-Text*, trans. Stephen Heath, 142–48. New York: Hill and Wang, 1977.

Baxter, Richard. *The Saints' Everlasting Rest.* 1759. Abridged by Benjamin Fawcett. New York: American Tract Society, n.d.

Bergman, David. "Marianne Moore and the Problem of 'Marriage.'" *American Literature* 60 (1988): 241–54.

Bloom, Harold. *The Anxiety of Influence: A Theory of Poetry.* London: Oxford UP, 1973.

Costello, Bonnie. *Marianne Moore: Imaginary Possessions.* Cambridge: Harvard UP, 1981.

Culler, Jonathan. "Presupposition and Intertextuality." In *The Pursuit of Signs* 100–18. Ithaca: Cornell UP, 1981.

Eliot, T. S. "In Memory of Henry James." *Egoist* 5 (1918): 1–2.

Eliot, T. S. "Tradition and the Individual Talent." In *Selected Essays of T. S. Eliot* 3–11. New York: Harcourt, Brace & World, 1950.

Eliot, T. S. *The Waste Land.* In *The Complete Poems and Plays, 1909–1950* 37–55. New York: Harcourt, Brace & World, 1952.

Eliot, T. S. "What Dante Means to Me." In *To Criticize the Critic and Other Writings.* New York: Farrar, Straus & Giroux, 1965.

Gradenwitz, Alfred. "Doing Two Things at Once: Multiple Consciousness, or Reflex Action of Unaccustomed Range?" *Scientific American,* January 1923, 17.

Holley, Margaret. *The Poetry of Marianne Moore: A Study in Voice and Value.* New York: Cambridge UP, 1987.

Keller, Lynn, and Cristanne Miller. "'The Tooth of Disputation': Marianne Moore's 'Marriage.'" *Sagetrieb* 6 (1987): 99–115.

Kenner, Hugh. *A Homemade World: The American Modernist Writers.* New York: William Morrow, 1975.

Milton, John. *Paradise Lost.* In *Complete Poems and Major Prose,* ed. Merritt Y. Hughes. Indianapolis: Bobbs-Merrill, 1957.

Moore, Marianne. *The Complete Poems of Marianne Moore.* New York: Macmillan, 1980.

Moore, Marianne. *The Complete Prose of Marianne Moore.* Ed. Patricia C. Willis. New York: Viking, 1986.

Moore, Marianne. *Observations*. New York: Dial, 1924.

Newlin, Margaret. "'Unhelpful Hymen!': Marianne Moore and Hilda Doolittle." *Essays in Criticism* 27 (1977): 216–30.

Reade, Charles. *Christie Johnstone*. Boston: Ticknor and Fields, 1855.

Riffaterre, Michael. "Syllepsis." *Critical Inquiry* 6 (1980): 625–38.

Rihbany, Abraham Mitrie. *The Syrian Christ*. Boston and New York: Houghton Mifflin, 1916.

Slatin, John M. "Advancing Backward in a Circle: Marianne Moore as (Natural) Historian." *Twentieth Century Literature* 30 (1984): 273–326.

Slatin, John M. *The Savage's Romance: The Poetry of Marianne Moore*. University Park: Pennsylvania State UP, 1986.

Smith, George Adam. *The Book of the Twelve Prophets*. Vol. 1. New York: A. C. Armstrong and Son, 1902.

Stapleton, Laurence. *Marianne Moore: The Poet's Advance*. Princeton: Princeton UP, 1978.

Thomas, Edward. *Feminine Influence on the Poets*. London: Martin Secker, 1910.

Tomlinson, Charles, ed. *Marianne Moore: A Collection of Critical Essays*. Englewood Cliffs, NJ: Prentice-Hall, 1969.

Williams, William Carlos. *The Autobiography of William Carlos Williams*. New York: New Directions, 1951.

Willis, Patricia C. "The Road to Paradise: First Notes on Marianne Moore's 'An Octopus.'" *Twentieth Century Literature* 30 (1984): 242–66.

CHAPTER 10

Sidney / Spenser / Shakespeare: Influence / Intertextuality / Intention

ANDREW D. WEINER

Although our collective project might seem to limit us to the two approaches of "influence" or "intertextuality," both the editors' introduction and Susan Friedman's essay remind us that the concept of influence does not really emerge until well after the deaths of Sidney, Spenser, and Shakespeare. Intextuality emerges at the same time, not as a term but as a complement, the productions of hack writers or of "folk." When ideas of originality and property altered in the later twentieth century, the idea of intextuality altered too, from complementing influence to rivaling or supplanting it. This collection of essays would have had a very different positioning in 1960; by analogy, one may ask if its terms pose useful questions about authorship and texts at a time when neither originality nor property had the legal, moral, and aesthetic weight that they attained after 1700. Nor, as I shall argue, did the text have an autonomous status. Might it then be anachronistic to apply these categories to sixteenth-century writers? The anachronism comes in the substitution of an emphasis that would have seemed irrelevant to the writers for an emphasis that would have seemed right. An example outside literary study is a historian's use of class terms instead of status terms for early English social history. Another is an anthropologist's following nineteenth-century predecessors in distinguishing scientific-rational from religious-magical actions when dealing with a society for whom these distinctions make no sense. My examples do not mean that historians today must limit themselves to early historians' techniques or that one must do all anthropology from the "inside." They mean that to avoid anachronism we should understand things in their own terms before we turn to other terms. The burden of proof is on "influence" and "intertextuality" to prove that they can do something that

245

a theory contemporary with the writers cannot *and* that they can do it from "without," so to speak, without writing over that contemporary history.

To explore these issues my specific project here is to address the question of how Shakespeare, in the process of authoring *King Lear,* might have responded to certain issues raised in Sidney's *Arcadia,* from which he drew the basic fable of the Gloucester-Edgar-Edmund subplot,[1] and in Spenser's *Faerie Queene,* in which, along with the most recent "true chronicle history" of King Lear / Leir / Leyr, he would have found several different versions of "history" and what it can mean to different "readers" of history or to differently inclined experiencers of history: I have in mind chiefly Arthur and Guyon, readers of two different written "histories" in Book II, and Britomart, Paridell, and Scudamour in Book III, whose experiences have taught each of them a different philosophy of history.

I am not, of course, alone in feeling some discomfort in trying to fit the interrelations of Renaissance texts into late-twentieth-century boxes. In an effort to identify "the structural element that informs the word and the text with whatever stability they succeed in achieving" (Greene 14)[2] within a Derridean universe, Thomas Greene has suggested that "the interplay between change and stability can be located most clearly in a work's intertextuality — the structural presence within it of elements from earlier works," noting further that "since a literary text that draws nothing from its predecessors is inconceivable, intertextuality is a universal literary constant." In the face of this universal constant, however, Greene, while acknowledging the "ultimate groundlessness and historicity of language," also acknowledges differences of degree of constancy to the principle of universal intertextuality: "some systems, some texts, make greater structural use of these elements than others; some insist on their own intertextual composition, but not all. . . . When a literary work does this, when it calls to the reader's attention its own deliberate allusiveness, it can be said to be affirming its own historicity, its own involvement in disorderly historical process. Allusions in these cases might be regarded as secondary etiologies, constructions of meaning connecting the past to the present" (Greene 16). All texts are intertextual, but some are more intertextual — at least more insistently and deliberately intertextual — than others. Rather than follow Greene in his employment of the term "etiology" to refer to the "process of creating signifying constructs" (Greene 16) and generate a new critical vocabulary to distinguish the more intertextual from the less, the more deliberately allusive from the less, I prefer to do what, as a historical critic, I am in any case inclined to do, explore the possibilites of using Renaissance terms and distinctions. I would at least begin by declaring revalorized the "poetics of intentionality" proclaimed in Sidney's *Defense of Poetry* (c. 1580), attributing intentionality not to the "literary work" but to the author of that work, as Sidney does, and referring to the language used in the Renaissance to describe the relation of texts to each other.[3]

Returning to the critical vocabulary of the late sixteenth-century offers readers of late-sixteenth-century poetry several advantages. First, it frees us from the ideological baggage that the debate about "influence" and "intertextuality" has made an almost inevitable adjunct to any critical journey. Much of this debate centers on the vicissitudes of personalism, with fetishizing ideas of (and denials of) originality and artistic autonomy that congeal what is fluid for Renaissance texts. Further, to employ "influence" and "intertextuality" is to accept the substitution of terms foreign to Renaissance writers and readers for terms familiar to them. In so doing, one cannot help distorting the web of belief woven into the texts, and thus compelling the modern critic to accept unnecessarily the added obligation of an elaborate and probably impossible job of translation. Perhaps most important for the argument that follows, "influence" and "intertextuality" cannot render the form of a Sidneyan mimesis because they fix attention on a text. In Sidney, the world being imitated is not a text—the "brazen" world of nature that we experience directly—but the nontextual intention, what Sidney calls the artificer's *"idea* or fore-conceit" (79), behind the text. To express that idea, the poet borrows, alludes to, takes from whatever source what he needs to figure the "golden" world the "brazen" cannot supply if he merely attempts to imitate it. The poet's "sources," then, are whatever has enabled him to glimpse that "golden" world—other texts, broadly accepted commonplaces, ideology—and his rhetoric is both influenced and intertextual. These terms now merely signal a distinction without difference and do no real work, except perhaps for a biographer.

Theories of influence and intertextuality are, to some degree, artifacts of what Habermas has called a "legitimation crisis": influence legitimates through the figure of the author as charismatic originator, intertextuality through the sheer existence of Barthes's ever-present "already read." Even in our times, the terms disappear as the need for individualized explanation disappears in the face of a rational practice. One does not say that Stephen Hawking was influenced by Einstein or even that Jung was influenced by Freud. Nor does one need a theory of intertextuality to explain the operation of Fermilab, NASA, the Center for Disease Control, or chiropractors. I mention Jung and chiropractic to suggest that one need not subscribe to a practice to find it rational in this sense. One must merely recognize it as based on what is taken to be some shared supervening truth which takes on the burden of legitimation. Sidney's "golden world" is such a truth. For the individual text, legitimation derives, as Sidney insists, from the reader's assent to the poet's representation of the golden world his poem presents. The poet's "invention" — his "*idea* or fore-conceit" — enables his "imitation" of the "golden" world; again, an analogy with scientific discovery may be helpful. Sidney's solution to an earlier crisis of legitimation does the same critical work that the theories of "influence" and "intertextuality" aspire to without being intrusively anachronistic. "Invention," which Sidney offers as the source from which the poet's golden world originates, and "imitation," the deliberate and deliberative process by which the poet reworks both the "facts" of the visible world and the materials inherited from his predecessors, offer themselves as potentially useful substitutes for both of our more modern ones in thinking about and describing the composition process.

This later term embraces the reworkings that Michael Baxandall so wonderfully exfoliates in his discussion of influence, a passage quoted in the introduction to this volume. Baxandall's inventory follows once again on the theory that it ought to be quoted as often as possible merely to counterbalance our overfamiliarity with the more limited concept that sees the later writer as the passive recipient of the earlier one, rather than as an active agent who can "draw on, resort to, avail oneself of, appropriate from, have recourse to, adapt, misunderstand, refer to, pick up, take on, engage with, react to, quote, differentiate oneself from, assimilate oneself to, assimilate, align oneself with, copy, address, paraphrase, absorb, make a variation on, revive, continue, remodel, ape, emulate, travesty, parody, extract from, distort, attend to, resist, simplify, reconstitute, elaborate on, develop, face up to, master, subvert, perpetuate, reduce, promote, respond to, transform, tackle . . ." the texts he or she incorporates within his or her own text (59, cited above, 6–7). The legitimacy of these procedures derives from the discovery that they present, the discovery that Sidney calls "invention."

Unfortunately, invention in the Renaissance was a much more complex term than our contemporary lexicon allows. Where a current dictionary (such as the *American Heritage Dictionary*) limits invention to the act of producing or contriving things previously unknown by the use of ingenuity or imagination, a historical dictionary reveals a far richer and complex association of meanings, linking the senses of discovering (accidentally or deliberately) with contriving or devising, including the possibilities of creating something new out of something preexistent as well as the possibility of devising something first, of originating it (see the various senses of both *invent* and *invention* in the *OED*). Poetic invention, then, involves both making something up and making it up out of previously invented materials. Above all, however, it involves deliberation. Sidney's exaltation of the poet's "golden" world over nature's "brazen" one thus acknowledges without disparagement that "the works of the one [nature] be essential, the other [the poet] in imitation or fiction" because what the poet brings forth is as "substantial" as nature's works, and it is why he insists that "any understanding knoweth that the skill of each artificer standeth in that *idea* or fore-conceit of the work and not in the work itself" (78, 79).

The reader of the poet's "imitation or fiction" furthers that poet's project "to bestow a Cyrus upon the world to make many Cyruses" either by remaking him- or herself or by making yet another representation of a "Cyrus" if the reader "will learn aright why and how that maker made him," i.e., his poetic image, Cyrus in the case of Sidney's example (79). Given that "first accursed fall of Adam" in consequence of which nature's "brazen" world cannot provide us with "essential" images of "virtues, vices, or what else" (81) as effective at moving as those to be found in the poet's feigned world, the poet's "imitation or fiction" must be primarily concerned with the creation of a fictional image, the "representing, counterfeiting, or figuring forth" of the "speaking picture" (79, 80) which will "delight, to move men to take that goodness in hand, which without delight they would fly as from a stranger; and teach, to make them know that goodness whereunto they are moved" (81). If nature is not a source of images that can delight and teach effectively, poets must look to their predecessors for "pictures" that can "strike, pierce, [and] . . . possess the sight of the soul" of their readers (85), pictures that can become the basis for the effects required within the poet's own "*idea* or fore-conceit." Poetic invention thus involves the search for images, whatever their source, adaptable to the poet's present need.

Imitation, the term most commonly used in the Renaissance to describe one writer's purposive use of another's writings, might be adequate to describe this process if we could agree to understand "imitation" as Richard Peterson has argued that Ben Jonson does ("the creative use of the thoughts and words of the ancients in a spirit of emulous rivalry" [xiii], "that process of judicious gathering in, assimilation, and transformation or turning whereby a good writer, and by extension a good man, shapes an original and coherent work of art or a virtuous life" [xiv]). But since "imitation" has acquired a set of irrelevant meanings that are likely to limit the bounds of critical inquiry severely, we might do well to consider the term used by Lynn Keller in an earlier study. The poet "makes" (Sidney's term for the activity of the poet) by "remaking . . . new" the works he or she uses according to his or her present project. It is this purposeful remaking of episodes from Sidney's *Arcadia* and Spenser's *Faerie Queene* that interests me, both for what it suggests about how Shakespeare's needs in *King Lear* differ from Sidney's and Spenser's in their works and for what it may suggest about why Shakespeare may have made *King Lear* as he did.

I

> I cannot fall worse than I am.
>
> Sidney, *Arcadia* 276

Sidney tells the story of the Paphlagonian king and his two sons, Leonatus and the bastard Plexirtus, as part of an intertwined series of retrospective narratives in book II of the revised *Arcadia*. Although Sidney insists upon the poet's obligation to create powerful images that can move the reader, he also insistently qualifies his "speaking pictures" with a dense linguistic commentary in which key terms are juxtaposed and echoed in order to force the reader to define more carefully the nature of those images, rejecting and transforming the Euphuistic play of sounds as a self-contained pleasure. In and through their stories, the two disguised princes Pyrocles and Musidorus woo their princesses by telling them of their adventures before they came to Arcadia. The story is a long and complex one and is heard in its entirety only by the reader. Perhaps as a consequence of his narrative technique, we should not be surprised to find ourselves pointed toward conclusions different from those the princes and their princesses reach. Despite its discontinuous narration, it is apparently of some importance within the *Arcadia,* where it ultimately explains how Pyrocles and Musidorus come to arrive, shipwrecked, in Arcadia, why they adopt the names they use in Arcadia before they don their disguises, why Pyrocles falls so quickly in love with Philoclea, and why he adopts the name of Zelmane when he dons his Amazonian persona. In addition to its importance to the plot of the *Arcadia,* it seems, in its extended relation, to insist upon some thematic issues important to the *Arcadia* as well. Obviously Shakespeare found this story sufficiently interesting that he not only based part of his plot upon Sidney's story but also incorporated numerous verbal details into his play.

Musidorus introduces the story to Pamela as one "worthy to be remembered for the unused examples therein as well of true natural goodness as of wretched ungratefulness" (275). As the princes, traveling in a winter storm, seek refuge in a hollow rock (much as Edgar will later find refuge in "the happy hollow of a tree" [II.iii.2]), they hear "a strange and pitiful disputation" between an aged blind man and a young man who leads him. The old man's insistence that Leonatus, the young man, leave him to his fate without fear for his welfare since "I cannot fall worse than I am" (276) provokes the princes to inquire into their history, and they learn that the old man, "lately rightful prince of the country of Paphlagonia," was "by the hard-hearted ungratefulness of a son of his deprived not only of his kingdom . . . but of his sight" (276). The king, who like Gloucester has at least acquired self-knowledge as a recompence for his blinding, interrupts his son Leonatus to accuse him of leaving out the "chief knot of all the discourse, my wickedness, my wickedness!" and refuses to provide them with the details of how his bastard son, Plexirtus, "with as much poisonous hypocrisy, desperate fraud, smooth malice, hidden ambition and smiling envy as in any living person could be harboured," deceived him, because he does not desire in any way to mitigate his own faults both in believing Plexirtus and in trying to destroy Leonatus (277). In time Plexirtus, having had the effective rule of the kingdom placed in his hands by his doting father, decides that rather than leave his father "nothing but the name of king" (278), he will leave him nothing but his misery, "full of wretchedness, fuller of disgrace, and fullest of guiltiness." Blinded by his bastard, thrust forth to wander through his former kingdom, and forbidden a guide for his "dark steps," he is succored by Leonatus, who refuses only to lead him to the top of a high rock from which his father might "free him from so serpentine a companion as I am" (279). A battle ensues when Plexirtus arrives with forty knights to kill his brother. Pyrocles and Musidorus join in, shortly to be seconded by an ally of theirs who has dreamed they were in danger.

Although Plexirtus escapes for the moment, he quickly finds himself besieged, his brother crowned king by their father, who, like Gloucester, then dies, "his heart broken with unkindness and affliction, stretched so far beyond his limits with this excess of comfort as it was no longer able to keep safe his vital spirits" (281). Plexirtus decides it is better "by humbleness to creep where by pride he could not march" (281) and submits to Leonatus, whose "ever-noble nature" (282) is quickly won from a desire for revenge to pity and finally to pardon by his brother's inexpressible cunning. For Musidorus, Plexirtus is an incomprehensible marvel of nature:

For certainly so had Nature formed him, and the exercise of craft conformed him to all turningness of sleights that, though no man had less goodness in his soul than he, no man could better find the places whence arguments might grow of goodness to another; though no man felt less pity, no man could tell better how to stir pity; no man more impudent to deny, where proofs were not manifest; no man more ready to confess with a repenting manner of aggravating his own evil, where denial would but make the fault fouler. (281)

Leaving the "reconciled brothers" (282) and the sphere of social justice, Pyrocles and Musidorus depart with Tydeus and Telenor, Plexirtus' chief supporters, to engage in "private chivalries" until Plexirtus recalls Tydeus and Telenor, "who willingly hoodwinking themselves from seeing his faults, and blinding themselves to believe what he said, often abused the virtue of courage to defend his foul vice of injustice" (283). At this point, Musidorus is forced to break off his narrative, which will be resumed only later by Pyrocles.

For Musidorus, the story thus far seems to be about how some virtuous people can, through love or weakness, so blind themselves to others' wickedness that they themselves lose their way and deviate from their own prescribed course of virtuous deeds to unworthiness. There is perhaps a certain irony in Musidorus' attitude, since love (which he had earlier called weakness), first of Pyrocles and then of Pamela, has transformed him from a prince into a shepherd and diverted him from the public and private chivalries to which he has devoted his life. Sidney, however, has not yet made this irony explicit when the narrative passes to Pyrocles.

After telling Philoclea of a number of other interlinked adventures, Pyrocles returns to Plexirtus via the conclusion of the story of the brothers Tydeus and Telenor. After "the noble prince Leonatus . . . forgetting all former injuries, had received that naughty Plexirtus into a strait degree of favour, his goodness being as apt to be deceived as the other's craft was to deceive" (361), he discovers that the "ungrateful" Plexirtus was trying to poison him. Once again, however, Leonatus, "would not suffer his kindness to be overcome, not by justice itself," and disregarding the counsel of those who would have him execute Plexirtus as one "likely to bring forth nothing but as dangerous, as wicked, effects" (361), offers to aid Plexirtus in the conquest of the city of Trebisond, which of right belongs to his kingdom, and to permit Plexirtus to rule it in the hope that "with less unnaturalness" Plexirtus can "glut" his ambition there, "and that done, if it be possible, learn virtue" (362). Like the "noble" Edgar, Leonatus has a "nature so far from doing harms / That he suspects none; on whose foolish honesty" the hypocrite's "practices ride easy" (I.ii.172–75). As Edmund will find, in a wicked world, honesty, goodness, and mercy merely offer opportunities to those who would abuse them for their own ends.

Achieving his conquest chiefly through the "virtue" (i.e. courage or force, *virtù*, not the more abstract concept that Leonatus had hoped Plexirtus might master) of Tydeus and Telenor, Plexirtus "(who by the rules of his own mind could construe no other end of men's doings but self-seeking) suddenly feared what they could do, and as suddenly suspected what they would do, and as suddenly hated them, as having both might and mind to do" (362). His fears, of course, are as groundless as Goneril's fears of what Lear's hundred knights might do (cf. *Lear* I.iv.313–21), since we have been frequently told that Tydeus and Telenor chose to aid him because they had determined rather to be "good friends than good men" (280). Using what Pyrocles calls his "devilish sleight" (362), Plexirtus engineers the destruction of the two brothers by engaging each, unknowingly, to fight the other, disguised, in a silent combat to the death. Musidorus, Pyrocles, and Pyrocles' page, Daiphantus, stumble upon the two brothers shortly before they expire from their wounds, discover each to the other, and hear them die, "detesting their unfortunately-spent time in having served so ungrateful a tyrant, and accusing their folly in having believed he could faithfully love who did not love faithfulness; wishing us to take heed how we placed our goodwill upon any other ground than proof of virtue, since length of acquaintance, mutual secrecies, nor height of bene-fits could bind a savage heart—no man being good to other that is not good in himself" (363). This lesson is not heeded. Hearing of Plexirtus' treachery, Pyrocles' page Daiphantus sickens "and hastily grew into the very extreme working of sorrowfulness" (364), until, on the point of death and hearing from one seeking Tydeus and Telenor that Plexirtus is "in present danger of a very cruel death" if he be not rescued, Daiphantus reveals "himself" as Plexirtus' daughter, Zelmane, thus disguised for love of Pyrocles and thus sickened out of fear that her father's habitual treachery would force Pyrocles to reject her.

As this doubling and redoubling of disguises suggests, the action of the *Arcadia* is taking place in a world where not only the evil disguise themselves through hypocrisy but the good mask themselves from reality in the pursuit of noble deeds and ends. "Amazed" at her speech, filled with sorrow and pity at her imminent death, Pyrocles yields "to the weakness of abundant weeping" (365, 366), and accedes to her dying wish that he "pardon my father the displeasure you have justly conceived against him, and for this once to succor him out of the danger wherein he is: I hope he will amend: and I pray you, whensoever you remember him to be the faulty Plexirtus, remember withal that he is Zelmane's father" (366–67). Like Leonatus, who will not put Plexirtus to death, remembering whose son he is (361), Pyrocles feels obliged to save Plexirtus, remembering at Zelmane's request whose father he is. Pyrocles, bound both by his oath and by what he complains to Philoclea is "the strange working of unjust fortune" (368), leaves his best friend Musidorus to stand alone in a battle while he goes to save the vicious Plexirtus from a "cruel and just" death ordained by an old nobleman who has bred a "beastly monster" to kill this "monstrous tyrant" (369). When Pyrocles kills the monster, the old nobleman, "only bewailing my virtue had been employed to save a worse monster than I killed" (369), frees Plexirtus and Pyrocles, who hasten to see if Musidorus still needs Pyrocles' help. He does not. Then Musidorus and Pyrocles, after being feted by an assembly of all of the grateful princes they have aided during their travels, leave for Greece in a ship "most royally furnished by Plexirtus" (371). Although this seems like folly, Pyrocles insists that Plexirtus, "seeming a quite altered man, had nothing but repentance in his eyes, friendship in his gesture, and virtue in his mouth; so that we, who had promised the sweet Zelmane to pardon him, now not only forgave but began to favour, persuading ourselves with a youthful credulity that perchance things were not so evil as we took them and, as it were, desiring our own memory that it might be so" (371). Despite their efforts to reconceive the past, Pyrocles and Musidorus' memories of Plexirtus are correct: he was and still is that evil, as they discover when, after the ship sails, one of his servants confesses to them that Plexirtus has ordered them killed before they reach Greece. Despite the servant's efforts, a kind of civil war breaks out on board the vessel between those of Plexirtus' servants who want to obey his orders and those who do not. In the resulting fighting, the ship is destroyed and everyone but Pyrocles and Musidorus perishes.

This disaster concludes Plexirtus' part in the *Arcadia* and returns us to the image of the shipwreck with which the work began:

they saw a sight of piteous strangeness: a ship, or rather the carcasse of a ship, or rather some few bones of the carcasse hulling there, part broken, part burned, part drowned—death having used more than one dart to that destruction. About it floated great store of very rich things and many chests which might promise no less. And amidst the precious things were a number of dead bodies, which likewise did not only testify both elements' violence, but that the chief violence was grown of human inhumanity; for their bodies were full of grisly wounds, and their blood had (as it were) filled the wrinkles of the sea's visage, which it seemed the sea would not wash away that it might witness that it is not always his fault when we condemn his cruelty. In sum, a defeat where the conquered kept both field and spoil; a shipwreck without storm or ill-footing, and a waste of fire in the midst of water. (66)

This shipwreck, which is played against the Neoplatonic fantasies of two shepherds in love with a shepherdess named Urania whom they seem to have equated with Venus Urania even though Sidney later has her communicating with them by mail and playing rustic shepherdish games with them, begins the work by pitting the characters' dreams of love against the reality of "human inhumanity" so prevalent throughout text. By the conclusion of the retrospective narrative of Book II, we can associate it with Plexirtus, whose commissioning of it is but one of many similar betrayals in a long and seemingly unstoppable career.

An expert at seeming to amend, Plexirtus never changes. Ruled by nothing but desire for self-aggrandizement and fear of the actions of others like himself, Plexirtus, like Goneril, believes it is safer to fear too far than trust too far (*Lear* I.iv.319). In the pagan world of the *Arcadia,* there can be no true repentance, only hypocritical disguisings to prey upon the noble natures and impulses to pity of others. Plexirtus, like the giants the princes kill immediately before their discovery of the Paphlagonian king and his son, is "so fleshed in cruelty as not to be reclaimed" (274), but until it pleases "the eternal justice" to make him "suffer death" at someone's hands, Plexirtus will merely continue his career. The ship filled with uncertain friends and unknown enemies mirrors the larger world of the work. The noble natured, thinking it "less evil to spare a foe than spoil a friend," will always be to some extent at risk: "Some of the wiser would call to parley and wish peace, but while the words of peace were in their mouths, some of their evil auditors gave them death for their hire" (373). The good and the evil are always at odds, but while fear of doing evil restrains the good, nothing restrains the evil, since it is "of such nature that it cannot stand but with strengthening one evil with another, and so multiply in itself till it came to the highest and then fall with his own weight" (392).

II

> Yours in the ranks of death.
> *Lear* IV.ii.25

Some of what Shakespeare found in Sidney is obvious: the king, content to pass on the burden of rule to his child and to be king in name only, who finds that power inevitably begets a desire for more power; the father, blinded by his bastard son's persuasions, who ends up blinded indeed, but who is saved by the son he has tried to kill when his despair leads him to attempt suicide by jumping off a cliff, and who dies when

> his flawed heart —
> Alack, too weak the conflict to support —
> 'Twixt two extremes of passion, joy and grief,
> Burst smilingly.
> (V.iii.197–200)

At least some of Shakespeare's reasons for wanting to incorporate a story like that of the Paphlagonian King and his two sons into the story of King Lear and his three daughters seem equally obvious. Throughout the play, Gloucester, Lear, and Edgar all comment upon the parallels between the two families, universalizing the cracking of the bond between parent and child into a sign of an unnatural scourging of nature, and even Edmund finds their belief apt for his plans. When Edmund first broaches Edgar's "plot" to Gloucester, Gloucester is already inclined to belief because of what has happened between Lear and Cordelia: "These late eclipses in the sun and moon portend no good to us. Though the wisdom of nature can reason it thus and thus, yet nature finds itself scourged by the sequent events. Love cools, friendship falls off, brothers divide. In cities, mutinies; in countries, discord; in palaces, treason; and the bond cracked 'twixt son and father. This villain of mine comes under the prediction, there's son against father; the King falls from the bias of nature, there's father against child" (I.ii.102–9).

Later Edmund plays against these normative beliefs in his claims that
Edgar was proof against appeals to natural law, showing his wounded arm in
testimony of Edgar's willingness to murder his brother as well as his father:

> I told him the revenging gods
> 'Gainst parricides did all the thunder bend;
> Spoke with how manifold and strong a bond
> The child was bound to the father — sir, in fine,
> Seeing how loathly opposite I stood
> To his unnatural purpose, in fell motion
> With prepared sword he charges home
> My unprovided body.
>
> (II.i.45–52)

During the storm, while Lear questions his philosopher, Poor Tom, about
the cause of thunder (III.iv.145–46), Gloucester confides to the disguised
Kent that similar effects grow from similar causes:

> Thou sayest the King grows mad — I'll tell thee, friend,
> I am almost mad myself. I had a son,
> Now outlawed from my blood; he sought my life
> But lately, very late. I loved him, friend,
> No father his son dearer. True to tell thee,
> The grief hath crazed my wits.
>
> (III.iv.156–61)

And after Gloucester sends the King from the hovel toward Dover, Edgar
reflects on the effects of the fellowship of pain between himself and the
King: "How light and portable my pain seems now, / When that which makes
me bend makes the King bow. / He childed as I fathered" (III.vi.106–8).

By doubling the Lear family history, Shakespeare economically achieves
the effect that Sidney retrospectively gains through his long narrative in
Book II of the *Arcadia:* our consent to Albany's rejection of Goneril, Regan,
and Cornwall's treatment of the King as unnatural, our recognition that
the unnatural has in the course of the play become "natural," and our acceptance of the need for extreme measures to stop its inevitable course:

> Wisdom and goodness to the vile seem vile;
> Filths savor but themselves. What have you done?
> Tigers not daughters, what have you performed?
>   . . .
> If that the heavens do not their visible spirits
> Send quickly down to tame these vile offenses,
> It will come,
> Humanity must perforce prey on itself,
> Like monsters of the deep.
>
> (IV.ii.38–50)

Where Sidney begins with a "speaking picture" of the triumph of "human inhumanity," Shakespeare's choric plotting weaves a tapestry of cruelty and apparent helplessness against it. As in Brueghel's "Triumph of Death" (1562–63),[4] in which an ever-increasing army of skeletons is waging relentless war upon an ever-diminishing number of living figures, the ranks of death, in which Edmund enrolls himself (IV.ii.25) and in which Goneril, Regan, Cornwall, and Oswald clearly belong, appear headed toward complete victory until shortly before the end of the play.

Shakespeare does not just adapt the raw materials he found in Sidney, however; he also transforms them. Plexirtus is silent in the *Arcadia;* Edmund is anything but. Interestingly, where Sidney simply presented Plexirtus as unnaturally evil—his father, brother, and daughter are all basically good—Shakespeare makes Edmund define himself as nature's worshiper ("Thou, Nature, art my goddess; to thy law / My services are bound" [I.ii.1–2]) and claim to be what he is by rational choice:

This is the excellent foppery of the world, that when we are sick in fortune, often the surfeits of our own behavior, we make guilty of our disasters the sun, moon, and stars; as if we were villains on necessity; fools by heavenly compulsion; knaves, thieves, and treachers by spherical predominance; drunkards, liars, and adulterers by an enforced obedience of planetary influence; and all that we are evil in, by a divine thrusting in. An admirable evasion of whoremaster man, to lay his goatish disposition on the charge of a star. (I.ii.115–24)

Where Sidney makes his *heroes* claim to be rational creatures free to choose whether to do good or evil—at least before love forces them to know themselves better (see, e.g., *Arcadia* 132–33 and 170)—Shakespeare makes his *villains* claim the greater freedom to unslip the bonds of nature and create themselves anew.

To Edmund his father's belief and his brother's nobility are merely signs of their weakness:

A credulous father, and a brother noble,
Whose nature is so far from doing harms
That he suspects none; on whose foolish honesty
My practises ride easy. I see the business.
Let me, if not by birth, have lands by wit;
All with me's meet that I can fashion fit.
(I.ii.172–77)

Edmund claims to be free to fashion himself as he sees fit, to be good or evil by choice, to ignore "the plague of custom" and the "curiosity of nations" (I.ii.3.4), and to make "Edmund the base / . . . top th' legitimate" (I.ii.20–21). In the end, however, both Sidney and Shakespeare show those claims to be equally illusory. Edmund ultimately goes to his death because he acts as he condemns others for doing. When challenged by the disguised Edgar, he accepts because "thy outside looks so fair and warlike, / And thy . . . tongue some say of breeding breaths" (V.iii.143–44); when he falls, Goneril mocks his departure from his principles: "Thou art not vanquished, / But cozened and beguiled" (V.iii.154–55). Like Plexirtus, Edmund has been a master at creating false appearances and using cunning words to make them real; the outlawed Edgar — legally a nonperson, his "name . . . lost, / By treason's tooth" (V.ii.121–22) — defeats him by using his own weapons against him. Among other things, Shakespeare's changed ending makes Edmund's assertion of freedom fail. When Edmund tries to choose goodness, he cannot. Dying, "pant[ing] for life," he proclaims, "Some good I mean to do, / Despite of my own nature" (V.iii.244–45), and urges Albany to send quickly so that he might save the lives of Lear and Cordelia. But Edmund, while he may be free to exercise his nature in doing evil, is not free to choose to be good. Shakespeare makes Lear enter almost immediately, carrying the dead Cordelia in his arms, to pronounce the failure of Edmund's attempt at conversion, at acting against his own nature.[5]

Shakespeare's other major change lies in his transformation of Leonatus, the "good" brother who yet seems impotent in the face of his brother's evil, into Edgar. Unlike the "ever-noble" (282) Leonatus, who sinks only so low as to become "a private soldier in a country hereby" who is about "to be greatly advanced for some noble pieces of service which he did" (278) when he comes to his father's aid, Edgar transforms himself into "the basest and most poorest shape, / That ever penury, in contempt of man, / Brought near to beast" (II.ii.7–9). In this shape, however, he becomes for Lear a mirror in which Lear can better see himself. When Edgar enters as Poor Tom, followed by "the foul fiend" (III.iv.45), Lear immediately seizes upon him: "Didst thou give all to thy daughters? And art thou come to this?" (III.iv.48–49). When Kent suggests that Poor Tom "hath no daughters" (III.iv.67), Lear rejects the idea as a violation of the natural order:

> Death, traitor! Nothing could have subdued nature
> To such a lowness but his unkind daughters.
> Is it the fashion that discarded fathers
> Should have thus little mercy on their flesh?
> Judicious punishment — 'twas this flesh begot
> Those pelican daughters.
>
> (III.iv.68–73)

Tom, naked except for his blanket, becomes for Lear the emblem of all mankind: "Is man no more than this? Consider him well. Thou ow'st the

worm no silk, the sheep no wool, the cat no perfume. Ha! here's three
on's are sophisticated. Thou art the thing itself; unaccommodated man
is no more but such a poor, bare, forked animal as thou art" (III.iv.97–
102). As an image, a Sidneyan "speaking picture," Tom is ambiguous – he
is not the "thing itself," but the thing disguised, the thing that makes
others think of other things. As Gloucester comments, when, after his
blinding, Tom is brought to lead him,

> I' the last night's storm, I such a fellow saw,
> Which made me think a man a worm. My son
> Came then into my mind, and yet my mind
> Was then scarce friends with him.
>   (IV.i.32–35)

Yet there is finally a sense that Edgar's disguise is also the means of his
salvation. When Gloucester addresses him as "thou whom the heavens'
plagues / Have humbled to all strokes," and prays that the "Heavens, deal
so still," that they "let the superfluous and lust-dieted man, / That slaves
your ordinance, that will not see / Because he does not feel, feel your
pow'r quickly" (IV.i.64–69), one cannot help feeling that as Poor Tom Edgar
has learned to see because he has been forced to feel. The contrast between
father and son is explicit, since Gloucester has just reflected on his own
lack of vision, in response to the Old Man's offer of aid because Gloucester
"cannot see . . . [his] way":

> I have no way, and therefore want no eyes;
> I stumbled when I saw. Full oft 'tis seen
> Our means secure us, and our mere defects
> Prove our commodities.
>   (IV.i.18–24)

Like Kent, who had earlier insisted that "Nothing almost sees miracles /
But misery" (II.ii.161–62), Edgar's misery teaches him how to "feel" not
just for those to whom we are linked by blood but for those to whom we
are linked by the common bond of humanity. He has become, as he tells
Gloucester, one "Who, by the art of known and feeling sorrows, / Am
pregnant to good pity" (IV.vi.218–19).

If Lear is correct in his analysis of the way this world goes ("Thou hast
seen a farmer's dog bark at a beggar? . . . And the creature run from the
cur. There thou mightst behold the great image of authority – a dog's
obeyed in office" [IV.vi.152–56]), Edgar learns the necessity never understood by Leonatus of keeping dogs out of office.[6] When Oswald tries to
kill Gloucester, Edgar dispatches him as "A serviceable villain, / As duteous
to the vices of thy mistress / As badness would desire" (IV.vi.248–50).

When Goneril and Edmund practice against the life of Albany, it is Edgar
who warns the Duke, Edgar who challenges Edmund, and Edgar who kills
Edmund in the name of justice:

> The gods are just, and of our pleasant vices
> Make instruments to plague us.
> The dark and vicious place where thee he got
> Cost him his eyes.
>
> (V.ii.171–74)

Edmund's "pleasant vices" against Edgar ultimately turn Edgar into the
instrument that plagues him. More than that, though, they make Edgar
an instrument fit to obey Albany's final command to "Rule in this realm,
and the gored state sustain" (V.iii.321). Edmund's casual viciousness transforms Edgar into one willing to attempt to "tame these vile offences" and
prevent "humanity" from preying upon itself "Like monsters of the deep."

Was Shakespeare influenced by Sidney? He was, in the sense that in
writing this essay I have been influenced by the term "influence" with its
resonances; he was not, in the sense that I have felt uncomfortable with
the term "influence" and its implied passivity on the part of the later
writer. Sidney's text offered a story to which Shakespeare was drawn and,
I suggest, by which he was troubled. Where Sidney sees evil as something
which, given human weakness, is inescapable and must be endured until
it providentially collapses under its own weight, Shakespeare presents
Edgar and ultimately Albany as attempting to halt and even to undo that
destruction caused by Goneril, Regan, Cornwall, and Edmund. Though
their success may be limited, Edgar and Albany are still there to attempt
to "sustain" the "gored state" at the end of the play. To say that Shakespeare was influenced by Sidney is either to generalize the term to the
point of destruction or to falsify the relation of their two texts. Was Shakespeare intertextual with Sidney then? To say that he was is to divert our
attention from the real similarity, a similarity of experience, including
belief, to a merely contingent one. When Shakespeare writes "Blow, winds,
and crack your cheeks" he perhaps draws on a truth he learned while
shivering in wintry gusts off the Thames, but he is not intertextual with
it or with any instance of it. One could say that Shakespeare is intertextual
with Sidney only if one departs from the priority given to the text so as
to add agency to intertextuality. Shakespeare does not merely recall Sidney's
text, he uses it deliberately, recalling it to challenge some of the truths it
presents as central to human existence. In short, he alludes to it in order
to remake it.[7] Shakespeare's remaking of Sidney is not, however, a Bloomian
competition between the poet and his forefather because the allusion is
a rhetorical convenience and not the central issue, which is the content.

Shakespeare is not remaking Sidney's text, he is clarifying what they both took to be fundamental truths. There is nothing in Sidney's poetics that precludes one text from existing in a complementary relationship to another since all texts are merely means to the discovery of the "*idea* or fore-conceit" that lies behind them. Like some of the extended essays that Erasmus writes as he transforms an adage set in one cultural matrix into a reflection upon life within a very different one, texts can exist in order to provide opportunities for commentary not upon other texts but upon the "golden world" that poetic creation discovers.

III

> Ripeness is all.
> *Lear* V.ii.11

Although Spenser's version of the story of Lear was not the only one available to Shakespeare — Holinshed and *The Mirror for Magistrates* also tell basically the same story — it is usually accepted as one of Shakespeare's sources, and only in *The Faerie Queene* does Cordelia commit suicide by hanging herself.[8] Once again, however, I wish to look at it not simply as a source but also as an occasion for "remaking" on Shakespeare's part. The most obvious difference between Shakespeare's history and those he might have used in constructing it is that in all of the other versions, the outcome of the battle is that summed up by Spenser:

> And after all an army strong she leau'd,
> To war on those, which had him of his realme bereau'd.

> So to his crowne she him restor'd againe,
>   In which he dyde, made ripe for death by eld,
>   And after wild, it should to her remaine:
>   Who peaceably the same long time did weld:
>   And all mens harts in dew obedience held:
>   Till that her sisters children, woxen strong
>   Through proud ambition, against her rebeld,
>   And ouercommen kept in prison long,
>   Till wearie of that wretched life, her selfe she hong.
>   (*Faerie Queene* II.x.31–32)

As every study of Shakespeare's use of other versions of the story recognizes, only in Shakespeare does Cordelia's army lose; only in Shakespeare is the captive Cordelia murdered.

Furthermore, Shakespeare fairly clearly plays off the contrary expectations of his audience in doing so.[9] Edgar and Gloucester enter; Edgar, who has not yet identified himself to his father, deposits him under a tree, and tells him to "Pray that the right may thrive," adding the promise of a reunion to come: "If ever I return to you again, / I'll bring you comfort" (V.ii.2–4). No sooner do we begin to anticipate a happy ending than, after an "alarum and retreat within," Edgar returns:

> Away, old man! Give me thy hand. Away!
> King Lear hath lost, he and his daughter ta'en.
> Give me thy hand. Come on.
>
> (V.ii.5–7)

Gloucester's immediate response is despair ("No further, sir. A man may rot even here" [V.ii.8]), but, since history is still on the side of "the right," an audience may not yet be too concerned. Even when Edmund sends a captain off to the prison with a note, warning him that "To be tender-minded / Does not become a sword" (V.ii.31–32), the prospect of our desired ending is not yet lost, especially when Albany arrests Edmund and Goneril "on capital treason" and Regan begins to experience the sickness worked on her by Goneril's "medicine" (V.ii.73–96).

With Edmund's defeat at Edgar's hands, a rescue seems even more inevitable until a gentleman enters with a "bloody knife," crying for help, exclaiming, "'Tis hot, it smokes. / It came even from the heart of – O, she's dead" (V.ii.224–25). With Albany, we have a pressing need to know, "Who dead? Speak, man" (V.ii.226). But on hearing that it is Goneril, we seem to have come closer to our desired port, especially after we learn that Regan is also dead. All of the evil characters seem to be meeting their just ends, and like Albany we may feel that "This judgment of the heavens, that makes us tremble, / Touches us not with pity" (V.ii.232–33). When Edmund suddenly remembers his commission for the life of Lear and Cordelia, it would appear that the final obstacle to a poetically "just" ending has been removed. As Albany and Edgar send a messenger to Edmund's captain to prevent the executions, we hear how "history" was to be enacted:

> He hath commission from thy wife and me
> To hang Cordelia in the prison and
> To lay the blame upon her own despair
> That she fordid herself.
>
> (V.ii253–56)

No sooner does disaster seem averted, however, than Lear enters, with Cordelia in his arms, howling: "She's gone forever. / I know when one is dead, and when one lives. / She's dead as earth" (V.ii.260–62).

The horror of this death seems to be made all the more intolerable by its incomprehensibility. History tells us Cordelia lived, only to kill herself in despair years later. Once again, however, Shakespeare appears to be

about to change directions when, in the midst of a chorus of lamentation
("Is this the promised end?" / "Or image of that horror?"), Lear again
cries out,

> This feather stirs; she lives! If it be so,
> It is a chance which does redeem all sorrows
> That ever I have felt.
>
> (V.ii.266–68)

Yet once again Shakespeare foils our expectations: Lear is wrong, Cordelia is dead, and sorrow is not to be redeemed by Cordelia's return from
the dead any more than Cordelia is to be the one who "redeems Nature
from the general curse / Which twain have brought her to" (IV.vi.202–3).

Despite Dr. Johnson's objections to the play's lack of poetic justice,
Shakespeare's ending appears to reflect the play's rejection of suicide —
Cordelia's eventual "fate" according to the histories — more than anything
else. Edgar's efforts for most of the last part of the play are directed toward curing his father's suicidal despair (IV.vi.33–34, 49–80, 213–16; V.ii.8–
11; V.iii.189–200), and Goneril's "desperate" (V.iii.162) death fills the Gentleman who reports it with horror and makes Albany "tremble," though not
with "pity" (V.iii.232, 233). It is not the fact of death that is horrible in
the play, but the manner of it. As the conversation between Lear and
Gloucester on the heath makes clear, it is not just Lear's hand that "smells
of mortality"; rather, "this great world / Shall so wear out to naught"
(IV.vi.132, 133–34). Although life may be precious ("O our lives' sweetness,
/ That we the pain of death would hourly die / Rather than die at once!"
[V.iii.185–87]), death itself can also be a release from life's tortures:

> Vex not his ghost. O let him pass! He hates him
> That would upon the rack of this tough world
> Stretch him out longer.
>
> (V.iii.314–16)

Cordelia's murder "prevents" the suicide to which history would lead her.
If Lear is "made ripe for death by eld" in Spenser's account, Cordelia is
already "ripe" in Shakespeare's:

> Patience and sorrow strove
> Who should express her goodliest. You have seen
> Sunshine and rain at one — her smiles and tears
> Were like, a better way. Those happy smilets
> That played on her ripe lip seemed not to know
> What guests were in her eyes, which parted thence
> As pearls from diamonds dropped.
>
> (IV.ii.16–22)

If "Ripeness is all" (V.ii.11), Cordelia is complete. Like Gloucester, who
learns that "Men must endure / Their going hence, even as their coming
hither" (V.ii.9–10), the play tries to teach us that Cordelia's death is preferable to the one history had in store for her.

In doing so, I suggest, Shakespeare is showing himself an apt student
of *The Faerie Queene*'s history lessons. In Books II and III, Spenser offers
us three versions of history. In the chamber of memory in the House of
Alma, Guyon and Arthur are introduced to an old man "of infinite remem-
braunce" who has recorded all "things foregone through many ages" in
his "immortal scrine, / Where they for euer incorrupted dweld" (II.ix.56).
Arthur and Guyon "chance" to discover the histories of their native lands,
which each eagerly reads. In *Briton moniments,* a chronicle of Britain
from its founding to the reign of Uther Pendragon, Arthur sees history
(from the point of view of the legend of Temperance) as one long unbroken record of human intemperance. Into this world the incarnate Christ
comes; from it he goes, after having "purge[d] away the guilt of sinfull
crime" from "wretched *Adams* line" (II.x.50), but subsequent history reveals no noticeable change in human behavior. Man is as intemperate as
ever he was in the remainder of the history Arthur reads. Guyon, in contrast, reads a history entitled "*Antiquitie* of *Faerie* lond" that shows an
unbroken string of successions and the successful building and defense
of Cleopolis, the city of glory, from the creation of Elfe and Fay by Pro-
metheus in the Gardens of Adonis to the reign of Gloriana in the poem's
present. History, *sub specie aeternitatis,* appears as an almost uneventful
progress toward the earthly equivalent ("for earthly frame, / The fairest
peece, that eye beholden can" [I.x.59]) of the New Jerusalem Redcrosse
was shown in Book I. What links the two histories, otherwise so contrasting, is a third, told Britomart by an inspired Merlin in Book III, who pro-
phesies from her present to what seems to be the Elizabethan "now." As
in Arthur's chronicle, wrath, lust, murder, betrayal, and pride loom large;
as in Guyon's history, all that happens is contained within what is now
explicitly "the streight course of heauenly destiny, / Led with eternall
prouidence . . . / . . . to bring his will to pas" (III.iii.24).

Britomart conveys her understanding of history both to Paridell, a de-
scendant of Paris, who sees history only as a record of "mans wretched
state" (III.ix.39), as emblematized by the fall of Troy, and to Scudamour,
for whom the loss of his bride is a sign that God has deserted mankind.
Britomart merely reminds Paridell of the second flourishing of Troy in
Rome and of the third that is to come in "*Troynouant* . . . that with the
waues / Of wealthy *Thamis* washed is along" (III.ix.44). Scudamour receives a more complex response when she finds him "groueling" on the
ground and sobbing out a "bitter" complaint:

> O soueraigne Lord that sit'st on hye,
> And raignst in blis emongst thy blessed Saintes,
> How suffrest thou such shamefull cruelty,
> So long vnwreaked of thine enimy?
> Or hast thou, Lord, of good mens cause no heed?
> Or doth thy iustice sleepe, and silent ly?
> What booteth then the good and righteous deed,
> If goodnesse find no grace, nor righteousness no meed?
>
> (III.xi.9)

Scudamour has been thrown into a state of despair, but for Britomart, if history is providential and God's grace has shaped its design and His justice its end, partial human interpretations are irrelevant; history answers instead to the rule of faith:

> Ah gentle knight, whose deepe conceiued griefe
>   Well seemes t'exceede the powre of patience,
>   Yet if that heauenly grace some good reliefe
>   You send, submit you to high prouidence,
>   And euer in your noble heart prepense,
>   That all the sorrow in the world is lesse,
>   Then virtues might and values confidence,
>   For who nill bide the burden of distresse,
> Must not here thinke to liue: for life is wretchednesse.
>
> (III.xi.14)

From this perspective, Lear's prayer on the heath ("Take physic, pomp; / Expose thyself to feel what wretches feel, / That thou mayest shake the superflux to them / And show the heavens more just" [III.iv.33–36]) belongs to the same world of measurement by which he has just concluded that Goneril loved him more than Regan: "Thy fifty yet doth double five-and-twenty, / And thou art twice her love" (II.iv.254–55), the world in which he had still earlier concluded that Cordelia did not love him at all. Yet what ultimately gives meaning to the world for Lear is not visible, quantifiable signs of love but the miracle that he "sees" when Cordelia kneels to ask his blessing and tells him that she has "no cause" not to love him (IV.vii.57–75). It is this moment that he remembers when Edmund orders Lear and Cordelia taken off to prison after their defeat in battle:

> Come, let's away to prison.
> We two alone will sing like birds i'th'cage.
> When thou dost ask me blessing, I'll kneel down
> And ask of thee forgiveness.

Spenser can allow Cordelia to commit suicide because he is going to provide alternate views of history that will render suicide an inadequate and unnecessary response to the world; Shakespeare, to the extent that he has internalized that "Spenserian" perspective, needs to preserve Cordelia from the "self-slaughter" against which Hamlet claimed "the Everlasting had . . . fixed / His canon" (I.ii.131–32). It is appropriate that Goneril, one of the leaders of the "ranks of death," kill herself. Trusting only in herself, she is made "desperate" (V.iii.162) by exposure; accepting no laws but her own, she will not be governed by the canons of others (V.iii.159–62). Her death, for Albany, finally manifests nothing more nor less than "the judgment of the heavens, that makes us tremble" though it "Touches us not with pity" (V.iii.232–33). From the beginning of the play, however, Cordelia has been presented as one who lives within "bonds," who sees life as a contract offered universally, and who is bound to it and by it. For Shakespeare to have followed Spenser in this detail would have been to depart from the general argument of Spenser's poem; by "correcting" Spenser's history, Shakespeare affirms the truth that both he and Spenser believed lies at the heart of life's mystery. His apparent cavalier departure from history is thus an affirmation of what he and most of his contemporaries would have believed to be the ultimate meaning of history. Once again, then, I would argue that what we see is neither a Shakespeare influenced by Spenser nor a *King Lear* intertextual with *The Faerie Queene*. Rather, we see Shakespeare engaging in Sidneyan imitation by remaking the fictive worlds of his predecessors so that they better express the truths presumed to underlie those worlds.

IV. THE INFLUENCE OF ANXIETY

We live in a critically anxious world, and recent theoretical concerns have made it even more so. But, to paraphrase John Donne's dictum in "Loves growth," criticism "sometimes would contemplate, sometimes do." Rather than worry whether my practice can be theoretically justified, I prefer to worry about whether theories can be practically justified. A crucial part of the practical justification for a historical critic like me comes from historical practice: what does what we may assume about Shakespeare's practice as a reader tell us about his practice as a writer and about the texts he produced. And what theory of ours will legitimate inclusion of his practices — practices that, if we want to avoid what I earlier called anachronism, precede our own — without simply seeming archaic?

Shakespeare's culture would have familiarized him with the assumption that a writer creates by taking the raw materials left him by his predecessors and transforming them into images that represent the "*idea* or fore-conceit" he wishes to present through his work. By investigating how he might have responded to two texts he is universally assumed to have read, we may come closer to a picture of Shakespeare as a "maker" that is more consistent with the poetics of the sixteenth century than with those of the nineteenth or twentieth century. My reading of all three poets is based upon a reading of what I believe are crucial elements of their cultural matrix, elements that could permit E.K. to gloss Colin's emblem ("La mort ny mord") to the *Nouember* eclogue of Spenser's *Shepheardes Calendar* in ways that his audience presumably did not find irrelevant:

For although by course of nature we be borne to dye, and being ripened with age, as with a timely haruest, we must be gathered in time, or els of our selues we fall like rotted ripe fruit fro the tree: yet death is not to be counted for euil, nor (as the Poete sayd a little before) as doome of ill desert. For though the trespasse of the first man brought death into the world, as the guerdon of sinne, yet being ouercome by the death of one, that dyed for al, it is now made (as Chaucer sayth) the grene path way to lyfe. So that it agreeth well with that was sayd, that Death byteth not (this is) hurteth not at all. (*Nouember,* "Glosse," lines 292–301)

But, of course, that Spenser's audience might have found these comments an applicable gloss on Spenser's Lear, who was "made ripe for death," does not mean that Shakespeare did or that we must.

To paraphrase Michael Baxandall, this essay does not urge "causal explanation" as the only course for literary criticism. It seems to me absurd to say that there is a proper way to read literature. Rather, the essay supposes that one of a number of unforced and unavoidable ways in which one can think of literature is as the product of purposeful activity, and therefore caused. Once we start inferring causes and intention in a literary work we are doing something that is obviously very precarious, and the reflective inferrer is likely to worry about the status of his or her inferences (Baxandall vi). Nonetheless, we all of us, every day, make inferences about belief, meaning, and intention when we speak with our family and friends, when we shop or vote or mark student papers or act as jurors in a law court. To expect our literary studies to have more certainty than we expect as spouses or jurors is to subscribe to an ideal of scientism that surely is as out of date in our skeptical times as it was unknown in Shakespeare's. Worry though I may about the status of my inferences, no worry will stop me for a moment from assuming what Baxandall calls "purposefulness — or intent or, as it were 'intentiveness'" (41) in both the writers and the works about which I have written. What I do not worry about is generating a universal theory of what literature is or how it works. I agree with many New Historicists at least in being concerned with "local knowledge," trying to recover a particular theory whose virtue is chiefly that it is the theory that shaped the historically specific mind-set imputable to Sidney, Spenser, and Shakespeare. While historical critics exist, this is ipso facto a useful and satisfying thing to do; and it is also economical in that the farther such a theory can take us, the more questions it can answer, the less we need to import more elaborate theories shaped by other, later histories. Thus I have tried to show that to impose "influence" and "intertextuality" upon three Renaissance works is unnecessary to describe the relationship among them, and misleading in the "spin" it gives to that relationship. In our present anxious theoretical climate, perhaps these reasons are reason enough.[10]

NOTES

1   For the "sources" upon which Shakespeare drew in the composition of *King Lear,* see Kenneth Muir's introduction to his New Arden edition of the play (xxi–xliii and 221–53), as well as Geoffrey Bullough, ed., *Narrative and Dramatic Sources of Shakespeare* (7:269–420). Throughout this paper, I cite the text of *King Lear* from Alfred Harbage's edition. Rather than limit my discussion of passages of interest to Shakespeare to the first brief telling of the story of the Paphlagonian king and his two sons, I have followed the story so far as Sidney treats it because I think Shakespeare would have seen it as one of the central motifs of the *Arcadia.* It is standard to see both Sidney's revised *Arcadia* and Spenser's version of the story of King Leyr in Book II of *The Faerie Queene* as "sources" for *King Lear.* My discussion will deal more extensively with their original contexts than is usual. I apologize in advance both to those sufficiently familiar with these texts not to require an extensive retelling of them and to those not sufficiently interested in them to desire such a retelling. My hope, however, is that through the details we may come to some general conclusions about the nature of the process of poetic composition—at least as it was believed to take place in the English Renaissance.

2   See also David Quint, *Origin and Originality in Renaissance Literature: Versions of the Source.* For the standard classical and Renaissance rhetorical treatments of discovery—*inventio*—see Wilbur Samuel Howell, *Logic and Rhetoric in England, 1500–1700.*

3   I have discussed Sidney's *Defense* in my *Sir Philip Sidney and the Poetics of Protestantism* and my forthcoming "'Unelected Vocation': Sir Philip Sidney's Literary Career."

4   Piero Bianconi, *The Complete Paintings of Brueghel,* plate X. The painting is currently in the Prado Museum (Madrid).

5   Cf. Phillip DuPlessis Mornay, *A Woorke concerning the trewnesse of the Christian Religion,* "Begunne to be translated into English by Sir *Philip Sidney* Knight, and at his request finished by *Arthur Golding*" (London, 1587): "We be free to followe our owne Nature, and our Nature is becomme euill through sinne. O wretched freedome, which bringeth vs vnder such bondage! And a fore this nature of ours, we can neither shun it nor drive it from vs:

for we be bondslaues to it, and to sinne, and there behoueth a stronger than ourselves to rid vs thereof. Therefore let vs pray God to bring the freedome of our wills in bondage to his will, and free our souls from this hard and damnable kind of freedome" (224).

6 For an argument on the central political importance in the play of the theme of the individual's responsibility to resist immoral princes, see Richard Strier, "Faithful Servants: Shakespeare's Praise of Disobedience" 104–33.

7 I have been influenced by Robert Alter's distinction between allusion and intertextuality: "Whereas allusion implies a writer's active, purposeful use of antecedent texts, intertextuality is something that can be talked about when two or more texts are set side by side . . . without regard to authorial intention" (112). It is also worth recalling Alter's dictum here that "in one way or another . . . all writers are forced to enter into a dialogue or debate with their predecessors, recycling bits and pieces of earlier texts, giving them a fresh application, a nuance of redefinition, a radically new meaning, a different function, an unanticipated elaboration" (114).

8 The old *King Leir* play (probably performed in the early 1590s and published in 1605 — possibly in response to Shakespeare's play) differs substantially both from the "historical" versions of the story and from Shakespeare's *King Lear.* Although it may have been the most important memory of the story for the nonliterate members of the audience (assuming any member of an audience can remember a play seen perhaps a decade earlier at all, let alone with any degree of clarity), its simplistic interpretation of Lear's character and its presentation of the society in which the action occurs mark it as a work that had little to contribute to the *idea* (as opposed to the plot) of Shakespeare's play.

9 I do not assume a familiarity with any particular version of the story, merely a knowledge that "history" tells a story with an immediately happy ending in which the French army defeats the English, Lear is reinstated to the kingship, and Cordelia is established as his successor. I assume that the literate members of the audience would have known as well what the *Leir* play does not deal with — that after a period of rule, Cordelia's nephews rebel against her, defeat her in battle, and imprison her, leading, ultimately, to her suicide. In the *Mirror for Magistrates,* Cordila's ghost laments that dying "a damned creature like" she has played the fool, for "Farre greater follye is it for to kill, / Themselves dispayring, then is any ill," since as a suicide she, a "damned wretch," sent her soul to hell (Bullough 7:332). The chronicles and Spenser leave the reader to draw his or her own conclusions, if any, about the fate of suicides' souls.

10 I would, in any case, endorse the position — asserted, not theorized — of Umberto Eco, *Postscript to The Name of the Rose* (8, 11): "The writer (or painter or sculptor or composer) always knows what he is doing and how much it costs him. He knows he has to solve a problem. Perhaps the original data are obscure, pulsive, obsessive, no more than a yearning or a memory. But then the problem is solved at the writer's desk as he interrogates the material on which he is working — material that reveals natural laws of its own, but at the same time contains the recollection of the culture with which it is loaded (the echo of intertextuality)."

270 ANDREW D. WEINER

WORKS CITED

Alter, Robert. *The Pleasures of Reading in an Ideological Age*. New York: Simon and Schuster, 1989.

Barthes, Roland. "From Work to Text." In *Textual Strategies: Perspectives in Post-Structuralist Criticism,* ed. Josué V. Harari. Ithaca: Cornell UP, 1979.

Baxandall, Michael. *Patterns of Intention: On the Historical Explanation of Pictures*. New Haven: Yale UP, 1985.

Bianconi, Piero. *The Complete Paintings of Brueghel*. New York: Abrams, 1967.

Bullough, Geoffrey, ed. *Narrative and Dramatic Sources of Shakespeare*. New York: Columbia UP, 1973.

Donne, John. *The Complete Poetry of John Donne*. Ed. John T. Shawcross. Garden City, New York: Anchor Books, 1969.

DuPlessis Mornay, Philip. *A Woorke concerning the trewnesse of the Christian Religion*. Trans. Sir Philip Sidney and Arthur Golding. London, 1587.

Eco, Umberto. *Postscript to The Name of the Rose*. Trans. William Weaver. New York: Harcourt Brace Jovanovich, 1984.

Greene, Thomas, *The Light in Troy: Imitation and Discovery in Renaissance Poetry*. New Haven: Yale UP, 1982.

Howell, Wilbur Samuel. *Logic and Rhetoric in England, 1500–1700*. Princeton: Princeton UP, 1956.

Peterson, Richard S. *Imitation and Praise in the Poems of Ben Jonson*. New Haven: Yale UP, 1982.

Quint, David. *Origin and Originality in Renaissance Literature: Versions of the Source*. New Haven: Yale UP, 1983.

Shakespeare, William. *King Lear*. Ed. Alfred Harbage. In *The Complete Works,* ed. Alfred Harbage. Baltimore: Penguin Books, 1969.

Shakespeare, William. *King Lear*. Ed. Kenneth Muir. Cambridge: Harvard UP, 1959.

Sidney, Sir Philip. *The Countess of Pembroke's Arcadia*. Ed. Maurice Evans. New York: Penguin Books, 1977.

Sidney, Sir Philip. *The Defense of Poetry*. In *Miscellaneous Prose,* ed. Katherine Duncan-Jones and Jan van Dorsten. Oxford: Clarendon, 1973.

Spenser, Edmund. *The Faerie Queene*. Ed. A. C. Hamilton. New York: Longman, 1977.

Spenser, Edmund. *The Shepheardes Calendar*. In *The Yale Edition of the Shorter Poems of Edmund Spenser,* ed. William A. Oram et al. New Haven: Yale UP, 1989.

Strier, Richard. "Faithful Servants: Shakespeare's Praise of Disobedience." In *The Historical Renaissance: New Essays on Tudor and Stuart Literature and Culture*, ed. Heather Dubrow and Richard Strier. Chicago: U of Chicago P, 1988

Weiner, Andrew D. *Sir Philip Sidney and the Poetics of Protestantism*. Minneapolis: U of Minnesota P, 1978.

CHAPTER 11

The Call of Eurydice:
Mourning and Intertextuality
in Margaret Fuller's Writing

JEFFREY STEELE

Sealed were my fountains and my heart-beats still. I felt that I had been that beauteous tree, but now only was — what — I knew not; yet I was, and the voices of men said, It is dead; cast it forth and plant another in the costly vase. A mystic shudder of pale joy then separated me from my former abode.

"The Magnolia of Lake Pontchartrain"

During the winter of 1840–41, Margaret Fuller entered a period of isolation and transformation that she imagined as a kind of death-in-life. Without any vestiges of recognizable identity, she had become distanced from her culture with its conventions of true womanhood. In her essay "The Magnolia of Lake Pontchartrain," Fuller alluded to her condition through the figure of a "beauteous tree" that had become dormant, a being that men rejected because they considered it "dead." But, in Fuller's fable, this moment of male rejection also marked the beginning of a new "abode," a changed sense of dwelling. Measuring the transformation of the self through figures of death and rebirth, she defined a moment of death that led effortlessly to a renewed being, standing on the margins of the dominant culture. The pain of rejection, as well as awareness of loss, simply vanishes in the face of a momentous personal metamorphosis that is identified, in the course of the essay, with a mystical feminism.

But Fuller's transformation into a writer who could define a new "abode" for herself was not a painless process. Behind the fabulous change portrayed in "The Magnolia of Lake Pontchartrain" lay a difficult shift in orientation from identity as a father's daughter, molded in his image, to

271

identity as a woman who could both challenge the authority of the Father and recover an enabling connection with what Fuller calls the "Mothers" (304). "The divine birds [of the self] need to be brooded into life and song by mothers," she was later to write in *Woman in the Nineteenth Century* (157), in a celebration of maternal power that depended upon diminishing the exclusive authority of the Father. Given the fact that Fuller's own father died prior to her assertion of a feminism that challenged paternal authority, one is intrigued by the possibility that her growing sense of power was linked to the process of mourning.

This supposition is strengthened by the recognition that, in the nineteenth century, images of selfhood were often mediated through representations of mourning, especially mourning for a dead father. The most famous examples of this process involve male writers who link assertions of independence with images of the dead. In this regard, Ralph Waldo Emerson's famous disavowal of mourning at the beginning of *Nature* confirms the very relationship that it seems to banish. "Our age is retrospective," he complains; "It builds the sepulchres of the fathers" (7). But the paradox of Emerson's position is that "it buries and commemorates in the same act, at once disposing of the fathers and erecting a monument to their vanquished power" (Sundquist 91–92). The Father's power, seemingly negated, returns to haunt the present under the guise of a refusal to mourn. In other terms, an image of the mourning process allows Emerson to absorb the power of the absent "fathers," at the same time that he celebrates his detachment from them — a classic oedipal move that constitutes his sense of personal autonomy.

During the American Renaissance, issues of authority and power, which are always tied to parent-child relations, were often inseparable from the complicated feelings engendered by the deaths of fathers. Both the self-image and the psychology of many writers during this period were shaped by their intimacy with death; for, frequently, the most profound emotional events of their childhoods had been acts of mourning. In the nineteenth century, death was a frequent visitor, and it was the rare individual who reached maturity without having experienced at least one process of grief. While Emerson simulated an escape from mourning, many of his contemporaries defined their creative power as an explicit relationship to the dead. Both Hawthorne and Melville, for example, lost their fathers during adolescence or earlier; and it should not surprise us that both *The House of the Seven Gables* and *Pierre* dwell upon the thanatoptic aspects of imaginative power, as artist figures learn to wrestle with and subdue the spirits of dead father figures.

Although it does not directly address the question of mourning, Harold Bloom's analysis of "the anxiety of influence" can be read as a paradigm of the male writer's relations with the dead. In Bloom's model, Oedipus and Laius struggle at the crossroads in a contest that leads eventually to the son's usurpation of the father's power (11). But what about the female writer, who was excluded from the patriarchal role? Unable to play the part of Oedipus, she was not freed from mourning or from the necessity of finding narratives that defined her relationship to the dead. In the case of Margaret Fuller, as we shall see, the myth of Oedipus held few attractions. But another classical tale, the narrative of Orpheus and Eurydice, evoked a model of mourning and personal transformation that provided an equivalent paradigm of being.

While the theories of Harold Bloom and others suggest the important relationship for the male writer between influence and mourning, few scholars have questioned whether analogous psychological connections existed for women as well. Because men and women in the nineteenth century occupied different positions in the economy of mourning, they tended to use representations of mourning in different ways. The mourning process, with its carefully prescribed rituals, intertextualizes grief. But in America, where "the burden of mourning fell primarily upon women" (Pike 310), men were more able to distance themselves from communal pressures by developing narratives of personal influence. While "the female mourner" was expected to act "as a public symbol of restrained grief" (Tolchin xii), men could often mystify their social enmeshment by employing images of mourning to mediate relations of influence with a clearly identifiable past, often equated with the absent Father. Male narratives of personal development repressed the intertexts circumscribing grief in favor of images of independence.

As Nancy Chodorow and others have shown, women have usually found themselves less able to imagine privileged positions in such oedipal transfers of power.[1] More enmeshed in socially defined networks, they are less attracted to *individualistic* paradigms of creative development. In the nineteenth century, women's lives were so overdetermined that it became difficult at times for them to identify individual antecedents. This was especially true in the case of mourning. Instead of promising a gateway to independence, the act of mourning replicated patterns of dependence and filiation that filtered through all aspects of female existence. Less able to escape from the home, where deathbeds were located, into a larger circle of nonfamilial concerns, nineteenth-century women found their lives and self-images inextricably involved with the mourning process.

Unlike her male counterpart, the female mourner was unable to repress burdensome recognition of her intertextuality. Instead, she found her grief textualized by cultural demands in ways that male grief was not. Positioned within a complicated fabric of social signification, a pattern she did not control, the grieving woman was transformed into a powerful signifier whose actions were defined by collective cultural expectations. Popular mourning rituals of decorum, dress, and artistic expression fell upon her, for her gestures of grief were considered culturally significant.[2] While "the question of men and how they mourned is little mentioned in the literature of the period," women observed a complicated set of "mourning rituals" that were "symbolic of [their] place in the world" (Pike 310, 312). Even during periods of mourning, male fashion remained relatively continuous; the male mourner expressed his grief with a black tie or a weed in his hat. But the female mourner followed an elaborate code of dress and seclusion that disrupted her life by turning her clothing and demeanor into public symbols.[3] This tendency crested in the 1850s and 1860s, when elaborate mourning rituals and dress were popularized by periodicals such as *Godey's Lady's Book* (Taylor 46).

During the first half of the nineteenth century, the iconography of mourning was a standard part of women's social indoctrination. In numerous finishing schools, girls were instructed in the composition of mourning pictures and samplers — training that imprinted the image of the female mourner as the natural signifier of grief. One widespread emblem was modeled upon an engraving by James Akin and William Farrison, Jr., entitled "America Lamenting Her Loss at the Tomb of General Washington" (Ring 160). Beneath a weeping willow, a grieving woman leans against a pyramid emblazoned with the bust of Washington.[4] Both the drapery and posture of the female mourner suggest grief but also total submission to an absent (yet omnipresent) male authority. Duplicated on numerous samplers, this popular icon represented a female passivity conjoined with a posture of grief and worship. It evoked images of woman's emotionality at the same time that it ornamentalized her by subordinating her to a rigidly codified system of gestures. Needless to say, male figures were rarely found in such abandoned poses in nineteenth-century prints and needlework patterns. When men are present, they are usually standing, often lending emotional support to women or children (Ring 188).

As a result of her different position within the economy of mourning, the nineteenth-century woman writer had a more difficult task as she attempted to define the sources of creative power. Since her sense of artistic persona was inextricably intertwined with collective forms of identity, affirmations of totally autonomous selfhood were an impossibility. But equally difficult was identification with paradigms of influence that threatened to silence her by subordinating her to a paternal economy of desire. Valued more as an evocative signifier than as a creative agent, the woman writer thus found that the traditional elegy held fewer attractions for her as a genre than for her male contemporaries. For representations of mourning did not produce the euphoria often found at the conclusion of male elegies. According to Celeste Schenck, the triumphant quality of the male elegy results from its staging of a scene of "initiation" in which the "poet separates himself from the forebear and simultaneously prepares to take his place" (15). Emphasizing oedipal "competition, separation, and individuation" (20), such works repress awareness of the self's intertextuality in favor of models of influence. In contrast, female elegies constitute a different pattern through the celebration of "connectedness" — the achievement of "poetic identity in relation to ancestresses" (15). Let us add that this discovery of the maternal intertexts of the female psyche is often preceded by a critique of the manifold ways in which woman's being has been inscribed by masculinist culture. In contrast to male contemporaries who celebrate their "liberation" from paternal authorities they have successfully learned to emulate, the female mourner had to learn both how to distance herself from self-destructive paradigms of patriarchal influence and to recover her connection with a chorus of women's voices.

A brief comparison of Walt Whitman's "When Lilacs Last in the Dooryard Bloom'd" and one of Emily Dickinson's poems highlights the different positions of the male and the female mourner. For Whitman, the death of Lincoln occasions the reassertion of a poetic power that has been chastened but not subdued in its claims of individual mastery. The poet emerges from the experience of mourning a more somber individual, yet one who is ready to assume again his position as spiritual and intellectual leader who has added another note to "the tally of my soul" (1.163). In contrast, the representation of mourning in Dickinson's poetry is devoted less to celebration of an arduous rite of passage than to the evocation of pervasive states of being that threaten to engulf the poet. Poem 280, "I felt a Funeral, in my Brain," for example, evokes processes of mourning and of self-mourning that have no determinable end. The unanchored, general quality of Dickinson's diction — describing a funeral that has no specific time or place — suggests that she is portraying an experience that recurs. Pain and mourning, Dickinson implies, are not distinct experiences related to the death of specific individuals, but rather general aspects of female existence. At the same time, Dickinson's language compels the reader to position her poem intertextually. Terms such as "Service," "Drum," "Box," "Boots of Lead," and "Bell" are all examples of "intratextual anomalies — obscure wordings, phrasings that the context alone will not suffice to explain" that "set in train an intertextual reading" (Riffaterre 627). Each of these words points toward cultural practices that shape intertextualized patterns of consciousness that take the mourning process as a model.

If we turn to a prose example such as Fanny Fern's *Ruth Hall*, we find something very similar. The story of a woman writer's education, Fern's

novel takes as its point of departure the dislocation and turmoil occasioned by the death of Ruth Hall's husband. Unlike a work such as Hawthorne's *The House of the Seven Gables*, where Judge Pyncheon's death
functions as a carefully controlled emotional and narrative climax, death
in Fern's fiction is positioned within an expanding circle of scenes that
point outward toward a multitude of cultural practices. As a grieving
widow, Ruth Hall becomes the subject of other characters' commentary.
They discuss her appearance, her financial prospects, even the proper
width of her veil. More than a mere contextualizing of grief, such scenes
establish a series of intertexts that force the reader to recognize the ways
in which women's lives are written by the pervasive codes of nineteenth-
century popular culture. The female self, both Dickinson and Fern suggest, is a text inscribed by a variety of signifying practices that become
discernible at the moment that the self's intertextuality is focused. To
speak of the "self's intertextuality" is to recognize something that feminist
theorists have known for a long while — that the actions, ideas, and dispositions of each person are encoded within an array of discourses and ideologies that determine the signifiers of feeling, thought, and behavior.

But if this critical insight is now widely available, it was the product
of a painful process of self-examination for Margaret Fuller — one of America's first feminist theorists. Preceding Fern and Dickinson by more than
a decade, she too came to see women's lives as texts crisscrossed by the
discursive practices of her culture. It is the central premise of this essay
that Fuller's feminist insight evolved out of a series of self-representations
shaped by nineteenth-century discourses of mourning. Her writing is filled
with narrative vignettes and implicit narratives that thematize issues of
death, abandonment, grief, and mourning. Linked initially by Fuller to
images of her dead father and absent father figures, these narratives of
mourning enable her to measure at progressive stages her sense of her self
and its powers. Yet, at a crucial moment, they elide into narratives that
link Fuller's own recovery from grief with the position of other women,
who have their own grief-work to perform, whether it is mourning for their
own damaged selves or for destructive patriarchal images that must be successfully "buried" before a new woman can be reborn.

As Fuller's representations of the self evolved, she slowly discovered
that the self is not a natural and independent entity (as Emerson might
suggest) but a text, inscribed with the multiple codes of one's culture. This
recognition can be measured by analyzing the ways Fuller's narratives of
mourning shift from a focus upon paternal influence to patriarchal intertextuality, and — finally — matriarchal intertextuality. The term "intertextuality" draws attention to the ways that Fuller's self-representations depend
upon the depiction of relationships between the self and figures that are

sometimes historical, often literary or mythical. Her self-images are placed within more and more complicated networks of figuration, culminating in the intertextual panorama of *Woman in the Nineteenth Century*. Rather than substantiating Julia Kristeva's famous assertion that "the notion of *intertextuality* replaces that of intersubjectivity" ("Word" 37), Fuller's depictions of selfhood suggest that intersubjectivity *is* intertextuality.

Initially, Fuller's confrontation with mourning involves the double bind of a woman who was trained by her father to appreciate the attractions of the oedipal position (with its narrative of paternal influence), but who was forced by personal circumstances to occupy a more traditional female narrative.[5] Coming to terms with her grief after her father's death, Fuller began to recognize the destructiveness of his influence, which presented her with a masculinized model of development that repressed female being. The contrast between the "oedipal" role that Fuller's father had created for her and her limited social position as a nineteenth-century woman highlighted the limitations of paternal influence.[6] At the same time, Fuller came to see that the process of mourning failed to empower her but replicated disabling relations between female selfhood and male power. For the traditional stance of female mourner continued to subordinate her both to the influence of her father and, in more general terms, to an intertextualized patriarchal authority.

As a first stage of recovery, Fuller used portrayals of the mourning process to highlight her awareness of the ways in which women's lives were absorbed and dispersed by signifying pressures. Behind her father's influence, she came to see, lay a disabling array of patriarchal intertexts that reinforced his authority. Initially, this intertextual awareness empowered Fuller, since it disclosed the patriarchal pressures warping female being. But, ultimately, Fuller felt compelled to balance this negative hermeneutic, disclosing the limitations of masculinist role models for the female writer, against a positive hermeneutic that uncovered a network of empowering matriarchal intertexts. Unable to assume the mantle of oedipal heir in a narrative of paternal influence, unwilling to embrace the passive female role assigned within intertextualized patriarchal narratives, she connected images of the self to a collective ground of female myth that—in effect—established an intertextualized model of female community. As a result, Fuller was able to replace disabling models of self-development with images of female selfhood that established constructive connections with others and creative agency.

In this regard, Fuller's developing narratives of mourning substantiate Nancy Miller's contention that women writers, excluded from patriarchal modes of identity formation, have a different relation to textuality than men.[7] Instead of erasing the subject, Fuller's analysis provides the means of comprehending a prior erasure of female experience mystified by narratives of paternal influence and by patriarchal intertexts that enforce an economy of male power. Disclosing a palimpsest of erased and suppressed texts lying behind the female subject, Fuller reconstructs a "political intertextuality"—to use Miller's phrase (111)—that bypasses the death of the subject often associated with masculinist theories of intertextuality.[8] In her writing, the rediscovery of forgotten narratives and antecedents does not erode female selfhood, for she does not tie her image of the self to an oedipal model of development in which recognition of the other's power erodes self-esteem. The other does not steal power in Fuller's world, but gives it. In contrast to Emerson's assertions of independence, Fuller articulates a self taking its stand in social and textual fields shaped by others. The power of each person, she asserts, is not the product of individual will but rather is the function of his or her relationships with others. Friends, she observes "not only know themselves more, but *are* more for having met, and regions of their being, which would else have laid sealed in cold obstruction, burst into leaf and bloom and song" (*M* 1:37).

Fuller's sense of the other involves a political awareness of the ways in which being always is with-and-for-others. In contrast, Fuller scholars who strive to determine the date of Fuller's political activism—usually linked with her move from Boston to New York—tend to enforce a public/private contrast that negates many of her best insights.[9] While the sphere of Fuller's action enlarged as she matured, her agency—from the first—had been politicized by virtue of her existence within a hierarchical system of gender relations, embodied in a set of intertexts that her writing eventually discloses. Fuller did not *become* political on a certain date. Instead, as she examined the contours of her own existence, she discovered that the politics of selfhood extended back to her earliest tutelage.

This recognition becomes apparent between 1839 and the fall of 1840, as Fuller's self-conscious articulation of her position as mourner coincided with a growing awareness of the ways in which her being was intertwined with others.[10] Confronting the ways in which grief had frozen her into a mute adoration of the Father, Fuller began to analyze the psychological and political expense of such dependence. This process of self-interpretation convinced her of the insufficiency of individualistic paradigms of the self, such as solitary models of self-reliance, with their reliance upon models of personal influence. But only after she began to escape from her father's influence could Fuller see the paradigm of male influence as a mystification of an underlying intertextuality.

In order to trace the relationship between Margaret Fuller's mourning and her gradual shift from paradigms of influence to models of intertextuality, we need to return to the shock she felt at her father's sudden death from cholera on October 1, 1835. A distinguished graduate of Harvard College who was active in various branches of Massachusetts state government and a four-term congressman, Timothy Fuller exerted a strong influence over Margaret, his oldest child, whose personality had been inextricably enmeshed with that of her powerful father.[11] When he died at age fifty-seven, Margaret was twenty-five. His death precipitated a prolonged and complicated period of grieving that lasted five years.

Fuller's professions of serenity and self-control, during the winter of 1835–36, suggest the extent to which she was trapped in the vicious cycle of what has been called "disordered mourning," a process in which "grief becomes *frozen*, or blocked" until "the mourner works though the conflicts he or she feels toward the deceased" (Tolchin 5). Entries in Fuller's letters and journals indicate that the full impact of her grief was quickly submerged, only to surface years later. "But my hard-won faith has not deserted me," she wrote to a friend four months after the event, "and I have so far preserved a serenity which might seem heartlessness to a common observer" (*L* 1:244). In her journal, she testified to "an awful calm" she felt after his death (*M* 1:155) and to the ambition to be a "strong soul" (*M* 1:158). Relinquishing her plans to travel to Europe and committing herself to a life of renunciation in support of her family, she exhorted herself in a letter "to try to forget myself, and act for others' sakes" (*L* 1:254).

In the unconscious logic of anniversary compulsion, each subsequent autumn and winter became for Fuller a time of isolation, depression, and sickness, as her unresolved mourning inscribed itself in a succession of ailments.[12] Never having properly mourned her father, she found herself trapped each year in a wintry mood that repeated the death encrypted within her. In the *Memoirs of Margaret Fuller Ossoli*, Emerson noted her tendency to be trapped in cycles of repetition, a sure sign of unresolved unconscious material. "The same dream," he wrote, "returns to her periodically, annually, and punctual to its night" (1:221). It was only when Fuller began to confront these buried forces four years later that she was able to mold them into a consciously controlled creative power.

Let me emphasize that, despite her ill health, Fuller in the years immediately following her father's death functioned effectively as the head of her family and as a teacher in both Boston and Providence. The point is not that she was incapacitated by grief, but just the opposite—that her functional behavior disguised a mourning process that had never been completed. As a result of this imposed tranquility, Fuller's delayed mourning hit her all the harder when it was finally reawakened by the engagement and marriage in 1839–40 of two of Fuller's closest friends, Samuel Ward and Anna Barker. There are clear indications in Fuller's letters and journals during this period that the altered relationships between Fuller and these two persons precipitated a period of reawakened grief during which she began to construct for herself narratives of the mourning process.[13] Confronting the psychological expense of losing Ward and Barker, she returned to the ghost of her unmourned father, measuring the hidden powers that had first been repressed by his influence and then fixed by her failure to mourn.

In terms of Fuller's grief-work, this process centered on two wounds: (1) the unexpressed anguish she felt when the "feminine" part of her self "died" as the result of her father's instruction, and (2) the pain occasioned by his death, which left her transfixed in an alienating identification with paternal values. Split into two opposing sides, the dominant "Father" and the buried "Mother," Fuller was unable for a period to confront that schism. Only as she faced the necessary grief-work was she able to recognize the extent to which she had incorporated into her personality the powerful voice of the unmourned Father, a voice that had alienated her from the Mother who was buried deeply within. Beginning to name those separate areas through a complex series of dichotomies, she began to free herself from an exclusive identification with paternal values at the same time that she rediscovered the existence of a core of maternal values that corresponded to a submerged aspect of the self.[14] As we shall see, the process of balancing Mother and Father led Fuller from paradigms of paternal influence toward intertextual models of the self's maternal antecedents. The power of the Mother, she ultimately discovered, could not be evoked by reference to the influence of a single figure, but only through a process of reconstruction that gathered the scattered fragments of the maternal image.

Quickly translating her reawakened mourning into a sophisticated reflection upon the psychology of melancholy and grief, Fuller observed in January 1840 that she had come to imagine her life in narrative terms as "a subject for a metaphysical romance" (L 2:113). She especially displayed this tendency to narrativize her experience in the construction of narratives of mourning. Among the most striking of such narratives are passages in which Fuller identifies herself with the *mater dolorosa*, the Virgin weeping at the sepulchre. Writing at different times to both Samuel Ward and William H. Channing, she imagined herself as the Virgin Mary waiting for Christ's resurrection. In September 1839, as she prayed for a full emotional response from Ward, who was drawing away from her, Fuller complained that "it is waiting like the Mother beside the sepulchre for the resurrection, for all I loved in you is dead and buried" (L 2:91). Over a year and a half later, writing to Channing of her devotion to him, Fuller again imagined herself "at the foot of the cross, at the door of the sepulchre" awaiting "the prince my youthful thought elected" (L 2:215). In both letters, Fuller depicted herself in the classic nineteenth-century stance of mourning—that of the "Mourning Madonna with "head . . . bowed in a posture of eloquent resignation" (Schorsch 15), a posture that replicated the gestures on countless American samplers of female mourners at the foot of tombs.[15]

But by mourning images of an absent male divinity associated with men she idolized, Fuller replicated a posture of grief that reinforced an economy of male influence. This idolatry deflected attention from her damaged self. Instead, it was a displaced worship of the men that Fuller admired (Ward, Emerson, Channing), all of whom seemed committed to a masculine ideal of individual perfection that excluded her troubling shifts of mood and spirit. But as Fuller continued to meditate upon the "dark hour" of reawakened mourning, the "sepulchre" at which she waited shifted its referent. Instead of pointing toward an image of male authority, it began to signify a damage in the depths of her own psyche. Ultimately, this displacement of the act of mourning from external to internal objects enabled Fuller to escape from the passivity of the conventional female mourner. Instead of elaborating her grief into a culturally reassuring signifier that reinforced the secondary status of women, she began to use representations of female mourning as the occasion for a process of reflection that highlighted the intertextual basis of women's experience. No longer positioning herself as an object within patriarchal discourse, she called that very process of objectification into question.

As she turned inward toward the self, Fuller began to transfer her attention from the "dead" to the act of mourning itself, turning away from Christianized images of female mourners lamenting the departed Father toward images in which the *activity* of mourning dominated the stage. In this way, Fuller began to generalize her sense of loss as a trait typical of many women. By 1840, she was thus able to link her sense of "the limitations of human nature" to her awareness of "my position as a woman" (*L* 2:109). Ultimately, as a result of reframing her grief, Fuller came to an understanding of the ways in which her psychological dependence upon the frozen image of her dead father recapitulated the dependence of women in general upon patriarchal narratives. In other words, Fuller's feminism began to develop as she confronted her ambivalence over the influence of her dead father, an ambivalence that became symbolic for Fuller of similar conflicts that women in general felt in the face of patriarchal influence.

In this context, Fuller's 1840 "Autobiographical Romance" takes on special interest because in it Fuller uses an analysis of her dead father's influence as the first step toward an intertextual feminist critique. "My father," Fuller begins and then, over the next eleven pages, presents her often-quoted account of her early instruction at the hands of her father.

Casting him in the role of villain, she asserts that his miseducation of her resulted from an incapacity to comprehend the emotional and imaginative depths of her nature — an incapacity that she presents as typical not only of her father but of nineteenth-century masculine character with its "Roman" ideals.

It is worth noting that the opening pages of Fuller's analysis are interrupted by a startling digression on the third page — an account of her "earliest recollection," "the death of a sister, two years younger than myself" (*M* 1:13). It is no accident that Fuller associates the image of her father with death; however, it is surprising that she omits all mention of *his* death, displacing attention instead to the earlier loss of a *female* relative. The result of this displacement is to shift attention from her father to herself and to make the condition of mourning the touchstone of her entire existence.

This image of woman as mourner takes on even greater significance as Fuller returns to the portrait of her dead father. For the effect of this transition is not to highlight Fuller's grief for her father, but rather to emphasize her grief for herself as a suffering woman for whom the act of mourning is a representative posture. In this regard, Fuller's famous account of the deleterious personal effects of her father's instruction demonstrates one of her first sustained attempts to interpret the grief that she feels for herself. A narrative of paternal influence, it is also a veiled account of mourning. Her description of one of her nightmares during this period clarifies the connection between paternal influence and female grief. In recounting her dream that she was "following to the grave the body of her mother, as she had done that of her sister" (*M* 1:16), Fuller connects the question of paternal influence with a recognition of woman's pain. Rather than mourning the father, this dream — identifying Fuller and her mother with a dead sister — suggests that the proper focus of Fuller's mourning is that part of her self killed by her father's instruction.

Foregrounding the damage done to her, Fuller began to transform her sense of loss into insight, passive suffering into an active engagement with the ideological pressures that diminish women's being. Fuller argues in her "Autobiographical Romance" that the damage wrought by her father's instruction was both psychological and spiritual. Demanding common sense and accuracy, he repressed deep within her the imaginative world that she associates with her mother's garden. In the place of imaginative reverie, he taught Fuller the "heroic" discipline of Roman ideals represented by "Man present in nature, commanding nature too sternly to be inspired by it, standing like the rock amid the sea, or moving like the fire over the land, either impassive or, irresistible; knowing not the soft mediums or fine flights of life, but by the force which he expresses, piercing to the centre" (*M* 1:19). By linking her father's authority to the image of Rome, and indirectly to the Romanized image of George Washington that inspired much nineteenth-century mourning art, Fuller discloses one of the patriarchal intertexts that lies behind — and, in a sense, validates — his myth of instruction. She was once committed to this image of masculine authority, having "steadily loved this ideal in my childhood" (20); but, now, she reflects, "A Caesar seemed great enough. I did not then know that such men impoverish the treasury to build the palace" (22).

Fuller increases her distance both from her father's influence and from patriarchal intertexts in a remarkable letter written several months after her "Autobiographical Romance." Confiding in her close friend Caroline Sturgis on October 22, she more explicitly connects her sense of emotional trauma to her father's death. But instead of prostrating herself before an external sepulchre as a "Virgin" lamenting an absent male divinity, Fuller internalizes the image of mourning — an imaginative act that replicates her sense of loss but expresses as well an intuition of power buried within. "Yet the cross, the symbol you have chosen seems indeed the one. Daily, hourly it is laid upon me. Tremulously I feel that a wound is yet to be given" (*L* 2:167). Identifying with both the grieving Mary and the crucified Christ, she turns the process of mourning into a self-conscious principle of psychic organization. Personal fulfillment, she now asserts, depends upon accepting the pain of self-division: "the One divides itself to win the last divinest birth of Love"; "from the darkest comes by brightness, from Chaos depths my love" (167, 168). Such statements might seem a displacement of a familiar language of Christian suffering and fortitude — an *imitatio Christi*. But as we shall see, the "brightness" that Fuller approaches manifests the face of the Mother not the Father.

Imagining herself as experiencing an agonizing process of death and rebirth, Fuller portrays herself in the midst a "Northern winter from which Phenix [*sic*] like rises the soul into the tenderest spring" (*L* 2:169). Metaphors of seasonal change and of dying and reborn vegetation evoke familiar images from Christian liturgy, but also pagan rituals of dying and reborn gods; while in an intertextual overlay, the deaths and resurrections of Christ, Osiris, and Persephone lie just behind the page as models of transformation. In many respects, the heterodox use of Christian imagery is the most striking, as Fuller longs to "bless myself like the holy Mother" and "like her . . . to be virgin" (167). But in contrast to earlier images of herself as the Virgin passively waiting at the sepulchre, Fuller's identification here is more active, enabling her to embody emotional impulses that had become Other for the "Roman" men that she was leaving behind her. Imagining herself as "Virgin bride" or "weeping mother," Fuller gives shape to heterodox feelings that challenge her earlier identification with the intellectual world of Emerson and her father.[16] In the words of Julia Kristeva, "The Mother and her attributes, evoking sorrowful humanity, thus become representatives of a 'return of the repressed' in monotheism. They re-establish what is non-verbal and show up as the receptacle of a signifying disposition that is closer to so-called primary processes" ("Stabat" 174).

Fuller complicates her identification with the Virgin Mary through thinly veiled references to the vicissitudes of her own sexuality. Longing "to be a virgin" like the "holy Mother," she imagines being impregnated by a divine wind analogous to the Holy Spirit of Christ's conception. As her "soul swells," she senses the divine "child" that will gestate within. The "desire" for "nun like dedication," it is clear, does not preclude the representation of sexual desire. Distancing herself from patriarchal definitions that limit female sexual power, Fuller combines the wish to be impregnated by divine spirit with autoerotic images that suggest her increasing control of sexual and spiritual energies. She has longed, she confesses, "to make a virtue bloom in my particular garden." Having pursued both "the graceful nymph" (Barker?) and "the slimiest monster" (Ward?), she has been led to "my deep mysterious grottoes" where "I feared no rebuff." "I could not pause," she continues, "yet ever I sobbed and wailed over my endless motion and foamed angrily to meet the storm-winds which kept me pure." Now, she would progress further into "the very heart of the untrodden mountain" where she hopes to find new power growing within her. The autoerotic quality of this imagery is reinforced by the assertion that "I cannot plunge into myself enough. I cannot dedicate myself sufficiently" (L 2:167).

Displacing the sexual charge of this material into a model of spiritual quest, Fuller imagines her psyche as receptive womb that is fertilized by a divine spirit. Opening herself to the possibility of psychic mitosis, she imagines that her emotional "winter," a representation of her grief, has been the occasion for a spiritual insemination and pregnancy that will lead to the birth within of spiritual powers imagined as a divine "child," "seed," and "Phenix" (L 2:167–69). This desire to be ravished by the Holy Spirit, to be a woman "betrothed to the sun" in the later phraseology of *Woman in the Nineteenth Century* (89), ultimately turns Fuller away from the worship of specific men such as her father, Samuel Ward, or Emerson. By releasing a maternal energy that is paired with a paternal energy found *within*, this figure incorporates masculine features inside of the psyche, instead of subordinating Fuller to the male world outside of her (Harding 153, 187). Such a maneuver enables Fuller to circumscribe and limit masculine traits as *part* of her being. Instead of identifying herself with masculinity, she becomes able to limit its influence and to explore areas of awareness that stand outside of it.

Equally important, Fuller connects her sense of spiritual transformation, born out of "renunciation" (*L* 2:167), with her complex emotional response to her father's death five years earlier. For the first time, she associates the discovery of powerful symbols of transformation with the prolonged process of grieving initiated by her father's death. After recounting a moment of spiritual revelation experienced as she attended the bed of a dying woman, Fuller remembers a moment of vigil kept in her father's bedroom the winter after his death:

I returned with the morning star. No one was with me in the house. I unlocked the door went into the silent room where but late before my human father dwelt. It was the first winter of my suffering health the musings and vigils of the night had exhausted while exalting me. The cold rosy winter dawn and then the sun. I had forgotten to wind up the clock the day marked itself. I lay there, I could not resolve to give myself food[.] The day was unintentionally a fast. Sacredest thoughts were upon it, and I comprehended the meaning of an ascetic life. (*L* 2:168)

Here, Fuller makes the connection between her illness and her grief that was unavailable to her in her "Autobiographical Romance." More significantly, her re-presentation of grief, a delayed reworking of her emotional response, becomes the occasion for insight.[17] Rather than being the source of creative blockage, her father's death is now reframed as an incident adumbrating the later discovery of creative power within.

Fuller's grief at her estrangement in the fall of 1840 from Ward, Barker, and Emerson reawoke an emotional pattern that she had been grappling with since 1835. But this time, something—perhaps the coincidence of a double grief, the echo of the previous loss of her father combined with a fresh cycle of mourning—precipitated a way out of emotional winter. Fuller's letter to William H. Channing, written October 25–28, 1840, reveals her sense that the moment had come to face her emotional blockage: "soon the winter winds will chant matins and vespers, which may make my house a cell, and in a snowy veil enfold me for my prayer. If I cannot dedicate myself this time, I will not expect it again" (*L* 2:171).

In Fuller's developing narratives of mourning, the failure of the father's influence and the limitations of patriarchal intertexts were compensated for by the discovery of an alternative realm of maternal value. While the Father's world was relatively easy to portray within "Romanized" American culture, representation of the realm of female value posed special problems. Unless she wished to replicate the patriarchal terms of the nineteenth-century "cult of true womanhood," the female writer was forced to adopt a literary strategy that both exposed and circumvented the lines of power behind such cultural myths. In practice, such strategies were often pluralogic, since no single representation of female experience carried the cultural weight to offset patriarchal pressure. As twentieth-century French theorists have since rediscovered, only a succession of terms and a constant proliferation of positions can escape the imaginative and ideological pressure of the status quo.[18] In Fuller's case, this meant the substitution of intertextual models of female being for debilitating models of paternal influence. Linking the female subject to a succession of intertexts, instead of to a single subordinated position, Fuller began to free herself from fixation within any single posture.

The most famous of Fuller's maternal realms is the mother's garden celebrated in her "Autobiographical Romance" as a refuge from her father's study. The terms of discussion here evoke the familiar nineteenth-century language of flowers — a striking example of the intertextual nature of Fuller's symbols of female being:

> I loved to gaze on the roses, the violets, the lilies, the pinks; my mother's hand had planted them, and they bloomed for me. I culled the most beautiful. I looked at them on every side. I kissed them, I pressed them to my bosom with passionate emotions, such as I have never dared express to any human being. An ambition swelled my heart to be as beautiful, as perfect as they. I have not kept my vow. (*M* 1:23–24)

This evocative passage asserts maternal value at the same time as it clarifies the difficulty of realizing it. One of the problems faced by Fuller is that female passion is inhibited by cultural pressures that make it virtually unutterable. More specifically, passion for the mother or for another woman (possible antecedents for these flowers) is beyond the pale — Fuller *dare not express it.*

As she continues, Fuller asks to be forgiven by the "wild asters" and "golden autumn flowers" for failing them; for "living and blooming in your unchecked law, ye know nothing of the blights, the distortions, which beset the human being . . . " (*M* 1:24). One half of Fuller's reawakened mourning process involved the "burial" of her father, an act that allowed Fuller to achieve an emotional distance from patriarchal influence; the other half became a lament for the Mother within herself, who had suffered a deformation and silencing. These two acts of mourning are reciprocal in their effect; as the Father is distanced through mourning, the Mother is brought closer.

It is as if Fuller realizes that her grief has been misplaced. By devoting herself exclusively to the Father's memory, she has neglected to mourn the maternal side that has been blighted and distorted by the Father's imperialistic rule. By expanding her mourning from Father to Mother, Fuller restores the psychological equilibrium that was disrupted by her earlier grief. At the same time, she recognizes that a woman's mourning is inevitably a mourning for the female condition. Fuller's reframing of grief supplements oedipal models of paternal influence with an excavation of her pre-oedipal identification with the mother. The ensuing merger with the maternal image, releasing a "more permeable" sense of "ego boundaries" (Chodorow 93), leads Fuller from the mere recognition of intertextuality toward an intertextual style of writing—a development that is most apparent in the complex textual overlay of *Woman in the Nineteenth Century*. The self and its maternal antecedents, the "mothers" that Fuller celebrates in her feminist writing, are perceived less as distinct entities and more as interconnected beings that form a mythic analogue to Carroll Smith-Rosenberg's "female world of love and ritual"—an extended network of female relationships modeled upon an "intimate mother-daughter relationship" (65).

In Fuller's narratives of mourning, this second grief carries a more intense erotic charge, suggesting that the bond snapped by the loss of Samuel Ward was matched (perhaps overbalanced) by an even more charged attachment to Anna Barker. Fuller's letters suggest that her feelings for Barker—her "eldest and divinest love," her "beloved" (*L* 2:93)—were more intense than those for Ward. After the initial shock of the Ward-Barker engagement, for example, she was soon able to write Ward that "my attachment . . . is sufficiently disinterested for me to be sure of it" (96). But over a year later, Fuller was so affected by seeing Anna, who "sat beside me, all glowing" and "kindled" a month after her marriage, that she returned home from one of her conversation classes with "a long attack of nervous headach [*sic*]" and began composing a mystical essay on the power of female attraction, "The Magnolia of Lake Pontchartrain" (*L* 2:183–84).

It should not surprise us that Fuller, whose psychic being had been split into "paternal" and "maternal" sides, should love both a man and a woman simultaneously. While Samuel Ward connected her to her father's world, Anna Barker linked her to a female world that represented a separate sphere of feeling and relationship. Emerson later acknowledged the importance for Fuller of this realm by citing in the *Memoirs* Fuller's most succinct statement of same-sex attraction: "It is so true that a woman may be in love with a woman, and a man with a man . . . " (*M* 1:283). In the continuation of this passage, from which Emerson excised the name "Anna," Fuller emphasized the emotional and spiritual value of her relationship with Anna Barker:

I loved Anna for a time I think with as much passion as I was then strong enough to feel. Her face was always gleaming before me, her voice was echoing in my ear, all poetic thoughts clustered round the dear image. This love was for me a key which unlocked many a treasure which I still possess, it was the carbuncle (emblematic gem) which cast light into many of the darkest corners of human nature.[19]

This passage begins to reveal the central importance for Fuller of her deep bond with Anna Barker — an attachment that provided an entry to an intertextual world of maternal value that counterbalanced her father's influence and its Roman antecedents.

Fuller's letters and journals of 1840, as well as the mystical sketches she published during the next two years, expanded her image of Barker into a meditation upon the self's relationship to a succession of powerful female images. Having once felt the presence of "poetic thoughts" clustering around the image of Anna, she later associated, in December of 1840, her internalized image of Barker with a corresponding image of the Goddess: "It is strange that these people should think her artificial because she is so natural. They do not think the *Diana* unnatural because her attitude is more free and noble than those they see every day. How lost they must be to every noble joy which our strength employs not to recognize such sweetness when it flows on them."[20] In the continuation of this passage, Fuller blessed God "for awakening my inward life" to the "ever flowing spirit." In many respects, we can conclude from such evidence, Fuller's love for Anna opened up for her a mythologized realm of female value that countered the patriarchal values of her father.[21]

Fuller's mystical sketch "The Magnolia of Lake Pontchartrain" provides the clearest link between Fuller's representation of mourning and the discovery of a maternal power that stands outside the realm of the Father. We can surmise the connection between this essay and Fuller's image of Anna Barker from the fact that Anna hailed from New Orleans, the site of Lake Pontchartrain. An additional link is provided by the goddess imagery of the essay — language that Fuller first discovered as she meditated upon the image of her "beloved," Anna. In structure, "The Magnolia" is loosely an elegy presented by a female speaker to an unnamed male protagonist. Although Emerson interpreted this piece as a commentary upon his relationship with Fuller,[22] it is more likely that it analyzes changes that Fuller felt were taking place in her personality as her grief for the Father was being replaced by a discovery of the buried Mother.

"The Magnolia of Lake Pontchartain" concludes with an assertion of the existence of a matriarchal power that stands outside of the dominant values of Fuller's patriarchal culture. Having stepped "inward," into a realm of "deeper thought" (304), the Magnolia tells her male auditor that "I cannot speak to thee in any language now possible betwixt us" (303). Finally, she asserts that she has totally rejected patriarchal terminology: "nor shall I again subject myself to be questioned by an alien spirit to tell the tale of my being in words that divide it from itself" (303–4). The essay closes with the male figure, left to muse on the meaning of the strange being he has just encountered — a conclusion that highlights a confrontation between patriarchal and matriarchal values.

Two years later, in her 1843 *Dial* essay "The Great Lawsuit" (which became the nucleus of *Woman in the Nineteenth Century*), Fuller shifts completely to an intertextual and pluralogic style of writing. Here, she is much less concerned with detailing the influence of one individual than in creating a self-image placed within an extended web of female models, a pantheon of representative women that functions as a template of potential postures. As a result of the plethora of citations and allusions, Fuller's representation of the self takes on an overdetermined quality. The allusiveness and nonlinearity of Fuller's style have been a source of embarrassment for most critics, who measure "The Great Lawsuit" and *Woman in the Nineteenth Century* by standards of unity and linear development. What disturbs readers the most, one assumes, is the seemingly casual way in which the thread of Fuller's argument is obscured by her interpolation of numerous anecdotes, quotations, and biographical sketches. But those troublesome digressions are not an afterthought or a stylistic flaw but rather a new way of viewing and writing the self's development — one that supplants Emerson's individualistic vision of self-reliance with a communal vision of intertextuality.

Relying on both herself and a medley of voices, Fuller articulates an *other-reliance* that asserts social connection, relationship with an other, in opposition to an implicit model of self-reliance. Defining the self through extended reference to the lives of numerous women, both real and imaginary, Fuller transcends individual influence. We see this redefinition in Fuller's portrait of herself as Miranda. Perhaps the most striking aspect of this passage is that Fuller refrains from expressing a relation of similitude (she is *like* Miranda) in favor of asserting one of identity (she *is* Miranda).[23] This act of identification suggests that the self cannot be defined without reference to external narratives. Shakespeare's portrait of Miranda in *The Tempest* is not merely an allusion that illuminates aspects of Fuller's being, as if her being were separable from the dramatic character, but rather a life that intersects Fuller's by providing the terms that illuminate it. In this regard, Fuller's use of Miranda is not that different from Freud's use of Oedipus. In both instances, a dramatic character forms part of an intertextual network that sets the very terms of self-understanding.

Within the context of Fuller's life, of course, the figure of Miranda has great resonance. The accomplished daughter of an illustrious father, she successfully negotiates the transition from father-love to extrafamilial relationships. At the same time, the implicit comparison between Timothy Fuller and Prospero elevates the image of the Father, an idealization that is continued when Fuller later celebrates the "Minerva" side of woman's being, since Minerva (Athena) was born from the head of her father, Jupiter. In modern terms, Fuller's idealization of paternal images does not seem to represent a wholly satisfactory conclusion of mourning, for it suggests the continued investment of libido in an idealized image of the dead father. But it is important to note that by 1843 Fuller was able to dissociate the image of Timothy Fuller from that of the destructive patriarchal Father, an identification that she had made three years earlier in her "Autobiographical Romance" when she identified her father's Roman character as the source of her psychological and physical suffering.

In "The Great Lawsuit" Fuller acknowledges her father's beneficent influence at the same time that she celebrates her escape from it. The feminism of Miranda/Minerva is made possible by Fuller's passage through the paralysis of early grief to a recognition of the limits between self and other, mourner and the dead. Successfully "burying" her father, she achieves a measurable distance from his influence. At that point, Fuller is in the position to reveal the links between her paralyzing grief for her father, her grief for herself, and the paralysis of other women who are trapped in a similar dependency. One signal that Fuller's discovery of her feminism coincides with the resolution of her mourning process is the striking assertion that "the time is come when Euridice is to call for an Orpheus, rather than Orpheus for Euridice" (7).

Occupying a cultural position analogous in many ways to that later occupied by Oedipus, the nineteenth-century figure of Orpheus was associated with male mastery over nature, death, the unconscious, and woman.[24] Orpheus, as Fuller defines him, "understood nature, and made *her* forms move to his music" (6, italics mine). Journeying into the underworld, after the death of his beloved wife Eurydice, he exhibited the bravado celebrated by male Romantic artists. But in Fuller's hands, this figure takes on a complexity and irony lacking in the more celebratory allusions of Emerson or Bronson Alcott. Fuller knew that Orpheus' flaw was lack of faith in Eurydice's presence. Having been told by Death that he could rescue her if he did not look back until after they returned to the world of the living, Orpheus succumbed to curiosity, only to lose her once again. Interpreting Orpheus as a symbol of man in general, Fuller suggests that he failed to trust Eurydice (woman) enough to raise her up to his level; instead, he left her in the underworld of a half-completed psychological process. Or as Fuller later phrases it later in *Woman in the Nineteenth Century,* "Man, in order of time, was developed first. . . . Woman was therefore under his care as an elder. He might have been her guardian and teacher. But . . . he misunderstood and abused his advantages, and became her temporal master instead of her spiritual sire" (155–56). Man's having failed to rescue woman, Fuller suggests, it is time to reverse the process and allow woman to rescue man ("Euridice is to call for an Orpheus"). Saving him from his own underworld, the chasm of patriarchal prejudice, she will raise him to a higher level of self-realization.

As Fuller knew well from her study of book X of Ovid's *Metamorphoses*, the call of Orpheus, the discovery of his poetic vocation, resulted from the loss of Eurydice to Hades.[25] Ovid's narrative popularized a model of the male artist that found its nineteenth-century analogue in Poe's (in)famous assertion that "the death . . . of a beautiful woman is, unquestionably, the most poetical topic in the world" (535). Silenced and objectified by male discourse, Eurydice became the occasion of male artistic production. As Poe phrases it, "the lips best suited for such topic are those of a bereaved lover." But by reversing the equation and constructing an antithetical intertext, Fuller's narrative disrupts the dominant tradition of male discourse. In place of a passive and mute Eurydice, Orpheus' muse who occasioned an endless cycle of poetic mourning, Fuller imagines a female agent who escapes from an economy of grief in which woman remains the most evocative signifier.

By calling Orpheus, Eurydice inaugurates a new vocation—one in which woman finds a role as the agent of artistic production, not just its subject. Within the context of "The Great Lawsuit" and of Fuller's biography, the act of calling Orpheus from his underworld involves much more than the familiar nineteenth-century myth of the inspirational true woman. In Fuller's hands, the myth of Orpheus and Eurydice links the process of psychological development with an encounter with death. Before she can call Orpheus, a woman must face both his absence and her own paralyzing grief. In order to overcome the patriarchal pressure of the more familiar Orphic narrative, Fuller suggests, the woman writer must realize that the "death" of Orpheus has engendered a corresponding death that she carries within herself. Only by facing that death within, the part of her that has been paralyzed and killed, can she help both of them on the long journey back toward life. Fuller, in other words, suggests that the nineteenth-century woman must mourn man, trapped in the underworld of dysfunctional patriarchal attitudes; but, even more important, she must mourn herself. In this way, she can recuperate that part of her self that has been trapped with him in the underworld.

Lying behind Fuller's image of Eurydice calling for Orpheus, we begin to see a psychological and textual palimpsest, a succession of similar narratives, all of which focus images of the mourning process. Immediately below the surface is the image of Isis, journeying into the underworld to rescue Osiris.[26] At even deeper levels are images that occur even earlier in Fuller's writing, such as the portrait of herself as the Virgin Mary waiting at Christ's sepulchre. In an intertextual overlay, Fuller's image of Eurydice conflates aspects of Virgin Mother (from the Bible), Isis (from Plutarch's *Morals*), and Eurydice (from Ovid's *Metamorphoses*). Scholars have noted the connection between images of the Virgin and of Isis, going so far as to suggest that the iconography of the nursing and weeping Mary was indebted to similar images found in the cult of Isis (Warner 193, 208, 256). Like Mary, Isis mourns the death of a god. Her cult in Egypt, Marina Warner notes, "centred on the death of her spouse and son Osiris, for whom the goddess weeps bitterly *before she triumphantly resuscitates him*" (208, italics mine). But the classical account of Isis evokes a female power lacking in the Christian narrative. There is a great difference between identifying with Mary the "mother of God" and identifying with a Goddess as "God the Mother" (Christ 244). The first confirms the paradigm of male influence by subordinating woman to the worship of a male divinity, while the second provides "a symbol that points to the rooting of feminism in the nature of being" (Christ 250). The grief of Mary was static, but the mourning of Fuller's Isis/Eurydice becomes the occasion of female-directed energies.

By 1843, Fuller was able to construct narratives that enabled her to escape from the vicious cycle of disordered mourning. Evoking the loss of her father, of Barker and Ward, and part of herself, they superimposed multiple female mourners — Eurydice, Isis, and Virgin Mother — who both suggested Fuller's historical life situation and allegorized her sense of female psychology. Distancing herself from images of the mourned "Father" (whether Orpheus, Osiris, or Christ), Fuller was able to place him as a component, but not the ruling deity, of her psyche. Having been forced by unforeseen circumstances to work through the disordered mourning of her father, she had learned that the process of mourning could be a source of female strength as well as weakness. In a succession of mourning narratives between 1839 and 1843, she had shifted her attention from the loss of one individual, an act of mourning that emphasized relationships of influence, to a series of similar losses that echoed each other. Ultimately, this repetition and modulation of patterns of grief led Fuller to reflect upon the psychology of mourning, a state that she defined as typical both of her existence and of women in general. In her explicitly political writings, Fuller defined female loss intertextually; the style of "The Great Lawsuit" and of *Woman in the Nineteenth Century* suggested that women's lives are inextricably bound in a network of relationships. In contrast to the Emersonian model of an independent male heroism that triumphs over relations of influence, Fuller offered a politicized model of the female self that opens up questions of ideological determination. The motives of nineteenth-century women, she suggested, were determined not in isolation but rather within an intricate set of intertexts that includes figures from the present, the past, mythology, and literature.

NOTES

1 See Nancy Chodorow, *The Reproduction of Mothering*, chap. 6, and Carol Gilligan, *In a Different Voice*, chap. 2.

2 According to Barton Levi St. Armand, "The image of the mourning maiden had archetypal resonances for the popular culture" of mid-nineteenth-century America (42).

3 For a detailed discussion of mourning dress as a sign of middle-class culture see Halttunen.

4 Numerous illustrations of this pose are represented in Ring (171–89).

5 Paula Blanchard argues that, as Fuller matured, her father shifted from requiring her to be "the perfect scholar" to demanding that she be "the perfect lady" (47).

6 According to Paula Blanchard, Fuller — after her father's death — was expected to be "both father and mother" to her siblings (93).

7 "Because the female subject," Miller argues, "has juridically been excluded from the polis, and hence decentered . . . her relation to integrity and textuality, desire and authority, is structurally different" (106).

8 For the idea of palimpsest, I am indebted to Susan Friedman's work on H.D., as expressed both in private conversations and in *Psyche Reborn* (29).

9 See Bell Gale Chevigny, "Growing Out of New England" and "To the Edges of Ideology."

10 Fuller's decision in the fall of 1839 to begin offering "Conversations" for Boston women was an important act that provided intellectual training for an influential group of female reformers (Capper 513). Similarly, Fuller's acceptance the following year of the editorship of the *Dial* magazine, the Transcendentalists' journal, placed her in a position of power that enabled her to generalize her experience into aesthetic and spiritual principles. While not overtly political, in the sense of espousing particular programs of reform, such actions expanded Fuller's field of concern by involving her in public forums in which many of the leading ideas of the age were being debated.

11 According to Thomas Wentworth Higginson, who was a personal friend of the family, Fuller's mother, Margarett Crane Fuller, was a "self-effacing" woman ruled by a "strong-willed spouse" (17). Margaret Fuller's education, her dress, and even her social life were strictly controlled by her father; "for almost all purposes of direction and guidance," Higginson observes, "she was her father's child" (29).

12 During the months of October and November between 1837 and 1839, for example, Fuller was "miserably unwell" (*L* 1:303), so ill that she "could attend to nothing that was not absolutely necessary" (*L* 1:310), convinced that "the secret of all things is pain" (*L* 1:347), praying that she might find some peace in "vestal solitudes" (*L* 1:351), hoping that she might recover "my natural tone of health and spirits" (*L* 1:352), and the victim of a three-week long headache (*L* 2:98).

13 According to Bell Gale Chevigny, both Ward and Barker "roused tumultuous feelings in her" (*Woman* 77). It is one of the goals of this paper to clarify the nature of Fuller's tumult.

14 Fuller's "Autobiographical Romance," written in 1840–41, describes this process. Within the context of her letters, the account given there suggests that she is just becoming aware of a psychological schism that has been unconscious.
15 During this period, "Woman Weeping was Christianized and romanticized until she took on a Madonna-like calm" (St. Armand 46).
16 In a letter three days later to Caroline Sturgis, Fuller complains about Emerson's blindness to a realm of being that stands outside of nineteenth-century patriarchal values, "the world of feeling" and "Love" (*L* 2:170).
17 Freud has called this process *Nachträglichkeit*. The classic discussion of *Nachträglichkeit* is found in "From the History of an Infantile Neurosis" in passages such as the following: "An analysis of a childhood disorder through the medium of recollection in an intellectually mature adult is free from these limitations; but it necessitates our taking into account the distortion and refurbishing to which a person's own past is subjected when it is looked back upon from a later period" (189).
18 See, for example, Jacques Derrida's discussion of the *pharmakon* in *Dissemination* (65–75).
19 Fuller MSS, Houghton Library, Harvard, bMs Am 1086 (Box A).
20 Fuller MSS, Boston Public Library, Ms Am 1450 (90), journal fragment, my italics.
21 According to Kathryn Rabuzzi, this process of "learning to love other women" is a necessary step toward the full realization of the female power found in goddess images (175–209).
22 See Emerson's letter to Fuller of January 19, 1841, in which he comments of "The Magnolia of Lake Pontchartrain" that "I read it with gladness & good will: Depart ye profane this is of me & mine!" (2:377–78).
23 Fuller made this identification explicit in an entry in her 1844 journal that was recorded in the notebook Emerson compiled as he was writing his section of the posthumous *Memoirs*: "Last year, I wrote of Woman, & proudly painted myself as Miranda" (Emerson, "Margaret Fuller Ossoli" 498–99).
24 For discussions of the meaning of Orpheus for nineteenth-century Americans, see Yoder and Richardson (55–60).
25 In her "Autobiographical Romance," Fuller remarks that "Ovid gave me not Rome, nor himself, but a view into the enchanted gardens of the Greek mythology. This path I followed, have been following ever since . . . " (*M* 1:21). As further confirmation of Fuller's knowledge of Ovid, it is worth noting that she refers three times in *Woman in the Nineteenth Century* to the account of Hercules and Dejanira found in book IX of the *Metamorphoses*.
26 For a detailed discussion of the significance of Isis for Fuller, see my book *The Representation of the Self in the American Renaissance* (114–21).

WORKS CITED

Blanchard, Paula. *Margaret Fuller: From Transcendentalism to Revolution*. New York: Dell, 1979.

Bloom, Harold. *The Anxiety of Influence: A Theory of Poetry*. New York: Oxford UP, 1973.

Capper, Charles. "Margaret Fuller as Cultural Reformer: The Conversations in Boston." *American Quarterly* 39 (1987): 509–28.

Chevigny, Bell Gale. "Growing Out of New England: The Emergence of Margaret Fuller's Radicalism." *Women's Studies* 5 (1977): 65–100.

Chevigny, Bell Gale. "To the Edges of Ideology: Margaret Fuller's Centrifugal Evolution." *American Quarterly* 38 (1986): 173–201.

Chevigny, Bell Gale. *The Woman and the Myth: Margaret Fuller's Life and Writings*. Old Westbury, NY: Feminist P, 1976.

Chodorow, Nancy. *The Reproduction of Mothering: Psychoanalysis and the Sociology of Gender*. Berkeley and Los Angeles: U of California P, 1978.

Christ, Carol P. "Symbols of Goddess and God in Feminist Theology." In *The Book of the Goddess Past and Present: An Introduction to Her Religion*, ed. Carl Olson. New York: Crossroad, 1986.

Derrida, Jacques. *Dissemination*. Trans. and introd. Barbara Johnson. Chicago: U of Chicago P, 1981.

Emerson, Ralph Waldo. *The Letters of Ralph Waldo Emerson*, ed. Ralph Rusk. 6 vols. New York: Columbia UP, 1939.

Emerson, Ralph Waldo. "Margaret Fuller Ossoli." In *The Journals and Miscellaneous Notebooks of Ralph Waldo Emerson*, ed. William H. Gilman, Alfred R. Ferguson, Harrison Hayford et al. Vol. ll, 1848–51. Cambridge: Harvard UP, 1975.

Emerson, Ralph Waldo. *Nature*. In *Nature, Addresses, and Lectures*, ed. Robert E. Spiller and Alfred R. Ferguson. Cambridge: Harvard UP, 1971.

Freud, Sigmund. "From the History of an Infantile Neurosis." In *Three Case Histories*, ed. Philip Rieff. New York: Collier Books, 1963.

Friedman, Susan Stanford. *Psyche Reborn: The Emergence of H.D.* Bloomington: Indiana UP, 1981.

Fuller, Margaret. "Autobiographical Romance." In *Memoirs of Margaret Fuller Ossoli*, vol. 1.

Fuller, Margaret. "The Great Lawsuit. Man *versus* Men. Woman *versus* Women." *Dial* 4 (1843): 1–47.

Fuller, Margaret. Journal fragment. Fuller Ms Am 1450 (90). Boston Public Library.

Fuller, Margaret. Journal fragment. Fuller bMs Am 1086 (Box A). Houghton Rare Book Library, Harvard University.

Fuller, Margaret. *The Letters of Margaret Fuller*. Ed. Robert N. Hudspeth. 5 vols. to date. Ithaca, NY: Cornell UP, 1983– . (Cited as *L*.)

Fuller, Margaret. "The Magnolia of Lake Pontchartrain." *Dial* 1 (1841): 299–305.

Fuller, Margaret. *The Memoirs of Margaret Fuller Ossoli*. Ed. Ralph Waldo Emerson, James Freeman Clarke, and William Henry Channing. 2 vols. Boston: Phillips, Sampson, 1852. (Cited as *M*.)

Fuller, Margaret. *Woman in the Nineteenth Century: A Facsimile of the 1845 Edition*. Ed. Joel Myerson. Columbia: U of South Carolina P, 1980.

Gilligan, Carol. *In a Different Voice: Psychological Theory and Women's Development*. Cambridge and London: Harvard UP, 1982.

Halttunen, Karen. "Mourning the Dead: A Study in Sentimental Ritual." Chap. 5 in *Confidence Men and Painted Women: A Study in Middle-Class Culture in America, 1830–1870*. New Haven: Yale UP, 1982.

Harding, Esther. *Woman's Mysteries: Ancient and Modern*. New York: Harper & Row, 1976.

Higginson, Thomas Wentworth. *Margaret Fuller Ossoli*. 1884. Rpt. New York: Confucian P, 1980.

Kristeva, Julia. "Stabat Mater." In *The Kristeva Reader*, ed. Toril Moi, 160–86. New York: Columbia UP, 1986.

Kristeva, Julia. "Word, Dialogue, and Novel." In *The Kristeva Reader* 34–61.

Miller, Nancy K. "Changing the Subject: Authorship, Writing, and the Reader." In *Feminist Studies/ Critical Studies*, ed. Teresa de Lauretis, 102–20. Bloomington: Indiana UP, 1986.

Pike, Martha. "In Memory Of: Artifacts Relating to Mourning in Nineteenth-Century America." In *Rituals and Ceremonies in Popular Culture*, ed. Ray B. Browne. Bowling Green, Ohio: Bowling Green UP, 1980.

Poe, Edgar Allan. *Great Short Works*. Ed. G. R. Thompson. New York: Harper & Row, 1970.

Rabuzzi, Kathryn Allen. *Motherself: A Mythic Analysis of Motherhood*. Bloomington: Indiana UP, 1988.

Richardson, Robert D., Jr. *Myth and Literature in the American Renaissance*. Bloomington and London: Indiana UP, 1978.

Riffaterre, Michael. "Syllepsis." *Critical Inquiry* 6 (1980): 625–38.

Ring, Betty. *Let Virtue Be a Guide to Thee: Needlework in the Education of Rhode Island Women, 1730–1830*. Providence: Rhode Island Historical Society, 1983.

St. Armand, Barton Levi. "Dark Parade: Dickinson, Sigourney, and the Victorian Way of Death." Chap. 2 of *Emily Dickinson and Her Culture: The Soul's Society*. Cambridge: Cambridge UP, 1984.

Schenck, Celeste M. "Feminism and Deconstruction: Re-Constructing the Elegy." *Tulsa Studies in Women's Literature* 5 (1986): 13–27.

Schorsch, Anita. *Mourning Becomes America: Mourning Art in the New Nation*. Clinton, NJ: Main Street, P 1976.

Smith-Rosenberg, Carroll. "The Female World of Love and Ritual: Relations between Women in Nineteenth-Century America." *Disorderly Conduct: Visions of Gender in Victorian America*. New York: Alfred A. Knopf, 1985.

Steele, Jeffrey. *The Representation of the Self in the American Renaissance*. Chapel Hill: U of North Carolina P, 1987.

Sundquist, Eric J. *Home As Found: Authority and Genealogy in Nineteenth-Century American Literature*. Baltimore: Johns Hopkins UP, 1979.

Taylor, Lawrence. "Symbolic Death: An Anthropological View of Mourning Ritual." In *A Time to Mourn: Expressions of Grief in Nineteenth Century America*, ed. Martha V. Pike and Janice Gray Armstrong. Stony Brook, NY: The Museums at Stony Brook, 1980.

Tolchin, Neal. *Mourning, Gender, and Creativity in the Art of Herman Melville*. New Haven & London: Yale UP, 1988.

Warner, Marina. *Alone of All Her Sex: The Myth and the Cult of the Virgin Mary.* 1976. Rpt. New York: Vintage Books, 1983.

Welter, Barbara. "The Cult of True Womanhood: 1800–1860." *Dimity Convictions: The American Woman in the Nineteenth Century.* Athens, Ohio: Ohio UP, 1976.

Yoder, R. A. *Emerson and the Orphic Poet in America.* Berkeley, Los Angeles, and London: U of California P, 1978.

CHAPTER 12

Inter(racial)textuality in Nineteenth-Century Southern Narrative

WILLIAM L. ANDREWS

Writing about the plantation in the nineteenth-century South, W. J. Cash calls the relationship between blacks and whites who lived and died under the aegis of that system "nothing less than organic." The intimacy born of black mammies nursing white infants, elderly black storytellers bewitching master's children, and virtually unrestricted companionship between the enslaved and the freeborn youth of the plantation all guaranteed that "Negro entered into white man as profoundly as white man entered into Negro—subtly influencing every gesture, every word, every emotion and idea, every attitude" (Cash 51). This acknowledgment of the integrated character of "the mind of the South" was not as fashionable in Cash's time as it is now. With the hindsight that the relative success of integration in the South has given to southern pundits, Marshall Frady, a South Carolina journalist, has no difficulty asserting that black and white Southerners have become after three centuries "a single people—or rather, two halves of a single people artificially divided by the arbitrary laws and institutions of fear and guilt and greed" (Frady 136). This may be so, but critics and historians of southern literature have not yet confirmed it. Nor has there been, thus far, much work on whether the intuitions of commentators like Cash and Frady are grounded in discernible evidence.

To be sure, students of southern literature have ceased to think of their field as a cotton patch—all white, except for an occasional dark-skinned tiller of the subsoil. This is an inference easily drawn from even a cursory look at the monumental and to a significant extent revisionist *The History of Southern Literature* (1985). Within the scope of this book, black and white writers are no longer segregated; indeed major themes and leaders of the Harlem Renaissance of the 1920s are proudly claimed for the South

The early black novelists William Wells Brown and Martin R. Delany are reviewed in detail in the conclusion of a chapter on antebellum fiction, where the likes of John Pendleton Kennedy and John Esten Cooke would once have reigned supreme. Yet even in this able discussion by Mary Ann Wimsatt (Rubin 92–107), the problem of how to locate the work of Brown and Delany in the romance tradition of antebellum fiction is not addressed, let alone resolved. To make this observation is not to fault a critic who undoubtedly found that describing the relationship of black and white southern writing in a given period of literary history is problematic. Anyone who explores this issue, from Ladell Payne's introductory (and in my view unsatisfying) monograph, *Black Novelists and the Southern Literary Tradition* (1981), to Minrose Gwin's provocative feminist study, *Black and White Women of the Old South* (1985), knows that we are not likely to reckon adequately with the relationship of black and white letters in the South without first reexamining our assumptions about the ways in which authors and texts interact and/or influence each other. This essay, despite the pretense of its title to breadth and definitiveness, is intended only to show how a concept of intertextuality can be applied to southern writing in its earliest biracial manifestations — before the collapse of slavery — and what that application reveals about the interracial textuality of southern narrative.

The familiar way of talking about the relationship of black and white writers and texts in southern literature has been to discuss the influence of white writers on black writers. Vernon Loggins' pioneering *The Negro Author: His Development in America to 1900* (1931) grants high marks for imitation of white models to many black writers from Phillis Wheatley to Charles W. Chesnutt, but he has nothing to say of the impact of Negro authors on white American literature other than to remark, offhandedly, that a book like *Up from Slavery* "is possibly as familiar to American readers as Franklin's *Autobiography*" (266). Loggins' successors, Hugh M. Gloster and Robert Bone most notably, also suggest that African American fiction writers were influenced by whites and (less often) by each other without exploring the degree to which influence moved in the other direction. Work on the impact of black writing on white writers is beginning to be done, but most of it concerns more recent writers.[1] Questions about the possible reciprocity of literary discourse across the color line during the formative era of modern southern literature remain largely unasked, though they would seem to be fundamental to the many attempts going on today to reconstruct the literary history of the South.

Approaching the problem of southern interracial textuality via questions about influence has not taken us very far toward understanding the degree to which black and white discourse has been reciprocal or dialogic.

From the end of the eighteenth to the beginning of the twentieth century, black southern writers do seem to have reacted, often defensively, to the work of whites, as Benjamin Banneker did to Jefferson's disparagement of Phillis Wheatley in *Notes on the State of Virginia* (Jefferson 140; Barksdale and Kinnamon 50–52), as George Moses Horton did to the poetry of Byron and the hymns of Wesley, as James Edwin Campbell and Daniel Webster Davis did to the dialect verse of Irwin Russell and white minstrel song writers (Brown 32–38), and as Chesnutt did to the fiction of Joel Chandler Harris and Thomas Nelson Page (Andrews, *Literary Career* 48–52). The mutedness of black writing in the South of slavery and white supremacy helped assure the unlikelihood of specific black literary influence on white writers. Yet acquiescing to a notion of influence that grants only to literary texts the power to shape the structure and significance of other literary texts leaves us with a shortsighted view of the dynamics of southern literary history. No one can dispute the fact that Irwin Russell, traditionally known as the first of the southern dialect poets, owed his inspiration to the black dialect he heard in his native Mississippi before the Civil War. Joel Chandler Harris' debt to black folklore and storytelling is also well known, as is the immense contribution of that folklore and the ex-slave as narrating voice to popular southern writing, white and black, in the late nineteenth and early twentieth centuries. It may be impossible to say that Russell and Harris were influenced by particular black writers or texts, but it is certain that the oral culture of black Southerners provided the pre-text for Russell's classic "Christmas Night in the Quarters" and Harris' Uncle Remus tales. It may be equally impossible to isolate or recover the origins of the white writers' texts in a black pre-text, but it may very well be possible to assess the effect of such interplay on what Jonathan Culler calls "the discursive space of a culture" (103), namely, southern culture in its biracial dimensions.

The linkage between antebellum black folk culture, Joel Chandler Harris' Uncle Remus tales of the 1880s, and the conjure stories of Charles W. Chesnutt in the 1890s is but one testimonial to the existence of southern inter(racial)textuality in the nineteenth century. At issue in this essay is not whether such intertextuality existed in the South but how various intertextual relationships are manifested in particular types of discourse in specific historical instances. Julia Kristeva stresses that intertextuality entails a "transposition of one (or several) sign system(s) into another," resulting in "a new articulation . . . of enunciative and denotative positionality" (59–60). This transposition works by both the absorption and destruction of other texts that occupy "the intertextual space," i.e., the realm in which all signifying practices — from the supposedly original to the clichéd, from the idiolect to the sociolect — exist in the consciousness of

writers and readers. Like outer space, intertextual space in a given culture
would seem to be constantly expanding. But how can we tell *when* and
how such expansion of discursive space takes place? Did Joel Chandler
Harris expand the discursive space of southern literature by creating the
Uncle Remus who told the animal fables of black folk culture? Or does
Harris' work indicate that the discursive space had already been expanded
sufficiently to allow writers like him to exploit it? Does a given text, in
this case one as unprecedented as *Uncle Remus: His Songs and His Sayings*
(1880), create its discursive space, or does the space necessitate, eventually,
the creation of a text to give it form and signify its potential? In this essay
I will address this question by examining the relationship of *The Confessions of Nat Turner* (1831), a peculiar kind of biracial intertext in its own
right, and John Pendleton Kennedy's *Swallow Barn* (1832), generally considered the first important novel of the plantation tradition in southern
literature.

During the last twenty years slave narratives, including Turner's, have
been read with increasing care as self-conscious texts,[2] though only recently, again in *The History of Southern Literature*, have they been offi-
cially included in the southern literary tradition (Rubin 85–86). Still, the
role that such narratives played in southern literature of the nineteenth century remains undetermined. It is not hard to see in former slaves like
Frederick Douglass, William Wells Brown, and Harriet Jacobs the fore-
runners of twentieth-century southern literary expatriates who had to
leave the South to find the opportunity and freedom to write frankly
about it. Unquestionably slave narratives were among the most widely
read and influential writing that the South produced, willy-nilly, before
the Civil War. Didn't Harriet Beecher Stowe, author of the biggest best-
seller in the United States during the nineteenth century, cite as direct literary influences the memoirs of Douglass, Lewis Clarke, and Josiah Henson
in her intertextual *Key to Uncle Tom's Cabin* (1853)?[3] And through the
medium of *Uncle Tom's Cabin*, didn't the slave narratives, in addition to
provoking wrathful reviews in the South, also compel the South to produce numerous anti-Tom novels in defense of the "peculiar institution"?[4]

Taking a somewhat larger view of the slave narratives' place on the
southern literary scene, we might argue that the first important tradition
in the southern novel — that centering on the image of the Old South
plantation — represents only one side, one version, of that much-studied
tradition. The darker, "other" side of that tradition, which first claimed
national attention with the publication of *The Confessions of Nat Turner*,
reveals not just an alternative perspective on the plantation. A text such
as the *Confessions* calls attention to some of the discursive conditions out
of which the antebellum white plantation tradition, epitomized by Kennedy's

Swallow Barn, emerged. My purpose in this essay is to map out the intertextual (if not influential) relationship between the *Confessions* and *Swallow Barn*, so as to suggest some of the ways in which black and white texts have competed for the right to define the discursive space in which "the Negro" would be signified.

In the first sentence of the *Confessions*, Thomas R. Gray, the Virginia lawyer who wrote this pamphlet after interviewing Nat Turner in jail, announces: "The late insurrection in Southampton has greatly excited the public mind, and led to a thousand idle, exaggerated and mischievous reports" (Tragle 303). Gray suggests that his account of the "insurrection" will help to calm the public by enabling whites "to understand the origin and progress of this dreadful conspiracy, and the motives which influence its diabolical actors." Simply by naming Turner's action an "insurrection," Gray offers from the outset of the *Confessions* a clearly defined interpretation of what Turner was about. He was leading a revolt against civil authority and the constituted government. Yet the first time Turner gets a chance to speak in the *Confessions*, in the opening statement of what is purportedly the slave's oral narrative, we read: "SIR, — You have asked me to give a history of the motives which induced me to undertake the late insurrection, *as you call it*" (306, emphasis added). Turner apparently had no intention of accepting Gray's label as an interpretation of his actions during August 21–23, 1831. Nor does an alternative to Gray's term appear anywhere in Turner's narration. He refers once to "the great work laid out for me to do" as an obligation, borne out by heavenly promptings, to "slay my enemies with their own weapons" (310).[5] But this language is much more descriptive than normative. In the final part of the *Confessions*, which contains a brief account of Turner's trial, we find further indication that, to Turner, his action could not be classified according to standard white moral or political norms. Upon arraignment, we are informed, the prisoner "pleaded *Not guilty*; saying to his counsel, that he did not feel so" (318).

Even a cursory reading of Turner's narrative will suggest why he did not feel guilty about what he had done. He had always enjoyed considerable respect from whites and blacks alike, who treated him with respect, if not awe, because of his intelligence, piety, and leadership potential. By the time he was twenty-five years old, he had devoted himself "more than ever to obtain true holiness before the great day of judgment should appear" (309), eventually coming to the conviction that he had been "made perfect" and was in direct communion with the Holy Spirit. This search for "true holiness" and the slave's belief that he had been made perfect in and through the Holy Spirit were by no means peculiar to Turner. Wesleyan perfectionism had traditionally promised a "second blessing" to Christians who, like Turner, sought to obtain radical holiness, or sanctification, as many American Methodists, black and white, termed it in the nineteenth century.[6] The visions, the sense of having received a second baptism, and the intimate communion with the Holy Spirit that Turner recounts are all consistent with the experiences of others in the holiness movement of the nineteenth century. What made Nat Turner unique, of course, is that once he "began to receive the true knowledge of faith" (309), he came gradually to the conclusion that he had a special role to play in what he interpreted as the impending eschaton, "when the first should be last and the last should be first" (310).

Pervasive in Turner's notion of the "great day of judgment" is a reversal of the instituted order of things. Not only will "the last" and "the first" change places; Turner also inherits Christ's apocalyptic role as the leader of those who must do battle with the loosened Serpent (310).[7] Just who Turner thought the Serpent was is not specified in his narration, but it is clear that he felt himself Christ's vicar and that Gray could not argue him out of his identification with the Messiah in His Second Coming.[8] In the midst of this invoking of Christian eschatology, however, Turner also makes plain allusions to the political scripture of the United States. He mentions that he planned to begin "the work of death" on the Fourth of July, 1831. He also recalls encouraging Will, one of his best "soldiers," in that desperate slave's determination to obtain "his liberty" or "lose his life" in the effort (310). This sort of mixing of the religious and the secular enabled Turner to bridge the gaps between Jesus and Jefferson, Patrick Henry and John the Revelator, as prophets and revolutionaries. No wonder Gray appears at such pains in his comments on Turner to explain him away as "a gloomy fanatic," whose mind, demented by persistent attempts "to grapple with things beyond its reach," could not help but be subverted to "hellish purposes" (304). Nat Turner, self-authorized black messianic scourge of the southern serpent, had utterly collapsed the distinctions between history and eternity, heaven and hell, right and wrong, the sacerdotal and the political. To an antebellum Southerner and a man of the law as well, a product of a society that, in Carl Degler's words, refused "to open up to challenge any facet of the social order" for fear that slavery itself might be threatened (61), Turner must have represented the ultimate horror — the slave, foundation of the socio-economic superstructure, displaced and run amuck.

Yet if we read the *Confessions* closely, we find that perhaps it was not Nat Turner the blindly mad and murderous slave that disturbed Gray the most. At the end of the *Confessions*, Gray lists and dismisses popular misinterpretations of Turner's motives partly to quiet rumors and partly to give the devil his due. After stressing that Turner was not stupid or cowardly, that he was not out to rob and murder in order to finance an escape to the North, and that he was not drunk, the lawyer reiterates his preferred interpretation of Turner as crazed by religious enthusiasm.[9] This time, however, he makes a significant qualification: "He is a complete fanatic, or plays his part most admirably" (317). Here Gray implicitly confirms the deepest anxiety aroused by Nat Turner in the antebellum southern mind: maybe this slave was not what he seemed; maybe the category of last resort — that of religious madman — did *not* explain him; maybe he was *beyond* explanation except in accordance with his own masked intentions.[10] This would imply that a black man like Turner could not be situated in the known order of things. It also implies that in this man's mind another order of things existed that would explain why he played his part so expertly before the white man.[11] Faced with this prospect, Gray understandably shied away. Instead he leaves his reader with a final Byronic image of Turner that betrays the white man's own unresolved impressions of a Negro who could be "calm and deliberate" in speech, yet "fiendlike" in visage "when excited by enthusiasm," who though marked by the blood of his innocent victims, "yet dar[ed] to raise his manacled hands to heaven, with a spirit soaring above the attributes of man" (317). The implicit contradictions in this image of Turner — is he fiend or victim, a transcendent spirit or a debased intellect? — attest to the unclassifiable space in southern racist discourse that Turner opened up, for which Gray could find no closure.

The problems that Thomas Gray faced in reading and writing Nat Turner were unprecedented in southern literature. Before the Turner uprising, southern narrative had enjoyed the luxury of ignoring blacks as anything more than a picturesque part of plantation scenery (McDowell 56). George Tucker's *The Valley of the Shenandoah* (1824) was a notable exception to this rule because it not only included black characters but also admitted some of the uglier aspects of the slave system. Yet even in this novel the Negroes who are individualized are thoroughly acculturated into the mores of "the peculiar institution." They are uniformly happy with their lot and celebrated especially for their "undeviating loyalty" to their master (McDowell 57). Jean Fagan Yellin points out that the black characters in this novel are used mainly "to convey a sense of loss through their recollection of the heroic Revolutionary past" (28). She finds it paradoxical that it should be left to the slaves to voice such nostalgia for an idealized southern past. Yet from the hindsight we gain from the *Confessions*, it is not hard to understand Tucker's reasons for making his slaves the principal spokespersons for the old order. Their nostalgia for the heroic days of the past exemplifies a deep-seated resistance to change, a conservatism that would become increasingly militant among southern writers and politicians after the Turner uprising and the nullification controversies of the 1830s. Tucker's slaves not only endorse southern conservatism; they also give voice to the increasing fear in the slaveocracy that the drift of the era was against it, that its struggle was to hold the line against the advancing tide of "isms" that threatened to sweep away southern civilization in the name of misbegotten "reform."

Slaves, according to southern ideology, quite naturally fear change and long for stasis. According to a dominant stereotype of the Negro in the early nineteenth century, one maintained by such European philosophers as Hegel and Hume, the African was incapable of change, except for the worse, unless carefully supervised by whites. Hegel called Africa the land of perpetual childhood whose denizens were "capable of no development or culture." "As we see them at this day, such have they always been" (quoted in Gates 19-20). "No change of their nature can be expected to result" from any efforts to elevate them from slavery to freedom, argued an early defender of slavery in the United States, and plenty of antebellum southern writers echoed the notion that blacks were predestined to occupy their peculiar station in the scheme of things, both ethnologically and socio-economically (Fredrickson 49-51). It is not surprising, then, that Tucker made his Negroes such ardent conservatives. The Negro of antebellum southern myth and propaganda is and must always be a constant, constitutionally averse and impervious to change, for the sake of himself, his white folks, and the southern ideal of civilization.

The Confessions of Nat Turner plainly challenged this image of the Negro as a constant, lacking the motive or potential for change unless and until factored into the white man's equation. Let us not overlook the important fact that the *Confessions* contains the first significant chronology of an African American life in southern literature. The simple but unprecedented import of the "confession" Turner recounts, when compared with earlier treatments of blacks in southern narrative, lies in Turner's making a history of *himself*, when all his white interviewer asked him for was "a history of the motives" that led to his uprising. From the outset of his portion of the *Confessions*, Turner announces that, to give a proper accounting of his motives, "I must go back to the days of my infancy, and even before I was born" (Tragle 306). He then makes a crucial statement that interjects him irreversibly into history: "I was thirty-one years of age the 2nd of October last, and born the property of Benj. Turner, of this county." What follows is Turner's personal story, carried through a discernible beginning, middle, and end, and bearing the authority and sense of reality that seem immanent in the structure of narrative itself.[12] Ironically, Gray's attempts to enclose Turner's narrative in a web of explanation and moralizing only heighten its claim to authority, since only a powerful and trenchant version of history could inspire such an intense counterargument. By the end of the *Confessions*, Turner successfully resists Gray's attempt to explain, categorize, and enclose him primarily because he has been allowed to represent himself through the dynamics of narrative. Regardless of how truthful that dictated narrative was, it testified convincingly to the potential of black reality to be narrativized. It opened up southern narrative to the idea that the slave not only could change, but could do so in a way that was meaningful to white reality, indeed, that was capable of enlarging and rewriting southern history.

The idea of a Negro who could change, and thereby alter the entire sociopolitical structure of the slaveocracy, shook the South. Nat Turner did not, however, revolutionize white southern depictions of the slave in the antebellum era. The demand for political orthodoxy in polite southern letters helps explain why the dominant image of the slave for two decades after the Turner uprising remained Sambo-like.[13] Only a writer who did not toe the political line of his region and who was not caught up in the idealization of the "Old South" (about which antebellum southern literature became increasingly preoccupied) could imagine the timeless, edenic southern plantation threatened by a black serpent of change.[14]

John Pendleton Kennedy was just such a writer. *Swallow Barn* retains its currency in southern literature mainly because its portrayal of a Tidewater Virginia plantation treats many southern institutions with gentle irony and many southern shibboleths with skepticism.[15] Given Kennedy's unorthodox attitudes, one would be surprised to find him conducting literary business as usual in his depiction of slavery at Swallow Barn. Moreover, because *Swallow Barn* was completed scarcely four months after Turner's uprising, it is unlikely that Kennedy could have escaped the influence of contemporary events when he thought about the character of the slaves in his book. Whether the young Baltimore lawyer actually read the *Confessions*, which were published in the District of Columbia almost two months before Kennedy finished his book, is not known. That he knew about Turner and the rumors and controversy that his uprising occasioned is unquestionable. No informed Southerner could not have known about Turner; no thoughtful Southerner, as Kennedy was on the slavery question, could have ignored the implications of Turner's act.[16] A slave from the Tidewater region of Virginia had upset the presuppositions upon which the treatment of slavery in southern literature had been based. The author of the first southern novel published after the uprising could hardly have ignored the idea, as Lewis P. Simpson puts it, that "out of the heart of the garden of the chattel in its most idealized image there might come forth a slave who, potentially at any rate, could become an apostatic figure" (50). The key to the appearance of such a figure in *Swallow Barn* lies, ultimately, not in its revolutionary alterity, however.[17] Rather, what is significant in this novel is, first, its capacity to make room for the alien, Turner-inspired idea of the slave as apostate to the social and moral order, and second, its ability to domesticate that seemingly alien idea as an intertextual variant of the Western European literary tradition.

The slave in question is named Abe, and he makes his appearance in an extended tale-within-a-tale that comes just before the conclusion of *Swallow Barn*. The son of the most treasured slaves of the former owner of Swallow Barn, Abe is "a singularly active" youth, "noted for his spirit, and his occasional bursts of passion" as well as for his "shrewdness of intellect, and an aptitude for almost every species of handicraft" (Kennedy 2:239). Unfortunately, Abe is also readily "corrupted" by an early association with "the most profligate menials" of Swallow Barn. By his young manhood he has hardened into "the most irreclaimable of spirits," known to be part of "a band of out-lying negroes, who had secured themselves, for some weeks, in the fastnesses of the low country swamps, from whence they annoyed the vicinity by nocturnal incursions of the most lawless character" (2:240–41). Only Abe's mother, who dotes on him, and his master, who abhors the idea of selling any of his slaves, stand between him and "public justice." Frank Meriwether, lord of the manor, decides that the best solution to the problem of his "refractory bondman" is to remove him from the estate and hire him out to a Chesapeake Bay pilot.

After a few years of sea life, "great changes" become evident in Abe. "The fearless qualities of his mind" are "greatly developed to the advantage of his character" by "the hardy discipline of his calling." "The vagrant, sunshiny, and billowy life of a sailor" casts a salutary spell over "the heedless and irresponsible temperament" of this Negro. One might say that he finds himself on the sea; he becomes "well content" with "his various destiny between the lowest trough of the sea, and the highest whitecap of the billow" (2:249–50). When asked to captain a rescue boat for the crew of a brig stranded in a February storm, Abe does not hesitate to accept the assignment. Nor does he ask for anything in return but his choice of a boat and crew. White seamen argue that the expedition is doomed, but Abe replies, "We can try, you know; and if no good comes on it, let them that *saunt* me judge of that. I always obeys orders!" (2:253). Faithful to his charge, Abe succeeds in reaching the wrecked brig not once but three times in a superhuman attempt to save the stranded white men. But he and his intrepid black crew are lost in the furious weather, leaving the narrator of *Swallow Barn* to eulogize their gallantry. The narrator, a Northerner not given to romantic excess, declares that Abe and his fellow blacks were "swayed by a noble emulation to relieve the distressed" and "impelled by that love of daring which the romancers call chivalry" (2:258).

"Such heroism," the narrator avers, though it came from "an humble and unknown negro," deserves comparison to the acts of white heroes immortalized in history.

The key issue in an examination of Abe vis-à-vis Nat Turner is not how much Kennedy's concept of a "lawless" and "outcast" slave was influenced by Turner. There are some similarities as well as some differences between Abe and Prophet Nat, which make the question of influence debatable and probably unresolvable. It is more profitable to investigate how Turner — as either a historical phenomenon or a figure in a text — affected the discursive space in which the slave would be reconceived in a subsequent southern text such as *Swallow Barn*. We have already seen the problems that Turner presented to one southern writer who attempted to formulate an explanation of the otherness that this black man so forcibly represented. Does *Swallow Barn* register similar problems and anxieties? If so, how does it accommodate itself to black difference, or that difference to the discourse of *Swallow Barn*?

Swallow Barn is unprecedented in southern literature in admitting to the ranks of the hero a proud, intelligent, and capable black man whose behavior plainly indicates "resentment at the authority that was exercised over him" by whites (2:245). This "outcast" black man, admired and feared by his fellow slaves and unmanageable by whites, represents the most serious attempt that southern literature had yet made in conceiving of black difference. Abe is in several important respects unclassifiable and perhaps unknowable. The reasons for his resistance to white authority are not probed in *Swallow Barn*, as Turner's motives are in the *Confessions*. We know that Abe's fractiousness is not attributable to mistreatment, for Meriwether has permitted Abe "to take his own way" without even the usual supervision. We also know that Abe is not motivated by a desire for emancipation. He tells his mother that he "never cared for" freedom (2:248), and he does not bargain for his freedom when he has the chance to set conditions before undertaking the rescue mission on the Chesapeake Bay. The narrator of the novel states that Abe's early involvement with "the most profligate menials" of Swallow Barn "corrupted" him and rendered him "offensive to the whole plantation." But nothing is said about why he became so involved, when his abilities and opportunities might just as easily have induced him in the opposite direction. In the absence of any explicit explanation, therefore, one can easily deduce from Abe's career that a proud, intelligent slave might, in the natural course of events, feel resentful toward white authority and demonstrate his resentment through antisocial behavior, without having any larger or deeper motive such as Gray tried to assign to Nat Turner. The absence of easily nameable motive in Abe may suggest that he is simply a rebel without a cause. But the question of Abe's motive is a singular question to beg in antebellum white southern literature, for it makes posssible the conclusion that an able, spirited, and intelligent black man needs no particular motive for resisting his bondage.

Another striking aspect of Abe is his ability to change. The familiar "before and after" pattern of the American success story structures the narrrative of this unlikely hero. In view of the stereotype of the Negro as inherently unchangeable, there is something very unusual about the narrator's assertion that "great changes had been wrought upon" Abe after working several years as a sailor 2:249). Abe's intellectual and moral qualities "greatly develop" without any evident direction or supervision from a white master. Once placed in an environment congenial to "the temper and cast of his constitution," the slave attains "the full perfection of manhood" (2:252) apparently on his own. Compared with Gray's explicit demand for more rigid regulation of slaves in the aftermath of Turner's uprising, Kennedy's implied message in the case of Abe seems almost heretical. Kennedy might be read as suggesting that every black did not have a place in the plantation order — and more radically, that slavery and its traditional means of regulating black behavior were not the best ways to ensure that superior blacks would become heroes like Abe, rather than horrors like Nat Turner.

By opening up his novel to a narrative treatment of a slave who changes from incipient rebel to chivalric hero, Kennedy takes a leaf from the text of the Turner phenomenon,[18] we might say, but only to write it in reverse. In light of Turner it was impossible to deny that a slave could evolve on his own into spiritual, political, and moral dimensions hitherto unimagined in southern literature. What Kennedy did with Abe was to accept the premise that a Negro could be converted from social conformism to militant antisocial activism, only to assert its opposite, that a Negro could be reformed to take exactly the reverse of Turner's path. Thus Kennedy's story of Abe exists as a kind of intertextual complement to Gray's story of Turner. Just as every sign in a text has its obverse in an intertext that complements the text in reverse, as a negative complements a photograph (Riffaterre 627, 629), so a plot may also have its complement in a similar sort of intertextual negative whose presence-in-reverse appears inescapably in the unfolding of the plot. In this case, the *Confessions* serves as the dark "negative" of Kennedy's "positive" variant of the narrative of the transformed Negro. In writing Abe's story, Kennedy may be seen as plotting against Turner himself and the innumerable rumors about him that had so indelibly narrativized this black man in southern discourse.

The Turner phenomenon unleashed upon the South numerous competing narratives of Turner the arch-conspirator, the "great bandit," the ma-

rauder crazed by abolitionist propaganda. The multiplicty of these versions of Turner did much to exacerbate the hysteria that swept the South
in the fall of 1831.[19] Gray tried (unsuccessfully, as we have seen) to invent
a single authoritative Turner story that would halt the proliferation of
Turners and establish an official southern line on Turner, a manageable
myth of the man and his actions. Meanwhile, abolitionists like William
Lloyd Garrison entered the discursive fray with their own version of Turner
and their own interpretations of his antislavery significance.[20] When *Swallow Barn* was published, southern narratives of the Negro,[21] especially
those newly inspired by the Turner phenomenon, were in a state of flux
and open to replotting and reinterpretation in fiction. By plotting the
Turner-inspired narrative in reverse, Kennedy may be read as yet another
southern writer bent on somehow rechanneling and seizing control of the
power of the new narrative of the subversive Negro. What makes Kennedy
noteworthy, however, is that he *novelized* the narrative of the Negro subversive for the first time. Transforming Negro subversion into Negro heroism was something of a rhetorical risk for a Southerner writing at the
height of the Turner hysteria, but there was political compensation for this
act of southern literary accommodation. Admitting the Negro as hero
into southern *literary* narrative was one way of displacing the black man
as subversive from southern *historical* narrative.

    "It was a gallant sight," concludes the narrator of *Swallow Barn*, "to
see such heroism shining out in an humble slave of the Old Dominion!"
(2:258). But Abe pays a price for being the Negro as hero in white southern literature. His actions become explainable according to prevailing white
southern norms. He is "impelled by that love of daring which the romancers call chivalry." This kind of "daring" warmed the southern heart. It was
the antithesis of the "daring" that moved Nat Turner to "raise his manacled hands to heaven, with a spirit soaring above the attributes of man."
That image "curdled" Thomas Gray's blood in his veins (Tragle 317). The
"noble" self-sacrifice of Abe and his band transforms them into "our
argonauts" (2:259), subsuming their action under a white Western literary
category that further helps to naturalize these black sailors into Negroes
whom whites could comfortably understand and romanticize.[22]
One should also not miss the implication of this consignment of the Negro
as hero to the realm of romance and classical myth. The narrator of *Swallow
Barn* acknowledges the comparability of Abe and his men to "heroes
whose names have been preserved fresh in the verdure of history." But,
he goes on, "History is a step-mother, and gives the bauble fame to her
own children, with such favoritism as she lists" (2:258). Who are History's
own children? Clearly they are white men. Negro heroes who measure up
to the standards of History may be celebrated in white novels, or, in the

case of *Swallow Barn*, thinly disguised fictions got up to look like travel books. But *Swallow Barn*'s narrator ensures that they have never been and presumably never will be part of the narrative of History.

If the Negro as hero is fit material only for novels, not for history, in the view of a Southerner as open-minded as Kennedy, what possible place was there in nineteenth-century southern literature or history for a black man like Turner, the antithesis of the formulatable Negro as culture-affirming hero? The answer is plain enough, according to an impressive study of the Turner phenomenon and its historical aftermath. Writing in 1970 Henry Irving Tragle states that historians of Virginia tend to view the Southampton revolt as a nonevent and Turner as a nonperson (Tragle 1, 5–7). Yet while Turner's historical identity waned, the literary importance of Abe, his alter ego, grew in the nineteenth century. White novelists as different as Harriet Beecher Stowe and Mark Twain went on reinventing the Negro as hero, making Abe into Uncle Tom and Nigger Jim, who in turn made it more and more difficult for white Americans to recall Nat Turner. White southern literature embraced Abe and Jim and even Uncle Tom, while denying a place in its history to the text that enabled — or rather, forced — such narratives of the Negro to be conceived. Only in 1967, when William Styron's novel tapped into the power of the *Confessions* for good and for ill, did Southerners black and white begin to reread seriously and historically this crucial text of southern literature.

The fate of the *Confessions* is perhaps instructive, therefore, to those who want to reconstruct southern literary history along biracial lines. It may be that nineteenth-century southern narratives of the Negro are less significant for their admission of a version of blackness into literature than for their displacement of another version of blackness from history. If so, then inter(racial) textuality in the southern narrative tradition may be the product of attempts by culturally sanctioned literary texts to fill — or maybe just paper over — black holes created in the dominant discourse by texts that have been "forgotten" or banished from official southern historical consciousness.[23] Canonical southern narratives of the Negro like *Swallow Barn, Uncle Tom's Cabin, The Adventures of Huckleberry Finn*, and maybe even *Up from Slavery* might be usefully re-historicized as the intertextual complements of black narratives (like those of Turner, Josiah Henson, James W. C. Pennington, and Frederick Douglass)[24] whose problematic discourse was re-voiced in literature even as it was being de-voiced in and *as* history.

In postulating this notion of southern inter(racial)textuality, I do not wish to suggest that the process is simply one of (white) literature answering (black) history in order to silence it. This is only one hypothesis that might be tested regarding the dynamics of the interrelationship of literary works and cultural texts in southern history. It seems entirely possible that the autobiographies of white southern rebels and expatriates like Moncure Conway, whose opposition to slavery seemed the ultimate self-denigration in the eyes of his region, owe much more to the black southern autobiographical tradition, epitomized by Frederick Douglass's *My Bondage and My Freedom* (1855), than to classic white southern autobiographies like Jefferson's.[25] Only by rethinking southern culture in ways that enable us to conceive of the possible participation of a Turner and a Kennedy, a Douglass and a Conway in the full textuality of southern history can we begin to assess anew the biracial dimension of nineteenth-century southern literature.

NOTES

1   An important indication of recent critical interest in the influence of black literature on a particular white writer is Susan Stanford Friedman's "Modernism of the 'Scattered Remnant': Race and Politics in H.D.'s Development." See also Houston A. Baker's *Modernism and the Harlem Renaissance*.

2   See Andrews, *To Tell a Free Story*; Davis and Gates, *The Slave's Narrative*; Foster, *Witnessing Slavery*; and Sekora and Turner, *The Art of Slave Narrative* for a representative sample of recent scholarship.

3   See Stowe, *The Key to Uncle Tom's Cabin* 18–22, 24–29, 42–44. It is worth noting that in her second antislavery novel, *Dred: A Tale of the Great Dismal Swamp* (1856), Stowe was greatly influenced by the *Confessions of Nat Turner* (1831), a copy of which was appended to the text. Another best-seller of the antebellum era, Richard Hildreth's abolitionist novel *The Slave, or Memoirs of Archy Moore* (1836), was published anonymously under the guise of a slave narrative and was not recognized as a fiction until so acknowledged by its author in 1852.

4   For a list and discussion of the anti-Tom novels, see Jeannette Tandy, "Pro-Slavery Propaganda in American Fiction of the Fifties."

5   In my comments on what "he" refers to in the narrative part of the *Confessions*, "he" should be construed as the character, the voice, and the words assigned to Nat Turner by Thomas R. Gray, Turner's purported amanuensis. One cannot determine for certain the extent to which the Nat Turner who supposedly speaks through Gray in the *Confessions* is in fact Gray ventriloquizing through Nat Turner.

6   See Lindström (92, 113–20, 148) for a discussion of Wesleyan perfectionism. See also the chapters "The Holiness Revival at Oberlin" and "Sanctification in American Methodism" in Smith (103–34). For a discussion of black participation in the holiness movement in the nineteenth century, see Hardesty, Dayton, and Dayton, "Women in the Holiness Movement: Feminism in the Evangelical Tradition," and Andrews, *Sisters of the Spirit*.

7   According to Turner, on May 12, 1828, the Holy Spirit informed him that "the Serpent was loosened, and Christ had laid down the yoke he had borne for the sins of men, and that I should take it on and fight against the Serpent, for the time was fast approaching when the first should be last and the last should be first" (Tragle 167). Here Turner recalls the eschatological prophecies of Revelation 20:1–10. For further commentary on Turner's welding of black folk religion with the Old and New Testament prophecies, see Mathews (231–36).

8   After Turner puts himself in Christ's role in the apocalyptic battle with the Serpent, Gray interrupts with the question "Do you not find yourself mistaken now?" to which Turner replies, "Was not Christ crucified?" (Tragle 167).

9   In what is probably the most obvious interpolation of Gray's views and language into Turner's narration, Turner is made to say, "In my childhood a circumstance occurred which made an indelible impression on my mind, and laid the ground work of that enthusiasm, which has terminated so fatally to many, both white and black, and for which I am about to atone at the gallows" (Tragle 165). There is no evidence anywhere else in Turner's narration that he regarded himself as a victim of religious "enthusiasm" or that he needed to atone for that at the gallows.

10 A similar anxiety about the knowability of apparently contented and reliable slaves is expressed by Mary Boykin Chesnut in her journal entry dated July 24, 1861: "I am always studying these creatures. They are to me inscrutable in their ways and past finding out" (Chesnut 114).

11 For a discussion of the structure of Turner's worldview, see Mathews (222–26, 231–36). My concern in this paper is not with the particulars of Turner's worldview, only with the fact that even a man like Gray could not quell the idea that Turner had one.

12 These comments on narrative are based on ideas more fully developed in White's "The Value of Narrativity in the Representation of Reality."

13 *Uncle Tom's Cabin*, of course, forced white southern writers to give blacks prominent roles in the fiction of the 1850s.

14 For a discussion of the investment of southern reactionism in the idea of the plantation of the "Old South," a garden of "pastoral independence and pastoral permanence, redeemed from the ravages of history," see Simpson (17–25, 55–60).

15 See Lucinda H. MacKethan's introduction to the 1986 reprint of *Swallow Barn* for a thorough discussion of the novel's unorthodoxy.

16 Kennedy announced the completion of *Swallow Barn* in his journal on December 31, 1831. In 1830 he sold the only slave he ever owned. As a political man, Kennedy's positions were ambivalent on slavery. He could not convince himself that human bondage was morally acceptable, but he feared the social and economic ramifications of emancipation in the South. See Bohner (72, 169–71).

17 My discussion of *Swallow Barn* differs from that of Yellin in *The Intricate Knot*, who argues that the novel does not respond to the events of the Nat Turner uprising (50), and from that of Lewis P. Simpson in *The Dispossessed Garden*, who sees the black apostate of the novel as a revolutionary who yearns "to transform the garden of the chattel into a domain of pastoral freedom, an Eden of freed slaves" (50).

18 By "the text of the Turner phenomenon," I do not mean the *Confessions* pub-
    lished by Gray but rather all the narratives and reports printed in the after-
    math of the uprising. See the forty-four newspaper accounts published within
    two months of the uprising in Tragle (31–132). See also Samuel Warner's
    *Authentic and impartial narrative of the tragical scene which Was witnessed
    in southhampton county (virginia) on Monday the 22nd of august last*, which
    antedates Gray's account, in Tragle (280–300).
19 For documents attesting to the multiple rumors and interpretations of Turner,
    see Tragle (31–153), and Aptheker (38–41, 71–74).
20 William Lloyd Garrison pronounced Turner's uprising a manifestation of
    "the vengeance of Heaven" upon "this guilty land" and predicted more blood-
    shed unless immediate and unconditional emancipation was instituted in the
    South. See *Liberator*, September 3, 1831, as reprinted in Tragle (62–64).
21 My phrase "narrative of the Negro" denotes those narratives that portray "the
    Negro" in accordance with the presuppositions of the dominant (white) ideol-
    ogy of the South at the time. My use of "the Negro" in this way is indebted
    to Thadious Davis' *Faulkner's "Negro"* (1–4).
22 In *Heart in Conflict: Faulkner's Struggles with Vocation*, Michael Grimwood
    treats *Swallow Barn* as a useful example of how plantation fiction attempted
    to maintain the myth of southern "interracial comity" by turning Abe, a
    "renegade slave," into "a black saint" idealized because of his self-sacrificial
    behavior in the end (240). While Grimwood's assessment of the politics of
    Abe's transformation is unquestionable, it should be pointed out in light of
    Prophet Nat's self-identification with Christian tradition in the *Confessions*,
    that Kennedy specifically links Abe to classical, not Christian, heroic prece-
    dent. In making this link, Kennedy was again redirecting the very idea of slave
    resistance away from the unnerving eschatological associations that Turner
    conjured up and back toward familiar classical categories contained within
    the framework of Western history.
23 For another application of the idea of black holes to American literary his-
    tory, see John Sekora and Houston A. Baker, Jr., "Written Off" 52–53. Unlike
    Sekora and Baker, I would not insist that black textual holes are also (w)holes
    but rather that their lack of wholeness is what generates in literary texts the
    image of the Negro as what Thadious Davis calls "the possibility of whole-
    ness" (4).
24 For a discussion of the possible influence of Pennington's fugitive slave nar-
    rative on *Huckleberry Finn*, see Andrews, "Mark Twain and James W. C. Pen-
    nington: Huckleberry Finn's Smallpox Lie."
25 A reading of Conway's journal of 1852 reveals the degree to which he com-
    pared himself to a slave longing for freedom on the eve of his break with his
    father and his journey to the North in search of an antislavery community.
    See d'Entremont (65). Conway's *Testimonies Concerning Slavery* (1864) lends
    further support to the idea of an intertextual relationship between black and
    white antebellum southern dissenters. Moreover, the possible inter(racial)tex-
    tuality of white southern rebels and black southern heroes like Booker T.
    Washington should not be ignored in light of Conway's recommendation that

miscegenation would be of great value to America in creating "a new Race" and that the Negro "is quite essential to the work that all races have to do on that continent, and which they cannot do until all unite as the fingers of One Great Hand" (77). Conway the apostate was read out of southern history, of course, yet a tantalizing resurfacing of his image of miscegenation, utterly revised to soothe white southern fear of miscegenation in the 1890s, appears in Washington's famous Atlanta Exposition Address: "In all things that are purely social we can be as separate as the fingers, yet one as the hand in all things essential to mutual progress" (*Washington Papers* 1:332).

WORKS CITED

Andrews, William L. *The Literary Career of Charles W. Chesnutt.* Baton Rouge: Louisiana State UP, 1980.

Andrews, William L. "Mark Twain and James W. C. Pennington: Huckleberry Finn's Smallpox Lie." *Studies in American Fiction* 9 (1981): 103–12.

Andrews, William L. *To Tell a Free Story: The First Century of Afro-American Autobiography, 1760–1865.* Urbana: U of Illinois P, 1986.

Andrews, William L., ed. *Sisters of the Spirit: Three Black Women's Autobiographies of the Nineteenth Century.* Bloomington: Indiana UP, 1986.

Aptheker, Herbert. *Nat Turner's Slave Rebellion.* New York: Humanities P, 1966.

Baker, Houston A. *Modernism and the Harlem Renaissance.* Chicago: U of Chicago P, 1987.

Barksdale, Richard, and Keneth Kinnamon, eds. *Black Writers of America.* New York: Macmillan, 1972.

Bohner, Charles H. *John Pendleton Kennedy.* Baltimore: Johns Hopkins UP, 1961.

Bone, Robert A. *The Negro Novel in America.* New Haven, CT: Yale UP, 1965.

Brown, Sterling. *Negro Poetry and Drama.* 1937. New York: Atheneum, 1972.

Cash, W. J. *The Mind of the South.* New York: Vintage, n.d.

Chesnut, Mary Boykin. *Mary Chesnut's Civil War.* Ed. C. Vann Woodward. New Haven: Yale UP, 1981.

Conway, Moncure. *Testimonies concerning Slavery.* London: Chapman and Hall, 1864.

Culler, Jonathan. *The Pursuit of Signs.* Ithaca: Cornell UP, 1981.

Davis, Charles T., and Henry Louis Gates, Jr., eds. *The Slave's Narrative.* New York: Oxford UP, 1985.

Davis, Thadious. *Faulkner's "Negro".* Baton Rouge: Louisiana State UP, 1983.

Degler, Carl. *Place over Time: The Continuity of Southern Distinctiveness.* Baton Rouge: Louisiana State UP, 1977.

D'Entremont, John. *Southern Emancipator: Moncure Conway, the American Years, 1832–1865.* New York: Oxford UP, 1987.

Foster, Frances Smith. *Witnessing Slavery: The Development of Ante-bellum Slave Narratives.* Westport, CT: Greenwood P, 1979.

Frady, Marshall. *Southerners*. New York: New American Library, 1980.

Fredrickson, George M. *The Black Image in the White Mind*. 1971. Middletown, CT: Wesleyan UP, 1987.

Friedman, Susan Stanford. "Modernism of the 'Scattered Remnant': Race and Politics in H.D.'s Development." In *Feminist Issues in Literary Scholarship*, ed. Shari Benstock, 208–32. Bloomington: Indiana UP, 1987.

Gates, Henry Louis, Jr. *Figures in Black*. New York: Oxford UP, 1987.

Gloster, Hugh M. *Negro Voices in American Fiction*. Chapel Hill: U of North Carolina P, 1948.

Grimwood, Michael. *Heart in Conflict: Faulkner's Struggles with Vocation*. Athens: U of Georgia P, 1987.

Gwin, Minrose. *Black and White Women of the Old South*. Knoxville: U of Tennessee P, 1985.

Kennedy, John Pendleton. *Swallow Barn*. 2 vols. Philadelphia: Carey and Lea, 1832.

Hardesty, Nancy, Lucille Sider Dayton, and Donald W. Dayton. "Women in the Holiness Movement: Feminism in the Evangelical Tradition." In *Women of Spirit*, ed. Rosemary Ruether and Eleanor McLaughlin, 225–54. New York: Simon and Schuster, 1979.

Jefferson, Thomas. *Notes on the State of Virginia*. Ed. William Peden. New York: Norton, 1972.

Kristeva, Julia. *Revolution in Poetic Language*. Trans. Margaret Waller. New York: Columbia UP, 1984.

Lindström, Harald. *Wesley and Sanctification*. London: Epworth, 1950.

Loggins, Vernon. *The Negro Author: His Development in America to 1900*. Port Washington, NY: Kennikat P, 1964.

McDowell, Tremaine. "The Negro in the Southern Novel prior to 1850." *Journal of English and Germanic Philology* 25 (1926): 455–73. Rpt. in *Images of the Negro in American Literature*, Ed. Seymour L. Gross and John Edward Hardy, 54–70. Chicago: U of Chicago P, 1966.

MacKethan, Lucinda H. Introduction to *Swallow Barn*, by John Pendleton Kennedy. Baton Rouge: Louisiana State UP, 1986.

Mathews, Donald G. *Religion in the Old South*. Chicago: U of Chicago P, 1977.

Payne, Ladell. *Black Novelists and the Southern Literary Tradition*. Athens: U of Georgia P, 1981.

Riffaterre, Michael. "Syllepsis." *Critical Inquiry* 6 (1980): 625–638.

Rubin, Louis D., et al., eds. *The History of Southern Literature*. Baton Rouge: Louisiana State UP, 1985.

Sekora, John, and Houston A. Baker, Jr. "Written Off: Narratives, Master Texts, and Afro-American Writing from 1760–1945." In *Black American Prose Theory*, ed. Joe Weixlmann and Chester J. Fontenot, 43–62. Studies in Black American Literature 1. Greenwood, FL: Penkevill, 1983.

Sekora, John, and Darwin T. Turner, eds. *The Art of Slave Narrative*. Macomb, IL: Essays in Literature, 1982.

Simpson, Lewis P. *The Dispossessed Garden*. Baton Rouge: Louisiana State UP, 1975.

Smith, Timothy. *Revivalism and Social Reform in Mid-Nineteenth-Century America*. New York: Abingdon, 1957.

Starling, Marion Wilson. *The Slave Narrative*. Boston: G. K. Hall, 1981.

Stowe, Harriet Beecher. *The Key to Uncle Tom's Cabin*. Boston: John P. Jewett, 1853.

Tandy, Jeannette Reid. "Pro-Slavery Propaganda in American Fiction of the Fifties." *South Atlantic Quarterly* 21 (1922): 41–50, 170–78.

Tragle, Henry Irving. *The Southampton Slave Revolt of 1831*. Amherst: U of Massachusetts P, 1971.

Washington, Booker T. *The Autobiographical Papers*. Vol. 1 of *The Booker T. Washington Papers*, ed. Louis R. Harlan. Urbana: U of Illinois P, 1972.

White, Hayden. "The Value of Narrativity in the Representation of Reality." *Critical Inquiry* 7 (1980). Rpt. in *The Content of the Form* 1–25. Baltimore: Johns Hopkins UP, 1987.

Yellin, Jean Fagan. *The Intricate Knot: Black Figures in American Literature, 1776–1863*. New York: New York UP, 1972.

CHAPTER 13

Chronotope and Intertext: The Case of Jean Rhys's Quartet

BETSY DRAINE

Just about everyone but Jean Rhys has understood her first novel, *Quartet*, to be an autobiographical act of vengeance against her erstwhile lover and literary patron, Ford Madox Ford. Rhys herself found that view appalling. In a letter written a good thirty years after the publication of *Quartet*, Rhys claimed: "I was astonished when so many people thought it an auto-biography from page 1 onwards and told me it should never have been written. Well, I had to write it. Even in America it was supposed to be a roman à clef. . . . I think it is angry and uneven as you say, but it has some life and it wasn't an autobiography, as everyone here seemed to imagine though some of it was lived of course" (*Letters* 171). The "some of it [that] was lived" has, "of course," been treated as the *source* behind *Quartet*. Likewise, the lines of literary *influence* suggested by the story of Ford's mentorship of his talented mistress have proven an irresistible lure to those interested in documenting a modernism in which Ford's impres-sionism is a defining force.[1]

In the early 1980s, however, two students of the Ford/Rhys relationship quietly brought to a theoretical turning point the source-hunting, influence-tracing approach to Rhys's early novel. In an article ironically titled "Rhys Recalls Ford: *Quartet* and *The Good Soldier*," Judith Kegan Gardiner unraveled the prevailing notion that Rhys wrote her novel as a pure recol-lection of her affair with Ford. Instead, Gardiner argued, "Rhys trans-formed the naked autobiography of her experiences with Ford so that the plot and main characters of her novel would parallel those of *The Good Soldier*" (69). Far from imitating either life with Ford or Ford's most artful text, Rhys "disassembles and reuses" elements of both in order to expose the "specifically oppressive social reality in which her characters" — and

Ford's — "are enmeshed" (73). Gardiner's article is dominated not by the image of Rhys as the object of Ford's literary influence, but rather by a vision of Rhys as subject — as authorial agent, shaping "a countertext to Ford's" (68). Such a perspective is just as revolutionary as — and no more so than — Harold Bloom's theory of "revisionary" rewriting is in relation to theories of influence that privilege the precursor text. Just as Bloom emphasizes and admires the strong poet's "swerves" from the work of his predecessor, Gardiner stresses and honors the ways in which Rhys deviates, in *Quartet*, from the techniques, themes, and values of Ford's *The Good Soldier*. The theoretical advance consists in the shift of attention from the act of influence (on the part of the "prior" author) to the act of revision (on the part of the so-called disciple). This is an "advance" and a "revolution" in crudely political terms: the maneuver wrests power from an established author and grants it to an upstart hostile to the establishment. With Ford and Rhys, this is not merely an instance of generational succession. Rather, here the waif supplants her patron, the mistress bests her master, the social outcast embarrasses the social arbiters, the Creole immigrant unsettles "Anglo-Saxon" complacencies.

In terms of the history of the development of concepts of influence and intertextuality, Gardiner's move, like Bloom's, might be seen as conservative. It conserves the idea of the author as sovereign subject, in control of the text she produces, as of the text she revises. As Jay Clayton and Eric Rothstein suggest in the essay that introduces this volume, such a conservation of the authorial subject cuts both ways politically. On the one hand, with its focus on the author as originator and owner of her text, it reinforces the individualism that lies at the heart of the very social system that novels such as *Quartet* critique — that is, a patriarchal, hierarchical capitalism masking its rapaciousness with the occasional democratic or benevolent gesture. On the other hand, it is by recognizing Rhys's agency as author of her own text and as redactor of Ford's that Gardiner opens the way to an interpretation of *Quartet* in the light of its author's specific position in such a society. Once we have considered, with Gardiner, the ways in which Rhys re-vises Ford, we are led inevitably to speculate on Rhys's motives for revision — and these lie, at least in part, in her experience of oppression, as inflected by her gender, her social status, and her ethnicity. In this case, an author-centered study of influence and revision provides an obvious locus for the analysis of how gender, race, and class can make a difference in writing. Conservation of the idea of the author as agent is thus strategically valuable to a kind of criticism that attempts to situate writing in relationship to constructs such as gender, race, and class.[2]

Like Judith Gardiner, Paul Delany used his title to distance himself from critics who had taken too simplistic a view of the relation between

life and art in the Rhys/Ford affair. The title "Jean Rhys and Ford Madox
Ford: What 'Really' Happened?" announces with a simple pair of quotation marks that Delany does not expect his criticism, or any other, to determine a factual source for *Quartet*. On the contrary, Delany sets out "to
demonstrate the extreme and inescapable textuality of the Ford/Rhys affair"
(16). Delany was the first critic to point out that though "the affair between
Rhys and Ford in 1924-25 is well known in literary history" (15), this
"knowledge" is based almost entirely on the evidence of literary texts
written by the principals in the affair—Jean Rhys, her husband Jean Lenglet, Ford Madox Ford, and his common-law wife at the time of the affair,
Stella Bowen. Delany examines the work of each of these principals, searching out the ways in which each shaped a narrative of self-justification.
Like Gardiner, then, Delany retains a stress on authorial agency: "In *Quartet*,
Rhys clearly aligns herself with the powerless outcasts of society, and
against the hypocritical bourgeoisie" (19), painting poverty-striken Marya
as the pitiable victim of the plump and self-satisfied patron of the arts,
Heidler. In a "swerve" worthy of Bloomian analysis, Ford "vulgarized
Rhys in *When the Wicked Man* [his novel of 1931] into a hysterical drunk-
ard, harridan and blackmailer" (21); if Rhys wanted to claim alliance with
the lower classes, Ford could use his fictive powers to hoist her by her own
petard, attributing to her the sordidness and the vices that the bourgeoisie
associates with the lower orders. Delany shows that the spouses of Rhys
and Ford also crafted their textual versions of the affair into briefs for a
self-defense. In his novel *Sous les verrous* (1933), Jean Lenglet exculpates
himself from the implication in *Quartet* that by his criminal conduct,
which landed him in prison, he endangered the safety of a wife who had
no other means of support than himself; conversely, in *Sous les verrous*
it is the fictional wife of the imprisoned man who, in her recklessness and
indolence, ruins both herself and her husband. Similarly, more than a
decade after the publication of *Quartet*, Stella Bowen made her attempt
to combat *Quartet*'s image of the calculating bourgeois wife who tolerates
and even encourages her husband's affairs in order the better to keep him
close to home. In her memoir, *Drawn from Life*, Bowen is at pains to
depict herself as the primary victim of Ford's predatory egoism, deluded
by love into believing that Ford required affairs for the maintenance of
his mental and artistic health. Delany sums up his reading of these texts
and countertexts with the observation that "in the endless struggle for personal and collective justification, text contends with text, and it takes one
nail, always, to drive out another" (23).

   I find that summary phrase to be redolent with implications for the
critic who is drawn to an intertextual approach to writing but whose commitment to examine effects of gender, race, and class continually leads her

back to individual authors who have matters at stake within those cultural arenas. For, in this phrase, Delany imagines an encounter between texts in which such stakes are both personal and collective, both specific to individual authors and general to a cultural unit in which those authors operate. In his article on *Quartet* and its countertexts, Delany's focus is firmly on the matter of the individual author's struggle to justify herself or himself; "collective justification" enters into his analysis only insofar as each author speaks for a specifically situated group — Rhys for underclass women exploited by lustful members of the ruling class, Bowen for the suffering wives of philanders, etc. But it would be possible to understand the phrase "collective justification" in a broader sense than that. We could assume that these four authors, whose paths crossed so intimately in the years 1924–25, shared a collective consciousness — not only because they were involved in the same personal events in the same time and place, but also, and perhaps even more forcibly, because the times and places of their lives offered them a shared "text" with respect to the subject matter they shared. To act on such an assumption would require us to attend to the narrative and linguistic practices these texts share and to look for the pre-texts they might also share. It would allow us, on the other hand, to examine how each author, specifically situated by all sorts of cultural and historical factors, shapes a given set of textual resources "differently."

Rhys herself seemed to favor such a dual understanding of how texts are made. On March 3, 1953, Rhys wrote to an actress to whom she had recently sent a copy of *Quartet* and about whose reaction she was obviously anxious. There was one criticism in particular that she was eager to forestall. In inquiring about *Quartet* as a possible radio vehicle, the actress had let slip that someone had said Rhys's work "dated a bit." Rhys replies:

> I see what he means, but also doubt whether it is valid criticism.
>
> After all books and plays are written some time, some place, by some person affected by that time, that place, the clothes he sees and wears, other books, the air and the room and every damned thing. It *must* be so, and how can it be otherwise except his book is a copy? (*Letters* 101)

This view is both author-centered and history-centered. Texts are written by authors who are definitely situated in terms of time, place, and literary milieu. Yet, only two days later Rhys wrote ruminatively to another novelist:

> I don't believe in the individual Writer so much as in Writing. It uses you and throws you away when you are not useful any longer. But it does not do this until you are useless and quite useless too. (*Letters* 103)

Perhaps pressed by the compulsions of *Wide Sargasso Sea*, the text that she had left half written and the completion of which would be her final

fictional effort, Rhys here insists on a force beyond the individual historically situated author—the force of Writing itself.

Rhys leaves us with the challenge of fashioning a critical stance that
would acknowledge both the historically bounded author-ity of her texts
and the infinitely extending participation of those texts in the intertextual
field of Writing. Theoretically, this would entail refashioning the discourse
of intertextuality given us by Julia Kristeva and Roland Barthes—by calling them both back in the direction of M. M. Bakhtin, the figure to whom
Kristeva recurs repeatedly in the inaugural essay of intertextuality, "Word,
Dialogue, and Novel."

The passage in Kristeva's essay that first employs the term "intertextuality" links the concept to

an insight first introduced into literary theory by Bakhtin: any text is constructed
as a mosaic of quotations; any text is the absorption and transformation of another. The notion of *intertextuality* replaces that of intersubjectivity, and poetic
language is read as at least *double*. ("Word" 66)

une découverte que Bakhtine est le premier à introduire dans la théorie littéraire:
tout texte se construit comme mosaïque de citations, tout texte est absorption et
transformation d'un autre texte. A la place de la notion d'intersubjectivité s'in-
stalle celle d'*intertextualité*, et le langage poétique se lit, au moins, comme *double*.
("Le mot" 146)

Without question, the author is receding from view here, becoming a
ghost in the verbal constructions attached to "any text." Within the English translation, the text "*is* constructed"; we are not to ask the questions
"by whom?" or "by what?" In the French original, the text "constructs itself" without aid of any other agent. Likewise, the text "*is* the absorption
and transformation of another"; we are not to ask who—or what, beyond
text itself—precipitated the actions of absorbing and transforming. We
are to let pass the fading ghost of the subjectivity of authorship and enter
into the vital spirit of textuality. The exorcism of the one is depicted as
prerequisite to possession by the other. Henceforth, when "poetic language *is* read" (or, as in the French, when it reads itself) it is to *be* read
"as at least *double*"—as a palimpsest of intertexts, none of which is in itself possessed of subjectivity. And yet, even in this founding passage of
"intertextuality," the ghost of subjectivity hovers in the very grammar. In
the French text, the ambiguities of the reflexive constructions make it
uncertain whether we are to posit agency (and subjectivity?) to texts that
truly construct *themselves* or whether the reflexive form of "*tout texte se
construit*" simply deflects the question of who constructs the text. It seems
to me significant that the translators render two out of three of the French
reflexive constructions with English verbs in the passive voice. In their ver-

sion of the passage, verbs bereft of active subjects call out, however faintly, for the agents that no longer own them. One is left unsure of whether or where agency abides within texts.

In his essay "The Death of the Author," Roland Barthes was humorously obvious in the way he drew from and reworked passages from Kristeva's "Word, Dialogue, and Novel," which had been written two years before Barthes's essay, at a time when he was acting as her chief mentor (Moi 1, 34). Reassembling elements from the Kristeva passage treated above, he illustrates the central principle announced in her "prior" passage—that any text, even Barthes's, "is the absorption and transformation of another" ("Word" 66). He says:

We know now [that is, after Kristeva?] that a text is not a line of words releasing a single "theological" meaning (the "message" of the Author-God) but a multi-dimensional space in which a variety of writings, none of them original, blend and clash. The text is a tissue of quotations drawn from the innumerable centers of culture. ("Death" 146)

One of the fascinating aspects of this passage is the way that intersubjectivity, banished by Kristeva, returns in Barthes's figures for the text. Whereas Kristeva's text is a "mosaic of quotations," a construction composed from essentially inert elements, Barthes's text is "a tissue of quotations"—an organism within the space of which "writings" act as subjects of verbs: there, "a variety of writings, none of them original, blend and clash." There may be no single (original) subject animating the text in such a way as to give all the writings within it coherence, but those writings themselves act, dynamically, within the tissue of the text, making it a viable matrix for the intersubjective life of differing discourses. Thus, for Barthes, the agency that traditional criticism granted authors is better imagined as the property of the pieces of texts within texts. Subjectivity is not so easy a category to let go, even for Barthes.

Bakhtin himself considered subjectivity an indispensable category, as Kristeva notes. Even though she has just characterized the central Bakhtinian insight as requiring that intertextuality should *replace* intersubjectivity, Kristeva does acknowledge that "Bakhtinian dialogism identifies writing as both subjectivity and communication, or better, as intertextuality. Confronted with this dialogism, the notion of a 'person-subject of writing' becomes blurred, yielding to that of 'ambivalence of writing'" ("Word" 68). But neither a "blurred" notion of a writing subject nor the idea that writing carries "ambivalence" can cancel the reader's image of a person talking, from some other space and time, through the words on a page, made present through the activity of the reader's attention. And for all that Bakhtin wrote little about the author per se, his frequent use of the terms "dialogue," "conversation," "communication," and "reply" summon continually images of the "person-subjects" whose dialogue generates texts.

Kristeva retains traces of such language within most of her representations of Bakhtin's theory. The following formulation, for example, calls up the spirit of a "person-subject" who writes, reads, absorbs, and replies to texts: "Bakhtin considers writing as a reading of the anterior literary corpus and the text as an absorption of and a reply to another text" ("Word" 69). Literally, this sentence attributes to writing and to the text the actions of absorbing and replying, but the modus operandi of the writing/text is figured here as identical to, and becomes identified subliminally with, that of an author. It is, after all, to authors that we most habitually attribute the actions of reading, absorbing, and replying to texts other than their own. Interestingly, when Barthes echoes this Kristevan passage in "The Death of the Author," he leaches out of it anything that smacks of the intersubjective *dynamic* of dialogue, reducing the writer to the mechanical role of mixing inert bits of writing: "The writer can only imitate a gesture that is always anterior, never original. His only power is to mix writings, to counter the ones with the others, in such a way as never to rest on any of them" (146). Whereas in Kristeva's reading of Bakhtin, someone or something *absorbs* and *replies* to "the anterior literary corpus," in Barthes's version the writer merely *imitates* anterior writings and brings them into conjunction.

Bakhtin's conception of the dialogical text also insists on the text's relationship to history, whereas Barthes's view of intertextuality seems nearly ahistorical. As Kristeva explains, Bakhtin's understanding of the "ambivalence" of dialogical writing "implies the insertion of history (society) into a text and of this text into history" ("Word" 68). The texts in dialogue within any given piece of writing come from some place and some time, and they carry their histories with them. For Bakhtin, those texts have a profoundly historical dimension, and so does the text in which they interact. Kristeva sums it up: "Bakhtin situates the text within history and society, which are then seen as texts read by the writer, and into which he inserts himself by rewriting them" ("Word" 65). Bakhtin's writer is an agent, acting on and in relationship to the materials of history (which are always textual), and *as*serting a self as he "*in*serts" his writing-agency into the textual trajectory of history.

When Barthes describes the writer's resources, history fades away along with authorial identity:

Succeeding the Author, the scriptor no longer bears within him passions, humours, feelings, impressions, but rather this immense dictionary from which he draws a writing that can know no halt: life never does more than imitate the book, and the book itself is only a tissue of signs, an imitation that is lost, infinitely deferred. ("Death" 147)

The "scriptor" is emptied out of all but words, and these words present themselves as if they were without history. A dictionary is one of the more arbitary arrangements of words, no doubt. Did discourse ever present itself to a writer in a form quite so relentlessly truncated and shuffled? I doubt it. The discourses within the writer come thickly or thinly, in short or long strings, crossed and recrossed by others, but always bearing with them the "passions, humours, feelings, impressions" that sealed them, at some historical time, in the writer's memory. If to bear such historically rooted passions within one's word-hoard is to be authorial, not writerly, then every writer is in some sense authorial, just as every author is in some sense writerly — driven by the exigencies of language "itself." Barthes, however, rejects such a shifting gestalt, insisting on negating the possibility of author-ity in writing: "It is language which speaks, *not* the author; to write is, through a prerequisite *im*personality . . . , to reach that point where *only* language acts, 'performs,' and *not* 'me'" ("Death" 143, emphasis added).

A return to Bakhtin recovers the possibility of honoring, with Barthes, the power of discourses that inhabit the writing subject, while also recognizing that discourses develop and clash within history and that the act of writing requires the exercise of dominion over contending discourses. In contrast to Barthes, Bakhtin finds alien "the conception of a purely poetic, extrahistorical language, a language far removed from the petty rounds of everyday life, a language of the gods." On the contrary, for him,

the art of prose is close to a conception of languages as historically concrete and living things. The prose art presumes a deliberate feeling for the historical and social concreteness of living discourse, as well as its relativity, a feeling for its participation in historical becoming and in social struggle; it deals with discourse that is still warm from that struggle and hostility, as yet unresolved and still fraught with hostile intentions and accents; prose art finds discourse in this state and subjects it to the dynamic-unity of its own style. (331)

Such a perspective would encourage the critic to develop and to exercise "a deliberate feeling for the historical and social concreteness" of the discourses that contend within texts. It would be by no means out of bounds of such an intertextually oriented criticism to locate the previous lives of particular discourses in specific times, places, and texts. This would be more than "mere" source-hunting. It would be a "deliberate" attempt to develop a "feeling" for the past lives of discourses that live again in the text in question.

Bakhtin has another concept that may be helpful here — the idea of the "chronotope." Quite literally indicating the intersection of time and place, the "chronotope" proves most useful to Bakhtin as a means of categorizing kinds of fiction according to how they bring spaces and times together to different effect—the novel of adventure and ordeal, the adventure novel of everyday life, the biographical novel, etc. Along the way of using the term to make these generic distinctions, Bakhtin stresses continually both the inseparability of space and time and the concreteness of any instance of their conjunction. As he ends the massive essay "Forms of Time and of the Chronotope in the Novel," Bakhtin alludes to another potential use of the term—one he does not pursue but that might be just the concept needed to valorize a kind of critical attention to the discourses contending in texts that would grant importance to the historical provenance of those discourses. He begins with the theme of the interpenetration of work and world:

The work and the world represented in it enter the real world and enrich it, and the real world enters the work and its world as part of the process of its creation, as well as part of its subsequent life, in a continual renewing of the work through the creative perception of listeners and readers. Of course this process of exchange is itself chronotopic: it occurs first and foremost in the historically developing social world, but without ever losing contact with changing historical space. We might even speak of a special *creative* chronotope inside which this exchange between work and life occurs, and which constitutes the distinctive life of the work. (254)

In applying the chronotopic perspective to a text such as Jean Rhys's *Quartet*, one could focus on the place/time of either its creation or its reception. Both are crucial intersections at which work and world meet, within space and time, and through the contention of discourses. For the purposes of this argument, however, it would seem most useful to concentrate on the chronotope of composition. If we want to highlight the difference between the traditional source-hunting, influence-tracing approach to the novel and an approach that stresses the intertextuality of the "creative chronotope," the place/time to start with will be that of inscription—which, in the case of *Quartet*, is the most certain part of a story that is otherwise shot through with discrepancies.

From all accounts, Jean Rhys wrote *Quartet* during the space of about a year, composing most of it "in Paris in a rather horrid little rue" and finishing it in Amsterdam, in 1927 (*Letters* 101, 171; *Smile Please* 126).[3] Though Rhys, Stella Bowen, and Arthur Mizener, Ford's biographer, disagree by a full year on the dating of Rhys's liaison with Ford, they agree on the following sequence of events that led Rhys to the horrid little rue and her solitary effort of writing. In 1919, at the age of twenty-nine, Ella Gwendolyn Rhys Williams married Jean Lenglet (born Willem Johan Marie Lenglet; later to write under the pseudonym Edouard de Nève), a journalist from the Netherlands who was also a veteran of the French Foreign Legion, a victim of gas attacks in World War I, and currently a worker in War Intelligence for France (Hollander 159–60). In later years, Rhys said that the marriage to Jean Lenglet offered her a much-needed escape from the sad life she had been leading in London. As a young immigrant beauty from the West Indies she had found only meager financial and emotional support in her itinerant wanderings from job to job as chorus girl, artist's model, or canteen waitress, and from relationship to relationship as the lover of men who had the means to pension her off when they were ready to disentangle themselves (*Smile Please* 92–114). Her life with Lenglet did not greatly increase her security; they traveled from Holland to Paris, Vienna, Budapest, Prague, Brussels, and finally back to Paris. Neither Rhys nor any of the scholars who have written on this period of her life offers a clear explanation of Lenglet's employment at this time, though the story entails his using his contacts with the French, for whom he had done diplomatic (espionage?) work during the war, to obtain a job as an interpreter with the Inter-allied Disarmament Commission. How long he kept that job and what other activities he conducted during the period are unclear.[4] At any rate, he left Vienna hurriedly because he had been caught violating regulations concerning currency exchange. It was as a result of that charge, along with the offense of entering France without a passport, that he was arrested in Paris in 1923. In Brussels, on the way to that illegal entry into France, Rhys, who had two years earlier suffered the death of their three-week-old son, gave birth to a daughter and placed her immediately in foster care.

It was just before Lenglet's arrest, when she was scrambling for means to feed them both and to board their daughter, that Rhys made her first contact with Ford Madox Ford, who as editor of the *Translantic Review* was in a position to recognize and reward talent. He was impressed with the material that Rhys showed him — this was a set of semi-autobiographical pieces, some of which were later to become the stories that appeared in the *Transatlantic Review* and in Rhys's first collection of short stories, *The Left Bank* (1927), which was published under Ford's patronage. Ford immediately recognized the brilliance of Rhys's writings — and the extremity of her personal needs. The literary contact between them had hardly begun when Lenglet was arrested and imprisoned, leaving Rhys destitute, without a home, and with a child still living in foster care. Ford and Stella Bowen offered the desolate Rhys a temporary home, and it was in that home that the famous "entanglement" (to use Ford's word for the affair [Bowen 168]) began. Stella Bowen describes Rhys as "a doomed soul, violent and demoralised":

She took the lid off the world that she knew, and showed us an underworld of darkness and disorder, where officialdom, the bourgeoisie and the police were the eternal enemies and the fugitive the only hero. All the virtues, in her view, were summed up in "being a sport," which meant being willing to take risks and show gallantry, and share one's last crust; more attractive qualities, no doubt, than patience or honesty or fortitude. She regarded the law as the instrument of the "haves" against the "have nots" and was well acquainted with every rung of that long and dismal ladder by which the respectable citizen descends towards degradation. (166–67)

Bowen is gracious enough to admit that "it was not her [Rhys's] fault that she knew these things" — by which Bowen seems to mean that poverty had exposed Rhys to sordid conditions and had cast her "for the role of . . . the poor, brave and desperate beggar who was doomed to be let down by the bourgeoisie" (167). There is another sense, however, in which "it was not her fault that she knew these things." She "knew" them as a reader, as a woman of words, acutely attuned to the discourses of her place and time. The world she took the lid off, in the notebooks she showed Ford and Bowen, is a world she had known, through books, long before she set foot on European soil or herself saw the "underworld" of city life.

In her memoir, *Smile Please*, Rhys recounts an isolated youth in which she "was alone except for books" (19). These books embued in her the Manichean vision of life of which Bowen complains above.[5] At an early age, Rhys "skimmed through *Paradise Lost* because [she] was curious about Satan," whom she says "most people then" considered "the personification of evil, for some reason the ruler of this world" (47). Her most vivid memory of her mother has her stirring a pot of jam with one hand and holding in the other Marie Corelli's *The Sorrows of Satan* (27).[6] This book of her mother's, like *Paradise Lost*, offered the young girl a portrait of Satan as a supremely interesting figure, psychologically and morally — one who just might wrest her sympathies away from a stolid God (the God of Bowen's "bourgoisie and the police," who recommends "patience" and "honesty" and "fortitude").

Some years later, Rhys sought in her father's library answers to troubling questions about sex, race, and the meaning of propriety that were raised by her adolescent experiences as the daughter of a white doctor living in the racially mixed island of Dominica:

As soon as I could I lost myself in the immense world of books and tried to blot out the real world which was so puzzling to me. Even then I had a vague, persistent feeling that I'd always be lost in it, defeated.

However, books, too were all about the same thing I discovered, but in a different way. I could accept it in books *and from books (fatally) I gradually got most of my ideas and beliefs.* (50, emphasis added)

So, she says, she pursued her reading beyond the family bookshelves, to even the rare book section of the local public library. She mentions only one type of reading as that which dominated her adolescence:

I liked books about prostitutes, there were a good many then, and vividly recollect a novel called *The Sands of Pleasure* written by a man named Filson Young. It must have been well written, otherwise I would never have remembered it so perfectly to this day. It was about an Englishman's love affair with an expensive demimondaine in Paris. (50)

One might well treat *The Sands of Pleasure* (1905) as a direct influence on Rhys's *Quartet*. Correspondences in subject matter, vision, and phrasing abound. It is even more suggestive, however, to perceive the ways in which Filson Young's inscription of the market of sexual pleasure in turn-of-the-century Montmartre café society uses the same figures and participates in the same view of the woman of pleasure that surfaces not only in Bowen's characterization of Rhys and in Rhys's own *Quartet* but also in a book that Ford gave to Rhys in 1926.

The Manichean perspective on women (which has dominated Western culture for centuries but which takes on peculiar force in the late nineteenth century)[7] is voiced crudely in *The Sands of Pleasure* by one of the servants of the lighthouse—a prominent symbol of phallic civilization in this novel. He declares bluntly to the more cultivated lighthouse engineer, the hero of the novel: "Women's either angels or deevils, in my opinion, sir; just the one thing or the other!" (55). The hero, Richard Grey, laughs at this simplistic formulation, though in fact it haunts his later assessments of the women of Paris. When introduced to Toni, the expensive and charming prostitute with whom he will fall briefly in love, Richard classifies her as a "vampire" and recoils from the "perversity" of her greed for pleasure (179). The word perversity shadows all Richard's perceptions of Toni and is always linked with the fact of her refusal (or inability) to belong to one man sexually. The essence of her "waywardness and perversity"—that which makes her, in the words of Richard's more worldly friend John, "a perverse little devil" (139, 197)—is her unwillingness to curb her desire for happiness. This unbridled longing for happiness is also one of the most striking motifs in Rhys's characterization of Marya in *Quartet*. In his own way, Heidler plays the part that Richard Grey plays in *The Sands of Pleasure*—the part of the Victorian gentleman who classifies women into angels or monsters—when he responds to Marya's passion by calling her "savage" (131). In the eyes of both men, for a woman to desire may be natural, but it is unacceptable within the bounds of patriarchal civilization. As Richard Grey complains, just before he gives up the hope of securing Toni's lasting affections, he must accept that Toni "came of a different race, breathed a different atmosphere from his; that she, in her single-hearted service of pleasure, was a creature of nature, and he of civilization; that she was primitive and eternal, while he was of time and evolution" (357). If Toni is "perverse" — etymologically, "thoroughly turned" — it is the law of patriarchal civilization, the law enjoining a woman to cleave to one man only, that she is turned against, not the law of nature.

The portrait of Marya in *Quartet* participates, however unconsciously, in the representation of woman as natural and desirous, man as civilized and reconciled to limits on satisfaction. The difference between *Quartet* and *The Sands of Pleasure*, in this respect, is one of valence. And it is that difference which scandalized Bowen. For Rhys ridicules the sexlessness of a civilization that acquiesces to patriarchal rules (as exemplified by the sexlessness of both Heidler and Lois), while at the same time she exposes the cruelty — even the sadism — that accompanies civilization's repression of sexuality ("cold" and "cruel" are the two adjectives Marya attributes most often to Heidler and his wife). What I want to stress here is that, in spite of this change in emphasis, Rhys relies on the same series of dichotomies that structured the favorite novel of her youth: man/woman, civilization/nature, restraint/desire, human/savage or devil. In the place/ time of *Quartet*'s creation, the discourse of female sexuality was still under the control of these dichotomies.

In the same year that Rhys was trying to finish *Quartet*, while living in Holland (though separated definitively from her husband, Jean Lenglet), she was also earning some much-needed money from a commission that Ford had arranged for her. In *Drawn from Life*, Stella Bowen puts it pretty baldly: she and Ford could not in good conscience rid themselves of Rhys until a job materialized for her (167). The job that got Rhys out of the Ford/Bowen apartment was an insignificant ghostwriting assignment, helping a wealthy woman to write up her rather bizarre theories on antique furniture and metempsychosis.[8] The more serious job was the one Rhys took with her to Holland, the translation into English of a French novel by Francis Carco called *Perversité*. Ford had become acquainted with Carco in the winter of 1925–26, and as a result of that friendship, he arranged for Rhys to translate Carco's most recent novel. As it turned out, when the translation was published in 1928, it had Ford's name, not Rhys's, on the title page — an "error" that was never corrected, though Rhys protested to Covici, the publisher. Because the book was soon suppressed, Rhys gave up on the effort to claim credit for her translation. This story of literary patronage turning into exploitation creates a double irony in the epigraph of *Quartet* (published the same year as "Ford's" translation of *Perversité*):

> ... Beware
> Of good Samaritans — walk to the right
> Or hide thee by the roadside out of sight
> Or greet them with the smile that villains wear.
> — R. C. Dunning

Within the text of *Quartet*, the epigraph resonates with the references to Heidler as a patron of the arts and the pretense that Heidler and Lois are merely being kind when they bring Marya into their home for the purpose of concubinage. Set in relation to the publication of *Perversity*, the epigraph transfers to Ford the suspicions that the reader develops regarding Heidler: he poses as a benefactor, but he may be a thief in disguise.[9]

The fact that Rhys translated *Perversité* during the same time period when she was finishing *Quartet* is a significant element in the "creative chronotope" of her novel. It is surprising, in fact, that no critic has explored the striking parallels between the two novels. *Perversity* is, like *Quartet* (and like *The Sands of Pleasure*), set in the night world of Montmartre. Like *Quartet*, it is a study in passion and jealousy that ends in murder. Even more openly than *Quartet*, it explores the psychodynamics of masochism and sadism. Finally, Carco's novel takes up directly the topic of female prostitution and links its "perversity" to that of sadomasochism. The action of *Quartet* takes place several rungs up the social ladder from the underworld of Carco's brothels, but not so far up that Marya and Lois do not contemplate prostitution as a solution to Marya's economic dilemma. And, in fact, Marya's "arrangement" with the Heidlers is nothing more than a genteel version of the prostitution practiced more openly by the denizens of Carco's Montmartre. We may never know to what extent these similarities may be attributed to the direct influence of Carco's text on Rhys as she composed *Quartet*. We do not know exactly when Rhys began writing *Quartet*, but according to her letters it was not likely to be much before the autumn of 1925. On January 7, 1926, Carco sent Ford a copy of *Perversité*, along with a letter discussing the proposal that Ford would translate the book (Harvey 97). If Ford gave his copy of *Perversité* to Rhys soon after receiving it, Carco's novel could have been in her hands for all but the first few months of her work on *Quartet*. On the other hand, she might not have had the book or might not have read it until 1927, the year she names for her actual work on the translation and for her finishing of *Quartet*. In any case, the perspective of intertextuality puts such concerns into abeyance by focusing interest on the way the two texts share a discursive field that precedes them both. Moreover, a chronotopic reading of the intertextual field would call for attention both to the ways in which the two contemporary texts replicate the discourse of that intertextual field and to the ways in which the contemporary texts "swerve" in common from texts that entered the discursive field at an earlier time.

It is a radical shortcut to make Filson Young's *The Sands of Pleasure* stand for the discursive field into which both *Quartet* and *Perversity* enter in 1928. To do justice to the intertextual field that encompasses Carco's and Rhys's texts would entail exploring their relations to both the English novels of prostitution that Rhys was so fond of in her youth and French treatments of the *demi-monde*, from Baudelaire, to Proust, to Colette. The literature touching on sadomasochism, from the Marquis de Sade to *The Story of O*, would be germane, as would the vast number of texts that encode the sexually active woman as monstrous. There are interesting observations to be made, however, by taking Young's text of 1905 as paradigmatic of turn-of-the-century discourse around women, sexual pleasure, prostitution, and the pleasure-pain nexus. A comparison of Young's novel with Carco's and Rhys's reveals a striking similarity in plot, characterization, and language among the three texts, while the two texts of 1928 swerve markedly from the text of 1905 in mode and tone. *The Sands of Pleasure* is sentimental and poignantly comedic in its treatment of a young gentleman's initiation into and escape from the "gay markets" of prostitution (116), whereas *Perversity* and *Quartet* are harsh and naturalistic in their depictions of the degradation and the deaths wrought by the marketing of women's sexuality.

In all three novels, a relative innocent enters a world in which sex has been put on a commercial basis. Each becomes caught in a triangle of desire and jealousy, learning in the end the futility of seeking love or affection in a world where flesh and money are the only elements of exchange. In *The Sands of Pleasure*, however, the mistake is correctable. John Lauder, the hero's guide to the Montmartre underworld, loves "to be intimate with the sources and changes of the river of pleasure, and to trace in its deep and intricate channels those human tides that connect it with our common life and keep it, in spite of its terrible burden of moral sewage, harmless to the sound of head and heart" (116). Health of mind and spirit can protect the young gentleman from the infection that floats upon but is not intrinsic to the waters of pleasure. Likewise, though the institution of prostitution strikes Lauder as one of the "grim" facts of life, he had "an Alexandrian respect for it, when it was cleanly and decently conducted" (117). He admires those "women of the *demi-monde* . . . who had a genius for their calling and a sense of dignity and behavior in it" (118). He understands the prostitute to have chosen her trade and to have struck her bargain; the only duty of the gentleman is to keep to the terms of the trade by not letting himself promise anything more than money. Lauder cautions Richard about the prostitute Toni:

A girl like Toni has deliberately chosen to take her love, or what stands for it, into the market; and she is far too sensible not to see that she can't have it both ways; or, if she didn't see it, a man who should try to make her believe that it was possible would be, to say the least of it, damned unfriendly. (207)

The plot of *The Sands of Pleasure* is based on the progress of Richard Grey toward this knowledge and toward his relinquishment of his "unfriendly" love—a relinquishment that frees Toni to return to the dignified conduct of her chosen profession.

In *Perversity* and *Quartet*, no one has made a deliberate choice of prostitution, and it is impossible to conduct oneself with dignity within it. Instead, prostitution is a given, an inescapable and degrading fact of a poor woman's life. Carco introduces his prostitutes in language that contrasts starkly with John Lauder's pronouncement about a prostitute's deliberate choice:

The women lived in an utterly careless disorder. The miserable staircase was lit by oil lamps and smelt abominably of drains, the damp walls were covered with scratches, the doors were badly fitting, the floors uneven. Thus they had always lived and their sordid surroundings were a part of themselves. Irma was accustomed to it all. (10)

It is not choice that places Irma in a brothel but a combination of destitution and her thralldom to a brutal pimp. The plot of *Perversity* follows the psychological journey of Irma's brother Emile into imaginative identification with her abjection before the pimp and all he represents—the power of masculinity, money, and sadism. The novel ends with a sudden twist when Emile, having intended to shoot the pimp, instead kills his sister. It is safer to end the cycle of cruelty within prostitution by killing the prostitute than by confronting the pimp.

The ending of *Quartet* depicts a similar deflection of rage from the masculine enemy to his female victim. Just as Emile kills his sister, his only ally in the novel, because she is also the lover of his enemy, the pimp, Stephan Zelli kills his wife, Marya, because she is the lover of his enemy, Heidler. Both men are outraged that "their" women have been bought by other men, but neither is in a position (in terms of strength, class, or wealth) to defy the other man's power. The economic and social system that prostituted "their" women emasculates them. They, too, are corrupted by prostitution. The graceful escape back to normalcy that was available to Richard Grey, the gentleman dabbler in prostitution of *The Sands of Pleasure*, is not available to them—though it is available to Heidler. *Perversity* and *Quartet* differ from *The Sands of Pleasure* in showing who pays the long-term price for the gentleman's purchase of transient pleasure: first the prostitute herself (dead at the end of both novels); second, the men of her own class who feel betrayed by her.

True to their naturalist mode, neither *Quartet* nor *Perversity* suggests that the participants in the drama become enlightened by their sufferings. Even as Emile seeks his revenge against his sister's pimp, he retains "the disdain he had always felt for women of that sort" (112). *Quartet* ends with Stephan Zelli leaving his wife's body behind him, as he picks up "another tart" to accompany him on his escape from Paris: "At that moment women seemed to him loathsome, horrible—soft and disgusting weights suspended round the necks of men, dragging them downwards" (186). Emile and Stephan Zelli fail to understand the conditions that make women depend on men and that force the poorest women into prostitution. All their potential empathy is consumed by their jealousy and humiliation at being the men such women leave behind. The inhumanity of these endings, with their spectacles of brutality to sympathetic women and degradation of pathetic men, differs sharply from the sentimental conclusion of *The Sands of Pleasure*, in which, contentedly returned to England, Richard Grey remembers his affair with Toni as a spiritual exchange with "great gain" for them both (395).

Together, *Quartet* and *Perversity* might be seen as "an absorption of and a reply to" (Kristeva, "Word" 69) the romanticization of prostitution in turn-of-the-century novels such as *The Sands of Pleasure*. They retain the basic plot structure of such novels, sending a *naïf* into the *demi-monde* to learn the lesson that love is not available there. But they talk back to the complacencies of romantic bohemianism by putting the clichés about the courtesan's savagery, charm, perversity, deviltry, and cruelty in the mouths of men who destroy women. And they give the lie to John Lauder's contention that the courtesan has deliberately chosen to take her love into the marketplace. Instead, their courtesans survive for a while—and finally fail to survive—because they have fallen under the control of men who can feed them.

Quartet, in turn, could be seen as "an absorption of and a reply to" *Perversity*. It complicates Carco's naturalistic portrayal of the prostitute by moving her consciousness to center stage and by making her prey, at times, to the same mystifications of her position as grip the imaginations of her exploiters. Even to herself, Marya is "reckless, lazy, a vagabond by nature" (14), "happy, petted, charming" (18), yet "savage" (114) and "wild" (117) in her passions. She dies deluded by love for her exploiter—but even more deluded by the romantic discourse of the *demi-monde* which cast her in the role of the tragic courtesan. Whereas Carco's Irma is a pure victim, thoughtlessly immersed in the life of the brothel, Rhys's Marya is a half-conscious participant in the discourse of romantic concubinage that justifies the final death scene—somewhat more sordid than the death of La Dame aux Camélias, but an instance of the same myth.

The place/time of the composition of *Quartet* gives special interest to these speculations. Barthes pictured the "scriptor" as "no longer bear[ing] within him passions, humours, feelings, impressions, but rather this immense dictionary from which he draws a writing that can know no halt" ("Death" 147). Bakhtin encourages us to imagine a writer whose "passions, humours, feelings, impressions" have been formed by the words available at specific times and places. The fact that Jean Rhys had *Perversité* in hand while she finished *Quartet*, and the fact that in later years she remembered *The Sands of Pleasure* as one of the books that formed her attitudes toward love, do not exhaust the connections of *Quartet* to other discourses, even to discourses of prostitution, but these facts do help us to develop a "feeling for the historical and social concreteness" of the languages within *Quartet* that both reproduce and critique the myth of the romantic concubine.

NOTES

1 See Staley (35–36) and Bender.

2 For further arguments on this point see Gilbert and Gubar (xiii–xiv), and Nancy K. Miller.

3 Secondary sources agree on the basic facts about the time and place of *Quartet*'s composition. See Angier (50), Staley (14), Davidson (12). All seem to base their information on a combination of Rhys's own statements in her memoir and letters and Stella Bowen's account in her autobiography, *Drawn from Life*.

4 See Staley (8–9); Rhys (*Letters* 13; *Smile Please* 120); Hollander (160).

5 It would be interesting to investigate the degree to which Rhys's exposure to Obeah, through the oral tales of her nurse Meta, would have reinforced — or even temporally preceded — the influence of the Christian Manicheanism that affected Rhys through her parents and the texts they offered her.

6 Marie Corelli, who published *The Sorrows of Satan* in 1895, was Queen Victoria's favorite novelist.

7 See Dijkstra and Auerbach.

8 See Mizener (347), Staley (13–14), Davidson (11).

9 Rhys's own comments on the possible culpability of Ford in the affair of the translation are somewhat contradictory. In *Smile Please*, she gives the facts in such a terse manner as to invite the reader's speculation on how she had been mistreated. After stating that it was Ford who arranged for her the job of translating *Perversité*, Rhys states in parentheses: "When the book was published in English it came out under Ford's name, not mine. My agent wrote to ask why this was so. Ford answered that the publisher, not he, had insisted on his name, which had more drawing power" (126). This formulation

depicts Ford as a passive participant in the decision to use his name instead of Rhys's: when the publishers "insisted," Ford apparently acquiesced. In a letter to Francis Wyndham written in 1966, Rhys took Ford off the hook: "When it [*Perversité*] appeared my agent wrote to ask about it, for I hadn't been told that I was 'ghosting.' It was Covici the publisher's fault, and I know Ford did his best to put things right. Then the book was banned and I heard no more about it" (*Letters* 294–95). David Dow Harvey's bibliography of Ford's works lists evidence both that Carco thought Ford was doing the translating and that Ford protested Covici's attribution of the translation to him. Ford says in a letter, "The publishers fraudently [*sic*] attributed it to me, I suppose, because they thought it would sell better and I had the book suppressed and never heard anything more about it" (97). It is interesting to note the discrepancy between Rhys's impression that the book had been "banned," as if by a government that found the contents of the book obscene, and Ford's statement that it was he who took the translation out of circulation, on account of his embarrassment over its false attribution to him.

WORKS CITED

Angier, Carole. *Jean Rhys*. Harmondsworth, England: Penguin, 1985.

Auerbach, Nina. *Woman and the Demon: The Life of a Victorian Myth*. Cambridge: Harvard UP, 1982.

Bakhtin, M. M. *The Dialogic Imagination*. Ed. Michael Holquist. Trans. Caryl Emerson and Michael Holquist. Austin: U of Texas P, 1981.

Barthes, Roland. "The Death of the Author." Trans. Stephen Heath. *Image-Music-Text* 142–48. New York: Hill & Wang, 1977. First published in French as "La mort de l'auteur," *Mantéia* 5 (1968).

Barthes, Roland. "From Work to Text." Trans. Stephen Heath. In *Image-Music-Text* 155–64. First published in French as "De l'oeuvre au texte," *Revue d'esthétique* 3 (1971).

Bender, Todd. "Jean Rhys and the Genius of Impressionism." *Studies in the Literary Imagination* 11 (1978): 43–53.

Bowen, Stella. *Drawn from Life*. Rpt. London: Virago, 1984. London: Collins Publishers, 1941.

Carco, Francis. *Perversity*. Trans. "Ford Madox Ford" [actually translated by Jean Rhys]. Chicago: Pascal Covici, Publisher, 1928. First published in French as *Perversité*. Paris: J. Ferenczi et Fils, 1925.

Davidson, Arnold E. *Jean Rhys*. New York: Ungar, 1985.

Delany, Paul. "Jean Rhys and Ford Madox Ford: What 'Really' Happened?" *Mosaic* 16 (Fall 1983): 15–24.

Dijkstra, Bram. *Idols of Perversity: Fantasies of Feminine Evil in Fin-de-Siècle Culture*. New York: Oxford UP, 1986.

Ford, Ford Madox. *When the Wicked Man*. New York: Horace Liveright, 1931.

Gardiner, Judith Kegan. "Rhys Recalls Ford: *Quartet* and *The Good Soldier.*" *Tulsa Studies in Women's Literature* 1 (1982): 67–81.

Gilbert, Sandra M., and Susan Gubar. *No Man's Land: The Place of the Woman Writer in the Twentieth Century.* Vol 1: *The War of the Words.* New Haven: Yale UP, 1988.

Harvey, David Dow. *Ford Madox Ford, 1873–1939: A Bibliography of Works and Criticism.* Princeton, NJ: Princeton UP, 1962.

Hollander, Martien Kappers-den. "Jean Rhys and the Dutch Connection." *Journal of Modern Literature* 11 (Spring 1984): 159–73.

Kristeva, Julia. "Le mot, le dialogue et le roman." In *Sémiotiké: Recherches pour une sémanalyse* 143–73. Paris: Editions du Seuil, 1969. Dated in this text as 1966. First published as "Bakhtine, le mot, le dialogue et le roman," *Critique* 239 (April 1967): 438–65.

Kristeva, Julia. "Word, Dialogue and Novel." Trans. Thomas Gora, Alice Jardine and Leon S. Roudiez. In *Desire in Language: A Semiotic Approach to Literature and Art*, ed. Leon S. Roudiez, 64–91. New York: Columbia UP, 1980. Translation of "Le mot, le dialogue et le roman." See above.

Miller, Nancy K. "Changing the Subject: Authorship, Writing, and the Reader." In *Feminist Studies, Critical Studies*, ed. Teresa de Lauretis, 102–20. Bloomington: Indiana UP, 1986.

Mizener, Arthur. *The Saddest Story: A Biography of Ford Madox Ford.* New York: World, 1971.

Moi, Toril, ed. *The Kristeva Reader.* New York: Columbia UP, 1986.

Rhys, Jean. *The Letters of Jean Rhys.* Ed. Francis Wyndham and Diana Melly. New York: Viking, 1984.

Rhys, Jean. *Quartet.* Rpt. New York: Vintage, 1974. First published in England as *Postures.* London: Chatto & Windus, 1928.

Rhys, Jean. *Smile Please: An Unfinished Autobiography.* New York: Harper & Row, 1979.

Staley, Thomas F. *Jean Rhys: A Critical Study.* Austin: U of Texas P, 1979.

Young, Filson [Guy Thorpe]. *The Sands of Pleasure.* Boston: Dana Estes, 1905.

Index

Index

Abrams, M. H., 15
Adorno, Theodor, 193
Aeschylus, 169
Africa, 305
African-American criticism, 28
Akins, James, 274
Alcott, Bronson, 290
allusion: ideology of, 189, 190; in *The End of the Road*, 185–89. *See also* influence; intertextuality
Alter, Robert, 269*n7*
Althusser, Louis, 69, 73, 185
Altieri, Charles, 124, 142
American, 146, 153, 154, 155–57, 158, 159, 160–61
Andrews, William L., 30–31, 312*nn2, 6,* 314*n24*
Angier, Carole, 335*n3*
Anglo-Saxon Poetic Records (ASPR), 97–101, 109*n39*, 110*n41*
Aptheker, Herbert, 314*n19*
Aries, Philippe, 58*n4*
Ariosto, Ludovico, 234
ars dictaminis. See dictation
Athena, 289
audience. *See* orality
Auerbach, Nina, 335*n7*
author. *See* influence; intertextuality; orality

Bacon, Sir Francis, 224, 227–28, 233, 241*n11*
Baker, Houston, 28, 312*n1*, 314*n23*
Bakhtin, Mikhail, 4, 18–19, 32*n10*, 44, 63–66, 117, 132, 147, 149, 152, 154,

159–60, 172, 181–82, 322, 324–25, 335; chronotope in, 325–26
Banneker, Benjamin, 300
Barker, Anna, 279–80, 284, 285, 287, 288, 292
Barth, John, 30, 181, 183–84, 199–200. *See also End of the Road, The*
Barthes, Roland, 4, 21–23, 27, 49–50, 52, 63, 66, 70, 72–73, 139, 146, 148–53, 154, 156, 158, 172, 174, 182, 185, 200, 205, 221, 241*n12*, 322, 323, 324–25, 335; "Death of the Author," 148–51, 154; *S/Z*, 22–23; "From Work to Text," 150–51, 154
Bate, Walter Jackson, 7–8
Bateson, F. W., 5
Baxandall, Michael, 6–7, 208, 248, 267
Baxter, Richard, 233, 236
Baym, Nina, 157, 175
Beardsley, Monroe C., 16
Bede (Anglo-Saxon writer): *Death Song,* 86–7, 107*n24;* story of Caedmon, 87, 88, 107*nn24, 26,* 107–8*n29*
Bell, Daniel, 195
Benjamin, Walter, 106*n16*
Beowulf, 94, 102
Bergman, David, 241*n9*
Bessinger, J. B., 97, 100, 102
Bhaskar, Roy, 143
Bible, 231–32, 234
Blackmur, R. P., 240*n5*
Blake, William, 67–68, 70, 73
Blanchard, Paula, 293*n5*
Block, Haskell, 31*n2*
Bloom, Harold, 4, 7, 8–10, 14, 32*n5* 37, 44,

341

WITHDRAWN

Undergraduate Lending Library